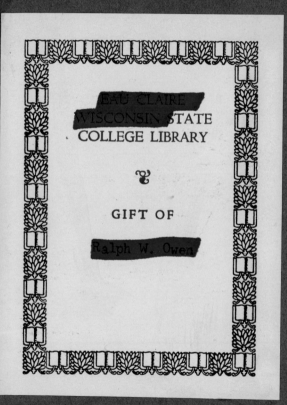

THE MERMAID SERIES.

THE BEST PLAYS OF THE OLD DRAMATISTS.

THOMAS MIDDLETON.

I.

"What things have we seen
Done at the Mermaid! heard words that have been
So nimble, and so full of subtle flame,
As if that every one from whence they came
Had meant to put his whole wit in a jest,
And had resolved to live a fool the rest
Of his dull life."

Master Francis Beaumont to Ben Jonson.

"Souls of Poets dead and gone,
What Elysium have ye known,
Happy field or mossy cavern,
Choicer than the Mermaid Tavern?"

Keats.

CONTENTS.

PAGE

THOMAS MIDDLETON vii

A TRICK TO CATCH THE OLD ONE 1

THE CHANGELING 83

A CHASTE MAID IN CHEAPSIDE 169

WOMEN BEWARE WOMEN 259

THE SPANISH GIPSY 367

THOMAS MIDDLETON.

IF it be true, as we are told on high authority, that the greatest glory of England is her literature, and the greatest glory of English literature is its poetry, it is not less true that the greatest glory of English poetry lies rather in its dramatic than its epic or its lyric triumphs. The name of Shakespeare is above the names even of Milton and Coleridge and Shelley: and the names of his comrades in art and their immediate successors are above all but the highest names in any other province of our song. There is such an overflowing life, such a superb exuberance of abounding and exulting strength, in the dramatic poetry of the half-century extending from 1590 to 1640, that all other epochs of English literature seem as it were but half awake and half alive by comparison with this generation of giants and of gods. There is more sap in this than in any other branch of the national bay-tree: it has an energy in fertility which reminds us rather of the forest than the garden or the park. It is true that the weeds and briars of the underwood are but too likely to embarrass and offend the feet of the rangers and the gardeners who trim the level flower-pots or preserve the domestic game of enclosed and ordered lowlands in the tamer demesnes of literature. The sun is strong and the wind sharp in the climate which reared the fellows and the followers of Shakespeare. The extreme inequality and roughness of the ground must also be taken into account when we are disposed, as I for one have often been disposed, to wonder beyond measure at the apathetic ignorance of average students in regard of the abundant treasure to be gathered from this widest and most fruitful province in the poetic empire of England. And yet, since Charles Lamb threw open its gates to all comers in the ninth year of the present century, it cannot but seem strange that comparatively so few should have availed themselves of the entry to so rich and royal an estate.

The first word of modern tribute to the tragic genius of Thomas Middleton was not spoken by Charles Lamb. Four years before the appearance of the priceless volume which established his fame for ever among all true lovers of English poetry by copious excerpts from five of his most characteristic works,

Walter Scott, in a note on the fifty-sixth stanza of the second fytte of the metrical romance of *Sir Tristrem*, had given a passing word of recognition to the "horribly striking" power of "some passages" in Middleton's masterpiece: which was first reprinted eleven years later in the fourth volume of Dilke's Old Plays. Lamb, surprisingly enough, has given not a single extract from that noble tragedy: it was reserved for Leigh Hunt, when speaking of its author, to remark that "there is one character of his (De Flores in *The Changeling*) which, for effect at once tragical, probable, and poetical, surpasses anything I know of in the drama of domestic life." The praise is not a whit too high: the truth could not have been better said.

Blurt, Master Constable, the play with which Mr. Bullen, altering the arrangement adopted by Mr. Dyce, opened his edition of Middleton, is a notable example of the best and the worst qualities which distinguish or disfigure the romantic comedy of the Shakespearean age. The rude and reckless composition, the rough intrusion of savourless farce, the bewildering combinations of incident and the far more bewildering fluctuations of character—all the inconsistences, incongruities, incoherences of the piece are forgotten when the reader remembers and reverts to the passages of exquisite and fascinating beauty which relieve and redeem the utmost errors of negligence and haste. To find anything more delightful, more satisfying in its pure and simple perfection of loveliness, we must turn to the very best examples of Shakespeare's youthful work. Nay, it must be allowed that in one or two of the master's earliest plays—in the *Two Gentlemen of Verona*, for instance—we shall find nothing comparable for charm and sincerity of sweet and passionate fancy with such enchanting verses as these

"O happy persecution, I embrace thee
With an unfettered soul! so sweet a thing
It is to sigh upon the rack of love,
Where each calamity is groaning witness
Of the poor martyr's faith. I never heard
Of any true affection, but 'twas nipt
With care, that, like the caterpillar, eats
The leaves off the spring's sweetest book, the rose.
Love, bred on earth, is often nursed in hell:
By rote it reads woe, ere it learn to spell."

Again: the "secure tyrant, but unhappy lover," whose prisoner and rival has thus expressed his triumphant resignation, is counselled by his friend to "go laugh and lie down," as not having slept for three nights; but answers, in words even more delicious than his supplanter's:

"Alas, how can I? he that truly loves
Burns out the day in idle fantasies;
And when the lamb bleating doth bid good night
Unto the closing day, then tears begin
To keep quick time unto the owl, whose voice
Shrieks like the bellman in the lover's ears:
Love's eye the jewel of sleep, O, seldom wears!
The early lark is wakened from her bed,
Being only by love's plaints disquieted;
And, singing in the morning's ear, she weeps,
Being deep in love, at lovers' broken sleeps:

> But say a golden slumber chance to tie
> With silken strings the cover of love's eye,
> Then dreams, magician-like, mocking present
> Pleasures, whose fading leaves more discontent."

Perfect in music, faultless in feeling, exquisite in refined simplicity of expression, this passage is hardly more beautiful and noble than one or two in the play which follows. *The Phœnix* is a quaint and homely compound of satirical realism in social studies with utopian invention in the figure of an ideal prince, himself a compound of Harun al-Rashid and "Albert the Good," who wanders through the play as a detective in disguise, and appears in his own person at the close to discharge in full the general and particular claims of justice and philanthropy. The whole work is slight and sketchy, primitive if not puerile in parts, but easy and amusing to read; the confidence reposed by the worthy monarch in noblemen of such unequivocal nomenclature as Lord Proditor, Lussurioso, and Infesto, is one of the signs that we are here still on the debatable borderland between the old Morality and the new Comedy—a province where incarnate vices and virtues are seen figuring and posturing in what can scarcely be called masquerade. But the two fine soliloquies of Phœnix on the corruption of the purity of law (Act i. scene iv.) and the profanation of the sanctity of marriage (Act ii. scene ii.) are somewhat riper and graver in style, with less admixture of rhyme and more variety of cadence, than the lovely verses above quoted. Milton's obligation to the latter passage is less direct than his earlier obligation to a later play of Middleton's, from which he transferred one of the most beautiful as well as most famous images in *Lycidas:* but his early and intimate acquaintance with Middleton had apparently (as Mr. Dyce seems to think) left in the ear of the blind old poet a more or less distinct echo from the noble opening verses of the dramatist's address to "reverend and honourable matrimony."[1]

In *Michaelmas Term* the realism of Middleton's comic style is no longer alloyed or flavoured with poetry or fancy. It is an excellent Hogarthian comedy, full of rapid and vivid incident, of pleasant or indignant humour. Its successor, *A Trick to Catch the Old One*, is by far the best

[1] "Reverend and honourable matrimony,
Mother of lawful sweets, unshamèd mornings,
Dangerless pleasures! thou that mak'st the bed
Both pleasant and legitimately fruitful!
Without thee,
All the whole world were soilèd bastardy.
Thou art the only and the greatest form
That putt'st a difference between our desires
And the disordered appetites of beasts,
Making their mates those that stand next their lusts.
Then,—
With what base injury is thy goodness paid!
First, rare to have a bride commence a maid,
But does beguile joy of the purity,
And is made strict by power of drugs and art,
An artificial maid, a doctored virgin,
And so deceives the glory of his bed;
A foul contempt against the spotless power
Of sacred wedlock! But if chaste and honest

play Middleton had yet written, and one of the best he ever wrote. The merit of this and his other good comedies does not indeed consist in any new or subtle study of character, any Shakespearean creation or Jonsonian invention of humours or of men: the spendthrifts and the misers, the courtesans and the dotards, are figures borrowed from the common stock of stage tradition: it is the vivid variety of incident and intrigue, the freshness and ease and vigour of the style, the clear straightforward energy and vivacity of the action, that the reader finds most praiseworthy in the best comic work of such ready writers as Middleton and Dekker. The dialogue has sometimes touches of real humour and flashes of genuine wit: but its readable and enjoyable quality is generally independent of these. Very witty writing may be very dreary reading, for want of natural animation and true dramatic movement: and in these qualities at least the rough and ready work of our old dramatists is seldom if ever deficient.

It is, however, but too probable that the

There is another devil haunts marriage—
None fondly loves but knows it—jealousy,
That wedlock's yellow sickness,
That whispering separation every minute,
And thus the curse takes his effect or progress.
The most of men in their sudden furies
Rail at the narrow bounds of marriage,
And call 't a prison; then it is most just,
That the disease a' th' prison, jealousy,
Should still affect 'em."

reader's enjoyment may be crossed with a dash of exasperation when he finds a writer of real genius so reckless of fame and self-respect as the pressure of want or the weariness of over-work seems but too often and too naturally to have made too many of the great dramatic journeymen whose powers were half wasted or half worn out in the struggle for bare bread. No other excuse than this can be advanced for the demerit of Middleton's next comedy. Had the author wished to show how well and how ill he could write at his worst and at his best, he could have given no fairer proof than by the publication of the two plays issued under his name in the same year, 1608. *The Family of Love* is in my judgment unquestionably and incomparably the worst of Middleton's plays: very coarse, very dull, altogether distasteful and ineffectual. As a religious satire it is so utterly pointless as to leave no impression of any definite folly or distinctive knavery in the doctrine or the practice of the particular sect held up by name to ridicule: an obscure body of feather-headed fanatics, concerning whom we can only be certain that they were decent and inoffensive in comparison with the yelling Yahoos whom the scandalous and senseless license of our own day allows to run and roar about the country unmuzzled and unwhipped.

There is much more merit in the broad comedy of *Your Five Gallants*, a curious burlesque study of manners and morals not generally commendable for imitation. The ingenious and humorous invention which supplies a centre for the picture and a pivot for the action is most singularly identical with the device of a modern detective as recorded by the greatest English writer of his day. "The Butcher's Story," told to Dickens by the policeman who had played the part of the innocent young butcher, may be profitably compared by lovers of detective humour with the story of Fitsgrave—a "thrice worthy" gentleman who under the disguise of a young gull fresh from college succeeds in circumventing and unmasking the five associated swindlers of variously villainous professions by whom a fair and amiable heiress is beleaguered and befooled. The play is somewhat crude and hasty in construction, but full of life and fun and grotesque variety of humorous event.

The first of Middleton's plays to attract notice from students of a later generation, *A Mad World, my Masters*, if not quite so thoroughly good a comedy as *A Trick to Catch the Old One*, must be allowed to contain the very best comic character ever drawn or sketched by the fertile and flowing pen of its author. The prodigal grandfather, Sir Bounteous Progress, is perhaps the most lifelike figure of a good-humoured and liberal old libertine that ever amused or scandalised a tolerant or intolerant reader. The chief incidents of the action are admirably humorous and ingenious; but the matrimonial part of the catastrophe is something more than repulsive, and the singular intervention of a real live succubus, less terrible in her seductions than her sister of the *Contes Drolatiques*, can hardly seem happy or seasonable to a generation which knows not King James and his Demonology.

Of the two poets occasionally associated with Middleton in the composition of a play, Dekker seems usually to have taken in hand the greater part, and Rowley the lesser part, of the composite poem engendered by their joint efforts. The style of *The Roaring Girl* is full of Dekker's peculiar mannerisms: slipshod and straggling metre, incongruous touches or flashes of fanciful or lyrical expression, reckless and awkward inversions, irrational and irrepressible outbreaks of irregular and fitful rhyme. And with all these faults it is more unmistakably the style of a born poet than is the usual style of Middleton. Dekker would have taken a high place among the finest if not among the greatest of English poets if he had but had the sense of form—the instinct of composition. Whether it was modesty, indolence, indifference or incompetence, some drawback or shortcoming there was which so far impaired the quality of his strong and delicate genius that it is impossible for his most ardent and cordial admirer to say or think of his very best work that it really does him justice—that it adequately represents the fullness of his unquestionable powers. And yet it is certain that Lamb was not less right than usual when he said that Dekker "had poetry enough for anything." But he had not constructive power enough for the trade of a playwright—the trade in which he spent so many weary years of ill-requited labour. This comedy, in which we first find him associated with Middleton, is well written and well contrived, and fairly diverting—especially to an idle or an uncritical reader: though even such an one may suspect that the heroine here represented as a virginal virago must have been in fact rather like Dr. Johnson's fair friend Bet Flint of whom the Great Lexicographer "used to say that she was generally slut and drunkard; occasionally whore and thief" (Boswell, May 8, 1781). The parallel would have been more nearly complete if Moll Cutpurse "had written her own life in verse," and brought it to Selden or Bishop Hall with a request that he would furnish her with a preface to it. But the seventeenth century was inadequate to so perfect a production of the kind; and we doubt not through the ages one increasing purpose runs, and the thoughts of girls are widened with the process of the suns.

The plays of Middleton are not so properly divisible into tragic and comic as into realistic and romantic—into plays of which the mainspring is essentially prosaic or photographic, and plays of which the mainspring is principally fanciful or poetical. Two only of the former class remain to be mentioned; *Anything for a Quiet Life*, and *A Chaste Maid in Cheapside*. There is very good stuff in the plot or groundwork of the former, but the workmanship is hardly worthy of the material. Mr. Bullen ingeniously and plausibly suggests the partnership of Shirley in this play; but the conception of the character in which he discerns a likeness to the touch of the lesser dramatist is happier and more original than such a comparison would indicate. The young stepmother whose affectation of selfish levity and grasping craft is really designed to cure her husband of his infatuation, and to reconcile him with the son who regards her as his worst enemy, is a figure equally novel, effective and attractive. The honest shopkeeper and his shrewish wife may remind us again of Dickens by their points of likeness to Mr. and Mrs. Snagsby; though the reformation of the mercer's jealous vixen is brought about by more humorous and less tragical means than the repentance of the law-stationer's "little woman." George the apprentice, through whose wit and energy this happy consummation becomes possible, is a very original and amusing example of the young Londoner of the period. But there is more humour, though very little chastity, in the *Chaste Maid;* a play of quite exceptional freedom and audacity, and certainly one of the drollest and liveliest that ever broke the bounds of propriety or shook the sides of merriment.

The opening of *More Dissemblers besides Women* is as full at once of comic and of romantic promise as the upshot of the whole is unsatisfactory —a most lame and impotent conclusion. But some of the dialogue is exquisite; full of flowing music and gentle grace, of ease and softness and fancy and spirit; and the part of a poetic or romantic Joseph Surface, as perfect in the praise of virtue as in the practice of vice, is one of Middleton's really fine and happy inventions. In the style of *The Widow* there is no less fluency and facility: it is throughout identical with that of Middleton's other comedies in metre; a style which has so many points in common with Fletcher's as to make the apocryphal attribution of a share in this comedy to the hand of the greater poet more plausible than many other ascriptions of the kind. I am inclined nevertheless to agree with Mr. Bullen's apparent opinion that the whole credit of this brilliant play may be reasonably assigned to Middleton; and especially with his remark that the only scene in which any resemblance to any manner of Ben Jonson can be traced by the most determined ingenuity of critical research is more like the work of a pupil than like a hasty sketch of the master's. There is no lack of energetic invention and beautiful versification in another comedy of adventure and intrigue, *No Wit, no Help like a Woman's:* the unpleasant or extravagant quality of certain incidents in the story is partly neutralised or modified by the unfailing charm of a style worthy of Fletcher himself in his ripest and sweetest stage of poetic comedy.

But high above all the works yet mentioned there stands and will stand conspicuous while noble emotion and noble verse have honour among English readers, the pathetic and heroic play so memorably appreciated by Charles Lamb, *A Fair Quarrel.* It would be the vainest and emptiest impertinence to offer a word in echo of his priceless and imperishable praise. The delicate nobility of the central conception on which the hero's character depends for its full relief and development should be enough to efface all remembrance of any defect or default in moral taste, any shortcoming on the æsthetic side of ethics, which may be detected in any slighter or hastier example of the poet's invention. A man must be dull and slow of sympathies indeed who cannot respond in spirit to that bitter cry of chivalrous and manful agony at sense of the shadow of a mother's shame :—

> "Quench my spirit,
> And out with honour's flaming lights within thee!
> Be dark and dead to all respects of manhood!
> I never shall have use of valour more."

Middleton has no second hero like Captain Ager;

but where is there another so thoroughly noble and lovable among all the characters of all the dramatists of his time but Shakespeare?

The part taken by Rowley in this play is easy for any tyro in criticism to verify. The rough and crude genius of that perverse and powerful writer is not seen here by any means at its best. I cannot as yet lay claim to an exhaustive acquaintance with his works, but judging from what I have read of them I should say that his call was rather towards tragedy than towards comedy; that his mastery of severe and serious emotion was more genuine and more natural than his command of satirical or grotesque realism. The tragedy[1] in which he has grappled with the subject afterwards so differently handled in the first and greatest of Landor's tragedies is to me of far more interest and value than such comedies as that[2] which kindled the enthusiasm of a loyal Londoner in the civic sympathies of Lamb. Disfigured as it is towards the close by indulgence in mere horror and brutality after the fashion of Andronicus or Jeronimo, it has more beauty and power and pathos in its best scenes than a reader of his comedies—as far as I know them—would have expected. There are noticeable points of likeness—apart from the coincidence of subject—between this and Mr. Caldwell Roscoe's noble tragedy of *Violenzia*. But

[1] *All's Lost by Lust.*

[2] *A New Wonder, a Woman Never Vext.*

in the underplot of *A Fair Quarrel* Rowley's besetting faults of coarseness and quaintness, stiffness and roughness, are so flagrant and obtrusive that we cannot avoid a feeling of regret and irritation at such untimely and inharmonious evidence of his partnership with a poet of finer if not of sturdier genius. The same sense of discord and inequality will be aroused on comparison of the worse with the better parts of *The Old Law.* The clumsiness and dulness of the farcical interludes can hardly be paralleled in the rudest and hastiest scenes of Middleton's writing: while the sweet and noble dignity of the finer passages have the stamp of his ripest and tenderest genius on every line and in every cadence. But for sheer bewildering incongruity there is no play known to me which can be compared with *The Mayor of Queenborough.* Here again we find a note so dissonant and discordant in the lighter parts of the dramatic concert that we seem at once to recognise the harsher and hoarser instrument of Rowley. The farce is even more extravagantly and preposterously mistimed and misplaced than that which disfigures the play just mentioned: but I thoroughly agree with Mr. Bullen's high estimate of the power displayed and maintained throughout the tragic and poetic part of this drama; to which no previous critic has ever vouchsafed a word of due acknowledgment. The story is ugly and unnatural, but its repulsive effect is transfigured or neutralised by the charm of tender or passionate poetry; and it must be admitted that the hideous villainy of Vortiger and Horsus affords an opening for subsequent scenic effects of striking and genuine tragical interest.

The difference between the genius of Middleton and the genius of Dekker could not be better illustrated than by comparison of their attempts at political and patriotic allegory. The lazy, slovenly, impatient genius of Dekker flashes out by fits and starts on the reader of the play in which he has expressed his English hatred of Spain and Popery, his English pride in the rout of the Armada, and his English gratitude for the part played by Queen Elizabeth in the crowning struggle of the time: but his most cordial admirer can hardly consider *The Whore of Babylon* a shining or satisfactory example of dramatic art. *A Game at Chess*, the play which brought Middleton into prison, and earned for the actors a sum so far beyond parallel as to have seemed incredible till the fullest evidence was procured, is one of the most complete and exquisite works of artistic ingenuity and dexterity that ever excited or offended, enraptured or scandalised an audience of friends or enemies—the only work of English poetry which may properly be called Aristophanic. It has the same depth of civic seriousness, the same earnest ardour and devotion to the old cause of the old country, the same solid fervour of enthusiasm and indignation which animated the third great poet of Athens against the corruption of art by the sophistry of Euripides and the corruption of manhood by the sophistry of Socrates. The delicate skill of the workmanship can only be appreciated by careful and thorough study; but that the infusion of poetic fancy and feeling into the generally comic and satiric style is hardly unworthy of the comparison which I have ventured to challenge, I will take but one brief extract for evidence.

> "Upon those lips, the sweet fresh buds of youth,
> The holy dew of prayer lies, like pearl
> Dropt from the opening eyelids of the morn
> Upon a bashful rose."

Here for once even "that celestial thief" John Milton has impaired rather than improved the effect of the beautiful phrase borrowed from an earlier and inferior poet. His use of Middleton's exquisite image is not quite so apt—so perfectly picturesque and harmonious—as the use to which it was put by the inventor.

Nothing in the age of Shakespeare is so difficult for an Englishman of our own age to realise as the temper, the intelligence, the serious and refined elevation of an audience which was at once capable of enjoying and applauding the roughest and coarsest kinds of pleasantry, the rudest and crudest scenes of violence, and competent to appreciate the finest and the highest reaches of poetry, the subtlest and the most sustained allusions of ethical or political symbolism. The large and long popularity of an exquisite dramatic or academic allegory such as *Lingua*, which would seem to appeal only to readers of exceptional education, exceptional delicacy of perception, and exceptional quickness of wit, is hardly more remarkable than the popular success of a play requiring such keen constancy of attention, such vivid wakefulness and promptitude of apprehension, as this even more serious than fantastic work of Middleton's. The vulgarity and puerility of all modern attempts at any comparable effect need not be cited to throw into relief the essential finish, the impassioned intelligence, the high spiritual and literary level, of these crowded and brilliant and vehement five acts. Their extreme cleverness, their indefatigable ingenuity, would in any case have been remarkable: but their fullness of active and poetic life gives them an interest far deeper and higher and more permanent than the mere sense of curiosity and wonder.

But if *A Game at Chess* is especially distinguished by its complete and thorough harmony of execution and design, the lack of any such artistic merit in another famous work of Middleton's is such as once more to excite that irritating sense of inequality, irregularity, inconstancy of genius and inconsequence of aim, which too often besets and bewilders the student of our early dramatists. There is poetry enough in *The Witch* to furnish forth a whole generation of poeticules: but the construction or composition of the play, the arrangement and evolution of event, the distinction or development of character, would do less than little credit to a boy of twelve; who at any rate would hardly have thought of patching up so ridiculous a reconciliation between intending murderers and intended victims as here exceeds in absurdity the chaotic combination of accident and error which disposes of inconvenient or superfluous underlings. But though neither Mr. Dyce nor Mr. Bullen has been at all excessive or unjust in his animadversions on these flagrant faults and follies, neither editor has given his author due credit for the excellence of style, of language and versification, which makes this play readable throughout with pleasure, if not always without impatience. Fletcher himself, the acknowledged master of the style here adopted by Middleton, has left no finer example of metrical fluency and melodious ease. The fashion of dialogue and composition is no doubt rather feminine than masculine: Marlowe and Jonson, Webster and Beaumont, Tourneur and Ford,—to cite none but the greatest of authorities in this kind—wrote a firmer if not a freer hand, struck a graver if not a sweeter note of verse: this rapid effluence of easy expression is liable to lapse into conventional efflux of facile improvisation: but such command of it as Middleton's is impossible to any but a genuine and a memorable poet.

As for the supposed obligations of Shakespeare to Middleton or Middleton to Shakespeare, the imaginary relations of *The Witch* to *Macbeth* or *Macbeth* to *The Witch*, I can only say that the investigation of this subject seems to me as profitable as a research into the natural history of snakes in Iceland. That the editors to whom we owe the miserably defaced and villainously garbled text which is all that has reached us of *Macbeth*, not content with the mutilation of the greater poet, had recourse to the interpolation of a few superfluous and incongruous lines or fragments from the lyric portions of the lesser poet's work—that the players who mangled Shakespeare were the pilferers who plundered Middleton—must be obvious to all but those (if any such yet exist anywhere) who are capable of believing the unspeakably impudent assertion of those mendacious malefactors that they have left us a pure and perfect edition of Shakespeare. These passages are all thoroughly in keeping with the general tone of the lesser work: it would be tautology to add that they are no less utterly out of keeping with the general tone of the other. But in their own way nothing can be finer: they have a tragic liveliness in ghastliness, a grotesque animation of horror, which no other poet has ever conceived or conveyed to us. The difference between Michel Angelo and Goya, Tintoretto and Gustave Doré, does not quite efface the right of the minor artists to existence and remembrance.

The tragedy of *Women beware Women*, whether or not it be accepted as the masterpiece of Middleton, is at least an excellent example of the facility and fluency and equable promptitude of style which all students will duly appreciate and applaud in the riper and completer work of this admirable poet. It is full to overflowing of noble eloquence, of inventive resource and suggestive effect, of rhetorical affluence and theatrical ability. The opening or exposition of the play is quite masterly: and the scene in which the forsaken husband is seduced into consolation by the temptress of his wife is worthy of all praise for the straightforward ingenuity and the serious delicacy by which the action is rendered credible and the situation endurable. But I fear that few or none will be found to disagree with my opinion that no such approbation or tolerance can be reasonably extended so as to cover or condone the offences of either the underplot or the upshot of the play. The one is repulsive beyond redemption by elegance of style, the other is preposterous beyond extenuation on the score of logical or poetical justice. Those who object on principle to solution by massacre must object in consistency to the conclusions of *Hamlet* and *King Lear:* nor are the results of Webster's tragic invention more questionable or less inevitable than the results of Shakespeare's: but the dragnet of murder which gathers in the characters at the close of this play is as promiscuous in its sweep as that cast by Cyril Tourneur over the internecine shoal of sharks who are hauled in and ripped open at the close of *The Revenger's Tragedy*. Had Middleton been content with the admirable subject of his main action, he might have given us a simple and unimpeachable masterpiece: and even as it is he has left us a noble and a memorable work. It is true that the irredeemable infamy of the leading characters degrades and deforms the nature of the interest excited: the good and gentle old mother whose affectionate simplicity is so gracefully and attractively painted passes out of the story and drops out of the list of actors just when some redeeming figure is most needed to assuage the dreariness of disgust with which we follow the fortunes of so meanly criminal a crew: and the splendid eloquence of the only other respectable person in the play is not of itself sufficient to make a living figure, rather than a mere mouthpiece for indignant emotion, of so subordinate and inactive a character as the Cardinal. The lower comedy of the play is identical in motive with that which defaces the master-work of Ford: more stupid and offensive it hardly could be. But the high comedy of the scene between Livia and the Widow is as fine as the best work in that kind left us by the best poets and humourists of the Shakespearean age; it is not indeed unworthy of the comparison with Chaucer's which it suggested to the all but impeccable judgment of Charles Lamb.

The lack of moral interest and sympathetic attraction in the characters and the story, which has been noted as the principal defect in the otherwise effective composition of *Women beware Women*, is an objection which cannot be brought against the graceful tragicomedy of *The Spanish Gipsy*. Whatever is best in the tragic or in the romantic part of this play bears the stamp of Middleton's genius alike in the sentiment and the style. "The code of modern morals," to borrow a convenient phrase from Shelley, may hardly incline us to accept as plausible or as possible the repentance and the redemption of so brutal a ruffian as Roderigo: but the vivid beauty of the dialogue is equal to the vivid interest of the situation which makes the first act one of the most striking in any play of the time. The double action has some leading points in common with two of Fletcher's, which have nothing in common with each other: Merione in *The Queen of Corinth* is less interesting than Clara, but the vagabonds of *Beggar's Bush* are more amusing than Rowley's or Middleton's. The play is somewhat deficient in firmness or solidity of construction: it is, if such a phrase be permissible, one of those half-baked or underdone dishes of various and confused ingredients, in which the cook's or the baker's hurry has impaired the excellent materials of wholesome bread and savoury meat. The splendid slovens who served their audience with spiritual work in which the gods had mixed "so much of earth, so much of heaven, and such impetuous blood"—the generous and headlong purveyors who lavished on their daily provision of dramatic fare such wealth of fine material and such prodigality of superfluous grace—the foremost followers of Marlowe and of Shakespeare were too prone to follow the reckless example of the first rather than the severe example of the second. There is perhaps not one of them—and Middleton assuredly is not one—whom we can reasonably imagine capable of the patience and self-respect which induced Shakespeare to rewrite the triumphantly popular parts of Romeo, of Falstaff, and of Hamlet, with an eye to the literary perfection and permanence of work which in its first light outline had won the crowning suffrage of immediate or spectacular applause.

The rough and ready hand of Rowley may be traced, not indeed in the more high-toned passages, but in many of the most animated scenes of *The Spanish Gipsy*. In the most remarkable[1] of the ten masques or interludes which appear among the collected works of Middleton the two names are again associated. To the freshness, liveliness, and spirited ingenuity of this little

[1] *The World Tost at Tennis.*

allegorical comedy Mr. Bullen has done ample justice in his excellent critical introduction. *The Inner-Temple Masque*, less elaborate than *The World Tost at Tennis*, shows no lack of homely humour and invention: and in the others there is as much waste of fine flowing verse and facile fancy as ever excited the rational regret of a modern reader at the reckless profusion of literary power which the great poets of the time were content to lavish on the decoration or exposition of an ephemeral pageant. Of Middleton's other minor works, apocryphal or genuine, I will only say that his authorship of *Microcynicon*—a dull and crabbed imitation of Marston's worst work as a satirist—seems to me utterly incredible. A lucid and melodious fluency of style is the mark of all his metrical writing: and this stupid piece of obscure and clumsy jargon could have been the work of no man endowed with more faculty of expression than informs or modulates the whine of an average pig. Nor is it rationally conceivable that the Thomas Middleton who soiled some reams of paper with what he was pleased to consider or to call a paraphrase of the *Wisdom of Solomon* can have had anything but a poet's name in common with a poet. This name is not like that of the great writer whose name is attached to *The Transformed Metamorphosis*: there can hardly have been two Cyril Tourneurs in the field, but there may well have been half a dozen

Thomas Middletons. And Tourneur's abortive attempt at allegoric discourse is but a preposterous freak of prolonged eccentricity: this paraphrase is simply a tideless and interminable sea of limitless and inexhaustible drivel. There are three reasons—two of them considerable, but the third conclusive—for assigning to Middleton the two satirical tracts in the style of Nash, or rather of Dekker, which appeared in the same year with his initials subscribed to their prefatory addresses. Mr. Dyce thought they were written by the poet whose ready verse and realistic humour are both well represented in their text: Mr. Bullen agrees with Mr. Dyce in thinking that they are the work of Middleton. And Mr. Carew Hazlitt thinks that they are not.

No such absolute and final evidence as this can be adduced in favour or disfavour of the theory which would saddle the reputation of Middleton with the authorship of a dull and disjointed comedy, the work (it has hitherto been supposed) of the German substitute for Shakespeare. Middleton has no doubt left us more crude and shapeless plays than *The Puritan;* none, in my opinion—excepting always his very worst authentic example of farce or satire, *The Family of Love*—so heavy and so empty and so feeble. If it must be assigned to any author of higher rank than the new Shakspeare, I would suggest that it is much more like Rowley's than like Middleton's worst work. Of the best qualities which distinguish either of these writers as poet or as humourist, it has not the shadow or the glimmer of a vestige.

In the last and the greatest work which bears their united names[1]—a work which should suffice to make either name immortal, if immortality were other than an accidental attribute of genius—the very highest capacity of either poet is seen at its very best. There is more of mere poetry, more splendour of style and vehemence of verbal inspiration in the work of other poets then writing for the stage: the two masterpieces of Webster are higher in tone at their highest, more imaginative and more fascinating in their expression of terrible or of piteous truth: there are more superb harmonies, more glorious raptures of ardent and eloquent music, in the sometimes unsurpassed and unsurpassable poetic passion of Cyril Tourneur. But even Webster's men seem but splendid sketches, as Tourneur's seem but shadowy or fiery outlines, beside the perfect and living figure of De Flores. The man is so horribly human, so fearfully and wonderfully natural, in his single-hearted brutality of devotion, his absolute absorption of soul and body by one consuming force of passionately cynical desire, that we must go to Shakespeare for an equally original and an equally unquestionable revelation of indubitable truth. And

[1] *The Changeling.*

in no play by Beaumont and Fletcher is the concord between the two partners more singularly complete in unity of spirit and of style than throughout the tragic part of this play. The underplot from which it most unluckily and absurdly derives its title is very stupid, rather coarse, and almost vulgar: but the two great parts of Beatrice and De Flores are equally consistent, coherent and sustained, in the scenes obviously written by Middleton and in the scenes obviously written by Rowley. The subordinate part taken by Middleton in Dekker's play of *The Honest Whore* is difficult to discern from the context or to verify by inner evidence: though some likeness to his realistic or photographic method may be admitted as perceptible in the admirable picture of Bellafront's morning reception at the opening of the second act of the first part. But here we may assert with fair confidence that the first and the last scenes of the play bear the indisputable sign-manual of William Rowley. His vigorous and vivid genius, his somewhat hard and curt directness of style and manner, his clear and trenchant power of straightforward presentation or exposition, may be traced in every line as plainly as the hand of Middleton must be recognised in the main part of the tragic action intervening. To Rowley therefore must be assigned the very high credit of introducing and of dismissing with adequate and even triumphant effect the strangely original tragic figure which owes its fullest and finest development to the genius of Middleton. To both poets alike must unqualified and equal praise be given for the subtle simplicity of skill with which they make us appreciate the fatal and foreordained affinity between the ill-favoured, rough-mannered, broken-down gentleman, and the headstrong unscrupulous unobservant girl whose very abhorrence of him serves only to fling her down from her high station of haughty beauty into the very clutch of his ravenous and pitiless passion. Her cry of horror and astonishment at first perception of the price to be paid for a service she had thought to purchase with mere money is so wonderfully real in its artless and ingenuous sincerity that Shakespeare himself could hardly have bettered it :

> "Why, 'tis impossible thou canst be so wicked,
> And shelter such a cunning cruelty,
> To make his death the murderer of my honour!"

That note of incredulous amazement that the man whom she has just instigated to the commission of murder "can be so wicked" as to have served her ends for any end of his own beyond the pay of a professional assassin is a touch worthy of the greatest dramatist that ever lived. The perfect simplicity of expression is as notable as the perfect innocence of her surprise; the candid astonishment of a nature absolutely incapable of seeing more than one thing or holding more than one thought at a time. That she, the first criminal, should be honestly shocked as well as physically horrified by revelation of the real motive which impelled her accomplice into crime, gives a lurid streak of tragic humour to the lifelike interest of the scene; as the pure infusion of spontaneous poetry throughout redeems the whole work from the charge of vulgar subservience to a vulgar taste for the presentation or the contemplation of criminal horror. Instances of this happy and natural nobility of instinct abound in the casual expressions which give grace and animation always, but never any touch of rhetorical transgression or florid superfluity, to the brief and trenchant sword-play of the tragic dialogue.

> "That sigh would fain have utterance: take pity on 't,
> And lend it a free word; 'las, how it labours
> For liberty! I hear the murmur yet
> Beat at your bosom."

The wording of this passage is sufficient to attest the presence and approve the quality of a poet: the manner and the moment of its introduction would be enough to show the instinctive and inborn insight of a natural dramatist. As much may be said of the few words which give us a ghostly glimpse of supernatural terror:—

> "Ha! what art thou that tak'st away the light
> Betwixt that star and me? I dread thee not:
> 'Twas but a mist of conscience."

But the real power and genius of the work

cannot be shown by extracts—not even by such extracts as these. His friend and colleague, Dekker, shows to better advantage by the process of selection: hardly one of his plays leaves so strong and sweet an impression of its general and complete excellence as of separate scenes or passages of tender and delicate imagination or emotion beyond the reach of Middleton: but the tragic unity and completeness of conception which distinguish this masterpiece will be sought in vain among the less firm and solid figures of his less serious and profound invention. Had *The Changeling* not been preserved, we should not have known Middleton: as it is, we are more than justified in asserting that a critic who denies him a high place among the poets of England must be not merely ignorant of the qualities which involve a right or confer a claim to this position, but incapable of curing his ignorance by any process of study. The rough and rapid work which absorbed too much of this poet's time and toil seems almost incongruous with the impression made by the noble and thoughtful face, so full of gentle dignity and earnest composure, in which we recognise the graver and loftier genius of a man worthy to hold his own beside all but the greatest of his age. And that age was the age of Shakespeare.

ALGERNON CHARLES SWINBURNE.

THOMAS MIDDLETON was born, probably in London, about 1570. He was the only son[1] of William Middleton, gentleman, who settled in London and there married Anne, daughter of William Snow. We know nothing in regard to his education. A Thomas Middleton was admitted member of Gray's Inn in 1596, and this may have been the dramatist. In 1597 was published *The Wisdom of Solomon Paraphrased*, by Thomas Middleton, and in 1599 *Microcynicon, Six Snarling Satyres*, in the manner of Marston and Hall, by "T. M. Gent." It is doubtful whether these were written by the dramatist. They are of little or no value; if he wrote them the young writer was here slowly feeling his way in diverse paths. A recent critic has noted his "imperial confidence in the use of words," and in all his genuine productions we feel the force and facility of the style. He appears to have learnt much from the swift incisive energy of Nash's prose, and in *Father Hubbard's Tale* he pays an admiring and affectionate tribute to Nash, cut off in his "best blooming May."

We do not know when Middleton first discovered his vocation, probably about 1600. In 1602 we find him, with Webster, Drayton, and Munday, occupied in writing a play called *Cæsar's Fall*, which has perished; and in the same year he received five shillings for writing a prologue and epilogue, which have also perished, for Greene's *Friar Bacon* on its revival at court.

Middleton married in (it is supposed) 1603 a daughter

[1] There was a daughter, who was younger, called Avicia.

of one of the six clerks of Chancery. A son was born the following year; there were no other children. About this time he published two curious pamphlets, written in excellent prose, *Father Hubbard's Tale* and *The Black Book.* In the former he told the history of a young spendthrift; in the latter he showed his familiarity with the lives and haunts of London thieves and prostitutes. Middleton had, however, now found his vocation. During the succeeding years he produced plays, and plays only, with an occasional masque, in fairly quick succession, though it is now impossible to arrange them in their order of production. In 1620 he was appointed City Chronologer, to "set down all memorable acts of this City and occurrences thereof, and for such other employments as this Court shall have occasion to use him in," at a salary of £6 13s. 4d., speedily raised to £10; and, unlike his successor, Ben Jonson, he faithfully executed the duties of this office.

In 1624 occurred the chief incident in Middleton's career. The Spanish marriage had just been broken off, and there was great satisfaction in England on account of supposed Spanish intrigues. This satisfaction found expression in Middleton's *Game at Chess.* Its popularity was immense. "I doubt not but you have heard of our famous play of Gondomar," we read in a contemporary letter, "which hath been followed with extraordinary curiosity, and frequented by all sorts of people, old and young, rich and poor, masters and servants, papists, wise men, etc., churchmen and Scotsmen." And the writer goes on to say that a certain Lady Smith would persuade him to take her to see it, but that he could not sit so long, since it was necessary to be there at one o'clock, two hours before the usual hour at which plays began. It was acted for no less than nine successive days, and it is said that during these nine days the receipts amounted to the enormous sum of fifteen hundred pounds.[1] On the ninth performance Gondomar, the Spanish ambassador, protested; the play had to be withdrawn, and author and actors were summoned to appear before the Privy Council. Middleton, "shifting out of the way," failed to attend with the players, who received "a round and sharp reproof." A few days later, however, his son Edward tendered his appearance in place of his father. The players were bound in £300, and for a short time forbidden altogether to play. Middleton was, according to one account, committed to prison for some time.

In 1623 Middleton was living at Newington Butts. Here he died, and, as Mr. Dyce discovered from the register of the parish church, was buried on the 4th July, 1627. In the following year his widow, Magdalen Middleton, applied to the civic authorities for pecuniary assistance, and received twenty nobles (£6 13s. 4d.). He was succeeded in his office of City Chronologer by Ben Jonson.

Middleton attracted little attention from his fellows. Ben Jonson said to Drummond in his dogmatic fashion that Middleton was "a base fellow." He said the same of Day and others, and had little good to say of any of his contemporaries beyond Chapman, Shakespeare, and Fletcher. It is impossible now to tell what value should be assigned to this utterance. It seems clear that

[1] Dyce regarded this statement as a gross exaggeration; Mr. Bullen seems inclined to accept it.

Middleton, notwithstanding his broad humanity, his sedate power, his industry and popularity as a writer, attracted little of the love of his fellow-dramatists. It is worth while to quote one of the few testimonies in his favour.

> "Facetious Middleton, thy witty Muse
> Hath pleasèd all that books or men peruse.
> If any thee despise, he doth but show
> Antipathy to wit in daring so:
> Thy fame's above his malice, and 'twill be
> Dispraise enough for him to censure thee."

Posterity has confirmed the judgment of the obscure contemporary who wrote these lines, and Middleton's fame is now above even the "malice" of Ben Jonson.

There are two admirable editions of Middleton's works, Mr. Dyce's and Mr. Bullen's. The text of the plays here given is founded on a careful collation of the two. The Essay which forms the Introduction has been revised by Mr. Swinburne since it appeared in the *Nineteenth Century* of Jan., 1886.

The only known portrait of Middleton is a wood-cut prefixed to *Two New Playes*, published in 1657. An etching from this by a French artist forms the frontispiece to the present volume.

H. E.

A TRICK TO CATCH THE OLD ONE.

A *Trick to Catch the Old One* was licensed for printing on the 7th October, 1607, and published in 1608. There was a second edition in 1616. The title was a proverbial expression. Massinger was probably indebted to this play for the central situation of his *New Way to Pay Old Debts*.

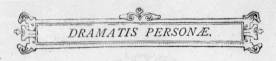

DRAMATIS PERSONÆ.

WITGOOD.
LUCRE, his uncle.
HOARD.
ONESIPHORUS HOARD, his brother.
LIMBER, KIX,[1] LAMPREY, SPICHCOCK, friends of HOARD.
DAMPIT.
GULF.
FREEDOM, son of MISTRESS LUCRE.
MONEYLOVE.
Host.
SIR LAUNCELOT.
Creditors.
Gentlemen.
GEORGE.
Drawer.
Boy.
Scrivener.
Servants, &c.

Courtesan.
MISTRESS LUCRE.
JOYCE, niece to HOARD.
LADY FOXSTONE.
AUDREY, servant to DAMPIT.

SCENE (except during the first two scenes of act i.)—
LONDON.

[1] Kix, or Kex, as it is indifferently spelt, means a dry stalk, and Dyce suggests that the name is evidently intended to apply to an elderly gentleman. It occurs again among the characters in *A Chaste Maid in Cheapside.*

A TRICK TO CATCH THE OLD ONE.

ACT THE FIRST.

SCENE I.

A Street in a Country Town.

Enter WITGOOD.

WIT. All's gone! still thou'rt a gentleman, that's all; but a poor one, that's nothing. What milk brings thy meadows forth now? where are thy goodly uplands, and thy down lands? all sunk into that little pit, lechery. Why should a gallant pay but two shillings for his ordinary that nourishes him, and twenty times two for his brothel[1] that consumes him? But where's Longacre[2]? in my uncle's conscience, which is three years' voyage about: he that sets out upon his conscience ne'er finds the way home again; he is either swallowed in the quicksands of law-quillets, or splits upon the piles of a *præmunire;* yet these old fox-brained and ox-browed uncles have still defences for their avarice, and apologies for their practices, and will thus greet our follies:

[1] Meaning here his harlot.

[2] A term applied to any estate.

He that doth his youth expose
To brothel, drink, and danger,
Let him that is his nearest kin
Cheat him before a stranger:

and that's his uncle; 'tis a principle in usury. I dare not visit the city: there I should be too soon visited by that horrible plague, my debts; and by that means I lose a virgin's love, her portion, and her virtues. Well, how should a man live now that has no living? hum,—why, are there not a million of men in the world that only sojourn upon their brain, and make their wits their mercers; and am I but one amongst that million, and cannot thrive upon't? Any trick, out of the compass of law, now would come happily to me.

Enter Courtesan.

Cour. My love!

Wit. My loathing! has thou been the secret consumption of my purse, and now comest to undo my last means, my wits? wilt leave no virtue in me, and yet thou ne'er the better?
Hence, courtesan, round-webbed tarantula,
That dry'st the roses in the cheeks of youth!

Cour. I've been true unto your pleasure; and all your lands
Thrice racked was never worth the jewel which
I prodigally gave you, my virginity:
Lands mortgaged may return, and more esteemed,
But honesty once pawned, is ne'er redeemed.

Wit. Forgive: I do thee wrong
To make thee sin, and then to chide thee for't.

Cour. I know I am your loathing now; farewell.

Wit. Stay, best invention, stay.

Cour. I that "have been the secret consumption of your purse," shall I stay now "to undo your last means, your wits? hence, courtesan," away!

Wit. I prithee, make me not mad at my own weapon:

stay (a thing few women can do, I know that, and therefore they had need wear stays), be not contrary: dost love me? Fate has so cast it that all my means I must derive from thee.

Cour. From me? be happy then;
What lies within the power of my performance
Shall be commanded of thee.

Wit. Spoke like
An honest drab, i'faith: it may prove something;
What trick is not an embryon at first,
Until a perfect shape come over it?

Cour. Come, I must help you: whereabouts left you?
I'll proceed:
Though you beget, 'tis I must help to breed.
Speak, what is't? I'd fain conceive it.

Wit. So, so, so: thou shalt presently take the name and form upon thee of a rich country widow, four hundred a-year valiant,[1] in woods, in bullocks, in barns, and in ryestacks; we'll to London, and to my covetous uncle.

Cour. I begin to applaud thee; our states being both desperate, they are soon resolute; but how for horses?

Wit. Mass, that's true; the jest will be of some continuance. Let me see; horses now, a bots on 'em! Stay, I have acquaintance with a mad host, never yet bawd to thee; I have rinsed the whoreson's gums in mull-sack many a time and often: put but a good tale into his ear now, so it come off cleanly, and there's horse and man for us, I dare warrant thee.

Cour. Arm your wits then
Speedily; there shall want nothing in me,
Either in behaviour, discourse, or fashion,
That shall discredit your intended purpose.
I will so artfully disguise my wants,
And set so good a courage on my state,
That I will be believed.

Wit. Why, then, all's furnished. I shall go nigh to

[1] Worth.

catch that old fox mine uncle: though he make but some amends for my undoing, yet there's some comfort in't, he cannot otherwise choose (though it be but in hope to cozen me again) but supply any hasty want that I bring to town with me. The device well and cunningly carried, the name of a rich widow, and four hundred a-year in good earth, will so conjure up a kind of usurer's love in him to me, that he will not only desire my presence,—which at first shall scarce be granted him, I'll keep off a' purpose,—but I shall find him so officious to deserve, so ready to supply! I know the state of an old man's affection so well: if his nephew be poor indeed, why, he let's God alone with him; but if he be once rich, then he'll be the first man that helps him.

Cour. 'Tis right the world; for, in these days, an old man's love to his kindred is like his kindness to his wife, 'tis always done before he comes at it.

Wit. I owe thee for that jest. Begone: here's all my wealth; prepare thyself, away. I'll to mine host with all possible haste; and with the best art, and most profitable form, pour the sweet circumstance into his ear, which shall have the gift to turn all the wax to honey. [*Exit Courtesan.*]—How now? O, the right worshipful seniors of our country!

Enter ONESIPHORUS HOARD, LIMBER, *and* KIX.

O. Hoa. Who's that?

Lim. O, the common rioter; take no note of him.

Wit. You will not see me now; the comfort is,
Ere it be long you will scarce see yourselves.
[*Aside, and exit.*

O. Hoa. I wonder how he breathes; has consumed all
Upon that courtesan.

Lim. We have heard so much.

O. Hoa. You've heard all truth. His uncle and my brother
Have been these three years mortal adversaries:

Two old tough spirits, they seldom meet but fight,
Or quarrel when 'tis calmest:
I think their anger be the very fire
That keeps their age alive.

Lim. What was the quarrel, sir?

O. Hoa. Faith, about a purchase, fetching over a young heir. Master Hoard, my brother, having wasted much time in beating the bargain, what did me old Lucre, but as his conscience moved him, knowing the poor gentleman, stept in between 'em and cozened him himself.

Lim. And was this all, sir?

O. Hoa. This was e'en it, sir; yet for all this, I know no reason but the match might go forward betwixt his wife's son and my niece; what though there be a dissension between the two old men, I see no reason it should put a difference between the two younger; 'tis as natural for old folks to fall out, as for young to fall in. A scholar comes a-wooing to my niece; well, he's wise, but he's poor: her son comes a wooing to my niece; well, he's a fool, but he's rich.

Lim. Ay, marry, sir.

O. Hoa. Pray, now, is not a rich fool better than a poor philosopher?

Lim. One would think so, i'faith.

O. Hoa. She now remains at London with my brother, her second uncle, to learn fashions, practise music; the voice between her lips, and the viol between her legs, she'll be fit for a consort[1] very speedily: a thousand good pound is her portion; if she marry, we'll ride up and be merry.

Kix. A match, if it be a match. [*Exeunt.*

[1] A play upon the word which signifies one of a band of musicians as well as a wife.

SCENE II.

Another Street in the same Town.

Enter WITGOOD, *meeting* Host.

Wit. Mine host!

Host. Young Master Witgood.

Wit. I have been laying[1] all the town for thee.

Host. Why, what's the news, bully Had-land?

Wit. What geldings are in the house, of thine own? Answer me to that first.

Host. Why, man, why?

Wit. Mark me what I say: I'll tell thee such a tale in thine ear, that thou shalt trust me spite of thy teeth, furnish me with some money willy nilly, and ride up with me thyself *contra voluntatem et professionem.*

Host. How? let me see this trick, and I'll say thou hast more art than a conjuror.

Wit. Dost thou joy in my advancement?

Host. Do I love sack and ginger?

Wit. Comes my prosperity desiredly to thee?

Host. Come forfeitures to a usurer, fees to an officer, punks to an host, and pigs to a parson desiredly? why, then, la.

Wit. Will the report of a widow of four hundred a-year, boy, make thee leap, and sing, and dance, and come to thy place again?

Host. Wilt thou command me now? I am thy spirit; conjure me into any shape.

Wit. I ha' brought her from her friends, turned back the horses by a slight; not so much as one among her six men, goodly large yeomanly fellows, will she trust with this her purpose: by this light, all unmanned, regardless of her state, neglectful of vain-glorious ceremony, all for my love. O, 'tis a fine little voluble tongue, mine host, that wins a widow!

[1] Searching.

Host. No, 'tis a tongue with a great T, my boy, that wins a widow.

Wit. Now, sir, the case stands thus : good mine host, if thou lovest my happiness, assist me.

Host. Command all my beasts i' th' house.

Wit. Nay, that's not all neither: prithee take truce with thy joy, and listen to me. Thou knowest I have a wealthy uncle i' th' city, somewhat the wealthier by my follies: the report of this fortune, well and cunningly carried, might be a means to draw some goodness from the usuring rascal; for I have put her in hope already of some estate that I have either in land or money: now, if I be found true in neither, what may I expect but a sudden breach of our love, utter dissolution of the match, and confusion of my fortunes for ever?

Host. Wilt thou but trust the managing of thy business with me?

Wit. With thee? why, will I desire to thrive in my purpose? will I hug four hundred a-year, I that know the misery of nothing? Will that man wish a rich widow that has ne'er a hole to put his head in? With thee, mine host? why, believe it, sooner with thee than with a covey of counsellors.

Host. Thank you for your good report, i'faith, sir; and if I stand you not in stead, why then let an host come off *hic et hæc hostis*, a deadly enemy to dice, drink, and venery. Come, where's this widow?

Wit. Hard at Park-end.

Host. I'll be her serving-man for once.

Wit. Why, there we let off together: keep full time; my thoughts were striking then just the same number?

Host. I knew't: shall we then see our merry days again?

Wit. Our merry nights—which ne'er shall be more seen. [*Aside.*] [*Exeunt.*

SCENE III.

A Street in London.

Enter LUCRE *and* HOARD *quarrelling;* LAMPREY, SPICHCOCK, FREEDOM, *and* MONEYLOVE, *coming between to pacify them.*

Lam. Nay, good Master Lucre, and you, Master Hoard, anger is the wind which you're both too much troubled withal.

Hoa. Shall my adversary thus daily affront me, ripping up the old wound of our malice, which three summers could not close up? into which wound the very sight of him drops scalding lead instead of balsamum.

Luc. Why, Hoard, Hoard, Hoard, Hoard, Hoard! may I not pass in the state of quietness to mine own house? answer me to that, before witness, and why? I'll refer the cause to honest, even-minded gentlemen or require the mere indifferences of the law to decide this matter. I got the purchase,[1] true: was't not any man's case? yes: will a wise man stand as a bawd, whilst another wipes his nose[2] of the bargain? no; I answer no in that case.

Lam. Nay, sweet Master Lucre.

Hoa. Was it the part of a friend—no, rather of a Jew; —mark what I say—when I had beaten the bush to the last bird, or, as I may term it, the price to a pound, then, like a cunning usurer, to come in the evening of the bargain, and glean all my hopes in a minute? to enter, as it were, at the back door of the purchase? for thou ne'er camest the right way by it.

Luc. Hast thou the conscience to tell me so without any impeachment to thyself?

Hoa. Thou that canst defeat thy own nephew, Lucre, lap his lands into bonds, and take the extremity of thy

[1] The booty. [2] Cheats him.

kindred's forfeitures, because he's a rioter, a wastethrift, a brothel-master, and so forth; what may a stranger expect from thee but *vulnera dilacerata*, as the poet says dilacerate dealing?

Luc. Upbraidest thou me with nephew? is all imputation laid upon me? what acquaintance have I with his follies? if he riot, 'tis he must want it; if he surfeit, 'tis he must feel it; if he drab it, 'tis he must lie by't: what's this to me?

Hoa. What's all to thee? nothing, nothing; such is the gulf of thy desire and the wolf of thy conscience: but be assured, old Pecunius Lucre, if ever fortune so bless me, that I may be at leisure to vex thee, or any means so favour me, that I may have opportunity to mad thee, I will pursue it with that flame of hate, that spirit of malice, unrepressed wrath, that I will blast thy comforts.

Luc. Ha, ha, ha!

Lam. Nay, Master Hoard, you're a wise gentleman——

Hoa. I will so cross thee——

Luc. And I thee.

Hoa. So without mercy fret thee——

Luc. So monstrously oppose thee——

Hoa. Dost scoff at my just anger? O, that I had as much power as usury has over thee!

Luc. Then thou wouldst have as much power as the devil has over thee.

Hoa. Toad!

Luc. Aspic!

Hoa. Serpent!

Luc. Viper!

Spi. Nay, gentlemen, then we must divide you perforce.

Lam. When the fire grows too unreasonable hot, there's no better way than to take off the wood.

[*Exeunt* LAMPREY *and* SPICHCOCK, *drawing off* LUCRE *and* HOARD *different ways.*

Free. A word, good signior.

Mon. How now, what's the news?

Free. 'Tis given me to understand that you are a rival of mine in the love of Mistress Joyce, Master Hoard's niece: say me ay, say me no?

Mon. Yes, 'tis so.

Free. Then look to yourself, you cannot live long: I'm practising every morning; a month hence I'll challenge you.

Mon. Give me your hand upon't; there's my pledge I'll meet you. [*Strikes him, and exit.*

Free. O, O! what reason had you for that, sir, to strike before the month? you knew I was not ready for you, and that made you so crank:[1] I am not such a coward to strike again, I warrant you. My ear has the law of her side, for it burns horribly. I will teach him to strike a naked face, the longest day of his life: 'slid, it shall cost me some money but I'll bring this box into the chancery. [*Exit.*

SCENE IV.

Another Street.

Enter WITGOOD *and* HOST.

Host. Fear you nothing, sir; I have lodged her in a house of credit, I warrant you.

Wit. Hast thou the writings?

Host. Firm, sir.

Wit. Prithee, stay, and behold two the most prodigious rascals that ever slipt into the shape of men; Dampit, sirrah, and young Gulf his fellow-caterpillar.

Host. Dampit? sure I have heard of that Dampit?

Wit. Heard of him? why, man, he that has lost both his ears may hear of him; a famous infamous trampler[2] of time; his own phrase. Note him well: that Dampit,

[1] Lively. [2] A term frequently applied at the time to lawyers.

sirrah, he in the uneven beard and the serge cloak, is the most notorious, usuring, blasphemous, atheistical, brothel-vomiting rascal, that we have in these latter times now extant; whose first beginning was the stealing of a masty[1] dog from a farmer's house.

Host. He looked as if he would obey the commandments well, when he began first with stealing.

Wit. True: the next town he came at, he set the dogs together by th' ears.

Host. A sign he should follow the law, by my faith.

Wit. So it followed, indeed; and being destitute of all fortunes, staked his masty against a noble,[2] and by great fortune his dog had the day; how he made it up ten shillings, I know not, but his own boast is, that he came to town with but ten shillings in his purse, and now is credibly worth ten thousand pound.

Host. How the devil came he by it?

Enter DAMPIT *and* GULF.

Wit. How the devil came he not by it? If you put in the devil once, riches come with a vengeance: has been a trampler of the law, sir; and the devil has a care of his footmen. The rogue has spied me now; he nibbled me finely once, too:—a pox search you! [*Aside.*]—O, Master Dampit!—the very loins of thee! [*Aside.*]—Cry you mercy, Master Gulf; you walk so low, I promise you I saw you not, sir.

Gulf. He that walks low walks safe, the poets tell us.

Wit. And nigher hell by a foot and a half than the rest of his fellows. [*Aside.*]—But, my old Harry!

Dam. My sweet Theodorus!

Wit. 'Twas a merry world when thou camest to town with ten shillings in thy purse.

Dam. And now worth ten thousand pound, my boy. Report it; Harry Dampit, a trampler of time, say, he

1 Mastiff.

2 A gold coin worth 6*s.* 8*d.*

would be up in a morning, and be here with his serge gown, dashed up to the hams in a cause; have his feet stink about Westminster Hall, and come home again; see the galleons, the galleasses,[1] the great armadas of the law; then there be hoys and petty vessels, oars and scullers of the time; there be picklocks of the time too: then would I be here; I would trample up and down like a mule: now to the judges, "May it please your reverend honourable fatherhoods;" then to my counsellor, "May it please your worshipful patience;" then to the examiner's office, "May it please your mastership's gentleness;" then to one of the clerks, "May it please your worshipful lousiness,"—for I find him scrubbing in his codpiece; then to the hall again, then to the chamber again——

Wit. And when to the cellar again?

Dam. E'en when thou wilt again: tramplers of time, motions[2] of Fleet Street, and visions of Holborn; here I have fees of one, there I have fees of another; my clients come about me, the fooliaminy and coxcombry of the country: I still trashed and trotted for other men's causes; thus was poor Harry Dampit made rich by others' laziness, who though they would not follow their own suits, I made 'em follow me with their purses.

Wit. Didst thou so, old Harry?

Dam. Ay, and I soused 'em with bills of charges, i'faith; twenty pound a-year have I brought in for boat-hire, and I ne'er stept into boat in my life.

Wit. Tramplers of time!

Dam. Ay, tramplers of time, rascals of time, bull-beggars![3]

Wit. Ah, thou'rt a mad old Harry!—Kind Master Gulf, I am bold to renew my acquaintance.

Gulf. I embrace it, sir. [*Exeunt.*

[1] Huge heavy-built galleys.
[2] Puppet-shows. [3] Hobgoblins.

ACT THE SECOND.

SCENE I.

A Room in LUCRE'S *House.*

Enter LUCRE.

LUC. My adversary evermore twits me with my nephew, forsooth, my nephew: why may not a virtuous uncle have a dissolute nephew? What though he be a brotheller, a wastethrift, a common surfeiter, and, to conclude, a beggar, must sin in him call up shame in me? Since we have no part in their follies, why should we have part in their infamies? For my strict hand toward his mortgage, that I deny not: I confess I had an uncle's pen'worth; let me see, half in half, true: I saw neither hope of his reclaiming, nor comfort in his being; and was it not then better bestowed upon his uncle than upon one of his aunts?—I need not say bawd, for every one knows what aunt stands for in the last translation.

Enter Servant.

Now, Sir?

Ser. There's a country serving-man, sir, attends to speak with your worship.

Luc. I'm at best leisure now; send him in to me.

[*Exit* Servant.

Enter Host *disguised as a serving-man.*

Host. Bless your venerable worship.

Luc. Welcome, good fellow.

Host. He calls me thief[1] at first sight, yet he little thinks I am an host. [*Aside.*

Luc. What's thy business with me?

Host. Faith, sir, I am sent from my mistress, to any sufficient gentleman indeed, to ask advice upon a doubtful point: 'tis indifferent, sir, to whom I come, for I know none, nor did my mistress direct me to any particular man, for she's as mere a stranger here as myself; only I found your worship within, and 'tis a thing I ever loved, sir, to be despatched as soon as I can.

Luc. A good, blunt honesty; I like him well. [*Aside.*] —What is thy mistress?

Host. Faith, a country gentlewoman, and a widow, sir. Yesterday was the first flight of us; but now she intends to stay till a little term business be ended.

Luc. Her name, I prithee?

Host. It runs there in the writings, sir, among her lands; Widow Medler.

Luc. Medler? mass, have I ne'er heard of that widow?

Host. Yes, I warrant you, have you, sir; not the rich widow in Staffordshire?

Luc. Cuds me, there 'tis indeed; thou hast put me into memory: there's a widow indeed; ah, that I were a bachelor again!

Host. No doubt your worship might do much then; but she's fairly promised to a bachelor already.

Luc. Ah, what is he, I prithee?

Host. A country gentleman too; one of whom your worship knows not, I'm sure; has spent some few follies in his youth, but marriage, by my faith, begins to call him home: my mistress loves him, sir, and love covers faults, you know: one Master Witgood, if ever you have heard of the gentleman.

Luc. Ha! Witgood, sayst thou?

[1] "Good fellow" was then the cant terms for a thief.

Host. That's his name indeed, sir; my mistress is like to bring him to a goodly seat yonder; four hundred a-year, by my faith.

Luc. But, I pray, take me with you.[1]

Host. Ay, sir.

Luc. What countryman might this young Witgood be?

Host. A Leicestershire gentleman, sir.

Luc. My nephew, by th' mass, my nephew? I'll fetch out more of this, i'faith: a simple country fellow, I'll work't out of him. [*Aside.*]—And is that gentleman, sayst thou, presently to marry her?

Host. Faith, he brought her up to town, sir; has the best card in all the bunch for't, her heart; and I know my mistress will be married ere she go down; nay, I'll swear that, for she's none of those widows that will go down first, and be married after; she hates that, I can tell you, sir.

Luc. By my faith, sir, she is like to have a proper gentleman, and a comely; I'll give her that gift.

Host. Why, does your worship know him, sir?

Luc. I know him? does not all the world know him? can a man of such exquisite qualities be hid under a bushel?

Host. Then your worship may save me a labour, for I had charge given me to inquire after him.

Luc. Inquire of him? If I might counsel thee, thou shouldst ne'er trouble thyself further; inquire of him no more, but of me; I'll fit thee. I grant he has been youthful; but is he not now reclaimed? mark you that, sir: has not your mistress, think you, been wanton in her youth? if men be wags, are there not women wagtails? [2]

Host. No doubt, sir.

Luc. Does not he return wisest that comes home whipt with his own follies?

Host. Why, very true, sir.

[1] *i.e.* Let me understand you. [2] Profligate women.

Luc. The worst report you can hear of him, I can tell you, is that he has been a kind gentleman, a liberal, and a worthy; who but lusty Witgood, thrice-noble Witgood!

Host. Since your worship has so much knowledge in him, can you resolve me, sir, what his living might be? my duty binds me, sir, to have a care of my mistress' estate; she has been ever a good mistress to me, though I say it: many wealthy suitors has she nonsuited for his sake; yet, though her love be so fixed, a man cannot tell whether his non-performance may help to remove it, sir; he makes us believe he has lands and living.

Luc. Who, young Master Witgood? why, believe it, he has as goodly a fine living out yonder.—what do you call the place.

Host. Nay, I know not, i'faith.

Luc. Hum—see, like a beast, if I have not forgot the name—pooh! and out yonder again, goodly grown woods and fair meadows: pax on't, I can ne'er hit of that place neither: he? why, he's Witgood of Witgood Hall; he an unknown thing!

Host. Is he so, sir? To see how rumour will alter! trust me, sir, we heard once he had no lands, but all lay mortgaged to an uncle he has in town here.

Luc. Pish, 'tis a tale, 'tis a tale.

Host. I can assure you, sir, 'twas credibly reported to my mistress.

Luc. Why, do you think, i'faith, he was ever so simple to mortgage his lands to his uncle? or his uncle so unnatural to take the extremity of such a mortgage?

Host. That was my saying still, sir.

Luc. Pooh, ne'er think it.

Host. Yet that report goes current.

Luc. Nay, then you urge me:
Cannot I tell that best that am his uncle?

Host. How, sir? what have I done!

Luc. Why, how now! in a swoon, man?

Host. Is your worship his uncle, sir?

Luc. Can that be any harm to you, sir?

Host. I do beseech you, sir, do me the favour to conceal it: what a beast was I to utter so much! pray, sir, do me the kindness to keep it in; I shall have my coat pulled o'er my ears, an't should be known; for the truth is, an't please your worship, to prevent much rumour and many suitors, they intend to be married very suddenly and privately.

Luc. And dost thou think it stands with my judgment to do them injury? must I needs say the knowledge of this marriage comes from thee? am I a fool at fifty-four? do I lack subtlety now, that have got all my wealth by it? There's a leash of angels[1] for thee: come, let me woo thee speak where lie they?

Host. So I might have no anger, sir——

Luc. Passion of me, not a jot: prithee, come.

Host. I would not have it known, sir, it came by my means.

Luc. Why, am I a man of wisdom?

Host. I dare trust your worship, sir; but I'm a stranger to your house; and to avoid all intelligencers, I desire your worship's ear.

Luc. This fellow's worth a matter of trust. [*Aside.*]—Come, sir. [Host *whispers to him.*] Why, now thou'rt an honest lad.—Ah, sirrah, nephew!

Host. Please you, sir, now I have begun with your worship, when shall I attend for your advice upon that doubtful point? I must come warily now.

Luc. Tut, fear thou nothing;
To-morrow's evening shall resolve the doubt.

Host. The time shall cause my attendance.

Luc. Fare thee well. [*Exit* Host.]—There's more true honesty in such a country serving-man than in a hundred of our cloak companions:[2] I may well call 'em companions, for since blue[3] coats have been turned into

[1] Gold coins, each worth from 6*s.* 8*d.* to 10*s.*
[2] Scurvy fellows. [3] The common livery of serving-men.

cloaks, we can scarce know the man from the master.—George!

Enter GEORGE.

Geo. Anon, sir.

Luc. List hither: [*whispers*] keep the place secret: commend me to my nephew; I knew no cause, tell him, but he might see his uncle.

Geo. I will, sir.

Luc. And, do you hear, sir?
Take heed to use him with respect and duty.

Geo. Here's a strange alteration; one day he must be turned out like a beggar, and now he must be called in like a knight. [*Aside, and exit.*

Luc. Ah, sirrah, that rich widow!—four hundred a-year! beside, I hear she lays claim to a title of a hundred more. This falls unhappily that he should bear a grudge to me now, being likely to prove so rich: what is 't, trow, that he makes me a stranger for? Hum,—I hope he has not so much wit to apprehend that I cozened him: he deceives me then. Good Heaven, who would have thought it would ever have come to this pass! yet he's a proper gentleman, i' faith, give him his due,—marry, that's his mortgage; but that I ne'er mean to give him: I'll make him rich enough in words, if that be good: and if it come to a piece of money, I will not greatly stick for't; there may be hope some of the widow's lands, too, may one day fall upon me, if things be carried wisely.

Re-enter GEORGE.

Now, sir, where is he?

Geo. He desires your worship to hold him excused; he has such weighty business, it commands him wholly from all men.

Luc. Were those my nephew's words?

Geo. Yes, indeed, sir.

Luc. When men grow rich, they grow proud too, I perceive that; he would not have sent me such an answer once within this twelvemonth : see what 'tis when a man's come to his lands ! [*Aside.*]—Return to him again, sir ; tell him his uncle desires his company for an hour ; I'll trouble him but an hour, say ; 'tis for his own good, tell him : and, do you hear, sir ? put "worship" upon him go to, do as I bid you ; he's like to be a gentleman of worship very shortly.

Geo. This is good sport, i' faith. [*Aside, and exit.*

Luc. Troth, he uses his uncle discourteously now : can he tell what I may do for him? goodness may come from me in a minute, that comes not in seven year again : he knows my humour ; I am not so usually good ; 'tis no small thing that draws kindness from me, he may know that an he will. The chief cause that invites me to do him most good is the sudden astonishing of old Hoard, my adversary : how pale his malice will look at my nephew's advancement ! with what a dejected spirit he will behold his fortunes, whom but last day he proclaimed rioter, penurious makeshift, despised brothel-master ! Ha, ha ! 'twill do me more secret joy than my last purchase, more precious comfort than all these widow's revenues.

Re-enter GEORGE, *showing in* WITGOOD.

Now, sir ?

Geo. With much entreaty he's at length come, sir. [*Exit.*

Luc. O, nephew, let me salute you, sir ! you're welcome, nephew.

Wit. Uncle, I thank you.

Luc. You've a fault, nephew ; you're a stranger here : Well, Heaven give you joy !

Wit. Of what, sir ?

Luc. Hah, we can hear !
You might have known your uncle's house, i'faith,
You and your widow : go to, you were to blame ;
If I may tell you so without offence.

Wit. How could you hear of that, sir ?

Luc. O, pardon me!
'Twas your will to have kept it from me, I perceive now.

Wit. Not for any defect of love, I protest, uncle.

Luc. Oh, 'twas unkindness, nephew! fie, fie, fie.

Wit. I am sorry you take it in that sense, sir.

Luc. Pooh, you cannot colour it, i'faith, nephew.

Wit. Will you but hear what I can say in my just excuse, sir.

Luc. Yes, faith, will I, and welcome.

Wit. You that know my danger i' th' city, sir, so well, how great my debts are, and how extreme my creditors, could not out of your pure judgment, sir, have wished us hither.

Luc. Mass, a firm reason indeed.

Wit. Else, my uncle's house! why, 't had been the only make-match.

Luc. Nay, and thy credit.

Wit. My credit? nay, my countenance: pish, nay, I know, uncle, you would have wrought it so by your wit, you would have made her believe in time the whole house had been mine.

Luc. Ay, and most of the goods too.

Wit. La, you there! well, let 'em all prate what they will, there's nothing like the bringing of a widow to one's uncle's house.

Luc. Nay, let nephews be ruled as they list, they shall find their uncle's house the most natural place when all's done.

Wit. There they may be bold.

Luc. Life, they may do anything there, man, and fear neither beadle nor somner:[1] an uncle's house! a very Cole-Harbour.[2] Sirrah, I'll touch thee near now: hast thou so much interest in thy widow, that by a token thou couldst presently send for her?

[1] Summoner.

[2] A corruption of Cold Harbour, a building in the parish of All-Hallows the Less, where debtors and vagabonds found sanctuary.

Wit. Troth, I think I can, uncle.

Luc. Go to, let me see that.

Wit. Pray, command one of your men hither, uncle.

Luc. George!

Re-enter GEORGE.

Geo. Here, sir.

Luc. Attend my nephew. [WITGOOD *whispers to* GEORGE, *who then goes out.*]—I love a' life to prattle with a rich widow; 'tis pretty, methinks, when our tongues go together: and then to promise much and perform little; I love that sport a' life, i' faith; yet I am in the mood now to do my nephew some good, if he take me handsomely. [*Aside.*]—What, have you despatched?

Wit. I ha' sent, sir.

Luc. Yet I must condemn you of unkindness, nephew.

Wit. Heaven forbid, uncle!

Luc. Yes, faith, must I. Say your debts be many, your creditors importunate, yet the kindness of a thing is all, nephew: you might have sent me close word on 't, without the least danger or prejudice to your fortunes.

Wit. Troth, I confess it, uncle; I was to blame there; but, indeed, my intent was to have clapped it up suddenly, and so have broke forth like a joy to my friends, and a wonder to the world: beside, there's a trifle of a forty pound matter toward the setting of me forth; my friends should ne'er have known on 't; I meant to make shift for that myself.

Luc. How, nephew? let me not hear such a word again, I beseech you: shall I be beholden to you?

Wit. To me? Alas, what do you mean, uncle?

Luc. I charge you, upon my love, you trouble nobody but myself.

Wit. You've no reason for that, uncle.

Luc. Troth, I'll ne'er be friends with you while you live, an you do.

Wit. Nay, an you say so, uncle, here's my hand; I will not do 't.

Luc. Why, well said! there's some hope in thee when thou wilt be ruled; I'll make it up fifty, faith, because I see thee so reclaimed. Peace; here comes my wife with Sam, her t'other husband's son.

Enter MISTRESS LUCRE *and* FREEDOM.

Wit. Good aunt.

Free. Cousin Witgood, I rejoice in my salute; you're most welcome to this noble city, governed with the sword in the scabbard.

Wit. And the wit in the pommel. [*Aside.*]—Good Master Sam Freedom, I return the salute.

Luc. By the mass, she's coming, wife; let me see now how thou wilt entertain her.

Mis. L. I hope I am not to learn, sir, to entertain a widow; 'tis not so long ago since I was one myself.

Enter Courtesan.

Wit. Uncle——

Luc. She's come indeed.

Wit. My uncle was desirous to see you, widow, and I presumed to invite you.

Cour. The presumption was nothing, Master Witgood: is this your uncle, sir?

Luc. Marry am I, sweet widow; and his good uncle he shall find me; ay, by this smack that I give thee [*Kisses her*], thou'rt welcome.—Wife, bid the widow welcome the same way again.

Free. I am a gentleman now too by my father's occupation, and I see no reason but I may kiss a widow by my father's copy: truly, I think the charter is not against it; surely these are the words, "The son once a gentleman may revel it, though his father were a dauber;" 'tis about the fifteenth page: I'll to her.

[*Aside, then offers to kiss the* Courtesan, *who repulses him.*

Luc. You're not very busy now; a word with thee, sweet widow.

Free. Coads-nigs! I was never so disgraced since the hour my mother whipt me.

Luc. Beside, I have no child of mine own to care for; she's my second wife, old, past bearing; clap sure to him, widow; he's like to be my heir, I can tell you.

Cour. Is he so, sir?

Luc. He knows it already, and the knave's proud on 't; jolly rich widows have been offered him here i' th' city, great merchants' wives; and do you think he would once look upon 'em? forsooth, he'll none: you are beholding to him i' th' country, then, ere we could be: nay, I'll hold a wager, widow, if he were once known to be in town, he would be presently sought after; nay, and happy were they that could catch him first.

Cour. I think so.

Luc. O, there would be such running to and fro, widow! he should not pass the streets for 'em: he'd be took up in one great house or other presently: faugh! they know he has it, and must have it. You see this house here, widow; this house and all comes to him; goodly rooms, ready furnished, ceiled with plaster of Paris, and all hung about with cloth of arras.—Nephew.

Wit. Sir.

Luc. Show the widow your house; carry her into all the rooms, and bid her welcome.—You shall see, widow.—Nephew, strike all sure above an thou beest a good boy,—ah! [*Aside to* WITGOOD.

Wit. Alas, sir, I know not how she would take it!

Luc. The right way, I warrant t'ye: a pox, art an ass? would I were in thy stead! get you up, I am ashamed of you. [*Exeunt* WITGOOD *and* Courtesan.] So: let 'em agree as they will now: many a match has been struck up in my house a' this fashion: let 'em try all manner of ways, still there's nothing like an uncle's house to strike the stroke in. I'll hold my wife in talk a little.—Now

Jenny, your son there goes a-wooing to a poor gentlewoman but of a thousand pound portion: see my nephew, a lad of less hope, strikes at four hundred a-year in good rubbish.

Mis. L. Well, we must do as we may, sir.

Luc. I'll have his money ready told for him against he come down: let me see, too;—by th' mass, I must present the widow with some jewel, a good piece of plate, or such a device; 'twill hearten her on well: I have a very fair standing cup; and a good high standing cup will please a widow above all other pieces. [*Exit.*

Mis. L. Do you mock us with your nephew?—I have a plot in my head, son;—i'faith, husband, to cross you.

Free. Is it a tragedy plot, or a comedy plot, good mother?

Mis. L. 'Tis a plot shall vex him. I charge you, of my blessing, son Sam, that you presently withdraw the action of your love from Master Hoard's niece.

Free. How, mother?

Mis. L. Nay, I have a plot in my head, i'faith. Here, take this chain of gold, and this fair diamond: dog me the widow home to her lodging, and at thy best opportunity, fasten 'em both upon her. Nay, I have a reach: I can tell you thou art known what thou art, son, among the right worshipful, all the twelve companies.

Free. Truly, I thank 'em for it.

Mis. L. He? he's a scab to thee: and so certify her thou hast two hundred a-year of thyself, beside thy good parts—a proper person and a lovely. If I were a widow, I could find in my heart to have thee myself, son; ay, from 'em all.

Free. Thank you for your good will, mother; but, indeed, I had rather have a stranger: and if I woo her not in that violent fashion, that I will make her be glad to take these gifts ere I leave her, let me never be called the heir of your body.

Mis. L. Nay, I know there's enough in you, son, if you once come to put it forth.

Free. I'll quickly make a bolt or a shaft on't.[1]

[*Exeunt.*

SCENE II.

A Street.

Enter HOARD *and* MONEYLOVE.

Mon. Faith, Master Hoard, I have bestowed many months in the suit of your niece, such was the dear love I ever bore to her virtues: but since she hath so extremely denied me, I am to lay out for my fortunes elsewhere.

Hoa. Heaven forbid but you should, sir! I ever told you my niece stood otherwise affected.

Mon. I must confess you did, sir; yet, in regard of my great loss of time, and the zeal with which I sought your niece, shall I desire one favour of your worship?

Hoa. In regard of those two, 'tis hard but you shall, sir.

Mon. I shall rest grateful: 'tis not full three hours, sir, since the happy rumour of a rich country widow came to my hearing.

Hoa. How? a rich country widow?

Mon. Four hundred a-year landed.

Hoa. Yea?

Mon. Most firm, sir; and I have learnt her lodging: here my suit begins, sir; if I might but entreat your worship to be a countenance for me, and speak a good word (for your words will pass), I nothing doubt but I might set fair for the widow; nor shall your labour, sir, end altogether in thanks; two hundred angels——[2]

[1] A proverb meaning to take the risk. A shaft was a sharp-pointed arrow, and a bolt an arrow with a round knob at its head.

[2] See note *ante*. p. 21.

Hoa. So, so: what suitors has she?

Mon. There lies the comfort, sir; the report of her is yet but a whisper; and only solicited by young riotous Witgood, nephew to your mortal adversary.

Hoa. Ha! art certain he's her suitor?

Mon. Most certain, sir; and his uncle very industrious to beguile the widow, and make up the match.

Hoa. So: very good.

Mon. Now, sir, you know this young Witgood is a spendthrift, dissolute fellow.

Hoa. A very rascal.

Mon. A midnight surfeiter.

Hoa. The spume of a brothel-house.

Mon. True, sir; which being well told in your worship's phrase, may both heave him out of her mind, and drive a fair way for me to the widow's affections.

Hoa. Attend me about five.

Mon. With my best care, sir. [*Exit.*

Hoa. Fool, thou hast left thy treasure with a thief,
To trust a widower with a suit in love!
Happy revenge, I hug thee! I have not only the means laid before me, extremely to cross my adversary, and confound the last hopes of his nephew, but thereby to enrich my estate, augment my revenues, and build mine own fortunes greater: ha, ha!
I'll mar your phrase, o'erturn your flatteries,
Undo your windings, policies, and plots,
Fall like a secret and despatchful plague
On your secured comforts. Why, I am able
To buy three of Lucre; thrice outbid him,
Let my out-monies be reckonèd and all.

Enter three of WITGOOD'S Creditors.

1st Cred. I am glad of this news.

2nd Cred. So are we, by my faith.

3rd Cred. Young Witgood will be a gallant again now.

Hoa. Peace. [*Listening.*

1st Cred. I promise you, Master Cockpit, she's a mighty rich widow.

2nd Cred. Why, have you ever heard of her?

1st Cred. Who? Widow Medler? she lies open to much rumour.

3rd Cred. Four hundred a-year, they say, in very good land.

1st Cred. Nay, take't of my word, if you believe that, you believe the least.

2nd Cred. And to see how close he keeps it!

1st Cred. O, sir, there's policy in that, to prevent better suitors.

3rd Cred. He owes me a hundred pound, and I protest I ne'er looked for a penny.

1st Cred. He little dreams of our coming; he'll wonder to see his creditors upon him.

[*Exeunt* Creditors.

Hoa. Good, his creditors: I'll follow. This makes
for me:
All know the widow's wealth; and 'tis well known
I can estate her fairly, ay, and will.
In this one chance shines a twice happy fate;
I both deject my foe and raise my state. [*Exit.*

ACT THE THIRD.

SCENE I.

WITGOOD'S *Lodgings.*

Enter WITGOOD *and three* Creditors.

WIT. Why, alas, my creditors, could you find no other time to undo me but now? rather your malice appears in this than the justness of the debt.

1st Cred. Master Witgood, I have forborne my money long.

Wit. I pray, speak low, sir: what do you mean?

2nd Cred. We hear you are to be married suddenly to a rich country widow.

Wit. What can be kept so close but you creditors hear on't! well, 'tis a lamentable state, that our chiefest afflictors should first hear of our fortunes. Why, this is no good course, i'faith, sirs: if ever you have hope to be satisfied, why do you seek to confound the means that should work it? there's neither piety, no, nor policy in that. Shine favourably now: why, I may rise and spread again, to your great comforts.

1st Cred. He says true, i'faith.

Wit. Remove me now, and I consume for ever.

2nd Cred. Sweet gentleman!

Wit. How can it thrive which from the sun you sever?

3rd Cred. It cannot, indeed.

Wit. O, then, show patience! I shall have enough
To satisfy you all.

1st Cred. Ay, if we could
Be content, a shame take us!
Wit. For, look you;
I am but newly sure[1] yet to the widow,
And what a rend might this discredit make!
Within these three days will I bind you lands
For your securities.
1st Cred. No, good Master Witgood:
Would 'twere as much as we dare trust you with!
Wit. I know you have been kind; however, now,
Either by wrong report or false incitement,
Your gentleness is injurèd: in such
A state as this a man cannot want foes.
If on the sudden he begin to rise,
No man that lives can count his enemies.
You had some intelligence, I warrant ye,
From an ill-willer.

2nd Cred. Faith, we heard you brought up a rich widow, sir, and were suddenly to marry her.

Wit. Ay, why there it was: I knew 'twas so: but since you are so well resolved[2] of my faith toward you, let me be so much favoured of you, I beseech you all——

All. O, it shall not need, i' faith, sir!——

Wit. As to lie still awhile, and bury my debts in silence, till I be fully possessed of the widow; for the truth is—I may tell you as my friends——

All. O, O, O!——

Wit. I am to raise a little money in the city, toward the setting forth of myself, for my own credit and your comfort; if my former debts should be divulged, all hope of my proceedings were quite extinguished.

1st Cred. Do you hear, sir? I may deserve your custom hereafter; pray, let my money be accepted before a stranger's: here's forty pound I received as I came to you; if that may stand you in any stead, make use on't

[1] Pledged. [2] Satisfied.

[*Offers him money, which he at first declines.*] Nay, pray, sir; 'tis at your service. [*Aside to* WITGOOD.

Wit. You do so ravish me with kindness, that
I am constrained to play the maid, and take it.

1*st Cred.* Let none of them see it, I beseech you.

Wit. Faugh!

1*st Cred.* I hope I shall be first in your remembrance
After the marriage rites.

Wit. Believe it firmly.

1*st Cred.* So.—What, do you walk, sirs?

2*nd Cred.* I go.—Take no care, sir, for money to furnish you; within this hour I send you sufficient. [*Aside to* WITGOOD.]—Come, Master Cockpit, we both stay for you.

3*rd Cred.* I ha' lost a ring, i'faith; I'll follow you presently [*exeunt* 1*st and* 2*nd* Creditors]—but you shall find it, sir; I know your youth and expenses have disfurnished you of all jewels: there's a ruby of twenty pound price, sir; bestow it upon your widow. [*Offers him the ring, which he at first declines*]—What, man! 'twill call up her blood to you; beside, if I might so much work with you, I would not have you beholden to those bloodsuckers for any money.

Wit. Not I, believe it.

3*rd Cred.* They're a brace of cut-throats.

Wit. I know 'em.

3*rd Cred.* Send a note of all your wants to my shop, and I'll supply you instantly.

Wit. Say you so? why, here's my hand then, no man living shall do't but thyself.

3*rd Cred.* Shall I carry it away from 'em both, then?

Wit. I'faith, shalt thou.

3*rd Cred.* Troth, then, I thank you, sir.

Wit. Welcome, good Master Cockpit. *Exit* 3rd Creditor.]—Ha, ha, ha! why, is not this better now than lying a-bed? I perceive there's nothing conjures up wit sooner than poverty, and nothing lays it down sooner than wealth and lechery: this has some savour yet. O that I had the mortgage from mine uncle as sure in possession as these trifles! I would forswear brothel at noonday, and muscadine[1] and eggs at midnight.

Cour. [*within*]. Master Witgood, where are you?

Wit. Holla!

Enter Courtesan.

Cour. Rich news?

Wit. Would 'twere all in plate!

Cour. There's some in chains and jewels: I am so haunted with suitors, Master Witgood, I know not which to despatch first.

Wit. You have the better term,[2] by my faith.

Cour. Among the number
One Master Hoard, an ancient gentleman.

Wit. Upon my life, my uncle's adversary.

Cour. It may well hold so, for he rails on you,
Speaks shamefully of him.

Wit. As I could wish it.

Cour. I first denied him, but so cunningly,
It rather promised him assurèd hopes,
Than any loss of labour.

Wit. Excellent!

Cour. I expect him every hour with gentlemen,
With whom he labours to make good his words,
To approve you riotous, your state consumed.
Your uncle——

Wit. Wench, make up thy own fortunes now; do thyself a good turn once in thy days: he's rich in money, movables, and lands; marry him: he's an old doating fool, and that's worth all; marry him: 'twould be a great comfort to me to see thee do well, i'faith; marry him: 'twould ease my conscience well to see thee well bestowed; I have a care of thee, i'faith.

[1] A sweet aromatic wine, the produce of the muscatel grape. The mixture in question was taken as an aphrodisiac.

[2] Witgood is playing on the double meaning attached to the word suitors.

Cour. Thanks, sweet Master Witgood.

Wit. I reach at farther happiness: first, I am sure it can be no harm to thee, and there may happen goodness to me by it: prosecute it well; let's send up for our wits, now we require their best and most pregnant assistance.

Cour. Step in, I think I hear 'em. [*Exeunt.*

Enter HOARD *and* Gentlemen, *with the* Host *as Servant.*

Hoa. Art thou the widow's man? by my faith, sh'as a company of proper men then.

Host. I am the worst of six, sir; good enough for blue [coats.

Hoa. Hark hither: I hear say thou art in most credit with her.

Host. Not so, sir.

Hoa. Come, come, thou'rt modest: there's a brace of royals,[1] prithee, help me to th' speech of her. [*Gives him money.*

Host. I'll do what I may, sir, always saving myself harmless.

Hoa. Go to, do't, I say; thou shalt hear better from me.

Host. Is not this a better place than five mark[2] a-year standing wages? Say a man had but three such clients in a day, methinks he might make a poor living on't; beside, I was never brought up with so little honesty to refuse any man's money; never: what gulls there are a this side the world! now know I the widow's mind; none but my young master comes in her clutches: ha, ha, ha! [*Aside, and exit.*

Hoa. Now, my dear gentlemen, stand firmly to me;
You know his follies and my worth.

1st Gent. We do, sir.

2nd Gent. But, Master Hoard, are you sure he is not i' th' house now?

Hoa. Upon my honesty, I chose this time
A' purpose, fit: the spendthrift is abroad:
Assist me; here she comes.

[1] Gold pieces 15s. in value. [2] The mark was worth 13*s.* 4*d.*

Enter Courtesan.

Now, my sweet widow.

Cour. You're welcome, Master Hoard.

Hoa. Despatch, sweet gentlemen, despatch.—
I am come, widow, to prove those my words
Neither of envy sprung nor of false tongues,
But such as their [1] deserts and actions
Do merit and bring forth; all which these gentlemen,
Well known, and better reputed, will confess.

Cour. I cannot tell
How my affections may dispose of me;
But surely if they find him so desertless,
They'll have that reason to withdraw themselves:
And therefore, gentlemen, I do entreat you,
As you are fair in reputation
And in appearing form, so shine in truth:
I am a widow, and, alas, you know,
Soon overthrown! 'tis a very small thing
That we withstand, our weakness is so great:
Be partial unto neither, but deliver,
Without affection, your opinion.

Hoa. And that will drive it home.

Cour. Nay, I beseech your silence, Master Hoard;
You are a party.

Hoa. Widow, not a word.

1st Gent. The better first to work you to belief,
Know neither of us owe him flattery,
Nor t'other malice; but unbribèd censure,[2]
So help us our best fortunes!

Cour. It suffices.

1st Gent. That Witgood is a riotous, undone man,
Imperfect both in fame and in estate,
His debts wealthier than he, and executions
In wait for his due body, we'll maintain
With our best credit and our dearest blood.

[1] *i.e.* Of Witgood and his uncle. [2] Judgment.

Cour. Nor land nor living, say you? Pray. take heed
You do not wrong the gentleman.
1st Gent. What we speak
Our lives and means are ready to make good.
Cour. Alas, how soon are we poor souls beguiled!
2nd Gent. And for his uncle——
Hoa. Let that come to me.
His uncle, a severe extortioner;
A tyrant at a forfeiture; greedy of others'
Miseries; one that would undo his brother,
Nay, swallow up his father, if he can,
Within the fathoms of his conscience.
1st Gent. Nay, believe it, widow,
You had not only matched yourself to wants,
But in an evil and unnatural stock.
Hoa. Follow hard, gentlemen, follow hard,
[*Aside to* Gent.
Cour. Is my love so deceived? Before you all
I do renounce him; on my knees I vow [*Kneeling.*
He ne'er shall marry me.
Wit. [*looking in*]. Heaven knows he never meant it!
[*Aside.*
Hoa. There take her at the bound. [*Aside to* Gent.
1st Gent. Then, with a new and pure affection,
Behold yon gentleman; grave, kind, and rich,
A match worthy yourself: esteeming him,
You do regard your state.
Hoa. I'll make her a jointure, say. [*Aside to* Gent.
1st Gent. He can join land to land. and will possess you
Of what you can desire.
2nd Gent. Come, widow, come,
Cour. The world is so deceitful!
1st Gent. There, 'tis deceitful,
Where flattery, want, and imperfection lie;
But none of these in him: pish!
Cour. Pray, sir——

1st Gent. Come, you widows are ever most backward when you should do yourselves most good; but were it to marry a chin not worth a hair now, then you would be forward enough. Come, clap hands, a match.

Hoa. With all my heart, widow. [HOARD *and* Courtesan *shake hands.*]—Thanks, gentlemen:
I will deserve your labour, and [*to* Courtesan] thy love.

Cour. Alas, you love not widows but for wealth!
I promise you I ha' nothing, sir.

Hoa. Well said, widow,
Well said; thy love is all I seek, before
These gentlemen.

Cour. Now I must hope the best.

Hoa. My joys are such they want to be expressed.

Cour. But, Master Hoard, one thing I must remember you of, before these gentlemen, your friends: how shall I suddenly avoid the loathed soliciting of that perjured Witgood, and his tedious, dissembling uncle? who this very day hath appointed a meeting for the same purpose too; where, had not truth come forth, I had been undone, utterly undone!

Hoa. What think you of that, gentlemen?

1st Gent. 'Twas well devised.

Hoa. Hark thee, widow: train out young Witgood single; hasten him thither with thee, somewhat before the hour; where, at the place appointed, these gentlemen and myself will wait the opportunity, when, by some slight removing him from thee, we'll suddenly enter and surprise thee, carry thee away by boat to Cole-Harbour, have a priest ready, and there clap it up instantly. How likest it, widow?

Cour. In that it pleaseth you, it likes me well.

Hoa. I'll kiss thee for those words. [*Kisses her.*]—
Come, gentlemen,
Still must I live a suitor to your favours,
Still to your aid beholden.

1st Gent. We're engaged, sir;
'Tis for our credits now to see't well ended.

Hoa. 'Tis for your honours, gentlemen; nay, look to't.
Not only in joy, but I in wealth excel:
No more sweet widow, but, sweet wife, farewell.

Cour. Farewell, sir. [*Exeunt* HOARD *and* Gentlemen.

Re-enter WITGOOD.

Wit. O for more scope! I could laugh eternally! Give you joy, Mistress Hoard, I promise your fortune was good, forsooth; you've fell upon wealth enough, and there's young gentlemen enow can help you to the rest. Now it requires our wits: carry thyself but heedfully now, and we are both——

Re-enter Host.

Host. Master Witgood, your uncle.

Wit. Cuds me! remove thyself awhile; I'll serve for him. [*Exeunt* Courtesan *and* Host.

Enter LUCRE.

Luc. Nephew, good morning, nephew.

Wit. The same to you, kind uncle.

Luc. How fares the widow? does the meeting hold?

Wit. O, no question of that, sir.

Luc. I'll strike the stroke, then, for thee; no more days.

Wit. The sooner the better, uncle. O, she's mightily followed!

Luc. And yet so little rumoured!

Wit. Mightily: here comes one old gentleman, and he'll make her a jointure of three hundred a year, forsooth; another wealthy suitor will estate his son in his lifetime, and make him weigh down the widow; here a merchant's son will possess her with no less than three goodly lordships at once, which were all pawns to his father.

Luc. Peace, nephew, let me hear no more of 'em;

it mads me. Thou shalt prevent[1] 'em all. No words to the widow of my coming hither. Let me see—'tis now upon nine: before twelve, nephew, we will have the bargain struck, we will, faith, boy.

Wit. O, my precious uncle! [*Exeunt.*

SCENE II.

A Room in HOARD'S *House.*

Enter HOARD *and* JOYCE.

Hoa. Niece, sweet niece, prithee, have a care to my house; I leave all to thy discretion. Be content to dream awhile; I'll have a husband for thee shortly: put that care upon me, wench, for in choosing wives and husbands I am only fortunate; I have that gift given me. [*Exit.*

Joy. But 'tis not likely you should choose for me,
Since nephew to your chiefest enemy
Is he whom I affect: but, O, forgetful!
Why dost thou flatter thy affections so,
With name of him that for a widow's bed
Neglects thy purer love? Can it be so,
Or does report dissemble?

Enter GEORGE.

How now, sir?

Geo. A letter, with which came a private charge.

Joy. Therein I thank your care. [*Exit* GEORGE.
—I know this hand—

[Reads.] Dearer than sight, what the world reports of me, yet believe not; rumour will alter shortly: be thou constant; I am still the same that I was in love, and I hope to be the same in fortunes. Theodorus Witgood.

[1] Anticipate.

I am resolved :[1] no more shall fear or doubt
Raise their pale powers to keep affection out. [*Exit.*

SCENE III.

A Tavern.

Enter HOARD, Gentlemen, *and* Drawer.

Dra. You're very welcome, gentlemen.—Dick, show those gentlemen the Pomegranate there.

Hoa. Hist!

Dra. Up those stairs, gentlemen.

Hoa. Hist! drawer!

Dra. Anon, sir.

Hoa. Prithee, ask at the bar if a gentlewoman came not in lately.

Dra. William, at the bar, did you see any gentlewoman come in lately? Speak you ay, speak you no?

[*Within.*] No, none came in yet, but Mistress Florence.

Dra. He says none came in yet, sir, but one Mistress Florence.

Hoa. What is that Florence? a widow?

Dra. Yes, a Dutch widow.[2]

Hoa. How?

Dra. That's an English drab, sir: give your worship good morrow. [*Exit.*

Hoa. A merry knave, i'faith! I shall remember a Dutch widow the longest day of my life.

1*st Gent.* Did not I use most art to win the widow?

2*nd Gent.* You shall pardon me for that, sir; Master Hoard knows I took her at best 'vantage.

Hoa. What's that, sweet gentlemen, what's that?

2*nd Gent.* He will needs bear me down, that his art only wrought with the widow most.

1 Convinced. 2 A cant term for a prostitute.

Hoa. O, you did both well, gentlemen, you did both well, I thank you.

1st Gent. I was the first that moved her.

Hoa. You were, i'faith.

2nd Gent. But it was I that took her at the bound.

Hoa. Ay, that was you: faith, gentlemen, 'tis right.

3rd Gent. I boasted least, but 'twas I joined their hands.

Hoa. By th' mass, I think he did: you did all well, Gentlemen, you did all well; contend no more.

1st Gent. Come, yon room's fittest.

Hoa. True, 'tis next the door. [*Exeunt.*

Enter WITGOOD, Courtesan, Host, *and* Drawer.

Dra. You're very welcome: please you to walk up stairs; cloth's laid, sir.

Cour. Up stairs? troth, I am very weary, Master [Witgood.

Wit. Rest yourself here awhile, widow; we'll have a cup of muscadine in this little room.

Dra. A cup of muscadine? You shall have the best, [sir.

Wit. But, do you hear, sirrah?

Dra. Do you call? anon, sir.

Wit. What is there provided for dinner?

Dra. I cannot readily tell you, sir: if you please you may go into the kitchen and see yourself, sir; many gentlemen of worship do use to do it, I assure you, sir. [*Exit.*

Host. A pretty familiar, prigging rascal; he has his part without book.

Wit. Against you are ready to drink to me, widow, I'll be present to pledge you.

Cour. Nay, I commend your care, 'tis done well of you. [*Exit* WITGOOD.]—'Las, what have I forgot!

Host. What, mistress?

Cour. I slipt my wedding ring off when I washed, and left it at my lodging: prithee, run; I shall be sad without it. [*Exit* Host.]—So, he's gone. Boy!

Enter Boy.

Boy. Anon, forsooth.

Cour. Come hither, sirrah: learn secretly if one Master Hoard, an ancient gentleman, be about house.

Boy. I heard such a one named.

Cour. Commend me to him.

Re-enter HOARD *and* Gentlemen.

Hoa. Ay, boy, do thy commendations.

Cour. O, you come well: away, to boat, begone.

Hoa. Thus wise men are revenged, give two for one.

[*Exeunt.*

Re-enter WITGOOD *and* Vintner.

Wit. I must request
You, sir, to show extraordinary care:
My uncle comes with gentlemen, his friends,
And 'tis upon a making.[1]

Vin. Is it so?
I'll give a special charge, good Master Witgood.
May I be bold to see her?

Wit. Who? the widow?
With all my heart, i'faith, I'll bring you to her.

Vin. If she be a Staffordshire gentlewoman, 'tis much if I know her not.

Wit. How now? boy! drawer!

Vin. Hie!

Re-enter Boy.

Boy. Do you call, sir?

Wit. Went the gentlewoman up that was here?

Boy. Up, sir? she went out, sir.

Wit. Out, sir?

Boy. Out, sir: one Master Hoard, with a guard of gentlemen, carried her out at back door, a pretty while since, sir.

Wit. Hoard? death and darkness? Hoard?

[1] *i.e.* Matching.

Re-enter Host.

Host. The devil of ring I can find.

Wit. How now? what news? where's the widow?

Host. My mistress? is she not here, sir?

Wit. More madness yet!

Host. She sent me for a ring.

Wit. A plot, a plot!—To boat! she's stole away.

Host. What?

Enter LUCRE *and* Gentlemen.

Wit. Follow! inquire old Hoard, my uncle's adversary. [*Exit* Host.

Luc. Nephew, what's that?

Wit. Thrice-miserable wretch!

Luc. Why, what's the matter?

Vin. The widow's borne away, sir.

Luc. Ha? passion of me!—A heavy welcome, gentlemen.

1*st Gent.* The widow gone?

Luc. Who durst attempt it?

Wit. Who but old Hoard, my uncle's adversary?

Luc. How?

Wit. With his confederates.

Luc. Hoard, my deadly enemy?—Gentlemen, stand to me,
I will not bear it; 'tis in hate of me;
That villain seeks my shame, nay, thirsts my blood;
He owes me mortal malice.
I'll spend my wealth on this despiteful plot,
Ere he shall cross me and my nephew thus.

Wit. So maliciously!

Re-enter Host.

Luc. How now, you treacherous rascal?

Host. That's none of my name, sir.

Wit. Poor soul, he knew not on't!

Luc. I'm sorry. I see then 'twas a mere plot.

Host. I traced em nearly——

Luc. Well?

Host. And hear for certain
They have took Cole-Harbour.

Luc. The devil's sanctuary!
They shall not rest; I'll pluck her from his arms—
Kind and dear gentlemen,
If ever I had seat within your breasts——

1st Gent. No more, good sir; it is a wrong to us
To see you injured; in a cause so just
We'll spend our lives but we will right our friends.

Luc. Honest and kind! come we've delayed too long;
Nephew, take comfort; a just cause is strong.

Wit. That's all my comfort, uncle. [*Exeunt all but* WITGOOD.] Ha, ha, ha!
Now may events fall luckily and well;
He that ne'er strives, says wit, shall ne'er excel. [*Exit.*

SCENE IV.

A Room in DAMPIT'S *House.*

Enter DAMPIT, *drunk.*

Dam. When did I say my prayers? In anno 88, when the great armada was coming; and in anno 89, when the great thundering and lightning was, I prayed heartily then, i'faith, to overthrow Poovies' new buildings; I kneeled by my great iron chest, I remember.

Enter AUDREY.

Aud. Master Dampit, one may hear you before they see you: you keep sweet hours, Master Dampit; we were all a-bed three hours ago.

Dam. Audrey?

Aud. O, you're a fine gentleman!

Dam. So I am i'faith, and a fine scholar: do you use to go to bed so early, Audrey?

Aud. Call you this early, Master Dampit?

Dam. Why, is't not one of clock i' th' morning? is not that early enough? fetch me a glass of fresh beer.

Aud. Here, I have warmed your nightcap for you, Master Dampit.

Dam. Draw it on then. I am very weak truly: I have not eaten so much as the bulk of an egg these three days.

Aud. You have drunk the more, Master Dampit.

Dam. What's that?

Aud. You mought, an you would, Master Dampit.

Dam. I answer you, I cannot: hold your prating; you prate too much, and understand too little: are you answered? Give me a glass of beer.

Aud. May I ask you how you do, Master Dampit?

Dam. How do I? i'faith, naught.

Aud. I ne'er knew you do otherwise.

Dam. I eat not one pen'north of bread these two years. Give me a glass of fresh beer. I am not sick, nor I am not well.

Aud. Take this warm napkin about your neck, sir, whilst I help to make you unready.[1]

Dam. How now, Audrey-prater, with your scurvy devices, what say you now?

Aud. What say I, Master Dampit? I say nothing, but that you are very weak.

Dam. Faith, thou hast more cony-catching[2] devices than all London.

Aud. Why, Master Dampit, I never deceived you in all my life.

Dam. Why was that? because I never did trust thee.

Aud. I care not what you say, Master Dampit.

Dam. Hold thy prating: I answer thee, thou art a beggar, a quean, and a bawd: are you answered?

[1] Undress you. [2] Cheating.

Aud. Fie, Master Dampit! a gentleman, and have such words?

Dam. Why, thou base drudge of infortunity, thou kitchen-stuff-drab of beggary, roguery, and coxcombry, thou cavernesed quean of foolery, knavery, and bawdreaminy, I'll tell thee what, I will not give a louse for thy fortunes.

Aud. No, Master Dampit? and there's a gentleman comes a-wooing to me, and he doubts[1] nothing but that you will get me from him.

Dam. I? If I would either have thee or lie with thee for two thousand pound, would I might be damned! why, thou base, impudent quean of foolery, flattery, and coxcombry, are you answered?

Aud. Come, will you rise and go to bed, sir?

Dam. Rise, and go to bed too, Audrey? How does Mistress Proserpine?

Aud. Fooh!

Dam. She's as fine a philosopher of a stinkard's wife, as any within the liberties. Faugh, faugh, Audrey!

Aud. How now, Master Dampit?

Dam. Fie upon't, what a choice of stinks here is! what hast thou done, Audrey? fie upon't, here's a choice of stinks indeed! Give me a glass of fresh beer, and then I will to bed.

Aud. It waits for you above, sir.

Dam. Foh! I think they burn horns in Barnard's Inn. If ever I smelt such an abominable stink, usury forsake me. [*Exit.*

Aud. They be the stinking nails of his trampling feet, and he talks of burning of horns. [*Exit.*

[1] Fears.

ACT THE FOURTH.

SCENE I.

An Apartment at Cole-Harbour.

Enter HOARD, Courtesan, LAMPREY, SPICHCOCK, *and* Gentlemen.

FIRST GENT. Join hearts, join hands.
In wedlock's bands,
Never to part
Till death cleave your heart.
[*To* HOARD.] You shall forsake all other women;
[*To* Courtesan.] You lords, knights, gentlemen, and yeomen.
What my tongue slips
Make up with your lips.

Hoa. [*kisses her.*] Give you joy, Mistress Hoard; let the kiss come about. [*Knocking.*
Who knocks? Convey my little pig-eater [1] out.

Luc. [*within.*] Hoard!

Hoa. Upon my life, my adversary, gentlemen!

Luc. [*within.*] Hoard, open the door, or we will force it ope:
Give us the widow.

Hoa. Gentlemen, keep 'em out.

Lam. He comes upon his death that enters here.

Luc. [*within.*] My friends, assist me!

Hoa. He has assistants, gentlemen.

[1] A term of endearment.

Lam. Tut, nor him nor them we in this action fear.

Luc. [*within.*] Shall I, in peace, speak one word with the widow?

Cour. Husband, and gentlemen, hear me but a word.

Lam. Freely, sweet wife.

Cour. Let him in peaceably;
You know we're sure from any act of his.

Hoa. Most true.

Cour. You may stand by and smile at his old weakness:
Let me alone to answer him.

Hoa. Content;
Twill be good mirth, i'faith. How think you, gentlemen?

Lam. Good gullery!

Hoa. Upon calm conditions let him in.

Luc. [*within.*] All spite and malice!

Lam. Hear me, Master Lucre:
So you will vow a peaceful entrance
With those your friends, and only exercise
Calm conference with the widow, without fury,
The passage shall receive you.

Luc. [*within.*] I do vow it.

Lam. Then enter and talk freely: here she stands.

Enter LUCRE, Gentlemen, *and* Host.

Luc. O, Master Hoard, your spite has watched the hour!
You're excellent at vengeance, Master Hoard.

Hoa. Ha, ha, ha!

Luc. I am the fool you laugh at:
You are wise, sir, and know the seasons well.—
Come hither, widow: why is it thus?
O, you have done me infinite disgrace,
And your own credit no small injury!
Suffer mine enemy so despitefully
To bear you from my nephew? O, I had
Rather half my substance had been forfeit
And begged by some starved rascal!

Cour. Why, what would you wish me do, sir?

I must not overthrow my state for love :
We have too many precedents for that ;
From thousands of our wealthy undone widows
One may derive some wit. I do confess
I loved your nephew, nay, I did affect him
Against the mind and liking of my friends ;
Believed his promises ; lay here in hope
Of flattered living, and the boast of lands :
Coming to touch his wealth and state, indeed,
It appears dross ; I find him not the man ;
Imperfect, mean, scarce furnished of his needs :
In words, fair lordships ; in performance, hovels :
Can any woman love the thing that is not ?

Luc. Broke you for this ?

Cour. Was it not cause too much ?
Send to inquire his state : most part of it
Lay two years mortgaged in his uncle's hands.

Luc. Why, say it did, you might have known my mind :
I could have soon restored it.

Cour. Ay, had I but seen any such thing performed,
Why, 'twould have tied my affection, and contained
Me in my first desires : do you think, i'faith,
That I could twine such a dry oak as this,
Had promise in your nephew took effect ?

Luc. Why, and there's no time past ; and rather than
My adversary should thus thwart my hopes,
I would——

Cour. Tut, you've been ever full of golden speech :
If words were lands, your nephew would be rich.

Luc. Widow, believe't, I vow by my best bliss,
Before these gentlemen, I will give in
The mortgage to my nephew instantly,
Before I sleep or eat.

1st Gent. [*friend to* LUCRE.] We'll pawn our credits,
Widow, what he speaks shall be performed
In fulness.

Luc. Nay, more ; I will estate him

In farther blessings; he shall be my heir;
I have no son;
I'll bind myself to that condition.

Cour. When I shall hear this done, I shall soon yield
To reasonable terms.

Luc. In the mean season,
Will you protest, before these gentlemen,
To keep yourself as you're now at this present?

Cour. I do protest, before these gentlemen,
I will be as clear then as I am now.

Luc. I do believe you. Here's your own honest servant,
I'll take him along with me.

Cour. Ay, with all my heart.

Luc. He shall see all performed, and bring you word.

Cour. That's all I wait for.

Hoa. What, have you finished, Master Lucre? ha, ha, ha, ha!

Luc. So laugh, Hoard, laugh at your poor enemy, do;
The wind may turn, you may be laughed at too;
Yes, marry may you, sir.—Ha, ha, ha!

[*Exeunt* LUCRE, Gentlemen, *and* Host.

Hoa. Ha, ha, ha! if every man that swells in malice
Could be revenged as happily as I,
He would choose hate, and forswear amity.—
What did he say, wife, prithee?

Cour. Faith, spoke to ease his mind.

Hoa. O, O, O!

Cour. You know now little to any purpose.

Hoa. True, true, true!

Cour. He would do mountains now.

Hoa. Ay, ay, ay, ay.

Lam. You've struck him dead, Master Hoard.

Spi. And his nephew desperate.

Hoa. I know't sirs, I.
Never did man so crush his enemy. [*Exeunt.*

SCENE II.

A Room in LUCRE'S *House.*

Enter LUCRE, Gentlemen, *and* Host, *meeting* FREEDOM.

Luc. My son-in-law, Sam Freedom, where's my nephew?

Free. O man in lamentation,[1] father.

Luc. How!

Free. He thumps his breast like a gallant dicer that has lost his doublet, and stands in's shirt to do penance.

Luc. Alas, poor gentleman!

Free. I warrant you may hear him sigh in a still evening to your house at Highgate.

Luc. I prithee send him in.

Free. Were it to do a greater matter, I will not stick with you, sir, in regard you married my mother. [*Exit.*

Luc. Sweet gentlemen, cheer him up; I will but fetch the mortgage and return to you instantly.

1st Gent. We'll do our best, sir. [*Exit* LUCRE.]—
See where he comes,
E'en joyless and regardless of all form.

Enter WITGOOD.

2nd Gent. Why, how now, Master Witgood? Fie! you a firm scholar, and an understanding gentleman, and give your best parts to passion?

1st Gent. Come, fie fie!

Wit. O, gentlemen——

1st Gent. Sorrow of me, what a sigh was there, sir! Nine such widows are not worth it.

Wit. To be borne from me by that lecher Hoard!

1st Gent. That vengeance is your uncle's; being done
More in despite to him than wrong to you:
But we bring comfort now.

Wit. I beseech you, gentlemen——

2nd Gent. Cheer thyself, man; there's hope of her, i'faith.

Wit. Too gladsome to be true.

[1] "O man in desperation" is the name of an old tune.

Re-enter LUCRE.

Luc. Nephew, what cheer?
Alas, poor gentleman, how art thou changed!
Call thy fresh blood into thy cheeks again:
She comes.

Wit. Nothing afflicts me so much,
But that it is your adversary, uncle,
And merely plotted in despite of you.

Luc. Ay, that's it mads me, spites me! I'll spend my wealth ere he shall carry her so, because I know 'tis only to spite me. Ay, this is it. Here, nephew [*giving a paper*], before these kind gentlemen, I deliver in your mortgage, my promise to the widow; see, 'tis done: be wise, you're once more master of your own. The widow shall perceive now you are not altogether such a beggar as the world reputes you; you can make shift to bring her to three hundred a-year, sir.

1st Gent. Byrlady,[1] and that's no toy, sir.

Luc. A word, nephew.

1st Gent. [*to* Host.] Now you may certify the widow.

Luc. You must conceive it aright, nephew, now;
To do you good I am content to do this.

Wit. I know it, sir.

Luc. But your own conscience can tell I had it
Dearly enough of you.

Wit. Ay, that's most certain.

Luc. Much money laid out, beside many a journey
To fetch the rent; I hope you'll think on't, nephew.

Wit. I were worse than a beast else, i'faith.

Luc. Although to blind the widow and the world,
I out of policy do't, yet there's a conscience, nephew.

Wit. Heaven forbid else!

Luc. When you are full possessed,
'Tis nothing to return it.

Wit. Alas, a thing quickly done, uncle!

Luc. Well said! you know I give it you but in trust.

[1] A corruption of "By our Lady."

Wit. Pray, let me understand you rightly, uncle:
You give it me but in trust?

Luc. No.

Wit. That is, you trust me with it?

Luc. True, true.

Wit. But if ever I trust you with it again,
Would I might be trussed up for my labour! [*Aside.*

Luc. You can all witness, gentlemen; and you, sir yeoman?

Host. My life for yours, sir, now, I know my mistress's mind so well toward your nephew, let things be in preparation, and I'll train her hither in most excellent fashion. [*Exit.*

Luc. A good old boy!—Wife! Jenny!

Enter MISTRESS LUCRE.

Mis. L. What's the news, sir?

Luc. The wedding-day's at hand: prithee, sweet wife, express thy housewifery; thou'rt a fine cook, I know't; thy first husband married thee out of an alderman's kitchen; go to, he raised thee for raising of paste What! here's none but friends; most of our beginnings must be winked at.—Gentlemen, I invite you all to my nephew's wedding against Thursday morning.

1st Gent. With all our hearts, and we shall joy to see
Your enemy so mocked.

Luc. He laughed at me, gentlemen; ha, ha, ha!
[*Exeunt all but* WITGOOD.

Wit. He has no conscience, faith, would laugh at them:
They laugh at one another;
Who then can be so cruel? troth, not I;
I rather pity now, than ought envy?
I do conceive such joy in mine own happiness,
I have no leisure yet to laugh at their follies.
Thou soul of my estate, I kiss thee! [*To the mortgage.*
I miss life's comfort when I miss thee
O, never will we part agen,

Until I leave the sight of men!
We'll ne'er trust conscience of our kin,
Since cozenage brings that title in. [*Exit.*

SCENE III.

A Street.

Enter three Creditors.

1st Cred. I'll wait these seven hours but I'll see him caught.

2nd Cred. Faith, so will I.

3rd Cred. Hang him, prodigal! he's stript of the widow.

1st Cred. A' my troth, she's the wiser; she has made the happier choice: and I wonder of what stuff those widows' hearts are made of, that will marry unfledged boys before comely thrum-chinned[1] gentlemen.

Enter Boy.

Boy. News, news, news!

1st Cred. What, boy?

Boy. The rioter is caught.

1st Cred. So, so, so, so! it warms me at the heart;
I love a' life to see dogs upon men.
O, here he comes.

Enter Sergeants, *with* WITGOOD *in custody.*

Wit. My last joy was so great, it took away the sense of all future afflictions. What a day is here o'ercast! how soon a black tempest rises!

1st Cred. O, we may speak with you now, sir! what's become of your rich widow? I think you may cast your cap at the widow, may you not, sir?

2nd Cred. He a rich widow? who, a prodigal, a daily

[1] Rough-chinned. "Thrum" is properly the end of the warp in weaving.

rioter, and a nightly vomiter? he a widow of account? he a hole[1] i' th' counter.

Wit. You do well, my masters, to tyrannise over misery, to afflict the afflicted; 'tis a custom you have here amongst you; I would wish you never leave it, and I hope you'll do as I bid you.

1st Cred. Come, come, sir, what say you extempore now to your bill of a hundred pound? a sweet debt for froating[2] your doublets.

2nd Cred. Here's mine of forty.

3rd Cred. Here's mine of fifty.

Wit. Pray, sirs,—you'll give me breath?

1st Cred. No, sir, we'll keep you out of breath still; then we shall be sure you will not run away from us.

Wit. Will you but hear me speak?

2nd Cred. You shall pardon us for that, sir; we know you have too fair a tongue of your own; you overcame us too lately, a shame take you! we are like to lose all that for want of witnesses: we dealt in policy then; always when we strive to be most politic we prove most coxcombs: *non plus ultra* I perceive by us, we're not ordained to thrive by wisdom, and therefore we must be content to be tradesmen.

Wit. Give me but reasonable time, and I protest I'll make you ample satisfaction.

1st Cred. Do you talk of reasonable time to us?

Wit. 'Tis true, beasts know no reasonable time.

2nd Cred. We must have either money or carcass.

Wit. Alas, what good will my carcass do you?

3rd Cred. O, 'tis a secret delight we have amongst us! we that are used to keep birds in cages, have the heart to keep men in prison, I warrant you.

Wit. I perceive I must crave a little more aid from my wits: do but make shift for me this once, and I'll forswear ever to trouble you in the like fashion hereafter;

[1] Where the poorest prisoners were confined.
[2] To froat a garment is to rub perfumed oil into it to sweeten it.

I'll have better employment for you, an I live. [*Aside.*] —You'll give me leave, my masters, to make trial of my friends, and raise all means I can?

1st Cred. That's our desire, sir.

Enter Host.

Host. Master Witgood.

Wit. O, art thou come?

Host. May I speak one word with you in private, sir?

Wit. No, by my faith, canst thou; I am in hell here, and the devils will not let me come to thee.

1st Cred. Do you call us devils? you shall find us puritans.—Bear him away; let 'em talk as they go: we'll not stand to hear 'em.—Ah, sir, am I a devil? I shall think the better of myself as long as I live: a devil, i'faith? [*Exeunt.*

SCENE IV.

A Room in HOARD'S *House.*

Enter HOARD.

Hoa. What a sweet blessing hast thou, Master Hoard, above a multitude! wilt thou never be thankful? how dost thou think to be blest another time? or dost thou count this the full measure of thy happiness? by my troth, I think thou dost: not only a wife large in possessions, but spacious in content; she's rich, she's young, she's fair, she's wise: when I wake, I think of her lands—that revives me; when I go to bed, I dream of her beauty—and that's enough for me: she's worth four hundred a-year in her very smock, if a man knew how to use it. But the journey will be all, in troth, into the country; to ride to her lands in state and order following; my brother, and other worshipful gentlemen, whose companies I ha' sent down for already, to ride along with us in their goodly decorum beards, their broad velvet cassocks, and chains of gold twice or thrice double; against which time I'll entertain some ten men of mine own into liveries, all of occupations or qualities; I will not keep an idle man about me: the sight of which will so vex my adversary Lucre—for we'll pass by his door of purpose, make a little stand for the nonce, and have our horses curvet before the window—certainly he will never endure it, but run up and hang himself presently.

Enter Servant.

How now, sirrah, what news? any that offer their service to me yet?

Ser. Yes, sir, there are some i' th' hall that wait for your worship's liking, and desire to be entertained.

Hoa. Are they of occupation?

Ser. They are men fit for your worship, sir.

Hoa. Sayest so? send 'em all in. [*Exit* Servant.]—To see ten men ride after me in watchet[1] liveries, with orange-tawny caps,—'twill cut his comb, i'faith.

Enter Tailor, Barber, Perfumer, Falconer, *and* Huntsman.

How now? of what occupation are you, sir?

Tai. A tailor, an't please your worship.

Hoa. A tailor? O, very good: you shall serve to make all the liveries.—What are you, sir?

Bar. A barber, sir.

Hoa. A barber? very needful: you shall shave all the house, and, if need require, stand for a reaper i' th' summer time.—You, sir?

Per. A perfumer.

Hoa. I smelt you before: perfumers, of all men, had need carry themselves uprightly; for if they were once knaves, they would be smelt out quickly.—To you, sir?

Fal. A falconer, an't please your worship.

[1] Light blue.

Hoa. Sa ho, sa ho, sa ho!—And you, sir?

Hunt. A huntsman, sir,

Hoa. There, boy, there, boy, there, boy! I am not so old but I have pleasant days to come. I promise, you, my masters, I take such a good liking to you, that I entertain you all; I put you already into my countenance, and you shall be shortly in my livery; but especially you two, my jolly falconer and my bonny huntsman; we shall have most need of you at my wife's manor-houses i' th' country; there's goodly parks and champion[1] grounds for you; we shall have all our sports within ourselves; all the gentlemen a' th' country shall be beholden to us and our pastimes.

Fal. And we'll make your worship admire, sir.

Hoa. Sayest thou so? do but make me admire, and thou shall want for nothing.—My tailor.

Tai. Anon, sir.

Hoa. Go presently in hand with the liveries.

Tai. I will, sir.

Hoa. My barber.

Bar. Here, sir.

Hoa. Make 'em all trim fellows, louse 'em well,—especially my huntsman,—and cut all their beards of the Polonian fashion.—My perfumer.

Per. Under your nose, sir.

Hoa. Cast a better savour upon the knaves, to take away the scent of my tailor's feet, and my barber's lotium-water.

Per. It shall be carefully performed, sir.

Hoa. But you, my falconer and huntsman, the welcomest men alive, i'faith!

Hunt. And we'll show you that, sir, shall deserve your worship's favour.

Hoa. I prithee, show me that.—Go, you knaves all, and wash your lungs i' th' buttery, go. [*Exeunt* Tailor, Barber, *&c.*]—By th' mass, and well remembered! I'll ask my wife that question.—Wife, Mistress Jane Hoard!

[1] Champaign.

Enter Courtesan, *altered in apparel.*

Cour. Sir, would you with me?

Hoa. I would but know, sweet wife, which might stand best to thy liking, to have the wedding dinner kept here or i' th' country?

Cour. Hum:—faith, sir, 'twould like me better here; here you were married, here let all rites be ended.

Hoa. Could a marquesse[1] give a better answer? Hoard, bear thy head aloft, thou'st a wife will advance it.

Enter Host *with a letter.*

What haste comes here now? yea, a letter? some dreg of my adversary's malice. Come hither; what's the news?

Host. A thing that concerns my mistress, sir.

[*Giving a letter to* Courtesan.

Hoa. Why then it concerns me, knave.

Host. Ay, and you, knave, too (cry your worship mercy): you are both like to come into trouble, I promise you, sir; a pre-contract.[2]

Hoa. How? a pre-contract, sayest thou?

Host. I fear they have too much proof on't, sir: old Lucre, he runs mad up and down, and will to law as fast as he can; young Witgood laid hold on by his creditors, he exclaims upon you a' t'other side, says you have wrought his undoing by the injurious detaining of his contract.

Hoa. Body a' me!

Host. He will have utmost satisfaction;
The law shall give him recompense, he says.

Cour. Alas, his creditors so merciless! my state being yet uncertain, I deem it not unconscionable to further him. [*Aside.*

Host. True, sir.

Hoa. Wife, what says that letter? let me construe it.

[1] Marchioness.

[2] A pre-contract of marriage could only be set aside with the consent of both parties.—*Bullen.*

Cour. Cursed be my rash and unadvisèd words!
[*Tears the letter and stamps on it.*
I'll set my foot upon my tongue,
And tread my inconsiderate grant to dust.

Hoa. Wife——

Host. A pretty shift, i'faith! I commend a woman when she can make away a letter from her husband handsomely, and this was cleanly done, by my troth. [*Aside.*

Cour. I did, sir;
Some foolish words I must confess did pass,
Which now litigiously he fastens on me.

Hoa. Of what force? let me examine 'em.

Cour. Too strong, I fear: would I were well freed of him!

Hoa. Shall I compound?

Cour. No, sir, I'd have it done some nobler way
Of your side; I'd have you come off with honour;
Let baseness keep with them. Why, have you not
The means, sir? the occasion's offered you.

Hoa. Where? how, dear wife?

Cour. He is now caught by his creditors; the slave's needy; his debts petty; he'll rather bind himself to all inconveniences than rot in prison; by this only means you may get a release from him: 'tis not yet come to his uncle's hearing; send speedily for the creditors; by this time he's desperate; he'll set his hand to anything: take order for his debts, or discharge 'em quite: a pax on him, let's be rid of a rascal!

Hoa. Excellent!
Thou dost astonish me.—Go, run, make haste;
Bring both the creditors and Witgood hither.

Host. This will be some revenge yet. [*Aside, and exit.*

Hoa. In the mean space I'll have a release drawn.—Within there!

Enter Servant.

Ser. Sir?

Hoa. Sirrah, come take directions; go to my scrivener.

Cour. [*aside, while* HOARD *gives directions to the*

Servant.] I'm yet like those whose riches lie in dreams,
If I be waked, they're false ; such is my fate,
Who venture deeper than the desperate state.
Though I have sinned, yet could I become new,
For where I once vow, I am ever true.

Hoa. Away, despatch, on my displeasure quickly.

[*Exit* Servant.

Happy occasion ! pray Heaven he be in the right vein now to set his hand to't, that nothing alter him ; grant that all his follies may meet in him at once, to besot him enough ! I pray for him, i'faith, and here he comes.

Enter WITGOOD *and* Creditors.

Wit What would you with me now, my uncle's spiteful adversary ?

Hoa. Nay, I am friends.

Wit. Ay, when your mischief's spent.

Hoa. I heard you were arrested.

Wit. Well, what then ?
You will pay none of my debts, I am sure.

Hoa. A wise man cannot tell ;
There may be those conditions 'greed upon
May move me to do much.

Wit. Ay, when ?—
'Tis thou, perjurèd woman ! (O, no name
Is vile enough to match thy treachery !)
That art the cause of my confusion.

Cour. Out, you penurious slave !

Hoa. Nay, wife, you are too froward ;
Let him alone ; give losers leave to talk.

Wit. Shall I remember thee of another promise
Far stronger than the first ?

Cour. I'd fain know that.

Wit. 'Twould call shame to thy cheeks.

Cour. Shame !

Wit. Hark in your ear.—[*They converse apart*].
Will he come off, think'st thou, and pay my debts roundly?

Cour. Doubt nothing; there's a release a-drawing and all, to which you must set your hand.

Wit. Excellent!

Cour. But methinks, i'faith, you might have made some shift to discharge this yourself, having in the mortgage, and never have burdened my conscience with it.

Wit. A' my troth, I could not, for my creditors' cruelties extend to the present.

Cour. No more.—
Why, do your worst for that, I defy you.

Wit. You're impudent: I'll call up witnesses.

Cour. Call up thy wits, for thou hast been devoted
To follies a long time.

Hoa. Wife, you're too bitter.—
Master Witgood, and you, my masters, you shall hear a mild speech come from me now, and this it is: 't has been my fortune, gentlemen, to have an extraordinary blessing poured upon me a' late, and here she stands; I have wedded her, and bedded her, and yet she is little the worse: some foolish words she hath passed to you in the country, and some peevish[1] debts you owe here in the city; set the hare's head to the goose-giblet,[2] release you her of her words, and I'll release you of your debts, sir.

Wit. Would you so? I thank you for that, sir; I cannot blame you, i'faith.

Hoa. Why, are not debts better than words, sir?

Wit. Are not words promises, and are not promises debts, sir?

Hoa. He plays at back-racket with me. [*Aside.*

1st Cred. Come hither, Master Witgood, come hither; be ruled by fools once.

2nd Cred. We are citizens, and know what belongs to't.

1st Cred. Take hold of his offer: pax on her, let her go; if your debts were once discharged, I would help you to a widow myself worth ten of her.

3rd Cred. Mass, partner, and now you remember me

[1] Trifling. [2] A proverbial phrase.

on't, there's Master Mulligrub's sister newly fallen a widow.

1st Cred. Cuds me, as pat as can be! there's a widow left for you; ten thousand in money, beside plate, jewels, *et cetera:* I warrant it a match; we can do all in all with her; prithee, despatch; we'll carry thee to her presently.

Wit. My uncle will ne'er endure me when he shall hear I set my hand to a release.

2nd Cred. Hark, I'll tell thee a trick for that: I have spent five hundred pound in suits in my time, I should be wise; thou'rt now a prisoner; make a release; take't of my word, whatsoever a man makes as long as he is in durance, 'tis nothing in law, not thus much.

[*Snaps his fingers.*

Wit. Say you so, sir?

3rd Cred. I have paid for't, I know't.

Wit. Proceed then; I consent.

3rd Cred. Why, well said.

Hoa. How now, my masters, what have you done with [him?

1st Cred. With much ado, sir, we have got him to consent.

Hoa. Ah—a—a! and what come his debts to now?

1st Cred. Some eight score odd pounds, sir.

Hoa. Naw, naw, naw, naw, naw! tell me the second time; give me a lighter sum; they are but desperate debts, you know; ne'er called in but upon such an accident; a poor, needy knave, he would starve and rot in prison: come, come, you shall have ten shillings in the pound, and the sum down roundly.

1st Cred. You must make it a mark, sir.

Hoa. Go to then, tell your money in the meantime; you shall find little less there. [*Giving them money.*]—Come, Master Witgood, you are so unwilling to do yourself good now!

Enter Scrivener.

Welcome, honest scrivener.—Now you shall hear the release read.

Scri. [*reads.*] Be it known to all men, by these presents, that I, Theodorus Witgood, gentleman, sole nephew to Pecunius Lucre, having unjustly made title and claim to one Jane Medler, late widow of Anthony Medler, and now wife to Walkadine Hoard, in consideration of a competent sum of money to discharge my debts, do for ever hereafter disclaim any title, right, estate, or interest in or to the said widow, late in the occupation of the said Anthony Medler, and now in the occupation of Walkadine Hoard; as also neither to lay claim by virtue of any former contract, grant, promise, or demise, to any of her manors, manor-houses, parks, groves, meadow-grounds, arable lands, barns, stacks, stables, dove-holes, and coney-burrows; together with all her cattle, money, plate, jewels, borders, chains, bracelets, furnitures, hangings, moveables or immoveables. In witness whereof, I the said Theodorus Witgood have interchangeably set to my hand and seal before these presents, the day and date above written.

Wit. What a precious fortune hast thou slipt here, like a beast as thou art!

Hoa. Come, unwilling heart, come.

Wit. Well, Master Hoard, give me the pen; I see
'Tis vain to quarrel with our destiny. [*Signs the paper.*

Hoa. O, as vain a thing as can be! you cannot commit a greater absurdity, sir. So, so; give me that hand now; before all these presents, I am friends for ever with thee.

Wit. Troth, and it were pity of my heart now, if I should bear you any grudge, i'faith.

Hoa. Content: I'll send for thy uncle against the wedding dinner; we will be friends once again.

Wit. I hope to bring it to pass myself, sir.

Hoa. How now? is't right, my masters?

1st Cred. 'Tis something wanting, sir; yet it shall be sufficient.

Hoa. Why, well said; a good conscience makes a fine

show now-a-days. Come, my masters, you shall all taste of my wine ere you depart.

All the Cred. We follow you, sir.

[*Exeunt* HOARD *and* Scrivener.

Wit. I'll try these fellows now. [*Aside.*]—A word, sir: what, will you carry me to that widow now?

1st Cred. Why, do you think we were in earnest, i'faith? carry you to a rich widow? we should get much credit by that: a noted rioter! a contemptible prodigal! 'twas a trick we have amongst us to get in our money: fare you well, sir. [*Exeunt* Creditors.

Wit. Farewell, and be hanged, you short pig-haired, ram-headed rascals! he that believes in you shall ne'er be saved, I warrant him. By this new league I shall have some access unto my love.

JOYCE *appears above.*

Joyce. Master Witgood!

Wit. My life!

Joyce. Meet me presently; that note directs you [*throws him a letter*]: I would not be suspected: our happiness attends us: farewell.

Wit. A word's enough. [*Exeunt severally.*

SCENE V.

DAMPIT'S *Bed-chamber.*

DAMPIT *in bed;* AUDREY *spinning by his side;* Boy.

Aud. [*singing.*]

Let the usurer cram him, in interest that excel,
There's pits enow to damn him, before he comes to hell;
In Holborn some, in Fleet Street some,
Where'er he come there's some, there's some.

Dam. Trahe, trahito, draw the curtain; give me a sip of sack more.

While he drinks, enter LAMPREY *and* SPICHCOCK.

Lam. Look you; did not I tell you he lay like the devil in chains, when he was bound for a thousand year?

Spi. But I think the devil had no steel bedstaffs; he goes beyond him for that.

Lam. Nay, do but mark the conceit of his drinking; one must wipe his mouth for him with a muckinder,[1] do you see, sir?

Spi. Is this the sick trampler? why, he is only bed-rid with drinking.

Lam. True, sir. He spies us.

Dam. What, Sir Tristram? you come and see a weak man here, a very weak man.

Lam. If you be weak in body, you should be strong in prayer, sir.

Dam. O, I have prayed too much, poor man!

Lam. There's a taste of his soul for you!

Spi. Faugh, loathsome!

Lam. I come to borrow a hundred pound of you, sir.

Dam. Alas, you come at an ill time! I cannot spare it i'faith; I ha' but two thousand i' th' house.

Aud. Ha, ha, ha!

Dam. Out, you gernative[2] quean, the mullipood[3] of villainy, the spinner of concupiscency!

Enter SIR LAUNCELOT *and others.*

Sir L. Yea, gentlemen, are you here before us? how is he now?

Lam. Faith, the same man still: the tavern bitch has bit him i' th' head.[4]

Sir L. We shall have the better sport with him: peace. —And how cheers Master Dampit now?

Dam. O, my bosom, Sir Launcelot, how cheer I! thy presence is restorative.

[1] Handkerchief.
[2] Bullen suggests that "gernative" means "grinning." To gern is to grin or to snarl.
[3] Multiple. [4] A proverb implying that a person was drunk.

Sir L. But I hear a great complaint of you, Master Dampit, among gallants.

Dam. I am glad of that, i'faith: prithee, what?

Sir L. They say you are waxed proud a' late, and if a friend visit you in the afternoon, you'll scarce know him.

Dam. Fie, fie; proud? I cannot remember any such thing: sure I was drunk then.

Sir L. Think you so, sir?

Dam. There 'twas, i'faith; nothing but the pride of the sack; and so certify 'em.—Fetch sack, sirrah.

Boy. A vengeance sack you once!

[*Exit, and returns presently with sack.*

Aud. Why, Master Dampit, if you hold on as you begin, and lie a little longer, you need not take care how to dispose your wealth; you'll make the vintner your heir.

Dam. Out, you babliaminy, you unfeathered, cremitoried quean, you cullisance of scabiosity!

Aud. Good words, Master Dampit, to speak before a maid and a virgin!

Dam. Hang thy virginity upon the pole of carnality!

Aud. Sweet terms! my mistress shall know 'em.

Lam. Note but the misery of this usuring slave: here he lies, like a noisome dunghill, full of the poison of his drunken blasphemies; and they to whom he bequeaths all, grudge him the very meat that feeds him, the very pillow that eases him. Here may a usurer behold his end: what profits it to be a slave in this world, and a devil i' th' next?

Dam. Sir Launcelot, let me buss thee, Sir Launcelot; thou art the only friend that I honour and respect.

Sir L. I thank you for that, Master Dampit.

Dam. Farewell, my bosom Sir Launcelot.

Sir L. Gentlemen, an you love me, let me step behind you, and one of you fall a talking of me to him.

Lam. Content.—Master Dampit——

Dam. So, sir.

Lam. Here came Sir Launcelot to see you e'en now.

Dam. Hang him, rascal!

Lam. Who? Sir Launcelot?

Dam. Pythagorical rascal!

Lam. Pythagorical?

Dam. Ay, he changes his cloak when he meets a sergeant.

Sir L. What a rogue's this!

Lam. I wonder you can rail at him, sir; he comes in love to see you.

Dam. A louse for his love! his father was a comb-maker; I have no need of his crawling love: he comes to have longer day,[1] the superlative rascal!

Sir L. 'Sfoot, I can no longer endure the rogue!—Master Dampit, I come to take my leave once again, sir.

Dam. Who? my dear and kind Sir Launcelot, the only gentleman of England? let me hug thee: "farewell, and a thousand."

Lam. Composed of wrongs and slavish flatteries!

Sir L. Nay, gentlemen, he shall show you more tricks yet; I'll give you another taste of him.

Lam. Is't possible?

Sir L. His memory is upon departing.

Dam. Another cup of sack!

Sir L. Mass, then 'twill be quite gone! Before he drink that, tell him there's a country client come up, and here attends for his learned advice.

Lam. Enough.

Dam. One cup more, and then let the bell toll: I hope I shall be weak enough by that time.

Lam. Master Dampit——

Dam. Is the sack spouting?

Lam. 'Tis coming forward, sir. Here's a countryman, a client of yours, waits for your deep and profound advice, sir.

[1] To postpone the payment of money he had borrowed.—*Bullen.*

Dam. A coxcombry, where is he? let him approach: set me up a peg higher.

Lam. [*to* Sir LAUN.] You must draw near, sir.

Dam. Now, good man fooliaminy, what say you to me now?

Sir L. Please your good worship, I am a poor man, sir——

Dam. What make you in my chamber then?

Sir L. I would entreat your worship's device[1] in a just and honest cause, sir.

Dam. I meddle with no such matters; I refer 'em to Master No-man's office.

Sir L. I had but one house left me in all the world, sir, which was my father's, my grandfather's, my great-grandfather's, and now a villain has unjustly wrung me out, and took possession on't.

Dam. Has he such feats? Thy best course is to bring thy *ejectione firmæ*, and in seven year thou mayst shove him out by the law.

Sir L. Alas, an't please your worship, I have small friends and less money!

Dam. Hoyday! this geer will fadge well:[2] hast no money? why, then, my advice is, thou must set fire a' th' house, and so get him out.

Lam. That will break strife, indeed.

Sir L. I thank your worship for your hot counsel, sir. —Altering but my voice a little, you see he knew me not: you may observe by this, that a drunkard's memory holds longer in the voice than in the person. But, gentlemen, shall I show you a sight? Behold the little dive-dapper[3] of damnation, Gulf the usurer, for his time worse than t'other.

Lam. What's he comes with him?

Sir L. Why, Hoard, that married lately the Widow Medler.

[1] Used designedly for "advice." [2] Answer well.

[3] The didapper or dabchick, an aquatic bird.

Lam. O, I cry you mercy, sir.

Enter HOARD *and* GULF.

Hoa. Now, gentlemen visitants, how does Master Dampit?

Sir L. Faith, here he lies, e'en drawing in, sir, good canary as fast as he can, sir; a very weak creature, truly, he is almost past memory.

Hoa. Fie, Master Dampit! you lie lazing a-bed here, and I come to invite you to my wedding-dinner: up, up, up!

Dam. Who's this? Master Hoard? who hast thou married, in the name of foolery?

Hoa. A rich widow.

Dam. A Dutch widow?[1]

Hoa. A rich widow; one Widow Medler.

Dam. Medler? she keeps open house.

Hoa. She did, I can tell you, in her t'other husband's days; open house for all comers; horse and man was welcome, and room enough for 'em all.

Dam. There's too much for thee, then; thou mayst let out some to thy neighbours.

Gulf. What, hung alive in chains? O spectacle! bed-staffs of steel? *O monstrum horrendum, informe, ingens, cui lumen ademptum!*[2] O Dampit, Dampit, here's a just judgment shown upon usury, extortion, and trampling villainy!

Sir L. This is excellent, thief rails upon the thief!

Gulf. Is this the end of cut-throat usury, brothel, and blasphemy? now mayst thou see what race a usurer runs.

Dam. Why, thou rogue of universality, do not I know thee? thy sound is like the cuckoo, the Welch ambassador:[3] thou cowardly slave, that offers to fight with a

[1] See note *ante*, p. 42. [2] Virg. *Æn.* iii. 658.

[3] So named, it is supposed, from the bird migrating hither from the west.

sick man when his weapon's down! rail upon me in my naked[1] bed? why, thou great Lucifer's little vicar! I am not so weak but I know a knave at first sight: thou inconscionable rascal! thou that goest upon Middlesex juries, and wilt make haste to give up thy verdict[2] because thou wilt not lose thy dinner! Are you answered?

Gulf. An't were not for shame——

[*Draws his dagger.*

Dam. Thou wouldst be hanged then.

Lam. Nay, you must exercise patience, Master Gulf, always in a sick man's chamber.

Sir L. He'll quarrel with none, I warrant you, but those that are bed-rid.

Dam. Let him come, gentlemen, I am armed: reach my close-stool hither.

Sir L. Here will be a sweet fray anon: I'll leave you, gentlemen.

Lam. Nay, we'll go along with you.—Master Gulf——

Gulf. Hang him, usuring rascal!

Sir L. Pish, set your strength to his, your wit to his!

Aud. Pray, gentlemen, depart; his hour's come upon him.—Sleep in my bosom, sleep.

Sir L. Nay, we have enough of him, i'faith; keep him for the house.
Now make your best:
For thrice his wealth I would not have his breast.

Gulf. A little thing would make me beat him now he's asleep.

Sir L. Mass, then 'twill be a pitiful day when he wakes: I would be loth to see that day: come.

Gulf. You overrule me, gentlemen, i'faith.

[*Exeunt.*

[1] *i.e.* Naked in bed.

[2] Did Pope remember this passage?

"The hungry judges soon the sentence sign,
And wretches hang, that jurymen may dine."
The Rape of the Lock, iii. 21.—*Dyce.*

ACT THE FIFTH.

SCENE I.

A Room in LUCRE'S *House.*

Enter LUCRE *and* WITGOOD.

WIT. Nay, uncle, let me prevail with you so much; I'faith, go, now he has invited you.

Luc. I shall have great joy there when he has borne away the widow!

Wit. Why, la, I thought where I should find you presently: uncle, a' ma troth, 'tis nothing so.

Luc. What's nothing so, sir? is not he married to the widow?

Wit. No, by my troth, is he not, uncle.

Luc. How?

Wit. Will you have the truth on't? he is married to a whore, i'faith.

Luc. I should laugh at that.

Wit. Uncle, let me perish in your favour if you find it not so; and that 'tis I that have married the honest woman.

Luc. Ha! I'd walk ten mile 'a foot to see that, i'faith.

Wit. And see't you shall, or I'll ne'er see you again.

Luc. A quean, i'faith? ha, ha, ha! [*Exeunt.*

SCENE II.

A Room in HOARD'S *House.*

Enter HOARD, *tasting wine,* Host *following in a livery cloak.*

Hoa. Pup, pup, pup, pup, I like not this wine: is there never a better tierce in the house?

Host. Yes, sir, there are as good tierces in the house as any are in England.

Hoa. Desire your mistress, you knave, to taste 'em all over; she has better skill.

Host. Has she so? the better for her, and the worse for you. [*Aside, and exit.*

Hoa. Arthur!

Enter ARTHUR.

Is the cupboard of plate set out?

Arth. All's in order, sir. [*Exit.*

Hoa. I am in love with my liveries every time I think on 'em; they make a gallant show, by my troth. Niece!

Enter JOYCE.

Joyce. Do you call, sir?

Hoa. Prithee, show a little diligence, and overlook the knaves a little; they'll filch and steal to-day, and send whole pasties home to their wives; an thou be'st a good niece, do not see me purloined.

Joyce. Fear it not, sir—I have cause: though the feast be prepared for you, yet it serves fit for my wedding-dinner too. [*Aside, and exit.*

Enter LAMPREY *and* SPICHCOCK.

Hoa. Master Lamprey and Master Spichcock, two the most welcome gentlemen alive! your fathers and mine were all free o' th' fishmongers.

Lam. They were indeed, sir. You see bold guests, sir; soon entreated.

Hoa. And that's best, sir.

Enter Servant.

How now, sirrah?

Ser. There's a coach come to th' door, sir. [*Exit.*

Hoa. My Lady Foxtone, a' my life!—Mistress Jane Hoard! wife!—Mass, 'tis her ladyship indeed!

Enter LADY FOXTONE.

Madam, you are welcome to an unfurnished house, dearth of cheer, scarcity of attendance.

L. Fox. You are pleased to make the worst, sir.

Hoa. Wife!

Enter Courtesan.

L. Fox. Is this your bride?

Hoa. Yes, madam.—Salute my Lady Foxtone.

Cour. Please you, madam, awhile to taste the air in the garden?

L. Fox. 'Twill please us well.

[*Exeunt* L. FOXTONE *and* Courtesan.

Hoa. Who would not wed? the most delicious life!
No joys are like the comforts of a wife.

Lam. So we bachelors think, that are not troubled with them.

Re-enter Servant.

Ser. Your worship's brother, with other ancient gentlemen, are newly alighted, sir. [*Exit.*

Hoa. Master Onesiphorus Hoard? why, now our company begins to come in.

Enter ONESIPHORUS HOARD, LIMBER, *and* KIX.

My dear and kind brother, welcome, i'faith.

O. Hoa. You see we are men at an hour, brother.

Hoa. Ay, I'll say that for you, brother; you keep as good an hour to come to a feast as any gentleman in the shire.—What, old Master Limber and Master Kix! do we meet, i'faith, jolly gentlemen?

Lim. We hope you lack guests, sir?

Hoa. O, welcome, welcome! we lack still such guests as your worships.

O. Hoa. Ah, sirrah brother, have you catched up Widow Medler?

Hoa. From 'em all, brother; and I may tell you I had mighty enemies, those that stuck sore; old Lucre is a sore fox, I can tell you, brother.

O. Hoa. Where is she? I'll go seek her out: I long to have a smack at her lips.

Hoa. And most wishfully, brother, see where she comes.

Re-enter Courtesan *and* LADY FOXTONE.

Give her a smack now we may hear it all the house over.

[Courtesan *and* O. Hoard *start and turn away.*

Cour. O Heaven, I am betrayed! I know that face.

Hoa. Ha, ha, ha! why, how now? are you both ashamed?—Come, gentlemen, we'll look another way.

O. Hoa. Nay, brother, hark you: come, you're disposed to be merry.

Hoa. Why do we meet else, man?

O. Hoa. That's another matter: I was ne'er so 'fraid in my life but that you had been in earnest.

Hoa. How mean you, brother?

O. Hoa. You said she was your wife.

Hoa. Did I so? by my troth, and so she is.

O. Hoa. By your troth, brother?

Hoa. What reason have I to dissemble with my friends, brother? if marriage can make her mine, she is mine. Why—— [O. HOARD *is about to retire.*

O. Hoa. Troth, I am not well of a sudden: I must crave pardon, brother; I came to see you, but I cannot stay dinner, i'faith.

Hoa. I hope you will not serve me so, brother?

Lim. By your leave, Master Hoard——

Hoa. What now? what now? pray, gentlemen:—you were wont to show yourselves wise men.

Lim. But you have shown your folly too much here.

Hoa. How?

Kix. Fie, fie! a man of your repute and name!
You'll feast your friends, but cloy 'em first with shame.

Hoa. This grows too deep; pray, let us reach the sense.

Lim. In your old age doat on a courtesan!

Hoa. Ha!

Kix. Marry a strumpet!

Hoa. Gentlemen!

O. Hoa. And Witgood's quean!

Hoa. O! nor lands nor living?

O. Hoa. Living!

Hoa. [*to* Courtesan.] Speak.

Cour. Alas, you know, at first, sir,
I told you I had nothing!

Hoa. Out, out! I am cheated; infinitely cozened!

Lim. Nay, Master Hoard——

Enter LUCRE, WITGOOD, *and* JOYCE.

Hoa. A Dutch widow![1] a Dutch widow! a Dutch widow!

Luc. Why, nephew, shall I trace thee still a liar?
Wilt make me mad? is not yon thing the widow?

Wit. Why, la, you are so hard a' belief, uncle! by my troth, she's a whore.

Luc. Then thou'rt a knave.

Wit. *Negatur argumentum*, uncle.

Luc. *Probo tibi*, nephew: he that knows a woman to be a quean must needs be a knave; thou sayst thou knowest her to be one; *ergo*, if she be a quean, thou'rt a knave.

Wit. *Negatur sequela majoris*, uncle; he that knows a woman to be a quean must needs be a knave; I deny that.

Hoa. Lucre and Witgood, you're both villains; get you out of my house!

[1] See note *ante*, p. 42.

Luc. Why, didst not invite me to thy wedding-dinner?

Wit. And are not you and I sworn perpetual friends before witness, sir, and were both drunk upon't?

Hoa. Daintily abused! you've put a punk [1] upon me!

Luc. Ha, ha, ha!

Hoa. A common strumpet!

Wit. Nay, now
You wrong her, sir; if I were she, I'd have
The law on you for that; I durst depose for her
She ne'er had common use nor common thought.

Cour. Despise me, publish me, I am your wife;
What shame can I have now but you'll have part?
If in disgrace you share, I sought not you;
You pursued, nay, forced me; had I friends would follow it,
Less than your action has been proved a rape.

O. Hoa. Brother!

Cour. Nor did I ever boast of lands unto you,
Money, or goods; I took a plainer course,
And told you true, I'd nothing:
If error were committed, 'twas by you;
Thank your own folly: nor has my sin been
So odious, but worse has been forgiven;
Nor am I so deformed, but I may challenge
The utmost power of any old man's love.
She that tastes not sin before twenty, twenty to one but she'll taste it after: most of you old men are content to marry young virgins, and take that which follows; where, marrying one of us, you both save a sinner and are quit from a cuckold for ever:
And more, in brief, let this your best thoughts win,
She that knows sin, knows best how to hate sin.

Hoa. Cursed be all malice! black are the fruits of spite,
And poison first their owners. O, my friends,
I must embrace shame, to be rid of shame!

[1] Prostitute. All the editions have "junt," but this is evidently a misprint.

Concealed disgrace prevents a public name.
Ah, Witgood! ah, Theodorus!

Wit. Alas, sir, I was pricked in conscience to see her well bestowed, and where could I bestow her better than upon your pitiful worship? Excepting but myself, I dare swear she's a virgin; and now, by marrying your niece, I have banished myself for ever from her: she's mine aunt now, by my faith, and there's no meddling with mine aunt, you know: a sin against my nuncle.

Cour. Lo, gentlemen, before you all [*Kneels.*
In true reclaimèd form I fall.
Henceforth for ever I defy
The glances of a sinful eye,
Waving of fans (which some suppose
Tricks of fancy [1]), treading of toes,
Wringing of fingers, biting the lip,
The wanton gait, th' alluring trip;
All secret friends and private meetings,
Close-borne letters and bawds' greetings;
Feigning excuse to women's labours
When we are sent for to th' next neighbour's;
Taking false physic, and ne'er start
To be let blood though sign [2] be at heart;
Removing chambers, shifting beds,
To welcome friends in husbands' steads,
Them to enjoy, and you to marry,
They first served, while you must tarry,
They to spend, and you to gather,
They to get, and you to father:
These, and thousand, thousand more,
New reclaimed, I now abhor.

Luc. [*to* WITGOOD.] Ah, here's a lesson, rioter, for you!

Wit. I must confess my follies; I'll down too: [*Kneels.*

[1] Love.

[2] "According to the directions for bleeding in old almanacs, blood was to be taken from particular parts under particular planets."—*Dyce.*

And here for ever I disclaim
The cause of youth's undoing, game,
Chiefly dice, those true outlanders,
That shake out beggars, thieves, and panders;
Soul-wasting surfeits, sinful riots,
Queans' evils, doctors' diets,
'Pothecaries' drugs, surgeons' glisters;
Stabbing of arms[1] for a common mistress;
Riband favours, ribald speeches;
Dear perfumed jackets, penniless breeches;
Dutch flapdragons,[2] healths in urine;
Drabs that keep a man too sure in:
I do defy[3] you all.
Lend me each honest hand, for here I rise
A reclaimed man, loathing the general vice.

Hoa. So, so, all friends! the wedding-dinner cools:
Who seem most crafty prove ofttimes most fools.

[*Exeunt.*

[1] "To stab their arms with daggers, and drink off the blood mixed with wine, to the health of their mistresses, was formerly a frequent practice among gallants."—*Dyce.*

[2] "Dutchmen had the reputation of being very expert in swallowing flapdragons."—*Bullen.*

[3] Renounce.

THE CHANGELING.

A "*Note of such Playes as were Acted at Court in* 1623 *and* 1624," in Sir Henry Herbert's Office-book, contains the entry: "Upon the Sonday after, beinge the 4 of January 1623, by the Queen of Bohemias company, *The Changelinge*, the prince only being there. Att Whitehall.' The play was published in 1653, as the joint work of Middleton and William Rowley, and in 1688 the unsold copies were reissued with a new title-page.

The story is taken from Reynolds's *God's Revenge against Murther* (first published in 1621), Book I. Hist. 4. Reynolds prefixed to the story the following argument: "Beatrice Joanna, to marry Alsemero, causeth De Flores to murder Alfonso Piracquo, who was a suitor to her. Alsemero marries her, and finding De Flores and her in adultery, kills them both. Thomaso Piracquo challengeth Alsemero for his brother's death. Alsemero kills him treacherously in the field, and is beheaded for the same, and his body thrown into the sea. At his execution he confesseth that his wife and De Flores murdered Alfonso Piracquo: their bodies are taken up out of their graves, then burnt, and their ashes thrown into the air." The dramatists do not follow the prose narrative closely. Rowley is probably responsible for the underplot (which gives the play its title) as well as for much in the treatment of the main story.

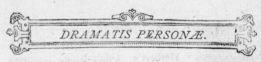

DRAMATIS PERSONÆ.

VERMANDERO, governor of the castle of Alicant.
ALONZO DE PIRACQUO, } brothers.
TOMASO DE PIRACQUO, }
ALSEMERO.
JASPERINO, his friend.
ALIBIUS, a doctor, who undertakes the cure of fools and madmen.
LOLLIO, his man.
ANTONIO, a pretended changeling.
PEDRO, his friend.
FRANCISCUS, a counterfeit madman.
DE FLORES, an attendant on Vermandero.
Madmen.
Servants.

BEATRICE-JOANNA, daughter of Vermandero.
DIAPHANTA, her waiting-woman.
ISABELLA, wife of Alibius.

SCENE—ALICANT.

THE CHANGELING.

ACT THE FIRST.

SCENE I.

A Street.

Enter ALSEMERO.

ALS. 'Twas in the temple where I first beheld her,
And now again the same: what omen yet
Follows of that? none but imaginary;
Why should my hopes or fate be timorous?
The place is holy, so is my intent:
I love her beauties to the holy purpose;
And that, methinks, admits comparison
With man's first creation, the place blessèd,
And is his right home back, if he achieve it.
The church hath first begun our interview,
And that's the place must join us into one;
So there's beginning and perfection too.

Enter JASPERINO.

Jas. O sir, are you here? come, the wind's fair with you;
You're like to have a swift and pleasant passage.

Als. Sure, you're deceived, friend, it is contrary,
In my best judgment.
Jas. What, for Malta?
If you could buy a gale[1] amongst the witches,
They could not serve you such a lucky pennyworth
As comes a' God's name.
Als. Even now I observed
The temple's vane to turn full in my face;
I know it is against me.
Jas. Against you?
Then you know not where you are.
Als. Not well, indeed.
Jas. Are you not well, sir?
Als. Yes, Jasperino,
Unless there be some hidden malady
Within me, that I understand not.
Jas. And that
I begin to doubt, sir: I never knew
Your inclination to travel at a pause,
With any cause to hinder it, till now.
Ashore you were wont to call your servants up,
And help to trap your horses for the speed;
At sea I've seen you weigh the anchor with 'em,
Hoist sails for fear to lose the foremost breath,
Be in continual prayers for fair winds;
And have you changed your orisons?
Als. No, friend;
I keep the same church, same devotion.
Jas. Lover I'm sure you're none; the stoic was
Found in you long ago; your mother nor
Best friends, who have set snares of beauty, ay,
And choice ones too, could never trap you that way:
What might be the cause?
Als. Lord, how violent

[1] "It has been observed by Steevens in a note on *Macbeth*, act i. sc. iii., that the selling of winds was an usual practice amongst the witches."—Editor of 1816.

Thou art! I was but meditating of
Somewhat I heard within the temple.

Jas. Is this
Violence? 'tis but idleness compared
With your haste yesterday.

Als. I'm all this while
A-going man.

Jas. Backwards, I think, sir. Look, your servants.

Enter Servants.

1st Ser. The seamen call; shall we board your trunks?

Als. No, not to day.

Jas. 'Tis the critical day, it seems, and the sign in Aquarius.

2nd Ser. We must not to sea to-day; this smoke will bring forth fire.

Als. Keep all on shore; I do not know the end,
Which needs I must do, of an affair in hand
Ere I can go to sea.

1st Ser. Well, your pleasure.

2nd Ser. Let him e'en take his leisure too; we are safer on land. [*Exeunt* Servants.

Enter BEATRICE, DIAPHANTA, *and* Servants: ALSEMERO *accosts* BEATRICE *and then kisses her.*

Jas. How now? the laws of the Medes are changed sure; salute a woman! he kisses too; wonderful! where learnt he this? and does it perfectly too; in my conscience, he ne'er rehearsed it before. Nay, go on; this will be stranger and better news at Valencia than if he had ransomed half Greece from the Turk. [*Aside.*

Beat. You are a scholar, sir?

Als. A weak one, lady.

Beat. Which of the sciences is this love you speak of?

Als. From your tongue I take it to be music.

Beat. You're skilful in it, can sing at first sight.

Als. And I have showed you all my skill at once;

I want more words to express me further,
And must be forced to repetition;
I love you dearly.

Beat. Be better advised, sir:
Our eyes are sentinels unto our judgments,
And should give certain judgment what they see;
But they are rash sometimes, and tell us wonders
Of common things, which when our judgments find,
They can then check the eyes, and call them blind.

Als. But I am further, lady; yesterday
Was mine eyes' employment, and hither now
They brought my judgment, where are both agreed:
Both houses then consenting, 'tis agreed;
Only there wants the confirmation
By the hand royal, that is your part, lady.

Beat. There's one above me, sir.—O, for five days past
To be recalled! sure mine eyes were mistaken;
This was the man was meant me: that he should come
So near his time, and miss it! [*Aside.*

Jas. We might have come by the carriers from Valencia,
I see, and saved all our sea-provision; we are at farthest
sure: methinks I should do something too;
I mean to be a venturer in this voyage:
Yonder's another vessel, I'll board her;
If she be lawful prize, down goes her topsail.
[*Accosts* DIAPHANTA.

Enter DE FLORES.

De F. Lady, your father——

Beat. Is in health, I hope.

De F. Your eye shall instantly instruct you, lady;
He's coming hitherward.

Beat. What needed then
Your duteous preface? I had rather
He had come unexpected; you must stale
A good presence with unnecessary blabbing;
And how welcome for your part you are,
I'm sure you know.

De F. Will't never mend, this scorn,
One side nor other? must I be enjoined
To follow still whilst she flies from me? well,
Fates, do your worst, I'll please myself with sight
Of her at all opportunities,
If but to spite her anger: I know she had
Rather see me dead than living; and yet
She knows no cause for't but a peevish will. [*Aside.*

Als. You seemed displeasèd, lady, on the sudden.

Beat. Your pardon, sir, 'tis my infirmity;
Nor can I other reason render you,
Than his or hers, of some particular thing
They must abandon as a deadly poison,
Which to a thousand other tastes were wholesome;
Such to mine eyes is that same fellow there,
The same that report speaks of the basilisk.

Als. This is a frequent frailty in our nature;
There's scarce a man amongst a thousand found
But hath his imperfection: one distastes
The scent of roses, which to infinites
Most pleasing is and odoriferous;
One oil, the enemy of poison;
Another wine, the cheerer of the heart
And lively refresher of the countenance:
Indeed this fault, if so it be, is general;
There's scarce a thing but is both loved and loathed:
Myself, I must confess, have the same frailty.

Beat. And what may be your poison, sir? I'm bold
with you.

Als. What might be your desire, perhaps; a cherry.

Beat. I am no enemy to any creature
My memory has, but yon gentleman.

Als. He does ill to tempt your sight, if he knew it.

Beat. He cannot be ignorant of that, sir,
I have not spared to tell him so; and I want
To help myself, since he's a gentleman
In good respect with my father, and follows him.

Als. He's out of his place then now. [*They talk apart.*

Jas. I am a mad wag, wench.

Dia. So methinks; but for your comfort, I can tell you, we have a doctor in the city that undertakes the cure of such.

Jas. Tush, I know what physic is best for the state of mine own body.

Dia. 'Tis scarce a well-governed state, I believe.

Jas. I could show thee such a thing with an ingredience that we two would compound together, and if it did not tame the maddest blood i' th' town for two hours after, I'll ne'er profess physic again.

Dia. A little poppy, sir, were good to cause you sleep.

Jas. Poppy? I'll give thee a pop i' th' lips for that first, and begin there: poppy is one simple indeed, and cuckoo-what-you-call't another: I'll discover no more now; another time I'll show thee all. [*Exit.*

Beat. My father, sir.

Enter VERMANDERO *and* Servants.

Ver. O Joanna, I came to meet thee;
Your devotion's ended?

Beat. For this time, sir.—
I shall change my saint, I fear me; I find
A giddy turning in me. [*Aside.*]—Sir, this while
I am beholden to this gentleman, who
Left his own way to keep me company,
And in discourse I find him much desirous
To see your castle; he hath deserved it, sir,
If ye please to grant it.

Ver. With all my heart, sir:
Yet there's an article between; I must know
Your country; we use not to give survey
Of our chief strengths to strangers; our citadels
Are placed conspicuous to outward view,
On promonts'[1] tops, but within our secrets.

Als. A Valencian, sir.

[1] Promontories.

Ver. A Valencian?
That's native, sir: of what name, I beseech you?
Als. Alsemero, sir.
Ver. Alsemero? not the son
Of John de Alsemero?
Als. The same, sir.
Ver. My best love bids you welcome.
Beat. He was wont
To call me so, and then he speaks a most
Unfeignèd truth.
Ver. O sir, I knew your father;
We two were in acquaintance long ago,
Before our chins were worth iulan [1] down,
And so continued till the stamp of time
Had coined us into silver: well, he's gone;—
A good soldier went with him.
Als. You went together in that, sir.
Ver. No, by Saint Jacques, I came behind him;
Yet I've done somewhat too: an unhappy day
Swallowed him at last at Gibraltar,
In fight with those rebellious Hollanders;
Was it not so?
Als. Whose death I had revenged,
Or followed him in fate, had not the late league
Prevented me.
Ver. Ay, ay, 'twas time to breathe.—
O Joanna, I should ha' told thee news;
I saw Piracquo lately.
Beat. That's ill news. [*Aside.*
Ver. He's hot preparing for this day of triumph:
Thou must be a bride within this sevennight.
Als. Ha! [*Aside.*
Beat. Nay, good sir, be not so violent; with speed
I cannot render satisfaction
Unto the dear companion of my soul,
Virginity, whom I thus long have lived with,
And part with it so rude and suddenly;

[1] From the Greek, meaning the first tender down.

Can such friends divide, never to meet again,
Without a solemn farewell?

Ver. Tush, tush! there's a toy.[1]

Als. I must now part, and never meet again
With any joy on earth. [*Aside.*]—Sir, your pardon;
My affairs call on me.

Ver. How, sir? by no means:
Not changed so soon, I hope? you must see my castle,
And her best entertainment, e'er we part,
I shall think myself unkindly usèd else.
Come, come, let's on; I had good hope your stay
Had been a while with us in Alicant;
I might have bid you to my daughter's wedding.

Als. He means to feast me, and poisons me beforehand.— [*Aside.*
I should be dearly glad to be there, sir,
Did my occasions suit as I could wish.

Beat. I shall be sorry if you be not there
When it is done, sir; but not so suddenly.

Ver. I tell you, sir, the gentleman's complete,
A courtier and a gallant, enriched
With many fair and noble ornaments;
I would not change him for a son-in-law
For any he in Spain, the proudest he,
And we have great ones, that you know.

Als. He's much
Bound to you, sir.

Ver. He shall be bound to me
As fast as this tie can hold him; I'll want
My will else.

Beat. I shall want mine, if you do it. [*Aside.*

Ver. But come, by the way I'll tell you more of him.

Als. How shall I dare to venture in his castle,
When he discharges murderers[2] at the gate?
But I must on, for back I cannot go. [*Aside.*

[1] Whim, fancy.
[2] Pieces of ordnance; also styled *murdering-pieces*.

Beat. Not this serpent gone yet?
[*Aside. Drops a glove.*

Ver. Look, girl, thy glove's fallen.
Stay, stay; De Flores, help a little.
[*Exeunt* VERMANDERO, ALSEMERO, *and* Servants.

De F. Here, lady. [*Offers her the glove.*

Beat. Mischief on your officious forwardness;
Who bade you stoop? they touch my hand no more:
There! for the other's sake I part with this;
[*Takes off and throws down the other glove.*
Take 'em, and draw thine own skin off with 'em!
[*Exit with* DIAPHANTA *and* Servants.

De F. Here's a favour come with a mischief now! I know
She had rather wear my pelt[1] tanned in a pair
Of dancing pumps, than I should thrust my fingers
Into her sockets here. I know she hates me,
Yet cannot choose but love her: no matter,
If but to vex her, I will haunt her still;
Though I get nothing else, I'll have my will. [*Exit.*

SCENE II.

A Room in the House of ALIBIUS.

Enter ALIBIUS *and* LOLLIO.

Alib. Lollio, I must trust thee with a secret,
But thou must keep it.

Lol. I was ever close to a secret, sir.

Alib. The diligence that I have found in thee,
The care and industry already past,
Assures me of thy good continuance.
Lollio, I have a wife.

[1] Skin.

Lol. Fie, sir, 'tis too late to keep her secret; she's known to be married all the town and country over.

Alib. Thou goest too fast, my Lollio; that knowledge
I allow no man can be barrèd it;
But there is a knowledge which is nearer,
Deeper, and sweeter, Lollio.

Lol. Well, sir, let us handle that between you and I.

Alib. 'Tis that I go about, man: Lollio,
My wife is young.

Lol. So much the worse to be kept secret, sir.

Alib. Why, now thou meet'st the substance of the point;
I am old, Lollio.

Lol. No, sir, 'tis I am old Lollio.

Alib. Yet why may not these concord and sympathise?
Old trees and young plants often grow together,
Well enough agreeing.

Lol. Ay, sir, but the old trees raise themselves higher and broader than the young plants.

Alib. Shrewd application![2] there's the fear, man;
I would wear my ring on my own finger;
Whilst it is borrowed, it is none of mine,
But his that useth it.

Lol. You must keep it on still then; if it but lie by, one or other will be thrusting into't.

Alib. Thou conceiv'st me, Lollio; here thy watchful eye
Must have employment; I cannot always be
At home.

Lol. I dare swear you cannot.

Alib. I must look out.

Lol. I know't, you must look out, 'tis every man's case.

Alib. Here, I do say, must thy employment be;
To watch her treadings, and in my absence
Supply my place.

1 "The 'shrewd application' is, I conceive, to that perpetual jest of the age, the cuckold's horns; which Lollio supposes might raise Alibius's head above his wife's."—Editor of 1816.

Lol. I'll do my best, sir; yet surely I cannot see who you should have cause to be jealous of.

Alib. Thy reason for that, Lollio? it is
A comfortable question.

Lol. We have but two sorts of people in the house, and both under the whip, that's fools [1] and madmen; the one has not wit enough to be knaves, and the other not knavery enough to be fools.

Alib. Ay, those are all my patients, Lollio;
I do profess the cure of either sort,
My trade, my living 'tis, I thrive by it;
But here's the care that mixes with my thrift;
The daily visitants, that come to see
My brain-sick patients, I would not have
To see my wife: gallants I do observe
Of quick enticing eyes, rich in habits,
Of stature and proportion very comely:
These are most shrewd temptations, Lollio.

Lol. They may be easily answered, sir; if they come to see the fools and madmen, you and I may serve the turn, and let my mistress alone, she's of neither sort.

Alib. 'Tis a good ward; [2] indeed, come they to see
Our madmen or our fools, let 'em see no more
Than what they come for; by that consequent
They must not see her, I'm sure she's no fool.

Lol. And I'm sure she's no madman.

Alib. Hold that buckler fast; Lollio, my trust
Is on thee, and I account it firm and strong.
What hour is't, Lollio?

Lol. Towards belly-hour, sir.

Alib. Dinner-time? thou mean'st twelve o'clock?

Lol. Yes, sir, for every part has his hour: we wake at six and look about us, that's eye hour; at seven we should pray, that's knee-hour; at eight walk, that's leg-hour; at nine gather flowers and pluck a rose,[3] that's

[1] Idiots. [2] *i.e.* Guard (in fencing).—*Dyce.*
[3] To pluck a rose is a euphemism of fairly obvious meaning.

nose-hour; at ten we drink, that's mouth-hour; at eleven lay about us for victuals, that's hand-hour; at twelve go to dinner, that's belly-hour.

Alib. Profoundly, Lollio! it will be long
Ere all thy scholars learn this lesson, and
I did look to have a new one entered;—stay,
I think my expectation is come home.

Enter PEDRO, *and* ANTONIO *disguised as an idiot.*

Ped. Save you, sir; my business speaks itself,
This sight takes off the labour of my tongue.

Alib. Ay, ay, sir, it is plain enough, you mean
Him for my patient.

Ped. And if your pains prove but commodious, to give but some little strength to the sick and weak part of nature in him, these are [*gives him money*] but patterns to show you of the whole pieces that will follow to you, beside the charge of diet, washing, and other necessaries, fully defrayed.

Alib. Believe it, sir, there shall no care be wanting.

Lol. Sir, an officer in this place may deserve something, the trouble will pass through my hands.

Ped. 'Tis fit something should come to your hands then, sir. [*Gives him money.*

Lol. Yes, sir, 'tis I must keep him sweet, and read to him: what is his name?

Ped. His name is Antonio; marry, we use but half to him, only Tony.

Lol. Tony, Tony, 'tis enough, and a very good name for a fool.—What's your name, Tony?

Ant. He, he, he! well, I thank you, cousin; he, he, he!

Lol. Good boy! hold up your head.—He can laugh; I perceive by that he is no beast.

Ped. Well, sir,
If you can raise him but to any height,
Any degree of wit, might he attain,

As I might say, to creep but on all four
Towards the chair of wit, or walk on crutches,
'Twould add an honour to your worthy pains,
And a great family might pray for you,
To which he should be heir, had he discretion
To claim and guide his own: assure you, sir,
He is a gentleman.

Lol. Nay, there's nobody doubted that; at first sight I knew him for a gentleman, he looks no other yet.

Ped. Let him have good attendance and sweet lodging.

Lol. As good as my mistress lies in, sir; and as you allow us time and means, we can raise him to the higher degree of discretion.

Ped. Nay, there shall no cost want, sir.

Lol. He will hardly be stretched up to the wit of a magnifico.

Ped. O no, that's not to be expected; far shorter will be enough.

Lol. I'll warrant you I'll make him fit to bear office in five weeks; I'll undertake to wind him up to the wit of constable.

Ped. If it be lower than that, it might serve turn.

Lol. No, fie; to level him with a headborough, beadle, or watchman, were but little better than he is: constable I'll able[2] him; if he do come to be a justice afterwards, let him thank the keeper: or I'll go further with you; say I do bring him up to my own pitch, say I make him as wise as myself.

Ped. Why, there I would have it.

Lol. Well, go to; either I'll be as arrant a fool as he, or he shall be as wise as I, and then I think 'twill serve his turn.

Ped. Nay, I do like thy wit passing well.

Lol. Yes, you may; yet if I had not been a fool, I had had more wit than I have too; remember what state you find me in.

[1] *i.e.* Answer for.

Ped. I will, and so leave you: your best cares, I beseech you.

Alib. Take you none with you, leave 'em all with us.

[*Exit* PEDRO.

Ant. O, my cousin's gone! cousin, cousin, O!

Lol. Peace, peace, Tony; you must not cry, child, you must be whipped if you do; your cousin is here still; I am your cousin, Tony.

Ant. He, he! then I'll not cry, if thou be'st my cousin; he, he, he!

Lol. I were best try his wit a little, that I may know what form to place him in.

Alib. Ay, do, Lollio, do.

Lol. I must ask him easy questions at first.—Tony, how many true[1] fingers has a tailor on his right hand?

Ant. As many as on his left, cousin.

Lol. Good: and how many on both?

Ant. Two less than a deuce, cousin.

Lol. Very well answered: I come to you again, cousin Tony; how many fools goes to a wise man?

Ant. Forty in a day sometimes, cousin.

Lol. Forty in a day? how prove you that?

Ant. All that fall out amongst themselves, and go to a lawyer to be made friends.

Lol. A parlous fool! he must sit in the fourth form at least, I perceive that.—I come again, Tony; how many knaves make an honest man?

Ant. I know not that, cousin.

Lol. No, the question is too hard for you: I'll tell you, cousin; there's three knaves may make an honest man, a sergeant, a jailor, and a beadle; the sergeant catches him, the jailor holds him, and the beadle lashes him; and if he be not honest then, the hangman must cure him.

Ant. Ha, ha, ha! that's fine sport, cousin.

[1] *i.e.* Honest.

Alib. This was too deep a question for the fool, Lollio.

Lol. Yes, this might have served yourself, though I say't.—Once more and you shall go play, Tony.

Ant. Ay, play at push-pin, cousin; ha, he!

Lol. So thou shalt: say how many fools are here——

Ant. Two, cousin; thou and I.

Lol. Nay, you're too forward there, Tony: mark my question; how many fools and knaves are here; a fool before a knave, a fool behind a knave, between every two fools a knave; how many fools, how many knaves?

Ant. I never learnt so far, cousin.

Alib. Thou puttest too hard questions to him, Lollio.

Lol. I'll make him understand it easily.—Cousin, stand there.

Ant. Ay, cousin.

Lol. Master, stand you next the fool.

Alib. Well, Lollio.

Lol. Here's my place: mark now, Tony, there's a fool before a knave.

Ant. That's I, cousin.

Lol. Here's a fool behind a knave, that's I; and between us two fools there is a knave, that's my master 'tis but we three, that's all.

Ant. We three, we three, cousin.

1st Mad. [*within.*] Put's head i' th' pillory, the bread's too little.

2nd Mad. [*within.*] Fly, fly, and he catches the swallow.

3rd Mad. [*within.*] Give her more onion, or the devil put the rope about her crag.[1]

Lol. You may hear what time of day it is, the chimes of Bedlam goes.

Alib. Peace, peace, or the wire[2] comes!

3rd Mad. [*within.*] Cat whore, cat whore! her parmasant, her parmasant![3]

[1] Neck. [2] Whip. [3] Parmesan cheese.

Alib. Peace, I say!—Their hour's come, they must be fed, Lollio.

Lol. There's no hope of recovery of that Welsh madman; was undone by a mouse that spoiled him a parmasant; lost his wits for't.

Alib. Go to your charge, Lollio; I'll to mine.

Lol. Go you to your madman's ward, let me alone with your fools.

Alib. And remember my last charge, Lollio. [*Exit.*

Lol. Of which your patients do you think I am?—Come, Tony, you must amongst your school-fellows now; there's pretty scholars amongst 'em, I can tell you; there's some of 'em at *stultus, stulta, stultum.*

Ant. I would see the madmen, cousin, if they would not bite me.

Lol. No, they shall not bite thee, Tony.

Ant. They bite when they are at dinner, do they not, coz?

Lol. They bite at dinner indeed, Tony. Well, I hope to get credit by thee; I like thee the best of all the scholars that ever I brought up, and thou shalt prove a wise man, or I'll prove a fool myself. [*Exeunt.*

ACT THE SECOND.

SCENE I.

An Apartment in the Castle.

Enter BEATRICE *and* JASPERINO *severally.*

BEAT. O sir, I'm ready now for that fair service
Which makes the name of friend sit glorious on you!
Good angels and this conduct be your guide! [*Giving a paper.*
Fitness of time and place is there set down, sir.
Jas. The joy I shall return rewards my service. [*Exit.*
Beat. How wise is Alsemero in his friend!
It is a sign he makes his choice with judgment;
Then I appear in nothing more approved
Than making choice of him; for 'tis a principle,
He that can choose
That bosom well who of his thoughts partakes,
Proves most discreet in every choice he makes.
Methinks I love now with the eyes of judgment,
And see the way to merit, clearly see it.
A true deserver like a diamond sparkles;
In darkness you may see him, that's in absence,
Which is the greatest darkness falls on love;
Yet is he best discernèd then
With intellectual eyesight. What's Piracquo,
My father spends his breath for? and his blessing

Is only mine as I regard his name,
Else it goes from me, and turns head against me,
Transformed into a curse: some speedy way
Must be remembered; he's so forward too,
So urgent that way, scarce allows me breath
To speak to my new comforts.

Enter DE FLORES.

De F. Yonder's she;
Whatever ails me, now a-late especially,
I can as well be hanged as refrain seeing her;
Some twenty times a day, nay, not so little,
Do I force errands, frame ways and excuses,
To come into her sight; and I've small reason for't,
And less encouragement, for she baits me still
Every time worse than other; does profess herself
The cruellest enemy to my face in town
At no hand can abide the sight of me,
As if danger or ill-luck hung in my looks.
I must confess my face is bad enough,
But I know far worse has better fortune,
And not endured alone, but doted on;
And yet such pick-haired faces, chins like witches',
Here and there five hairs whispering in a corner,
As if they grew in fear one of another,
Wrinkles like troughs, where swine-deformity swills
The tears of perjury, that lie there like wash
Fallen from the slimy and dishonest eye;
Yet such a one plucks sweets without restraint,
And has the grace of beauty to his sweet.
Though my hard fate has thrust me out to servitude,
I tumbled into th' world a gentleman.
She turns her blessèd eye upon me now,
And I'll endure all storms before I part with't. [*Aside.*

Beat. Again?
This ominous ill-faced fellow more disturbs me
Than all my other passions. [*Aside.*

De F. Now 't begins again ; [*Aside.*
I'll stand this storm of hail, though the stones pelt me.
Beat. Thy business? what's thy business?
De F. Soft and fair!
I cannot part so soon now. [*Aside.*
Beat. The villain's fixed.— [*Aside.*
Thou standing toad-pool——
De F. The shower falls amain now. [*Aside.*
Beat. Who sent thee? what's thy errand? leave my sight!
De F. My lord, your father, charged me to deliver
A message to you.
Beat. What, another since?
Do't, and be hanged then ; let me be rid of thee.
De F. True service merits mercy.
Beat. What's thy message?
De F. Let beauty settle but in patience,
You shall hear all.
Beat. A dallying, trifling torment!
De F. Signor Alonzo de Piracquo, lady,
Sole brother to Tomaso de Piracquo——
Beat. Slave, when wilt make an end?
De F. Too soon I shall.
Beat. What all this while of him?
De F. The said Alonzo,
With the foresaid Tomaso——
Beat. Yet again?
De F. Is new alighted.
Beat. Vengeance strike the news!
Thou thing most loathed, what cause was there in this
To bring thee to my sight?
De F. My lord, your father,
Charged me to seek you out.
Beat. Is there no other
To send his errand by?
De F. It seems 'tis my luck
To be i' th' way still.

Beat. Get thee from me!

De F. So:
Why, am not I an ass to devise ways
Thus to be railed at? I must see her still!
I shall have a mad qualm within this hour again,
I know't; and, like a common Garden-bull,[1]
I do but take breath to be lugged[2] again.
What this may bode I know not; I'll despair the less,
Because there's daily precedents of bad faces
Beloved beyond all reason; these foul chops
May come into favour one day 'mongst their fellows:
Wrangling has proved the mistress of good pastime;
As children cry themselves asleep, I ha' seen
Women have chid themselves a-bed to men.
[*Aside, and exit*

Beat. I never see this fellow but I think
Of some harm towards me, danger's in my mind still;
I scarce leave trembling of an hour after:
The next good mood I find my father in,
I'll get him quite discarded. O, I was
Lost in this small disturbance, and forgot
Affliction's fiercer torrent that now comes
To bear down all my comforts!

Enter VERMANDERO, ALONZO, *and* TOMASO.

Ver. You're both welcome,
But an especial one belongs to you, sir,
To whose most noble name our love presents
Th' addition of a son, our son Alonzo.

Alon. The treasury of honour cannot bring forth
A title I should more rejoice in, sir.

Ver. You have improved it well.—Daughter, prepare;
The day will steal upon thee suddenly.

[1] At Paris Garden, on the Bankside, bull-baiting and similar pastimes were carried on.

[2] "Dragged by the ear. The term 'lug' is usually found in connection with bull or bear-baiting. Falstaff protested that he was 'as melancholy as a gib cat or a *lugged* bear.'"—*Bullen.*

Beat. Howe'er I will be sure to keep the night,
If it should come so near me. [*Aside.*
[BEATRICE *and* VERMANDERO *talk apart.*

Tom. Alonzo.

Alon. Brother?

Tom. In troth I see small welcome in her eye.

Alon. Fie, you are too severe a censurer
Of love in all points, there's no bringing on you:
If lovers should mark everything a fault,
Affection would be like an ill-set book,
Whose faults might prove as big as half the volume.

Beat. That's all I do entreat.

Ver. It is but reasonable;
I'll see what my son says to't.—Son Alonzo,
Here is a motion made but to reprieve
A maidenhead three days longer; the request
Is not far out of reason, for indeed
The former time is pinching.

Alon. Though my joys
Be set back so much time as I could wish
They had been forward, yet since she desires it,
The time is set as pleasing as before,
I find no gladness wanting.

Ver. May I ever
Meet it in that point still! you're nobly welcome, sirs.
[*Exit with* BEATRICE.

Tom. So; did you mark the dulness of her parting now?

Alon. What dulness? thou art so exceptious still!

Tom. Why, let it go then; I am but a fool
To mark your harms so heedfully.

Alon. Where's the oversight?

Tom. Come, your faith's cozened in her, strongly cozened:
Unsettle your affection with all speed
Wisdom can bring it to; your peace is ruined else.
Think what a torment 'tis to marry one
Whose heart is leaped into another's bosom:

If ever pleasure she receive from thee,
It comes not in thy name, or of thy gift;
She lies but with another in thine arms,
He the half-father unto all thy children
In the conception; if he get 'em not,
She helps to get 'em for him; and how dangerous
And shameful her restraint may go in time to,
It is not to be thought on without sufferings.

Alon. You speak as if she loved some other, then.

Tom. Do you apprehend so slowly?

Alon. Nay, an that
Be your fear only, I am safe enough:
Preserve your friendship and your counsel, brother,
For times of more distress; I should depart
An enemy, a dangerous, deadly one,
To any but thyself, that should but think
She knew the meaning of inconstancy,
Much less the use and practice: yet we're friends;
Pray, let no more be urged; I can endure
Much, till I meet an injury to her,
Then I am not myself. Farewell, sweet brother;
How much we're bound to Heaven to depart lovingly
[*Exit.*

Tom. Why, here is love's tame madness; thus a man
Quickly steals into his vexation. [*Exit.*

SCENE II.

Another Apartment in the Castle.

Enter DIAPHANTA *and* ALSEMERO.

Dia. The place is my charge; you have kept your [hour,
And the reward of a just meeting bless you!
I hear my lady coming: complete gentleman,

I dare not be too busy with my praises,
They're dangerous things to deal with. [*Exit.*

Als. This goes well;
These women are the ladies' cabinets,
Things of most precious trust are locked into 'em.

Enter BEATRICE.

Beat. I have within mine eye all my desires:
Requests that holy prayers ascend Heaven for,
And brings 'em down to furnish our defects,
Come not more sweet to our necessities
Than thou unto my wishes.

Als. We're so like
In our expressions, lady, that unless I borrow
The same words, I shall never find their equals.

Beat. How happy were this meeting, this embrace,
If it were free from envy! this poor kiss
It has an enemy, a hateful one,
That wishes poison to 't: how well were I now,
If there were none such name known as Piracquo,
Nor no such tie as the command of parents!
I should be but too much blessed.

Als. One good service
Would strike off both your fears, and I'll go near't too,
Since you are so distressed; remove the cause,
The command ceases; so there's two fears blown out
With one and the same blast.

Beat. Pray, let me find you, sir:
What might that service be, so strangely happy?

Als. The honourablest piece about man, valour:
I'll send a challenge to Piracquo instantly.

Beat. How? call you that extinguishing of fear,
When 'tis the only way to keep it flaming?
Are not you ventured in the action,
That's all my joys and comforts? pray, no more, sir:
Say you prevailed, you're danger's and not mine then;
The law would claim you from me, or obscurity

Be made the grave to bury you alive.
I'm glad these thoughts come forth; O, keep not one
Of this condition, sir! here was a course
Found to bring sorrow on her way to death;
The tears would ne'er ha' dried, till dust had choked 'em.
Blood-guiltiness becomes a fouler visage;—
And now I think on one; I was to blame,
I ha' marred so good a market with my scorn;
'Thad been done questionless: the ugliest creature
Creation framed for some use: yet to see
I could not mark so much where it should be! [*Aside.*

Als. Lady——

Beat. Why, men of art make much of poison,
Keep one to expel another; where was my art? [*Aside.*

Als. Lady, you hear not me.

Beat. I do especially, sir:
The present times are not so sure of our side
As those hereafter may be; we must use 'em then
As thrifty folks their wealth, sparingly now,
Till the time opens.

Als. You teach wisdom, lady.

Beat. Within there! Diaphanta!

Re-enter DIAPHANTA.

Dia. Do you call, madam?

Beat. Perfect your service, and conduct this gentleman
The private way you brought him.

Dia. I shall, madam.

Als. My love's as firm as love e'er built upon.
[*Exit with* DIAPHANTA.

Enter DE FLORES.

De F. I've watched this meeting, and do wonder much
What shall become of t'other; I'm sure both
Cannot be served unless she transgress; haply
Then I'll put in for one; for if a woman
Fly from one point, from him she makes a husband,
She spreads and mounts then like arithmetic;
One, ten, a hundred, a thousand, ten thousand,

Proves in time sutler to an army royal.
Now do I look to be most richly railed at,
Yet I must see her. [*Aside.*

Beat. Why, put case I loathed him
As much as youth and beauty hates a sepulchre,
Must I needs show it? cannot I keep that secret,
And serve my turn upon him? See, he's here.— [*Aside.*
De Flores.

De F. Ha, I shall run mad with joy!
She called me fairly by my name De Flores,
And neither rogue nor rascal. [*Aside.*

Beat. What ha' you done
To your face a' late? you've met with some good physician;
You've pruned yourself, methinks: you were not wont
To look so amorously.[1]

De F. Not I;—
'Tis the same physnomy, to a hair and pimple,
Which she called scurvy scarce an hour ago:
How is this? [*Aside.*

Beat. Come hither; nearer, man.

De F. I'm up to the chin in Heaven! [*Aside.*

Beat. Turn, let me see;
Faugh, 'tis but the heat of the liver, I perceive't;
I thought it had been worse.

De F. Her fingers touched me!
She smells all amber.[2] [*Aside.*

Beat. I'll make a water for you shall cleanse this
Within a fortnight.

De F. With your own hands, lady?

Beat. Yes, mine own, sir; in a work of cure
I'll trust no other.

De F. 'Tis half an act of pleasure
To hear her talk thus to me. [*Aside.*

Beat. When we're used
To a hard face, it is not so unpleasing;

[1] *i.e.* An object of love. [2] Ambergris.

It mends still in opinion, hourly mends;
I see it by experience.
De F. I was blessed
To light upon this minute; I'll make use on't. [*Aside.*
Beat. Hardness becomes the visage of a man well;
It argues service, resolution, manhood,
If cause were of employment.
De F. 'Twould be soon seen
If e'er your ladyship had cause to use it;
I would but wish the honour of a service
So happy as that mounts to.
Beat. We shall try you:
O my De Flores!
De F. How's that? she calls me hers!
Already, *my* De Flores! [*Aside.*]—You were about
To sigh out somewhat, madam?
Beat. No, was I?
I forgot,—O!——
De F. There 'tis again, the very fellow on't.
Beat. You are too quick, sir.
De F. There's no excuse for't now; I heard it twice, madam;
That sigh would fain have utterance: take pity on't,
And lend it a free word; 'las, how it labours
For liberty! I hear the murmur yet
Beat at your bosom.
Beat. Would creation——
De F. Ay, well said, that is it.
Beat. Had formed me man!
De F. Nay, that's not it.
Beat. O, 'tis the soul of freedom!
I should not then be forced to marry one
I hate beyond all depths; I should have power
Then to oppose my loathings, nay, remove 'em
For ever from my sight.
De F. O blessed occasion! [*Aside.*
Without change to your sex you have your wishes;
Claim so much man in me.

Beat. In thee, De Flores?
There is small cause for that.

De F. Put it not from me,
It is a service that I kneel for to you. [*Kneels.*

Beat. You are too violent to mean faithfully:
There's horror in my service, blood, and danger;
Can those be things to sue for?

De F. If you knew
How sweet it were to me to be employed
In any act of yours, you would say then
I failed, and used not reverence enough
When I received the charge on't.

Beat. This is much, methinks;
Belike his wants are greedy; and to such
Gold tastes like angel's food. [*Aside.*]—De Flores, rise.

De F. I'll have the work first.

Beat. Possible his need
Is strong upon him. [*Aside.*]—There's to encourage thee; [*Gives money.*
As thou art forward, and thy service dangerous,
Thy reward shall be precious.

De F. That I've thought on;
I have assured myself of that beforehand,
And know it will be precious; the thought ravishes!

Beat. Then take him to thy fury!

De F. I thirst for him.

Beat. Alonzo de Piracquo.

De F. [*rising.*] His end's upon him;
He shall be seen no more.

Beat. How lovely now
Dost thou appear to me! never was man
Dearlier rewarded.

De F. I do think of that.

Beat. Be wondrous careful in the execution.

De F. Why, are not both our lives upon the cast?

Beat. Then I throw all my fears upon thy service.

De F. They ne'er shall rise to hurt you.

Beat. When the deed's done,

I'll furnish thee with all things for thy flight;
Thou may'st live bravely in another country.

De F. Ay, ay;
We'll talk of that hereafter.

Beat. I shall rid myself
Of two inveterate loathings at one time,
Piracquo, and his dog-face. [*Aside, and exit.*

De F. O my blood!
Methinks I feel her in mine arms already;
Her wanton fingers combing out this beard,
And, being pleasèd, praising this bad face.
Hunger and pleasure, they'll commend sometimes
Slovenly dishes, and feed heartily on 'em.
Nay, which is stranger, refuse daintier for 'em:
Some women are odd feeders.—I am too loud.
Here comes the man goes supperless to bed,
Yet shall not rise to-morrow to his dinner.

Enter ALONZO.

Alon. De Flores.

De F. My kind, honourable lord?

Alon. I'm glad I ha' met with thee.

De F. Sir?

Alon. Thou canst show me
The full strength of the castle?

De F. That I can, sir.

Alon. I much desire it.

De F. And if the ways and straits
Of some of the passages be not too tedious for you,
I'll assure you, worth your time and sight, my lord.

Alon. Pooh, that shall be no hindrance.

De F. I'm your servant, then:
'Tis now near dinner-time; 'gainst your lordship's rising
I'll have the keys about me.

Alon. Thanks, kind De Flores.

De F. He's safely thrust upon me beyond hopes.
[*Aside.*
[*Exeunt severally.*

ACT THE THIRD.

SCENE I.

A Narrow Passage in the Castle.

Enter ALONZO *and* DE FLORES. (*In the act-time* [1] DE FLORES *hides a naked rapier behind a door.*[2])

DE FLORES. Yes, here are all the keys;
I was afraid, my lord,
I'd wanted for the postern, this is it:
I've all, I've all, my lord: this for the
sconce. [nable fort.
Alon. 'Tis a most spacious and impreg-
De F. You will tell me more, my lord: this descent
Is somewhat narrow, we shall never pass
Well with our weapons, they'll but trouble us.
Alon. Thou sayest true.
De F. Pray, let me help your lordship.
Alon. 'Tis done: thanks, kind De Flores.

1 *i.e.* Between the acts.

2 "Whiles Piracquo is at dinner with Vermandero, De Flores is providing of a bloody banquet in the east casemate; where of purpose he goes and hides a naked sword and poniard behind the door. Now dinner being ended, Piracquo finds out De Flores, and summons him of his promise; who tells him he is ready to wait on him: so away they go from the walls to the ravelins, sconces, and bulwarks, and from thence by a postern to the ditches; and so in again to the casemates, whereof they have already viewed three, and are now going to the last, which is the theatre whereon we shall presently see acted a mournful and bloody tragedy. At the descent hereof De Flores puts off his rapier, and leaves it behind him; treacherously informing Piracquo that the descent is narrow and craggy. See here the policy and villainy of this devilish and

De F. Here are hooks, my lord,
To hang such things on purpose.
[*Hanging up his own sword and that of* ALONZO.
Alon. Lead, I'll follow thee. [*Exeunt.*

SCENE II.

A Vault.

Enter ALONZO *and* DE FLORES.

De F. All this is nothing; you shall see anon
A place you little dream on.
Alon. I am glad
I have this leisure; all your master's house
Imagine I ha' taken a gondola.
De F. All but myself, sir,—which makes up my safety.
[*Aside.*
My lord, I'll place you at a casement here
Will show you the full strength of all the castle.
Look, spend your eye awhile upon that object.
Alon. Here's rich variety, De Flores.
De F. Yes, sir.
Alon. Goodly munition.
De F. Ay, there's ordnance, sir,
No bastard metal, will ring you a peal like bells
At great men's funerals: keep your eye straight, my lord;

treacherous miscreant. Piracquo, not doubting nor dreaming of any treason, follows his example, and so casts off his rapier: De Flores leads the way, and he follows him; but, alas, poor gentleman, he shall never return with his life. They enter the vault of the casemate, De Flores opens the door, and throws it back, thereby to hide his sword and poniard: he stoops and looks through a port-hole, and tells him that that piece doth thoroughly scour the ditch. Piracquo stoops likewise down to view it, when (O grief to think thereon) De Flores steps for his weapons, and with his poniard stabs him through the back, and swiftly redoubling blow upon blow, kills him dead at his feet, and, without going farther, buries him there, right under the ruins of an old wall, whereof that casemate was built."—Reynolds's *Triumphs of God's Revenge against Murther*, pp. 54, 55, ed. 1635.

Take special notice of that sconce before you,
There you may dwell awhile.
[*Takes the rapier which he had hid behind the door.*
Alon. I am upon't.
De F. And so am I. [*Stabs him.*
Alon. De Flores! O De Flores!
Whose malice hast thou put on?
De F. Do you question
A work of secrecy? I must silence you. [*Stabs him.*
Alon. O, O, O!
De F. I must silence you. [*Stabs him.*
So here's an undertaking well accomplished:
This vault serves to good use now: ha, what's that
Threw sparkles in my eye? O, 'tis a diamond
He wears upon his finger; 'twas well found,
This will approve the work.[1] What, so fast on?
Not part in death? I'll take a speedy course then.
Finger and all shall off. [*Cuts off the finger.*] So, now I'll clear
The passages from all suspect or fear. [*Exit with body.*

SCENE III.

An Apartment in the House of ALIBIUS

Enter ISABELLA *and* LOLLIO.

Isa. Why, sirrah, whence have you commission
To fetter the doors against me?
If you keep me in a cage, pray, whistle to me,
Let me be doing something.

Lol. You shall be doing, if it please you; I'll whistle to you, if you'll pipe after.

Isa. Is it your master's pleasure, or your own,
To keep me in this pinfold?

Lol. 'Tis for my master's pleasure, lest being taken in

[1] *i.e.* Prove it has been done.

another man's corn, you might be pounded in another place.

Isa. 'Tis very well, and he'll prove very wise.

Lol. He says you have company enough in the house, if you please to be sociable, of all sorts of people.

Isa. Of all sorts? why, here's none but fools and madmen.

Lol. Very well: and where will you find any other, if you should go abroad? there's my master, and I to boot too.

Isa. Of either sort one, a madman and a fool.

Lol. I would even participate of both then if I were as you; I know you're half mad already, be half foolish too.

Isa. You're a brave saucy rascal! come on, sir,
Afford me then the pleasure of your bedlam;
You were commending once to-day to me
Your last-come lunatic; what a proper [1]
Body there was without brains to guide it,
And what a pitiful delight appeared
In that defect, as if your wisdom had found
A mirth in madness; pray, sir, let me partake,
If there be such a pleasure.

Lol. If I do not show you the handsomest, discreetest madman, one that I may call the understanding madman, then say I am a fool.

Isa. Well, a match, I will say so.

Lol. When you have had a taste of the madman, you shall, if you please, see Fool's College, o' th' other side. I seldom lock there; 'tis but shooting a bolt or two, and you are amongst 'em. [*Exit, and brings in* FRANCISCUS.] —Come on, sir; let me see how handsomely you'll behave yourself now.

Fran. How sweetly she looks! O, but there's a wrinkle in her brow as deep as philosophy. Anacreon, drink to my mistress' health, I'll pledge it; stay, stay, there's a spider in the cup! no, 'tis but a grape-stone; swallow it, fear nothing, poet; so, so, lift higher.

[1] Handsome.

Isa. Alack, alack, it is too full of pity
To be laughed at! How fell he mad? canst thou tell?

Lol. For love, mistress: he was a pretty poet too, and that set him forwards first: the muses then forsook him; he ran mad for a chambermaid, yet she was but a dwarf neither.

Fran. Hail, bright Titania!
Why stand'st thou idle on these flowery banks?
Oberon is dancing with his Dryades;
I'll gather daisies, primrose, violets,
And bind them in a verse of poesy.

Lol. [*holding up a whip.*] Not too near! you see your danger.

Fran. O, hold thy hand, great Diomede!
Thou feed'st thy horses well, they shall obey thee:
Get up, Bucephalus kneels. [*Kneels.*

Lol. You see how I awe my flock; a shepherd has not his dog at more obedience.

Isa. His conscience is unquiet; sure that was
The cause of this: a proper gentleman!

Fran. Come hither, Æsculapius; hide the poison.

Lol. Well, 'tis hid. [*Hides the whip.*

Fran. Didst thou ne'er hear of one Tiresias,
A famous poet?

Lol. Yes, that kept tame wild geese.

Fran. That's he; I am the man.

Lol. No?

Fran. Yes; but make no words on't: I was a man
Seven years ago.

Lol. A stripling, I think, you might.

Fran. Now I'm a woman, all feminine.

Lol. I would I might see that!

Fran. Juno struck me blind.

Lol. I'll ne'er believe that: for a woman, they say, has an eye more than a man.

Fran. I say she struck me blind.

Lol. And Luna made you mad: you have two trades to beg with.

Fran. Luna is now big-bellied, and there's room
For both of us to ride with Hecate;
I'll drag thee up into her silver sphere,
And there we'll kick the dog—and beat the bush—
That barks against the witches of the night;
The swift lycanthropi[1] that walks the round,
We'll tear their wolvish skins, and save the sheep.

[*Attempts to seize* LOLLIO.

Lol. Is't come to this? nay, then, my poison comes forth again [*showing the whip*]: mad slave, indeed, abuse your keeper!

Isa. I prithee, hence with him, now he grows dangerous.

Fran. [*sings.*] Sweet love, pity me,
Give me leave to lie with thee.

Lol. No, I'll see you wiser first: to your own kennel!

Fran. No noise, she sleeps; draw all the curtains round,
Let no soft sound molest the pretty soul,
But love, and love creeps in at a mouse-hole.

Lol. I would you would get into your hole! [*Exit* FRANCISCUS.]—Now, mistress, I will bring you another sort; you shall be fooled another while. [*Exit, and brings in* ANTONIO.]—Tony, come hither, Tony: look who's yonder, Tony.

Ant. Cousin, is it not my aunt?[2]

Lol. Yes, 'tis one of 'em, Tony.

Ant. He, he! how do you, uncle?

Lol. Fear him not, mistress, 'tis a gentle nigget;[3] you may play with him, as safely with him as with his bauble.

Isa. How long hast thou been a fool?

Ant. Ever since I came hither, cousin.

Isa. Cousin? I'm none of thy cousins, fool.

Lol. O, mistress, fools have always so much wit as to claim their kindred.

[1] Persons suffering from *lycanthropia*, or wolf-madness, at one time believed to be common.

[2] Cant term for procuress or bawd. [3] Nidget, *i.e.* idiot.

Madman [*within.*] Bounce, bounce! he falls, he falls!

Isa. Hark you, your scholars in the upper room
Are out of order.

Lol. Must I come amongst you there?—Keep you the fool, mistress; I'll go up and play left-handed Orlando amongst the madmen. [*Exit.*

Isa. Well, sir.

Ant. 'Tis opportuneful now, sweet lady! nay,
Cast no amazing eye upon this change.

Isa. Ha!

Ant. This shape of folly shrouds your dearest love,
The truest servant to your powerful beauties,
Whose magic had this force thus to transform me.

Isa. You're a fine fool indeed!

Ant. O, 'tis not strange!
Love has an intellect that runs through all
The scrutinous sciences, and, like a cunning poet,
Catches a quantity of every knowledge,
Yet brings all home into one mystery,
Into one secret, that he proceeds in.

Isa. You're a parlous fool.

Ant. No danger in me; I bring nought but love
And his soft-wounding shafts to strike you with:
Try but one arrow; if it hurt you, I
Will stand you twenty back in recompense.

Isa. A forward fool too!

Ant. This was love's teaching:
A thousand ways he fashioned out my way,
And this I found the safest and the nearest,
To tread the galaxia to my star.

Isa. Profound withal! certain you dreamed of this,
Love never taught it waking.

Ant. Take no acquaintance
Of these outward follies, there's within
A gentleman that loves you.

Isa. When I see him,
I'll speak with him; so, in the meantime, keep

Your habit, it becomes you well enough:
As you're a gentleman, I'll not discover you;
That's all the favour that you must expect:
When you are weary, you may leave the school,
For all this while you have but played the fool.

Re-enter LOLLIO.

Ant. And must again.—He, he! I thank you, cousin;
I'll be your valentine to-morrow morning.

Lol. How do you like the fool, mistress?

Isa. Passing well, sir.

Lol. Is he not witty, pretty well, for a fool?

Isa. If he holds on as he begins, he's like
To come to something.

Lol. Ay, thank a good tutor: you may put him to't; he begins to answer pretty hard questions.—Tony, how many is five times six?

Ant. Five times six is six times five.

Lol. What arithmetician could have answered better? How many is one hundred and seven?

Ant. One hundred and seven is seven hundred and one, cousin.

Lol. This is no wit to speak on!—Will you be rid of the fool now?

Isa. By no means; let him stay a little.

Madman [*within.*] Catch there, catch the last couple in hell! [1]

Lol. Again! must I come amongst you? Would my master were come home! I am not able to govern both these wards together. [*Exit.*

Ant. Why should a minute of love's hour be lost?

Isa. Fie, out again! I had rather you kept
Your other posture; you become not your tongue
When you speak from your clothes.

Ant. How can he freeze

[1] An allusion to the game of barley-break, the ground for which was divided into three compartments, of which the middle one was termed "hell."

Lives near so sweet a warmth? shall I alone
Walk through the orchard of th' Hesperides,
And, cowardly, not dare to pull an apple?

Enter LOLLIO *above.*

This with the red cheeks I must venture for.
[*Attempts to kiss her.*

Isa. Take heed, there's giants keep 'em.

Lol. How now, fool, are you good at that? have you read Lipsius?[1] he's past *Ars Amandi;* I believe I must put harder questions to him, I perceive that. [*Aside.*

Isa. You're bold without fear too.

Ant. What should I fear,
Having all joys about me? Do you but smile,
And love shall play the wanton on your lip,
Meet and retire, retire and meet again;
Look you but cheerfully, and in your eyes
I shall behold mine own deformity,
And dress myself up fairer: I know this shape
Becomes me not, but in those bright mirrors
I shall array me handsomely.

[*Cries of madmen are heard within, like those of birds and beasts.*

Lol. Cuckoo, cuckoo! [*Exit above.*

Ant. What are these?

Isa. Of fear enough to part us;
Yet are they but our schools of lunatics,
That act their fantasies in any shapes,
Suiting their present thoughts: if sad, they cry
If mirth be their conceit, they laugh again:
Sometimes they imitate the beasts and birds,
Singing or howling, braying, barking; all
As their wild fancies prompt 'em.

Ant. These are no fears.

Isa. But here's a large one, my man.

[1] "Is it necessary to notice that the name of this great scholar is ntroduced merely for the sake of its first syllable?"—*Dyce.*

Re-enter LOLLIO.

Ant. Ha, he! that's fine sport indeed, cousin.

Lol. I would my master were come home! 'tis too much for one shepherd to govern two of these flocks; nor can I believe that one churchman can instruct two benefices at once; there will be some incurable mad of the one side, and very fools on the other.—Come, Tony.

Ant. Prithee, cousin, let me stay here still.

Lol. No, you must to your book now; you have played sufficiently.

Isa. Your fool has grown wondrous witty.

Lol. Well, I'll say nothing: but I do not think but he will put you down one of these days.

[*Exit with* ANTONIO.

Isa. Here the restrainèd current might make breach,
Spite of the watchful bankers: would a woman stray,
She need not gad abroad to seek her sin,
It would be brought home one way or other:
The needle's point will to the fixèd north;
Such drawing arctics women's beauties are.

Re-enter LOLLIO.

Lol. How dost thou, sweet rogue?

Isa. How now?

Lol. Come, there are degrees; one fool may be better than another.

Isa. What's the matter?

Lol. Nay, if thou givest thy mind to fool's flesh, have at thee!

Isa. You bold slave, you!

Lol. I could follow now as t'other fool did:
"What should I fear,
Having all joys about me? Do you but smile,
And love shall play the wanton on your lip,
Meet and retire, retire and meet again;
Look you but cheerfully, and in your eyes
I shall behold my own deformity,

And dress myself up fairer: I know this shape
Becomes me not—"
And so as it follows: but is not this the more foolish way? Come, sweet rogue; kiss me, my little Lacedæmonian; let me feel how thy pulses beat; thou hast a thing about thee would do a man pleasure, I'll lay my hand on't.

Isa. Sirrah, no more! I see you have discovered
This love's knight errant, who hath made adventure
For purchase of my love: be silent, mute,
Mute as a statue, or his injunction
For me enjoying, shall be to cut thy throat;
I'll do it, though for no other purpose; and
Be sure he'll not refuse it.

Lol. My share, that's all;
I'll have my fool's part with you.

Isa. No more! your master.

Enter ALIBIUS.

Alib. Sweet, how dost thou?

Isa. Your bounden servant, sir.

Alib. Fie, fie, sweetheart,
No more of that.

Isa. You were best lock me up.

Alib. In my arms and bosom, my sweet Isabella,
I'll lock thee up most nearly.—Lollio,
We have employment, we have task in hand:
At noble Vermandero's, our castle's captain,
There is a nuptial to be solemnised—
Beatrice-Joanna, his fair daughter, bride—
For which the gentleman hath bespoke our pains,
A mixture of our madmen and our fools,[1]
To finish, as it were, and make the fag
Of all the revels, the third night from the first;
Only an unexpected passage over,

[1] "So Corax, a physician, in Ford's *Lover's Melancholy*, provides a 'Masque of Melancholy,' in which various forms of madness are represented, for the entertainment of Palador, Prince of Cyprus."—*Bullen*.

To make a frightful pleasure, that is all,
But not the all I aim at; could we so act it,
To teach it in a wild distracted measure,
Though out of form and figure, breaking time's head,
It were no matter, 'twould be healed again
In one age or other, if not in this:
This, this, Lollio, there's a good reward begun,
And will beget a bounty, be it known.

Lol. This is easy, sir, I'll warrant you: you have about you fools and madmen that can dance very well; and 'tis no wonder, your best dancers are not the wisest men; the reason is, with often jumping they jolt their brains down into their feet, that their wits lie more in their heels than in their heads.

Alib. Honest Lollio, thou giv'st me a good reason,
And a comfort in it.

Isa. You've a fine trade on't;
Madmen and fools are a staple commodity.

Alib. O wife, we must eat, wear clothes, and live:
Just at the lawyer's haven we arrive,
By madmen and by fools we both do thrive. [*Exeunt.*

SCENE IV.

An Apartment in the Castle.

Enter VERMANDERO, BEATRICE, ALSEMERO, *and* JASPERINO.

Ver. Valencia speaks so nobly of you, sir,
I wish I had a daughter now for you.

Als. The fellow of this creature were a partner
For a king's love.

Ver. I had her fellow once, sir,
But Heaven has married her to joys eternal;
'Twere sin to wish her in this vale again.

Come, sir, your friend and you shall see the pleasures
Which my health chiefly joys in.

Als. I hear
The beauty of this seat largely commended.

Ver. It falls much short of that.

[*Exit with* ALSEMERO *and* JASPERINO.

Beat. So, here's one step
Into my father's favour; time will fix him;
I've got him now the liberty of the house;
So wisdom, by degrees, works out her freedom:
And if that eye be darkened that offends me,—
I wait but that eclipse,—this gentleman
Shall soon shine glorious in my father's liking,
Through the refulgent virtue of my love.

Enter DE FLORES.

De F. My thoughts are at a banquet; for the deed,
I feel no weight in't; 'tis but light and cheap
For the sweet recompense that I set down for't. [*Aside.*

Beat. De Flores?

De F. Lady?

Beat. Thy looks promise cheerfully.

De F. All things are answerable, time, circumstance,
Your wishes, and my service.

Beat. It is done, then?

De F. Piracquo is no more.

Beat. My joys start at mine eyes; our sweet'st delights
Are evermore born weeping.

De F. I've a token for you.

Beat. For me?

De F. But it was sent somewhat unwillingly;
I could not get the ring without the finger.

[*Producing the finger and ring.*

Beat. Bless me, what hast thou done?

De F. Why, is that more
Than killing the whole man? I cut his heart-strings;

A greedy hand thrust in a dish at court,
In a mistake hath had as much as this.

Beat. 'Tis the first token my father made me send him.

De F. And I have made him send it back again
For his last token ; I was loth to leave it,
And I'm sure dead men have no use of jewels ;
He was as loth to part with't, for it stuck
As if the flesh and it were both one substance.

Beat. At the stag's fall, the keeper has his fees ;
'Tis soon applied, all dead men's fees are yours, sir :
I pray, bury the finger, but the stone
You may make use on shortly ; the true value,
Tak't of my truth, is near three hundred ducats.

De F. 'Twill hardly buy a capcase [1] for one's conscience though,
To keep it from the worm, as fine as 'tis :
Well, being my fees, I'll take it ;
Great men have taught me that, or else my merit
Would scorn the way on't.

Beat. It might justly, sir ;
Why, thou mistak'st, De Flores, 'tis not given
In state of recompense.

De F. No, I hope so, lady ;
You should soon witness my contempt to't then.

Beat. Prithee,—thou look'st as if thou wert offended.

De F. That were strange, lady ; 'tis not possible
My service should draw such a cause from you :
Offended ! could you think so ? that were much
For one of my performance, and so warm
Yet in my service.

Beat. 'Twere misery in me to give you cause, sir.

De F. I know so much, it were so : misery
In her most sharp condition,

Beat. 'Tis resolved then ;

[1] Band-box.

Look you, sir, here's three thousand golden florens;[1]
I have not meanly thought upon thy merit.

De F. What! salary? now you move me.

Beat. How, De Flores?

De F. Do you place me in the rank of verminous fellows,
To destroy things for wages? offer gold
For the life-blood of man? is anything
Valued too precious for my recompense?

Beat. I understand thee not.

De F. I could ha' hired
A journeyman in murder at this rate,
And mine own conscience might have slept at ease,
And have had the work brought home.

Beat. I'm in a labyrinth;
What will content him? I'd fain be rid of him. [*Aside.*
I'll double the sum, sir.

De F. You take a course
To double my vexation, that's the good you do.

Beat. Bless me, I'm now in worse plight than I was;
I know not what will please him. [*Aside*].—For my fear's sake,
I prithee, make away with all speed possible;
And if thou be'st so modest not to name
The sum that will content thee, paper blushes not,
Send thy demand in writing, it shall follow thee;
But, prithee, take thy flight.

De F. You must fly too then.

Beat. I?

De F. I'll not stir a foot else.

Beat. What's your meaning?

De F. Why, are not you as guilty? in, I'm sure,
As deep as I; and we should stick together:
Come, your fears counsel you but ill; my absence

[1] So called from having been first coined by the Florentines. Their value was 3*s*. 4*d*. each.

Would draw suspect upon you instantly;
There were no rescue for you.
Beat. He speaks home! [*Aside.*
De F. Nor is it fit we two, engaged so jointly,
Should part and live asunder.
Beat. How now, sir?
This shows not well.
De F. What makes your lip so strange?
This must not be betwixt us.
Beat. The man talks wildly!
De F. Come, kiss me with a zeal now.
Beat. Heaven, I doubt him! [*Aside.*
De F. I will not stand so long to beg 'em shortly.
Beat. Take heed, De Flores, of forgetfulness,
'Twill soon betray us.
De F. Take you heed first;
Faith, you're grown much forgetful, you're to blame in't.
Beat. He's bold, and I am blamed for't. [*Aside.*
De F. I have eased you
Of your trouble, think on it; I am in pain,
And must be eased of you; 'tis a charity,
Justice invites your blood to understand me.
Beat. I dare not.
De F. Quickly!
Beat. O, I never shall!
Speak it yet further off, that I may lose
What has been spoken, and no sound remain on't;
I would not hear so much offence again
For such another deed.
De F. Soft, lady, soft!
The last is not yet paid for: O, this act
Has put me into spirit; I was as greedy on't
As the parched earth of moisture, when the clouds weep:
Did you not mark, I wrought myself into't,
Nay, sued and kneeled for't? why was all that pains took?
You see I've thrown contempt upon your gold

Not that I want it not, for I do piteously,
In order I'll come unto't, and make use on't,
But 'twas not held so precious to begin with,
For I place wealth after the heels of pleasure;
And were not I resolved in my belief
That thy virginity were perfect in thee,
I should but take my recompense with grudging,
As if I had but half my hopes I agreed for.

Beat. Why, 'tis impossible thou canst be so wicked,
Or shelter such a cunning cruelty,
To make his death the murderer of my honour!
Thy language is so bold and vicious,
I cannot see which way I can forgive it
With any modesty.

De F. Pish! you forget yourself;
A woman dipped in blood, and talk of modesty!

Beat. O misery of sin! would I'd been bound
Perpetually unto my living hate
In that Piracquo, than to hear these words!
Think but upon the distance that creation
Set 'twixt thy blood and mine, and keep thee there.

De F. Look but into your conscience, read me there;
'Tis a true book, you'll find me there your equal:
Pish! fly not to your birth, but settle you
In what the act has made you; you're no more now.
You must forget your parentage to me;
You are the deed's creature; by that name
You lost your first condition, and I challenge you,
As peace and innocency has turned you out,
And made you one with me.

Beat. With thee, foul villain!

De F. Yes, my fair murderess; do you urge me,
Though thou writ'st maid, thou whore in thy affection?
'Twas changed from thy first love, and that's a kind
Of whoredom in the heart; and he's changed now
To bring thy second on, thy Alsemero,
Whom by all sweets that ever darkness tasted,

If I enjoy thee not, thou ne'er enjoyest!
I'll blast the hopes and joys of marriage,
I'll confess all; my life I rate at nothing.

Beat. De Flores!

De F. I shall rest from all plagues then;
I live in pain now; that love-shooting eye[1]
Will burn my heart to cinders.

Beat. O sir, hear me!

De F. She that in life and love refuses me,
In death and shame my partner she shall be.

Beat. [*kneeling.*] Stay, hear me once for all; I make thee master
Of all the wealth I have in gold and jewels;
Let me go poor unto my bed with honour,
And I am rich in all things!

De F. Let this silence thee:
The wealth of all Valencia shall not buy
My pleasure from me;
Can you weep Fate from its determined purpose?
So soon may you weep me.

Beat. Vengeance begins;
Murder, I see, is followed by more sins:
Was my creation in the womb so curst,
It must engender with a viper first?

De F. [*raising her.*] Come, rise and shroud your blushes in my bosom;
Silence is one of pleasure's best receipts:
Thy peace is wrought for ever in this yielding.
'Las! how the turtle pants! thou'lt love anon
What thou so fear'st and faint'st to venture on.

[*Exeunt.*

[1] In the old edition:—
"I shall rest from all love's plagues then;
I live in pain now; that shooting eye."
The correction was suggested by Dyce.

ACT THE FOURTH.

Dumb Show.

Enter Gentlemen, VERMANDERO *meeting them with action of wonderment at the disappearance of* PIRACQUO. *Enter* ALSEMERO *with* JASPERINO *and gallants:* VERMANDERO *points to him, the gentlemen seeming to applaud the choice.* ALSEMERO, VERMANDERO, JASPERINO, *and the others pass over the stage with much pomp,* BEATRICE *as a bride following in great state, attended by* DIAPHANTA, ISABELLA, *and other gentlewomen;* DE FLORES *after all, smiling at the accident:* ALONZO'S *ghost appears to him in the midst of his smile, and startles him, showing the hand whose finger he had cut off.*

SCENE I.

ALSEMERO'S *Apartment in the Castle.*

Enter BEATRICE.

BEAT. This fellow has undone me endlessly;
Never was bride so fearfully distressed:
The more I think upon th' ensuing night,
And whom I am to cope with in embraces,
One who's ennobled both in blood and mind,
So clear in understanding,—that's my plague now—
Before whose judgment will my fault appear
Like malefactors' crimes before tribunals

There is no hiding on't, the more I dive
Into my own distress: how a wise man
Stands for a great calamity! there's no venturing
Into his bed, what course soe'er I light upon,
Without my shame, which may grow up to danger;
He cannot but in justice strangle me
As I lie by him, as a cheater use me;
'Tis a precious craft to play with a false die
Before a cunning gamester. Here's his closet;
The key left in't, and he abroad i' th' park!
Sure 'twas forgot; I'll be so bold as look in't.

[*Opens closet.*

Bless me! a right physician's closet 'tis,
Set round with vials; every one her mark too:
Sure he does practise physic for his own use,
Which may be safely called your great man's wisdom.
What manuscript lies here?
[*Reads.*] "The Book of Experiment, called Secrets in Nature:"
So 'tis so:
[*Reads.*] "How to know whether a woman be with child or no:"
I hope I am not yet; if he should try though!
Let me see [*reads*] "folio forty-five," here 'tis,
The leaf tucked down upon't, the place suspicious:
[*Reads.*] "If you would know whether a woman be with child or not, give her two spoonfuls of the white water in glass C——"
Where's that glass C? O yonder, I see 't now—
[*Reads.*] "and if she be with child, she sleeps full twelve hours after; if not, not:"
None of that water comes into my belly;
I'll know you from a hundred; I could break you now,
Or turn you into milk, and so beguile
The master of the mystery; but I'll look to you.

[1] "In *Antonii Mizaldi Monluciani de Arcanis Naturæ Libelli Quatuor*, ed. tertia, 1558, 12mo, I find no passages resembling those which are read by Beatrice."– *Dyce.*

Ha! that which is next is ten times worse:
[*Reads.*] "How to know whether a woman be a maid or not:"
If that should be applied, what would become of me?
Belike he has a strong faith of my purity,
That never yet made proof; but this he calls
[*Reads.*] "A merry slight,[1] but true experiment; the author Antonius Mizaldus. Give the party you suspect the quantity of a spoonful of the water in the glass M, which, upon her that is a maid, makes three several effects; 'twill make her incontinently[2] gape, then fall into a sudden sneezing, last into a violent laughing; else, dull, heavy, and lumpish."
Where had I been?
I fear it, yet 'tis seven hours to bed-time.

Enter DIAPHANTA.

Dia. Cuds, madam, are you here?
Beat. Seeing that wench now,
A trick comes in my mind; 'tis a nice piece
Gold cannot purchase. [*Aside.*]—I come hither, wench,
To look my lord.
Dia. Would I had such a cause [madam.
To look him too! [*Aside.*]—Why, he's i' th' park,
Beat. There let him be.
Dia. Ay, madam, let him compass
Whole parks and forests, as great rangers do,
At roosting-time a little lodge can hold 'em:
Earth-conquering Alexander, that thought the world
Too narrow for him, in th' end had but his pit-hole.
Beat. I fear thou art not modest, Diaphanta.
Dia. Your thoughts are so unwilling to be known,
'Tis ever the bride's fashion, towards bed-time, [madam.
To set light by her joys, as if she owned 'em not.
Beat. Her joys? her fears thou wouldst say.
Dia. Fear of what?
Beat. Art thou a maid, and talk'st so to a maid?

[1] Trick. [2] Immediately.

You leave a blushing business behind;
Beshrew your heart for't!
Dia. Do you mean good sooth, madam?
Beat. Well, if I'd thought upon the fear at first,
Man should have been unknown.
Dia. Is't possible?
Beat. I'd give a thousand ducats to that woman
Would try what my fear were, and tell me true
To-morrow, when she gets from't; as she likes,
I might perhaps be drawn to't.
Dia. Are you in earnest?
Beat. Do you get the woman, then challenge me,
And see if I'll fly from't; but I must tell you
This by the way, she must be a true maid,
Else there's no trial, my fears are not her's else.
Dia. Nay, she that I would put into your hands, madam.
Shall be a maid.
Beat. You know I should be shamed else,
Because she lies for me.
Dia. 'Tis a strange humour!
But are you serious still? would you resign.
Your first night's pleasure, and give money too?
Beat. As willingly as live.—Alas, the gold
Is but a by-bet to wedge in the honour! [*Aside.*
Dia. I do not know how the world goes abroad
For faith or honesty; there's both required in this.
Madam, what say you to me, and stray no further?
I've a good mind, in troth, to earn your money.
Beat. You are too quick, I fear, to be a maid.
Dia. How? not a maid? nay, then you urge me, [madam;
Your honourable self is not a truer,
With all your fears upon you——
Beat. Bad enough then. [*Aside.*
Dia. Than I with all my lightsome joys about me.
Beat. I'm glad to hear't: then you dare put your [honesty
Upon an easy trial.
Dia. Easy? anything.

Beat. I'll come to you straight. [*Goes to the Closet.*
Dia. She will not search me, will she,
Like the forewoman of a female jury?[1]
Beat. Glass M: ay, this is it. [*Brings vial.*]—Look,
Diaphanta,
You take no worse than I do. [*Drinks.*
Dia. And in so doing,
I will not question what it is, but take it. [*Drinks.*
Beat. Now if th' experiment be true, 'twill praise itself,
And give me noble ease: begins already;
[DIAPHANTA *gapes.*
There's the first symptom; and what haste it makes
To fall into the second, there by this time!
[DIAPHANTA *sneezes.*
Most admirable secret! on the contrary,
It stirs not me a whit, which most concerns it. [*Aside.*
Dia. Ha, ha, ha!
Beat. Just in all things, and in order
As if 'twere circumscribed; one accident
Gives way unto another. [*Aside.*
Dia. Ha, ha, ha!
Beat. How now, wench?
Dia. Ha, ha, ha! I'm so, so light
At heart—ha, ha, ha!—so pleasurable!
But one swig more, sweet madam.
Beat. Ay, to-morrow,
We shall have time to sit by't.
Dia. Now I'm sad again.
Beat. It lays itself so gently too! [*Aside.*]—Come,
Most honest Diaphanta I dare call thee now. [wench.
Dia. Pray, tell me, madam, what trick call you this?
Beat. I'll tell thee all hereafter; we must study
The carriage of this business.
Dia. I shall carry't well,
Because I love the burthen.

[1] Mr. Bullen suspects that there is a reference here to the examination by matrons of the notorious Countess of Essex in the divorce suit brought by her against her husband a few years previously.

Beat. About midnight
You must not fail to steal forth gently,
That I may use the place.
Dia. O, fear not, madam,
I shall be cool by that time: the bride's place,
And with a thousand ducats! I'm for a justice now,
I bring a portion with me:. I scorn small fools. [*Exeunt.*

SCENE II.

Another Apartment in the Castle.

Enter VERMANDERO *and* Servant.

Ver. I tell thee, knave, mine honour is in question,
A thing till now free from suspicion,
Nor ever was there cause. Who of my gentlemen
Are absent?
Tell me, and truly, how many, and who?
Ser. Antonio, sir, and Franciscus.
Ver. When did they leave the castle?
Ser. Some ten days since, sir; the one intending to Briamata, th' other for Valencia.
Ver. The time accuses 'em; a charge of murder
Is brought within my castle-gate, Piracquo's murder;
I dare not answer faithfully their absence:
A strict command of apprehension
Shall pursue 'em suddenly, and either wipe
The stain off clear, or openly discover it.
Provide me wingèd warrants for the purpose.
[*Exit* Servant.
See, I am set on again.

Enter TOMASO.

Tom. I claim a brother of you.
Ver. You're too hot;
Seek him not here.

Tom. Yes, 'mongst your dearest bloods,
If my peace find no fairer satisfaction:
This is the place must yield account for him,
For here I left him; and the hasty tie
Of this snatched marriage gives strong testimony
Of his most certain ruin.

Ver. Certain falsehood!
This is the place indeed; his breach of faith
Has too much marred both my abusèd love,
The honourable love I reserved for him,
And mocked my daughter's joy; the prepared morning
Blushed at his infidelity; he left
Contempt and scorn to throw upon those friends
Whose belief hurt 'em: O, twas most ignoble
To take his flight so unexpectedly,
And throw such public wrongs on those that loved him!

Tom. Then this is all your answer?

Ver. 'Tis too fair
For one of his alliance; and I warn you
That this place no more see you. [*Exit.*

Enter DE FLORES.

Tom. The best is,
There is more ground to meet a man's revenge on.—
Honest De Flores?

De F. That's my name indeed.
Saw you the bride? good sweet sir, which way took she?

Tom. I've blessed mine eyes from seeing such a false one.

De F. I'd fain get off, this man's not for my company;
I smell his brother's blood when I come near him. [*Aside.*

Tom. Come hither, kind and true one; I remember
My brother loved thee well.

De F. O, purely, dear sir!—
Methinks I'm now again a-killing on him,
He brings it so fresh to me. [*Aside.*

Tom. Thou canst guess, sirrah—

An honest friend has an instinct of jealousy—
At some foul guilty person.
De F. Alas! sir,
I am so charitable, I think none
Worse than myself! you did not see the bride then?
Tom. I prithee, name her not: is she not wicked?
De F. No, no; a pretty, easy, round-packed sinner,
As your most ladies are, else you might think
I flattered her; but, sir, at no hand wicked,
Till they're so old their chins and noses[1] meet,
And they salute witches. I'm called, I think, sir.—
His company even overlays my conscience.
[*Aside, and exit.*

Tom. That De Flores has a wondrous honest heart;
He'll bring it out in time, I'm assured on't.
O, here's the glorious master of the day's joy!
'Twill not be long till he and I do reckon.

Enter ALSEMERO.

Sir.
Als. You're most welcome.
Tom. You may call that word back;
I do not think I am, nor wish to be.
Als. 'Tis strange you found the way to this house, then.
Tom. Would I'd ne'er known the cause! I'm none of those, sir,
That come to give you joy, and swill your wine;
'Tis a more precious liquor that must lay
The fiery thirst I bring.
Als. Your words and you
Appear to me great strangers.
Tom. Time and our swords
May make us more acquainted; this the business:
I should have had a brother in your place;
How treachery and malice have disposed of him,

1 Old ed. has "sins and vices." The correction was suggested by Dyce.

I'm bound to inquire of him which holds his right,
Which never could come fairly.

Als. You must look
To answer for that word, sir,

Tom. Fear you not,
I'll have it ready drawn at our next meeting.
Keep your day solemn; farewell, I disturb it not;
I'll bear the smart with patience for a time. [*Exit.*

Als. 'Tis somewhat ominous this; a quarrel entered
Upon this day; my innocence relieves me,

Enter JASPERINO.

I should be wondrous sad else.—Jasperino,
I've news to tell thee, strange news.

Jasp. I ha' some too,
I think as strange as yours: would I might keep
Mine, so my faith and friendship might be kept in't!
Faith, sir, dispense a little with my zeal,
And let it cool in this.

Als. This puts me on,
And blames thee for thy slowness.

Jas. All may prove nothing,
Only a friendly fear that leapt from me, sir.

Als. No question, 't may prove nothing; let's partake it though.

Jas. 'Twas Diaphanta's chance—for to that wench
I pretend[1] honest love, and she deserves it—
To leave me in a back part of the house,
A place we chose for private conference;
She was no sooner gone, but instantly
I heard your bride's voice in the next room to me;
And lending more attention, found De Flores
Louder than she.

Als. De Flores! thou art out now.

Jas. You'll tell me more anon.

Als. Still I'll prevent[2] thee,

[1] Offer.

[2] Anticipate.

The very sight of him is poison to her.
Jas. That made me stagger too; but Diaphanta
At her return confirmed it.
Als. Diaphanta!
Jas. Then fell we both to listen, and words passed
Like those that challenge interest in a woman.
Als. Peace; quench thy zeal, 'tis dangerous to thy bosom.
Jas. Then truth is full of peril.
Als. Such truths are.
O, were she the sole glory of the earth,
Had eyes that could shoot fire into king's breasts,
And touched,[1] she sleeps not here! yet I have time,
Though night be near, to be resolved hereof;
And, prithee, do not weigh me by my passions.
Jas. I never weighed friend so.
Als. Done charitably!
That key will lead thee to a pretty secret, [*Giving key.*
By a Chaldean taught me, and I have
My study upon some: bring from my closet
A glass inscribed there with the letter M,
And question not my purpose.
Jas. It shall be done, sir. [*Exit.*
Als. How can this hang together? not an hour since
Her woman came pleading her lady's fears,
Delivered her for the most timorous virgin
That ever shrunk at man's name, and so modest,
She charged her weep out her request to me,
That she might come obscurely to my bosom.

Enter BEATRICE.

Beat. All things go well; my woman's preparing yonder
For her sweet voyage, which grieves me to lose;
Necessity compels it; I lose all else. [*Aside.*
Als. Tush! modesty's shrine is set in yonder forehead:
I cannot be too sure though. [*Aside.*]—My Joanna!

[1] Tainted.

Beat. Sir, I was bold to weep a message to you;
Pardon my modest fears.

Als. The dove's not meeker;
She's abused, questionless. [*Aside.*

Re-enter JASPERINO *with vial.*

O, are you come, sir?

Beat. The glass, upon my life! I see the letter. [*Aside*

Jas. Sir, this is M. [*Giving vial.*

Als. 'Tis it.

Beat. I am suspected. [*Aside.*

Als. How fitly our bride comes to partake with us!

Beat. What is't, my lord?

Als. No hurt.

Beat. Sir, pardon me,
I seldom taste of any composition.

Als. But this, upon my warrant, you shall venture on.

Beat. I fear 'twill make me ill.

Als. Heaven forbid that.

Beat. I'm put now to my cunning: th' effects I know,
If I can now but feign'em handsomely. [*Aside, then drinks.*

Als. It has that secret virtue, it ne'er missed, sir.
Upon a virgin.

Jas. Treble-qualitied? [BEATRICE *gapes and sneezes.*

Als. By all that's virtuous it takes there! proceeds!

Jas. This is the strangest trick to know a maid by.

Beat. Ha, ha, ha!
You have given me joy of heart to drink, my lord.

Als. No, thou hast given me such joy of heart,
That never can be blasted.

Beat. What's the matter, sir?

Als. See now 'tis settled in a melancholy;
Keeps both the time and method. [*Aside.*]—My Joanna,
Chaste as the breath of Heaven, or morning's womb,
That brings the day forth! thus my love encloses thee.

[*Exeunt.*

SCENE III.

A Room in the House of ALIBIUS.

Enter ISABELLA *and* LOLLIO.

Isa. O Heaven! is this the waning moon?
Does love turn fool, run mad, and all at once?
Sirrah, here's a madman, akin to the fool too,
A lunatic lover.

Lol. No, no, not he I brought the letter from.

Isa. Compare his inside with his out, and tell me.

Lol. The out's mad, I'm sure of that; I had a taste on't.

Isa. [*reads letter.*] "To the bright Andromeda, chief chambermaid to the Knight of the Sun, at the sign of Scorpio, in the middle region, sent by the bellows-mender of Æolus. Pay the post."

Lol. This is stark madness!

Isa. Now mark the inside.
[*Reads.*] "Sweet lady, having now cast off this counterfeit cover of a madman, I appear to your best judgment a true and faithful lover of your beauty."

Lol. He is mad still.

Isa. [*reads.*] "If any fault you find, chide those perfections in you which have made me imperfect; 'tis the same sun that causeth to grow and enforceth to wither——"

Lol. O rogue!

Isa. [*reads.*] "Shapes and transhapes, destroys and builds again: I come in winter to you, dismantled of my proper ornaments; by the sweet splendour of your cheerful smiles, I spring and live a lover."

Lol. Mad rascal still!

Isa. [*reads.*] "Tread him not under foot, that shall appear an honour to your bounties. I remain—mad till I speak with you, from whom I expect my cure, yours all, or one beside himself, FRANCISCUS."

Lol. You are like to have a fine time on't; my master

and I may give over our professions; I do not think but you can cure fools and madmen faster than we, with little pains too.

Isa. Very likely.

Lol. One thing I must tell you, mistress; you perceive that I am privy to your skill; if I find you minister once, and set up the trade, I put in for my thirds; I shall be mad or fool else.

Isa. The first place is thine, believe it, Lollio,
If I do fall.

Lol. I fall upon you.

Isa. So.

Lol. Well, I stand to my venture.

Isa. But thy counsel now; how shall I deal with 'em?

Lol. Why, do you mean to deal with em?

Isa. Nay, the fair understanding, how to use 'em.

Lol. Abuse 'em! that's the way to mad the fool, and make a fool of the madman, and then you use 'em kindly.

Isa. 'Tis easy, I'll practise; do thou observe it;
The key of thy wardrobe.

Lol. There [*gives key*]; fit yourself for 'em, and I'll fit 'em both for you.

Isa. Take thou no further notice than the outside.

Lol. Not an inch [*Exit* ISABELLA]; I'll put you to the inside.

Enter ALIBIUS.

Alib. Lollio, art there? will all be perfect, think'st thou?
To-morrow night, as if to close up the
Solemnity, Vermandero expects us.

Lol. I mistrust the madmen most; the fools will do well enough; I have taken pains with them.

Alib. Tush! they cannot miss; the more absurdity,
The more commends it, so no rough behaviours
Affright the ladies; they're nice things, thou knowest.

Lol. You need not fear, sir; so long as we are there

with our commanding pizzles[1], they'll be as tame as the ladies themselves.

Alib. I'll see them once more rehearse before they go.

Lol. I was about it, sir: look you to the madmen's morris, and let me alone with the other: there is one or two that I mistrust their footing; I'll instruct them, and then they shall rehearse the whole measure.

Alib. Do so; I'll see the music prepared: but, Lollio,
By the way, how does my wife brook her restraint?
Does she not grudge at it?

Lol. So, so; she takes some pleasure in the house, she would abroad else; you must allow her a little more length, she's kept too short.

Alib. She shall along to Vermandero's with us,
That will serve her for a month's liberty.

Lol. What's that on your face, sir?

Alib. Where, Lollio? I see nothing.

Lol. Cry you mercy, sir, 'tis your nose; it showed like the trunk of a young elephant.

Alib. Away, rascal! I'll prepare the music, Lollio.

Lol. Do, sir, and I'll dance the whilst. [*Exit* ALIBIUS.]
—Tony, where art thou, Tony?

Enter ANTONIO.

Ant. Here, cousin; where art thou?

Lol. Come, Tony, the footmanship I taught you.

Ant. I had rather ride, cousin.

Lol. Ay, a whip take you! but I'll keep you out; vault in: look you, Tony; fa, la, la, la, la. [*Dances*

Ant. Fa, la, la, la, la. [*Sings and dances*

Lol. There, an honour.

Ant. Is this an honour, coz?

[1] In Dekker's *Wonder of a Kingdom*, Torrenti's brother says that he has been taken by the Turks and chained to the oar:

"If thou wouldst know more, read it on my back,
Printed with the bull's pizzle."

Lol. Yes, an it please your worship.

Ant. Does honour bend in the hams, coz?

Lol. Marry does it, as low as worship, squireship, nay, yeomanry itself sometimes, from whence it first stiffened: there rise, a caper.

Ant. Caper after an honour, coz?

Lol. Very proper, for honour is but a caper, rises as fast and high, has a knee or two, and falls to th' ground again: you can remember your figure, Tony?

Ant. Yes, cousin; when I see thy figure, I can remember mine. [*Exit* LOLLIO.

Re-enter ISABELLA, *dressed as a madwoman.*

Isa. Hey, how he treads the air! shough, shough, t'other way! he burns his wings else: here's wax enough below, Icarus, more than will he cancelled these eighteen moons: he's down, he's down! what a terrible fall he had!
Stand up, thou son of Cretan Dædalus,
And let us tread the lower labyrinth;
I'll bring thee to the clue.

Ant. Prithee, coz, let me alone.

Isa. Art thou not drowned?
About thy head I saw a heap of clouds
Wrapt like a Turkish turban; on thy back
A crooked chamelon-coloured rainbow hung
Like a tiara down unto thy hams:
Let me suck out those billows in thy belly;
Hark, how they roar and rumble in the straits!
Bless thee from the pirates!

Ant. Pox upon you, let me alone!

Isa. Why shouldst thou mount so high as Mercury,
Unless thou hadst reversion of his place?
Stay in the moon with me, Endymion,
And we will rule these wild rebellious waves,
That would have drowned my love.

Ant. I'll kick thee, if

Again thou touch me, thou wild unshapen antic;
I am no fool, you bedlam!

Isa. But you are, as sure as I am mad:
Have I put on this habit of a frantic,
With love as full of fury, to beguile
The nimble eye of watchful jealousy,
And am I thus rewarded?

Ant. Ha! dearest beauty!

Isa. No, I have no beauty now,
Nor never had but what was in my garments:
You a quick-sighted lover! come not near me:
Keep your caparisons, you're aptly clad;
I came a feigner, to return stark mad.

Ant. Stay, or I shall change condition,
And become as you are. [*Exit* ISABELLA.

Re-enter LOLLIO.

Lol. Why, Tony, whither now? why, fool——

Ant. Whose fool, usher of idiots? you coxcomb!
I have fooled too much.

Lol. You were best be mad another while then.

Ant. So I am, stark mad; I have cause enough;
And I could throw the full effects on thee,
And beat thee like a fury.

Lol. Do not, do not; I shall not forbear the gentleman under the fool, if you do: alas! I saw through your fox-skin before now! Come, I can give you comfort; my mistress loves you; and there is as arrant a madman i' th' house as you are a fool, your rival, whom she loves not: if after the masque we can rid her of him, you earn her love, she says, and the fool shall ride her.

Ant. May I believe thee?

Lol. Yes, or you may choose whether you will or no.

Ant. She's eased of him; I've a good quarrel on't.

Lol. Well, keep your old station yet, and be quiet.

Ant. Tell her I will deserve her love. [*Exit.*

Lol. And you are like to have your desert.

Enter FRANCISCUS.

Fran. [*sings.*] "Down, down, down a-down a-down,"—
and then with a horse-trick
To kick Latona's forehead, and break her bowstring.

Lol. This is t'other counterfeit; I'll put him out of his humour. [*Aside. Takes out a letter and reads.*] "Sweet lady, having now cast this counterfeit cover of a madman, I appear to your best judgment a true and faithful lover of your beauty." This is pretty well for a madman.

Fran. Ha! what's that?

Lol. [*reads.*] "Chide those perfections in you which have made me imperfect."

Fran. I am discovered to the fool.

Lol. I hope to discover the fool in you ere I have done with you. [*Reads.*] "Yours all, or one beside himself, FRANCISCUS." This madman will mend sure.

Fran. What do you read, sirrah?

Lol. Your destiny, sir; you'll be hanged for this trick, and another that I know.

Fran. Art thou of counsel with thy mistress?

Lol. Next her apron-strings.

Fran. Give me thy hand.

Lol. Stay, let me put yours in my pocket first [*putting letter into his pocket*]: your hand is true,[1] is it not? it will not pick? I partly fear it, because I think it does lie.

Fran. Not in a syllable.

Lol. So if you love my mistress so well as you have handled the matter here, you are like to be cured of your madness.

Fran. And none but she can cure it.

Lol. Well, I'll give you over then, and she shall cast your water next.

Fran. Take for thy pains past. [*Gives him money.*

Lol. I shall deserve more, sir, I hope: my mistress loves you, but must have some proof of your love to her.

[1] Honest.

Fran. There I meet my wishes.

Lol. That will not serve, you must meet her enemy and yours.

Fran. He's dead already.

Lol. Will you tell me that, and I parted but now with him?

Fran. Show me the man.

Lol. Ay, that's a right course now; see him before you kill him, in any case; and yet it needs not go so far neither, 'tis but a fool that haunts the house and my mistress in the shape of an idiot; bang but his fool's coat well-favouredly, and 'tis well.

Fran. Soundly, soundly!

Lol. Only reserve him till the masque be past; and if you find him not now in the dance yourself, I'll show you. In, in! my master! [*Dancing.*

Fran. He handles him like a feather. Hey! [*Exit.*

Enter ALIBIUS.

Alib. Well said: in a readiness, Lollio?

Lol. Yes, sir.

Alib. Away then, and guide them in, Lollio:
Entreat your mistress to see this sight.
Hark, is there not one incurable fool
That might be begged?[1] I have friends.

Lol. I have him for you,
One that shall deserve it too. [*Exit.*

Re-enter ISABELLA: *then re-enter* LOLLIO *with the madmen and fools, who dance.*

Alib. Good boy, Lollio!
'Tis perfect: well, fit but once these strains,
We shall have coin and credit for our pains. [*Exeunt.*

[1] Begging a person for a fool, meant applying to be his guardian, to whom the profits of his lands and the custody of his person were granted by the king.

ACT THE FIFTH.

SCENE I.

A Gallery in the Castle.

Enter BEATRICE : *a clock strikes one.*

BEAT. One struck, and yet she lies by't !
O my fears !
This strumpet serves her own ends, 'tis apparent now,
Devours the pleasure with a greedy appetite,
And never minds my honour or my peace,
Makes havoc of my right ; but she pays dearly for't ;
No trusting of her life with such a secret,
That cannot rule her blood to keep her promise ;
Beside, I've some suspicion of her faith to me,
Because I was suspected of my lord,
And it must come from her [*clock strikes two*] : hark ! by my horrors,
Another clock strikes two !

Enter DE FLORES.

De F. Hist ! where are you ?
Beat. De Flores ?
De F. Ay : is she not come from him yet ?
Beat. As I'm a living soul, not !
De F. Sure the devil
Hath sowed his itch within her ; who would trust
A waiting-woman ?
Beat. I must trust somebody.

De F. Tush! they're termagants;
Especially when they fall upon their masters
And have their ladies' first fruits; they're mad whelps,
You cannot stave 'em off from game royal: then
You are so rash and hardy, ask no counsel;
And I could have helped you to a 'pothecary's daughter
Would have fall'n off before eleven, and thanked you too.

Beat. O me, not yet! this whore forgets herself.

De F. The rascal fares so well: look, you're undone;
The day-star, by this hand! see Phosphorus plain yonder.

Beat. Advise me now to fall upon some ruin;
There is no counsel safe else.

De F. Peace! I ha't now,
For we must force a rising, there's no remedy.

Beat. How? take heed of that.

De F. Tush! be you quiet, or else give over all.

Beat. Prithee, I ha' done then.

De F. This is my reach:[1] I'll set
Some part a-fire of Diaphanta's chamber.

Beat. How? fire, sir? that may endanger the whole house.

De F. You talk of danger when your fame's on fire?

Beat. That's true; do what thou wilt now.

De F. Tush! I aim
At a most rich success strikes all dead sure:
The chimney being a-fire, and some light parcels
Of the least danger in her chamber only,
If Diaphanta should be met by chance then
Far from her lodging, which is now suspicious,
It would be thought her fears and affrights then
Drove her to seek for succour; if not seen
Or met at all, as that's the likeliest,
For her own shame she'll hasten towards her lodging;
I will be ready with a piece high-charged,
As 'twere to cleanse the chimney, there 'tis proper now
But she shall be the mark.

[1] Plan.

Beat. I'm forced to love thee now,
'Cause thou provid'st so carefully for my honour.

De F. 'Slid, it concerns the safety of us both,
Our pleasure and continuance.

Beat. One word now, prithee;
How for the servants?

De F. I will despatch them,
Some one way, some another in the hurry,
For buckets, hooks, ladders; fear not you,
The deed shall find its time; and I've thought since
Upon a safe conveyance for the body too:
How this fire purifies wit! watch you your minute.

Beat. Fear keeps my soul upon't, I cannot stray from't.

Enter Ghost of ALONZO.

De F. Ha! what art thou that tak'st away the light
Betwixt that star and me? I dread thee not:
'Twas but a mist of conscience; all's clear again. [*Exit.*

Beat. Who's that, De Flores? bless me, it slides by!
[*Exit Ghost.*
Some ill thing haunts the house; 't has left behind it
A shivering sweat upon me; I'm afraid now:
This night hath been so tedious! O this strumpet!
Had she a thousand lives, he should not leave her
Till he had destroyed the last. List! O my terrors!
[*Clock strikes three.*
Three struck by Sebastian's!

Voices [*within*]. Fire, fire, fire!

Beat. Already? how rare is that man's speed!
How heartily he serves me! his face loathes one;
But look upon his care, who would not love him?
The east is not more beauteous than his service.

Voices [*within*]. Fire, fire, fire!

Re-enter DE FLORES: Servants *pass over the stage.*

De F. Away, despatch! hooks, buckets, ladders! that's well said. [*Bell rings within.*

The fire-bell rings; the chimney works, my charge;
The piece is ready. [*Exit.*
Beat. Here's a man worth loving!

Enter DIAPHANTA.

O you're a jewel!
Dia. Pardon frailty, madam;
In troth, I was so well, I even forgot myself.
Beat. You've made trim work!
Dia. What?
Beat. Hie quickly to your chamber;
Your reward follows you.
Dia. I never made
So sweet a bargain. [*Exit.*

Enter ALSEMERO.

Als. O, my dear Joanna,
Alas! art thou risen too? I was coming,
My absolute treasure!
Beat. When I missed you,
I could not choose but follow.
Als. Thou'rt all sweetness:
The fire is not so dangerous.
Beat. Think you so, sir?
Als I prithee, tremble not; believe me, 'tis not.

Enter VERMANDERO *and* JASPERINO.

Ver. O bless my house and me!
Als. My lord your father.

Re-enter DE FLORES *with a gun.*

Ver. Knave, whither goes that piece?
De F. To scour the chimney.
Ver. O, well said, well said! [*Exit* DE FLORES.
That fellow's good on all occasions.
Beat. A wondrous necessary man, my lord.
Ver. He hath a ready wit; he's worth 'em all, sir;

Dog at a house of fire; I ha' seen him singed ere now.—
[*Gun fired off within.*
Ha, there he goes!
Beat. 'Tis done! [*Aside.*
Als. Come, sweet, to bed now;
Alas! thou wilt get cold.
Beat. Alas! the fear keeps that out!
My heart will find no quiet till I hear
How Diaphanta, my poor woman, fares;
It is her chamber, sir, her lodging chamber.
Ver. How should the fire come there?
Beat. As good a soul as ever lady countenanced,
But in her chamber negligent and heavy:
She 'scaped a mine twice.
Ver. Twice?
Beat. Strangely twice, sir.
Ver. Those sleepy sluts are dangerous in a house,
An they be ne'er so good.

Re-enter DE FLORES.

De F. O poor virginity,
Thou hast paid dearly for't!
Ver. Bless us, what's that?
De F. A thing you all knew once, Diaphanta's burnt.
Beat. My woman! O my woman!
De F. Now the flames
Are greedy of her; burnt, burnt, burnt to death, sir!
Beat. O my presaging soul!
Als. Not a tear more!
I charge you by the last embrace I gave you
In bed, before this raised us.
Beat. Now you tie me;
Were it my sister, now she gets no more.

Enter Servant.

Ver. How now?
Ser. All danger's past; you may now take

Your rests, my lords; the fire is throughly quenched:
Ah, poor gentlewoman, how soon was she stifled!

Beat. De Flores, what is left of her inter,
And we as mourners all will follow her:
I will entreat that honour to my servant
Even of my lord himself.

Als. Command it, sweetness.

Beat. Which of you spied the fire first?

De F. 'Twas I, madam.

Beat. And took such pains in't too? a double goodness!
'Twere well he were rewarded.

Ver. He shall be.—
De Flores, call upon me.

Als. And upon me, sir.

[*Exeunt all except* DE FLORES.

De F. Rewarded? precious! here's a trick beyond me:
I see in all bouts, both of sport and wit,
Always a woman strives for the last hit. [*Exit.*

SCENE II.

Another Apartment in the Castle.

Enter TOMASO.

Tom. I cannot taste the benefits of life
With the same relish I was wont to do:
Man I grow weary of, and hold his fellowship
A treacherous bloody friendship; and because
I'm ignorant in whom my wrath should settle,
I must think all men villains, and the next
I meet, whoe'er he be, the murderer
Of my most worthy brother. Ha! what's he?

DE FLORES *passes across the stage.*

O, the fellow that some call honest De Flores;
But methinks honesty was hard bested

To come here for a lodging; as if a queen
Should make her palace of a pest-house:
I find a contrariety in nature
Betwixt that face and me; the least occasion
Would give me game upon him; yet he's so foul
One would scarce touch him with a sword he loved
And made account of; so most deadly venomous,
He would go near to poison any weapon
That should draw blood on him; one must resolve
Never to use that sword again in fight
In way of honest manhood that strikes him;
Some river must devour it; 'twere not fit
That any man should find it. What, again?

Re-enter DE FLORES.

He walks a' purpose by, sure, to choke me up,
T' infect my blood.

De F. My worthy noble lord!

Tom. Dost offer to come near and breathe upon me? [*Strikes him.*

De F. A blow! [*Draws.*

Tom. Yea, are you so prepared?
I'll rather like a soldier die by the sword,
Than like a politician by thy poison. [*Draws.*

De F. Hold, my lord, as you are honourable!

Tom. All slaves that kill by poison are still cowards.

De F. I cannot strike; I see his brother's wounds
Fresh bleeding in his eye, as in a crystal.— [*Aside.*
I will not question this, I know you're noble;
I take my injury with thanks given, sir,
Like a wise lawyer, and as a favour
Will wear it for the worthy hand that gave it.—
Why this from him that yesterday appeared
So strangely loving to me?
O, but instinct is of a subtler strain!
Guilt must not walk so near his lodge again;
He came near me now. [*Aside and exit.*

Tom. All league with mankind I renounce for ever,
Till I find this murderer; not so much
As common courtesy but I'll lock up;
For in the state of ignorance I live in,
A brother may salute his brother's murderer,
And wish good speed to the villain in a greeting.

Enter VERMANDERO, ALIBIUS, *and* ISABELLA.

Ver. Noble Piracquo!
Tom. Pray, keep on your way, sir;
I've nothing to say to you.
Ver. Comforts bless you, sir!
Tom. I've forsworn compliment, in troth I have, sir;
As you are merely man, I have not left
A good wish for you, nor for any here.
Ver. Unless you be so far in love with grief,
You will not part from't upon any terms,
We bring that news will make a welcome for us.
Tom. What news can that be?
Ver. Throw no scornful smile
Upon the zeal I bring you, 'tis worth more, sir;
Two of the chiefest men I kept about me
I hide not from the law of your just vengeance.
Tom. Ha!
Ver. To give your peace more ample satisfaction,
Thank these discoverers.
Tom. If you bring that calm,
Name but the manner I shall ask forgiveness in
For that contemptuous smile I threw upon you,
I'll perfect it with reverence that belongs
Unto a sacred altar. [*Kneels.*
Ver. [*raising him.*] Good sir, rise;
Why, now you overdo as much 'a this hand
As you fell short 'a t'other.—Speak, Alibius.
Alib. 'Twas my wife's fortune, as she is most lucky
At a discovery, to find out lately,
Within our hospital of fools and madmen,

Two counterfeits slipp'd into these disguises,
Their names Franciscus and Antonio.

Ver. Both mine, sir, and I ask no favour for 'em.

Alib. Now that which draws suspicion to their habits,
The time of their disguisings agrees justly
With the day of the murder.

Tom. O blest revelation!

Ver. Nay, more, nay, more, sir—I'll not spare mine [own
In way of justice—they both feigned a journey
To Briamata, and so wrought out their leaves;
My love was so abused in it.

Tom. Time's too precious
To run in waste now; you have brought a peace
The riches of five kingdoms could not purchase:
Be my most happy conduct; I thirst for 'em:
Like subtle lightning will I find about 'em,
And melt their marrow in 'em. [*Exeunt.*

SCENE III.

ALSEMERO'S *Apartment in the Castle.*

Enter ALSEMERO *and* JASPERINO.

Jas. Your confidence, I'm sure, is now of proof;
The prospect from the garden has showed
Enough for deep suspicion.

Als. The black mask
That so continually was worn upon't
Condemns the face for ugly ere't be seen,
Her despite to him, and so seeming bottomless.

Jas. Touch it home then; 'tis not a shallow probe
Can search this ulcer soundly; I fear you'll find it
Full of corruption: 'tis fit I leave you,
She meets you opportunely from that walk;
She took the back door at his parting with her. [*Exit.*

Als. Did my fate wait for this unhappy stroke
At my first sight of woman? She is here.

Enter BEATRICE.

Beat. Alsemero!
Als. How do you?
Beat. How do I?
Alas, sir! how do you? you look not well.
Als. You read me well enough, I am not well.
Beat. Not well, sir? is't in my power to better you?
Als. Yes.
Beat. Nay, then you're cured again.
Als. Pray, resolve me one question, lady.
Beat. If I can.
Als. None can so sure: are you honest?
Beat. Ha, ha, ha! that's a broad question, my lord.
Als. But that's not a modest answer, my lady:
Do you laugh? my doubts are strong upon me.
Beat. 'Tis innocence that smiles, and no rough brow
Can take away the dimple in her cheek:
Say I should strain a tear to fill the vault,
Which would you give the better faith to?
Als. 'Twere but hypocrisy of a sadder colour,
But the same stuff; neither your smiles nor tears
Shall move or flatter me from my belief:
You are a whore!
Beat. What a horrid sound it hath!
It blasts a beauty to deformity;
Upon what face soever that breath falls,
It strikes it ugly: O, you have ruined
What you can ne'er repair again!
Als. I'll all
Demolish, and seek out truth within you,
If there be any left; let your sweet tongue
Prevent your heart's rifling; there I'll ransack
And tear out my suspicion.
Beat. You may, sir;

It is an easy passage; yet, if you please,
Show me the ground whereon you lost your love;
My spotless virtue may but tread on that
Before I perish.
Als. Unanswerable;
A ground you cannot stand on; you fall down
Beneath all grace and goodness when you set
Your ticklish heel on it: there was a visor
Over that cunning face, and that became you;
Now impudence in triumph rides upon't;
How comes this tender reconcilement else
'Twixt you and your despite, your rancorous loathing,
De Flores? he that your eye was sore at sight of,
He's now become your arm's supporter, your
Lip's saint!
Beat. Is there the cause?
Als. Worse, your lust's devil,
Your adultery!
Beat. Would any but yourself say that,
'Twould turn him to a villain!
Als. It was witnessed
By the counsel of your bosom, Diaphanta.
Beat. Is your witness dead then?
Als. 'Tis to be feared
It was the wages of her knowledge; poor soul,
She lived not long after the discovery.
Beat. Then hear a story of not much less horror
Than this your false suspicion is beguiled with;
To your bed's scandal I stand up innocence,
Which even the guilt of one black other deed
Will stand for proof of; your love has made me
A cruel murderess.
Als. Ha!
Beat. A bloody one;
I have kissed poison for it, stroked a serpent:
That thing of hate, worthy in my esteem
Of no better employment, and him most worthy

To be so employed, I caused to murder
That innocent Piracquo, having no
Better means than that worst to assure
Yourself to me.

Als. O, the place itself e'er since
Has crying been for vengeance! the temple,
Where blood and beauty first unlawfully
Fired their devotion and quenched the right one;
'Twas in my fears at first, 'twill have it now:
O, thou art all deformed!

Beat. Forget not, sir,
It for your sake was done: shall greater dangers
Make the less welcome?

Als. O, thou should'st have gone
A thousand leagues about to have avoided
This dangerous bridge of blood! here we are lost.

Beat. Remember, I am true unto your bed.

Als. The bed itself's a charnel, the sheets shrouds
For murdered carcasses. It must ask pause
What I must do in this; meantime you shall
Be my prisoner only: enter my closet;

[*Exit* BEATRICE *into closet.*

I'll be your keeper yet. O, in what part
Of this sad story shall I first begin? Ha!
This same fellow has put me in.—

Enter DE FLORES.

De Flores!

De F. Noble Alsemero!

Als. I can tell you
News, sir; my wife has her commended to you.

De F. That's news indeed, my lord; I think she would
Commend me to the gallows if she could,
She ever loved me so well; I thank her.

Als. What's this blood upon your band, De Flores?

De F. Blood! no, sure 'twas washed since.

Als. Since when, man?

De F. Since t'other day I got a knock
In a sword-and-dagger school; I think 'tis out.
Als. Yes, 'tis almost out, but 'tis perceived though.
I had forgot my message; this it is,
What price goes murder?
De F. How, sir?
Als. I ask you, sir;
My wife's behindhand with you, she tells me,
For a brave bloody blow you gave for her sake
Upon Piracquo.
De F. Upon? 'twas quite through him sure:
Has she confessed it?
Als. As sure as death to both of you;
And much more than that.
De F. It could not be much more;
'Twas but one thing, and that—she is a whore.
Als. It could not choose but follow: O cunning devils!
How should blind men know you from fair-faced saints?
Beat. [*within.*] He lies! the villain does belie me!
De F. Let me go to her, sir.
Als. Nay, you shall to her.—
Peace, crying crocodile, your sounds are heard;
Take your prey to you;—get you in to her, sir:
[*Exit* DE FLORES *into closet.*
I'll be your pander now; rehearse again
Your scene of lust, that you may be perfect
When you shall come to act it to the black audience,
Where howls and gnashings shall be music to you:
Clip[1] your adulteress freely, 'tis the pilot
Will guide you to the *mare mortuum*,
Where you shall sink to fathoms bottomless.

Enter VERMANDERO, TOMASO, ALIBIUS, ISABELLA, FRANCISCUS, *and* ANTONIO.

Ver. O Alsemero! I've a wonder for you.
Als. No, sir, 'tis I, I have a wonder for you.

[1] Embrace.

Ver. I have suspicion near as proof itself
For Piracquo's murder.
Als. Sir, I have proof
Beyond suspicion for Piracquo's murder.
Ver. Beseech you, hear me; these who have been disguised
E'er since the deed was done.
Als. I have two other
That were more close disguised than your two could be
E'er since the deed were done.
Ver. You'll hear me—these mine own servants——
Als. Hear me—those nearer than your servants
That shall acquit them, and prove them guiltless.
Fran. That may be done with easy truth, sir,
Tom. How is my cause bandied through your delays!
'Tis urgent in my blood and calls for haste;
Give me a brother or alive or dead;
Alive, a wife with him; if dead, for both
A recompense, for murder and adultery.
Beat. [*within.*] O, O, O!
Als. Hark! 'tis coming to you.
De F. [*within.*] Nay, I'll along for company.
Beat. [*within.*] O, O!
Ver. What horrid sounds are these?
Als. Come forth, you twins
Of mischief!

Re-enter DE FLORES, *dragging in* BEATRICE *wounded.*

De F. Here we are; if you have any more
To say to us, speak quickly, I shall not
Give you the hearing else; I am so stout yet,
And so, I think, that broken rib of mankind.
Ver. An host of enemies entered my citadel
Could not amaze like this: Joanna! Beatrice! Joanna!
Beat. O, come not near me, sir, I shall defile you!
I that am of your blood was taken from you

For your better health; look no more upon't,
But cast it to the ground regardlessly,
Let the common sewer take it from distinction:
Beneath the stars, upon yon meteor
[*Pointing to* DE FLORES.
Ever hung my fate, 'mongst things corruptible;
I ne'er could pluck it from him; my loathing
Was prophet to the rest, but ne'er believed:
Mine honour fell with him, and now my life.—
Alsemero, I'm a stranger to your bed;
Your bed was cozened on the nuptial night,
For which your false bride died.

Als. Diaphanta?

De F. Yes, and the while I coupled with your mate
At barley-break; now we are left in hell.[1]

Ver. We are all there, it circumscribes us here.

De F. I loved this woman in spite of her heart:
Her love I earned out of Piracquo's murder.

Tom. Ha! my brother's murderer?

De F. Yes, and her honour's prize
Was my reward; I thank life for nothing
But that pleasure; it was so sweet to me,
That I have drunk up all, left none behind
For any man to pledge me.

Ver. Horrid villain!
Keep life in him for further tortures.

De F. No!
I can prevent you; here's my pen-knife still;
It is but one thread more [*stabbing himself*], and now 'tis cut.—
Make haste, Joanna, by that token to thee,
Canst not forget, so lately put in mind;
I would not go to leave thee far behind. [*Dies.*

Beat. Forgive me, Alsemero, all forgive!
'Tis time to die when 'tis a shame to live. [*Dies.*

[1] See note *ante*, p. 129.

Ver. O, my name's entered now in that record
Where till this fatal hour 'twas never read.

Als. Let it be blotted out; let your heart lose it,
And it can never look you in the face,
Nor tell a tale behind the back of life
To your dishonour; justice hath so right
The guilty hit, that innocence is quit
By proclamation, and may joy again.—
Sir, you are sensible of what truth hath done;
'Tis the best comfort that your grief can find.

Tom. Sir, I am satisfied; my injuries
Lie dead before me; I can exact no more,
Unless my soul were loose, and could o'ertake
Those black fugitives that are fled from hence,
To take a second vengeance; but there are wraths
Deeper than mine, 'tis to be feared, about 'em.

Als. What an opacous body had that moon
That last changed on us! here is beauty changed
To ugly whoredom; here servant-obedience
To a master-sin, imperious murder;
I, a supposed husband, changed embraces
With wantonness,—but that was paid before.—
Your change is come too, from an ignorant wrath
To knowing friendship.—Are there any more on's?

Ant. Yes, sir, I was changed too from a little ass as I was to a great fool as I am; and had like to ha' been changed to the gallows, but that you know my innocence[1] always excuses me.

Fran. I was changed from a little wit to be stark mad,
Almost for the same purpose.

Isa. Your change is still behind,
But deserve best your transformation:
You are a jealous coxcomb, keep schools of folly,
And teach your scholars how to break your own head.

[1] Idiocy.

Alib. I see all apparent, wife, and will change now
Into a better husband, and ne'er keep
Scholars that shall be wiser than myself.

Als. Sir, you have yet a son's duty living,
Please you, accept it; let that your sorrow,
As it goes from your eye, go from your heart,
Man and his sorrow at the grave must part.

EPILOGUE.

Als. All we can do to comfort one another,
To stay a brother's sorrow for a brother,
To dry a child from the kind father's eyes,
Is to no purpose, it rather multiplies:
Your only smiles have power to cause re-live
The dead again, or in their rooms to give
Brother a new brother, father a child;
If these appear, all griefs are reconciled. [*Exeunt.*

A CHASTE MAID IN CHEAPSIDE.

NO record exists of the date when *A Chaste Maid in Cheapside* was first performed, although it is known to have been often acted at the "Swan," on the Bankside, by "the Lady Elizabeth's Servants"; in 1630 it was published in quarto, with Middleton's name on the title-page, as "a Pleasant conceited Comedy neuer before printed." It is the only play now extant known to have been acted at the "Swan."

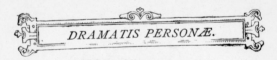

DRAMATIS PERSONÆ.

SIR WALTER WHOREHOUND.
SIR OLIVER KIX.
TOUCHWOOD senior.
TOUCHWOOD junior.
ALLWIT.
YELLOWHAMMER, a goldsmith.
TIM, his son.
Tutor to Tim.
DAVY DAHANNA, Sir Walter's poor kinsman and attendant.
Parson.
WAT, } sons of Sir Walter by Mistress Allwit.
NICK, }
Two Promoters.
Porter, Watermen, &c.

LADY KIX.
MISTRESS TOUCHWOOD, wife of TOUCHWOOD senior.
MISTRESS ALLWIT.
MAUDLIN, wife of YELLOWHAMMER.
MOLL, her daughter.
Welshwoman, mistress to SIR W. WHOREHOUND.
Country Girl.
SUSAN.
Maid, Midwife, Nurses, Puritans, and other Gossips, &c.

SCENE—LONDON.

A CHASTE MAID IN CHEAPSIDE.

ACT THE FIRST.

SCENE I.

YELLOWHAMMER'S *Shop.*

Enter MAUDLIN *and* MOLL.

MAUD. Have you played over all your old lessons o' the virginals?[1]

Moll. Yes.

Maud. Yes? you are a dull maid a' late; methinks you had need have somewhat to quicken your green sickness—do you weep?—a husband: had not such a piece of flesh been ordained, what had us wives been good for? to make salads, or else cried up and down for samphire. To see the difference of these seasons! when I was of your youth, I was lightsome and quick two years before I was married. You fit for a knight's bed! drowsy-browed, dull-eyed, drossy-spirited! I hold my life you have forgot your dancing: when was the dancer with you?

Moll. The last week.

Maud. Last week? when I was of your bord[2]

[1] The Elizabethan ancestor of the piano.

[2] *i.e.* Bore (of a gun), capacity.

He missed me not a night; I was kept at it;
I took delight to learn, and he to teach me;
Pretty brown gentleman! he took pleasure in my company:
But you are dull, nothing comes nimbly from you;
You dance like a plumber's daughter, and deserve
Two thousand pound in lead to your marriage,
And not in goldsmith's ware.

Enter YELLOWHAMMER.

Yel. Now, what's the din
Betwixt mother and daughter, ha?
Maud. Faith, small;
Telling your daughter, Mary, of her errors.
Yel. Errors? nay, the city cannot hold you, wife,
But you must needs fetch words from Westminster:
I ha' done, i'faith.
Has no attorney's clerk been here a' late,
And changed his half-crown-piece his mother sent him,
Or rather cozened you with a gilded twopence,
To bring the word in fashion for her faults
Or cracks in duty and obedience?
Term 'em even so, sweet wife,
As there's no woman made without a flaw;
Your purest lawns have frays, and cambrics bracks.[1]
Maud. But 'tis a husband solders up all cracks.
Moll. What, is he come, sir?
Yel. Sir Walter's come: he was met
At Holborn Bridge, and in his company
A proper fair young gentlewoman, which I guess,
By her red hair and other rank descriptions,
To be his landed niece, brought out of Wales,
Which Tim our son, the Cambridge boy, must marry:
'Tis a match of Sir Walter's own making,
To bind us to him and our heirs for ever.
Maud. We're honoured then, if this baggage would be humble,

[1] Flaws.

And kiss him with devotion when he enters.
I cannot get her for my life
To instruct her hand thus, before and after,—
Which a knight will look for,—before and after:
I've told her still 'tis the waving of a woman
Does often move a man, and prevails strongly.
But, sweet, ha' you sent to Cambridge? has Tim word on't?

Yel. Had word just the day after, when you sent him
The silver spoon to eat his broth in the hall
Amongst the gentlemen commoners.

Maud. O, 'twas timely.

Enter Porter.

Yel. How now?

Por. A letter from a gentleman in Cambridge.

[*Gives letter to* YELLOWHAMMER.

Yel. O, one of Hobson's[1] porters: thou art welcome.—
I told thee, Maud, we should hear from Tim. [*Reads.*]
Amantissimis carissimisque ambobus parentibus, patri et matri.

Maud. What's the matter?

Yel. Nay, by my troth, I know not, ask not me:
He's grown too verbal; this learning's a great witch.

Maud. Pray, let me see it; I was wont to understand him. [*Reads.*] *Amantissimis carissimis*, he has sent the carrier's man, he says; *ambobus parentibus*, for a pair of boots; *patri et matri*, pay the porter, or it makes no matter.

Por. Yes, by my faith, mistress; there's no true construction in that: I have took a great deal of pains, and come from the Bell sweating. Let me come to't, for I was a scholar forty years ago; 'tis thus, I warrant you: [*Reads.*] *Matri*, it makes no matter; *ambobus parentibus*, for a pair of boots; *patri*, pay the porter; *amantissimis*

[1] The Cambridge carrier, for whom Milton wrote an epitaph and who is immortalised in the proverb "Hobson's choice," which originated in his never allowing his customers to choose their horses, the animals being always let out by him in succession.

carissimis, he's the carrier's man, and his name is Sims; and there he says true, forsooth, my name is Sims indeed; I have not forgot all my learning: a money-matter, I thought I should hit on't.

Yel. Go, thou'rt an old fox; there's a tester[1] for thee. [*Gives money.*

Por. If I see your worship at Goose-fair, I have a dish of birds for you.

Yel. Why, dost dwell at Bow?

Por. All my lifetime, sir; I could ever say bo to a goose. Farewell to your worship. [*Exit.*

Yel. A merry porter.

Maud. How can he choose but be so,
Coming with Cambridge letters from our son Tim.

Yel. What's here? *maximus diligo;* faith, I must to my learned counsel with this gear,[2] 'twill ne'er be discerned else.

Maud. Go to my cousin then, at Inns of Court.

Yel. Fie, they are all for French, they speak no Latin.

Maud. The parson then will do it.

Yel. Nay, he disclaims it,
Calls Latin papistry, he will not deal with it.—

Enter a Gentleman.

What is't you lack, gentleman?

Gent. Pray, weigh this chain.

[*Gives chain, which* YELLOWHAMMER *weighs.*

Enter Sir WALTER WHOREHOUND, Welshwoman, *and* DAVY.

Sir Wal. Now, wench, thou art welcome
To the heart of the city of London.

Welsh. Dugat a whee.

Sir Wal. You can thank me in English, if you list.

Welsh. I can, sir, simply.

Sir Wal. 'Twill serve to pass, wench;

[1] Sixpence. [2] Business.

'Twas strange that I should lie with thee so often.
To leave thee without English, that were unnatural.
I bring thee up to turn thee into gold, wench,
And make thy fortune shine like your bright trade;
A goldsmith's shop sets out a city maid.—
Davy Dahanna, not a word.
Davy. Mum, mum, sir.
Sir Wal. Here you must pass for a pure virgin.
Davy. Pure Welsh virgin!
She lost her maidenhead in Brecknockshire. [*Aside.*
Sir Wal. I hear you mumble, Davy.
Davy. I have teeth, sir;
I need not mumble yet this forty years.
Sir Wal. The knave bites plaguily!
Yel. What's your price, sir?
Gent. A hundred pound, sir.
Yel. A hundred marks [1] the utmost;
'Tis not for me else.—What, Sir Walter Whorehound?
[*Exit* Gentleman.
Moll. O death! [*Exit.*
Maud. Why, daughter—Faith, the baggage is
A bashful girl, sir; these young things are shamefaced;
Besides, you have a presence, sweet Sir Walter,
Able to daunt a maid brought up i' the city:
A brave court-spirit makes our virgins quiver,
And kiss with trembling thighs; yet see, she comes, sir.

Re-enter MOLL.

Sir Wal. Why, how now, pretty mistress? now I've caught you:
What, can you injure so your time to stray
Thus from your faithful servant?
Yel. Pish, stop your words, good knight,—'twill make her blush else,—
Which wound [2] too high for the daughters of the freedom.
Honour and faithful servant! they are compliments

[1] The mark was worth 13*s.* 4*d.*
[2] Dyce suggests "sound."

For the worthies of Whitehall or Greenwich;
E'en plain, sufficient subsidy words serves us, sir.
And is this gentlewoman your worthy niece?

Sir Wal. You may be bold with her on these terms; 'tis she, sir,
Heir to some nineteen mountains.

Yel. Bless us all!
You overwhelm me, sir, with love and riches.

Sir Wal. And all as high as Paul's.

Davy. Here's work, i'faith! [*Aside.*

Sir Wal. How sayst thou, Davy?

Davy. Higher, sir, by far;
You cannot see the top of 'em.

Yel. What, man!—
Maudlin, salute this gentlewoman, our daughter,
If things hit right.

Enter TOUCHWOOD *junior.*

Touch. jun. My knight, with a brace of footmen,
Is come, and brought up his ewe-mutton to find
A ram at London; I must hasten it,
Or else pick[1] a' famine; her blood is mine,
And that's the surest. Well, knight, that choice spoil
Is only kept for me. [*Aside.*

Moll. Sir——

Touch. jun. Turn not to me till thou mayst lawfully; it but whets my stomach, which is too sharp-set already. Read that note carefully [*giving letter to* MOLL]; keep me from suspicion still, nor know my zeal but in thy heart:
Read, and send but thy liking in three words;
I'll be at hand to take it.

Yel. O turn, sir, turn.
A[2] poor, plain boy, an university man;
Proceeds next Lent to a bachelor of art;

[1] Peak, grow meagre.
[2] Some previous lines referring to Tim seem to have dropped out.

He will be called Sir Yellowhammer then
Over all Cambridge, and that's half a knight.

Maud. Please you, draw near
And taste the welcome of the city, sir.

Yel. Come, good Sir Walter, and your virtuous niece here.

Sir Wal. 'Tis manners to take kindness.

Yel. Lead 'em in, wife.

Sir Wal. Your company, sir?

Yel. I'll give't you instantly.

[*Exeunt* MAUDLIN, Sir W. WHOREHOUND, *Welshwoman, and* DAVY.

Touch. jun. How strangely busy is the devil and riches!
Poor soul! kept in too hard, her mother's eye
Is cruel toward her, being to him.
'Twere a good mirth now to set him a-work
To make her wedding-ring; I must about it:
Rather than the gain should fall to a stranger,
'Twas honesty in me t' enrich my father. [*Aside.*

Yel. The girl is wondrous peevish. I fear nothing
But that she's taken with some other love,
Then all's quite dashed: that must be narrowly looked to;
We cannot be too wary in our children.— [*Aside.*
What is't you lack?

Touch. jun. O, nothing now; all that I wish is present:
I'd have a wedding-ring made for a gentlewoman
With all speed that may be.

Yel. Of what weight, sir?

Touch. jun. Of some half ounce, stand fair
And comely, with the spark of a diamond;
Sir, 'twere pity to lose the least grace.

Yel. Pray, let's see it.

[*Takes stone from* TOUCHWOOD *junior.*

Indeed, sir, 'tis a pure one.

Touch. jun. So is the mistress.

Yel. Have you the wideness of her finger, sir?

Touch. jun. Yes, sure, I think I have her measure about me:
Good faith, 'tis down, I cannot show it you;
I must pull too many things out to be certain.
Let me see—long and slender, and neatly jointed;
Just such another gentlewoman—that's your daughter, sir?

Yel. And therefore, sir, no gentlewoman.

Touch. jun. I protest
I ne'er saw two maids handed more alike;
I'll ne'er seek farther, if you'll give me leave, sir.

Yel. If you dare venture by her finger, sir.

Touch. jun. Ay, and I'll bide all loss, sir.

Yel. Say you so, sir?
Let us see.—Hither, girl.

Touch. jun. Shall I make bold
With your finger, gentlewoman?

Moll. Your pleasure, sir.

Touch. jun. That fits her to a hair, sir.

[*Trying ring on* MOLL'S *finger.*

Yel. What's your posy now, sir?

Touch. jun. Mass, that's true: posy? i'faith, e'en thus, sir:

"Love that's wise
Blinds parents' eyes."

Yel. How, how? if I may speak without offence, sir,
I hold my life——

Touch. jun. What, sir?

Yel. Go to,—you'll pardon me?

Touch. jun. Pardon you? ay, sir.

Yel. Will you, i'faith?

Touch. jun. Yes, faith, I will.

Yel. You'll steal away some man's daughter: am I near you?
Do you turn aside? you gentlemen are mad wags!

I wonder things can be so warily carried,
And parents blinded so: but they're served right,
That have two eyes and were so dull a' sight.

Touch. jun. Thy doom take hold of thee! [*Aside.*

Yel. To-morrow noon
Shall show your ring well done.

Touch. jun. Being so, 'tis soon.—
Thanks, and your leave, sweet gentlewoman.

Moll. Sir, you're welcome.—

[*Exit* TOUCHWOOD *junior.*

O were I made of wishes, I went with thee! [*Aside.*

Yel. Come now, we'll see how the rules [1] go within.

Moll. That robs my joy; there I lose all I win.

[*Aside. Exeunt.*

SCENE II.

A Hall in ALLWIT'S *House.*

Enter DAVY *and* ALLWIT *severally.*

Davy. Honesty wash my eyes! I've spied a wittol.[2]

[*Aside.*

Allwit. What, Davy Dahanna? welcome from North Wales, i'faith!
And is Sir Walter come?

Davy. New come to town, sir.

Allwit. In to the maids, sweet Davy, and give order
His chamber be made ready instantly.
My wife's as great as she can wallow, Davy, and longs
For nothing but pickled cucumbers and his coming;
And now she shall ha't, boy.

Davy. She's sure of them, sir.

Allwit. Thy very sight will hold my wife in pleasure

[1] Games. [2] A contented cuckold.

Till the knight come himself; go in, in, in, Davy.
[*Exit* DAVY.
The founder's come to town: I'm like a man
Finding a table furnished to his hand,
As mine is still to me, prays for the founder,—
Bless the right worshipful the good founder's life!
I thank him, has maintained my house this ten years;
Not only keeps my wife, but 'a keeps me
And all my family; I'm at his table:
He gets me all my children, and pays the nurse
Monthly or weekly; puts me to nothing, rent,
Nor church-duties, not so much as the scavenger:
The happiest state that ever man was born to!
I walk out in a morning; come to breakfast,
Find excellent cheer; a good fire in winter;
Look in my coal-house about midsummer eve,
That's full, five or six chaldron new laid up;
Look in my back-yard, I shall find a steeple
Made up with Kentish faggots, which o'erlooks
The water-house and the windmills: I say nothing,
But smile and pin the door. When she lies in,
As now she's even upon the point of grunting,
A lady lies not in like her; there's her embossings,
Embroiderings, spanglings, and I know not what,
As if she lay with all the gaudy-shops[1]
In Gresham's Burse[2] about her; then her restoratives,
Able to set up a young 'pothecary,
And richly stock the foreman of a drug-shop;
Her sugar by whole loaves, her wines by rundlets.
I see these things, but, like a happy man,
I pay for none at all; yet fools think's mine;
I have the name, and in his gold I shine:
And where some merchants would in soul kiss hell
To buy a paradise for their wives, and dye
Their conscience in the bloods of prodigal heirs

[1] Where articles of finery were sold.
[2] The Royal Exchange.

To deck their night-piece, yet all this being done,
Eaten with jealousy to the inmost bone,—
As what affliction nature more constrains,
Than feed the wife plump for another's veins?—
These torments stand I freed of; I'm as clear
From jealousy of a wife as from the charge:
O, two miraculous blessings! 'tis the knight
Hath took that labour all out of my hands:
I may sit still and play; he's jealous for me,
Watches her steps, sets spies; I live at ease,
He has both the cost and torment: when the string
Of his heart frets, I feed, laugh, or sing,
La dildo, dildo la dildo, la dildo dildo de dildo! [*Sings.*

Enter two Servants.

1st Ser. What, has he got a singing in his head now?
2nd Ser. Now's out of work, he falls to making dildoes.
Allwit. Now, sirs, Sir Walter's come.
1st Ser. Is our master come?
Allwit. Your master! what am I?
1st Ser. Do not you know, sir?
Allwit. Pray, am not I your master?
1st Ser. O, you're but
Our mistress's husband.
Allwit. *Ergo*, knave, your master.
1st Ser. *Negatur argumentum.*—Here comes Sir Walter:

Enter Sir WALTER *and* DAVY.

Now 'a stands bare as well as we; make the most of him,
He's but one peep above a serving-man,
And so much his horns make him.
Sir Wal. How dost, Jack?
Allwit. Proud of your worship's health, sir.
Sir Wal. How does your wife?
Allwit. E'en after your own making, sir;
She's a tumbler, a' faith, the nose and belly meets.

Sir Wal. They'll part in time again.

Allwit. At the good hour they will, an't please your worship.

Sir Wal. Here, sirrah, pull off my boots.—Put on,[1] put on, Jack. [Servant *pulls off his boots.*

Allwit. I thank your kind worship, sir.

Sir Wal. Slippers! heart, you are sleepy!

[Servant *brings slippers.*

Allwit. The game begins already. [*Aside.*

Sir Wal. Pish, put on, Jack.

Allwit. Now I must do't, or he'll be as angry now,
As if I had put it on at first bidding;
'Tis but observing,
'Tis but observing a man's humour once,
And he may ha' him by the nose all his life. [*Aside.*

Sir Wal. What entertainment has lain open here?
No strangers in my absence?

1*st Ser.* Sure, sir, not any.

Allwit. His jealousy begins: am not I happy now,
That can laugh inward whilst his marrow melts? [*Aside.*

Sir Wal. How do you satisfy me?

1*st Ser.* Good sir, be patient!

Sir Wal. For two months' absence I'll be satisfied.

1*st Ser.* No living creature entered——

Sir Wal. Entered? come, swear!

1*st Ser.* You will not hear me out, sir——

Sir Wal. Yes, I'll hear't out, sir.

1*st Ser.* Sir, he can tell himself——

Sir Wal. Heart, he can tell?
Do you think I'll trust him? as a usurer
With forfeited lordships:—him? O monstrous injury!
Believe him? can the devil speak ill of darkness?—
What can you say, sir?

Allwit. Of my soul and conscience, sir,
She's a wife as honest of her body to me
As any lord's proud lady e'er can be!

[1] *i.e.* Put on your hat.

Sir Wal. Yet, by your leave, I heard you were once offering
To go to bed to her.

Allwit. No, I protest, sir!

Sir Wal. Heart, if you do, you shall take all! I'll marry.

Allwit. O, I beseech you, sir!

Sir Wal. That wakes the slave,
And keeps his flesh in awe. [*Aside.*

Allwit. I'll stop that gap
Where'er I find it open: I have poisoned
His hopes in marriage already with
Some old rich widows, and some landed virgins;
And I'll fall to work still before I'll lose him;
He's yet too sweet to part from. [*Aside.*

Enter WAT *and* NICK.

Wat. God-den,[1] father.

Allwit. Ha, villain, peace!

Nick. God-den, father.

Allwit. Peace, bastard!
Should he hear 'em! [*Aside.*]—These are two foolish children,
They do not know the gentleman that sits there.

Sir Wal. O, Wat—how dost, Nick? go to school, ply your books, boys, ha!

Allwit. Where's your legs, whoresons?—They should kneel indeed,
If they could say their prayers.

Sir Wal. Let me see, stay,—
How shall I dispose of these two brats now [*Aside.*
When I am married? for they must not mingle
Amongst my children that I get in wedlock;
'Twill make foul work that, and raise many storms.
I will bind Wat prentice to a goldsmith,

[1] A corruption of "good evening."

My father Yellowhammer, as fit as can be;
Nick with some vintner; good, goldsmith and vintner ·
There will be wine in bowls, i'faith.

Enter Mistress ALLWIT.

Mis. All. Sweet knight,
Welcome! I've all my longings now in town;
Now welcome the good hour!

Sir Wal. How cheers my mistress?

Mis. All. Made lightsome e'en by him that made me heavy.

Sir Wal. Methinks she shows gallantly, like a moon at full, sir.

Allwit. True, and if she bear a male child, there's the man in the moon, sir.

Sir Wal. 'Tis but the boy in the moon yet, goodman calf.

Allwit. There was a man, the boy had ne'er been there else.

Sir Wal. It shall be yours, sir.

Allwit. No, by my troth, I'll swear
It's none of mine; let him that got it keep it!—
Thus do I rid myself of fear,
Lie soft, sleep hard, drink wine, and eat good cheer.
[*Aside. Exeunt.*

ACT THE SECOND.

SCENE I.

A Street.

Enter TOUCHWOOD *senior and* Mistress TOUCHWOOD.

Mis. Touch. 'Twill be so tedious, sir, to live from you,
But that necessity must be obeyed.

Touch. sen. I would it might not, wife! the tediousness
Will be the most part mine, that understand
The blessings I have in thee; so to part,
That drives the torment to a knowing heart.
But, as thou sayst, we must give way to need,
And live awhile asunder; our desires
Are both too fruitful for our barren fortunes.
How adverse runs the destiny of some creatures!
Some only can get riches and no children;
We only can get children and no riches:
Then 'tis the prudent'st part to check our wills,
And, till our state rise, make our bloods lie still.
'Life, every year a child, and some years two!
Besides drinkings abroad, that's never reckoned;
This gear will not hold out.

Mis. Touch. Sir, for a time
I'll take the courtesy of my uncle's house,
If you be pleased to like on't, till prosperity
Look with a friendly eye upon our states.

Touch. sen. Honest wife, I thank thee! I never knew
The perfect treasure thou brought'st with thee more
Than at this instant minute: a man's happy

When he's at poorest, that has matched his soul
As rightly as his body: had I married
A sensual fool now, as 'tis hard to 'scape it
'Mongst gentlewomen of our time, she would ha' hanged
About my neck, and never left her hold
Till she had kissed me into wanton businesses,
Which at the waking of my better judgment
I should have cursed most bitterly,
And laid a thicker vengeance on my act
Than misery of the birth; which were enough
If it were born to greatness, whereas mine
Is sure of beggary, though 't were got in wine.
Fulness of joy showeth the goodness in thee;
Thou art a matchless wife: farewell, my joy!

Mis. Touch. I shall not want your sight?

Touch. sen. I'll see thee often,
Talk in mirth, and play at kisses with thee;
Anything, wench, but what may beget beggars:
There I give o'er the set, throw down the cards,
And dare not take them up.

Mis. Touch. Your will be mine, sir! [*Exit.*

Touch. sen. This does not only make her honesty perfect,
But her discretion, and approves her judgment.
Had her desires been wanton, they'd been blameless,
In being lawful ever; but of all creatures,
I hold that wife a most unmatchèd treasure,
That can unto her fortunes fix her pleasure,
And not unto her blood: this is like wedlock;
The feast of marriage is not lust, but love,
And care of the estate. When I please blood,
Merrily I sing and suck out others' then:
'Tis many a wise man's fault; but of all men
I am the most unfortunate in that game
That ever pleased both genders; I ne'er played yet
Under a bastard; the poor wenches curse me
To the pit where'er I come; they were ne'er served so,

But used to have more words than one to a bargain:
I've such a fatal finger in such business,
I must forth with't; chiefly for country wenches,
For every harvest I shall hinder haymaking;
I had no less than seven lay in last progress,[1]
Within three weeks of one another's time.

Enter a Country Girl *with a child.*

C. Girl. O snaphance,[2] have I found you?
Touch. sen. How snaphance?
C. Girl. Do you see your workmanship? nay, turn not from't,
Nor offer to escape; for if you do,
I'll carry it through the streets, and follow you.
Your name may well be called Touchwood,—a pox on you!
You do but touch and take; thou hast undone me:
I was a maid before, I can bring a certificate
For it from both the churchwardens.
Touch. sen. I'll have
The parson's hand too, or I'll not yield to't.
C. Girl. Thou shalt have more, thou villain! Nothing grieves me
But Ellen my poor cousin in Derbyshire;
Thou'st cracked her marriage quite; she'll have a bout with thee.
Touch. sen. Faith, when she will, I'll have a bout with her.
C. Girl. A law bout, sir, I mean.
Touch. sen. True, lawyers use
Such bouts as other men do; and if that
Be all thy grief, I'll tender her a husband;
I keep of purpose two or three gulls in pickle
To eat such mutton with, and she shall choose one.
Do but in courtesy, faith, wench, excuse me

[1] Royal journey.
[2] A spring-lock to a gun: hence applied to anything that strikes sharply.—*Bullen.*

Of this half yard of flesh, in which, I think,
It wants a nail or two.

C. Girl. No; thou shalt find, villain,
It hath right shape, and all the nails it should have.

Touch. sen. Faith, I am poor; do a charitable deed, wench;
I am a younger brother, and have nothing.

C. Girl. Nothing? thou hast too much, thou lying villain,
Unless thou wert more thankful!

Touch. sen. I've no dwelling;
I brake up house but this morning; pray thee, pity me;
I'm a good fellow, faith; have been too kind
To people of your gender; if I ha't
Without my belly, none of your sex shall want it;
That word has been of force to move a woman.
There's tricks enough to rid thy hand on't, wench;
Some rich man's porch to-morrow before day,
Or else anon i' the evening; twenty devices.
Here's all I have, i'faith; take purse and all,
And would I were rid of all the ware i' the shop so!
[*Gives money.*

C. Girl. Where I find manly dealings, I am pitiful:
This shall not trouble you.

Touch. sen. And I protest, wench,
The next I'll keep myself.

C. Girl. Soft, let it be got first.
This is the fifth; if e'er I venture more,
Where I now go for a maid, may I ride for a whore![1]
[*Exit.*

Touch. sen. What shift she'll make now with this piece of flesh
In this strict time of Lent, I cannot imagine;
Flesh dare not peep abroad now: I have known
This city now above this seven years,
But, I protest, in better state of government

[1] An allusion to the carting of prostitutes.

I never knew it yet, nor ever heard of;
There have been more religious wholesome laws
In the half-circle of a year erected
For common good than memory e'er knew of,
Setting apart corruption of promoters,[1]
And other poisonous officers, that infect
And with a venomous breath taint every goodness.

Enter Sir OLIVER KIX *and* Lady KIX.

Lady Kix. O that e'er I was begot, or bred, or born!
Sir Ol. Be content, sweet wife.
Touch. sen. What's here to do now?
I hold my life she's in deep passion[2]
For the imprisonment of veal and mutton,
Now kept in garrets; weeps for some calf's head now:
Methinks her husband's head might serve, with bacon.
[*Aside.*

Enter TOUCHWOOD *junior.*

Touch. jun. Hist!
Sir Ol. Patience, sweet wife.
Touch. jun. Brother, I've sought you strangely.
Touch. sen. Why, what's the business?
Touch. jun. With all speed thou canst
Procure a license for me.
Touch. sen. How, a license?
Touch. jun. Cud's foot, she's lost else! I shall miss her ever.
Touch. sen. Nay, sure thou shalt not miss so fair a mark
For thirteen shillings fourpence.[3]
Touch. jun. Thanks by hundreds!
[*Exeunt* TOUCHWOOD *senior and junior.*
Sir Ol. Nay, pray thee, cease; I'll be at more cost yet,
Thou know'st we're rich enough.

[1] Common informers.
[2] Sorrow.
[3] The worth of a mark.

Lady Kix. All but in blessings,
And there the beggar goes beyond us: O-o-o!
To be seven years a wife, and not a child!
O, not a child!

Sir Ol. Sweet wife, have patience.

Lady Kix. Can any woman have a greater cut?

Sir Ol. I know 'tis great, but what of that, sweet wife?
I cannot do withal;[1] there's things making,
By thine own doctor's advice, at pothecary's:
I spare for nothing, wife; no, if the price
Were forty marks a spoonful, I would give
A thousand pound to purchase fruitfulness:
It is but bating so many good works
In the erecting of bridewells and spittlehouses,
And so fetch it up again; for having none,
I mean to make good deeds my children.

Lady Kix. Give me but those good deeds, and I'll find children.

Sir Ol. Hang thee, thou'st had too many!

Lady Kix. Thou liest, brevity.

Sir Ol. O horrible! dar'st thou call me brevity?
Dar'st thou be so short with me?

Lady Kix. Thou deserv'st worse:
Think but upon the goodly lands and livings
That's kept back through want on't.

Sir Ol. Talk not on't, pray thee;
Thou'lt make me play the woman and weep too.

Lady Kix. 'Tis our dry barrenness puffs up Sir Walter;
None gets by your not getting but that knight;
He's made by th' means, and fats his fortunes shortly
In a great dowry with a goldsmith's daughter.

Sir Ol. They may be all deceived; be but you patient, wife.

Lady Kix. I've suffered a long time.

Sir Ol. Suffer thy heart out;
A pox suffer thee!

[1] *i.e.* I cannot help it.

Lady Kix. Nay, thee, thou desertless slave!
Sir Ol. Come, come, I ha' done: you'll to the gossiping
Of Master Allwit's child?
Lady Kix. Yes, to my much joy!
Every one gets before me; there's my sister
Was married but at Bartholomew Eve last,
And she can have two children at a birth:
O, one of them, one of them, would ha' served my turn!
Sir Ol. Sorrow consume thee! thou'rt still crossing me,
And know'st my nature.

Enter Maid.

Maid. O mistress!—weeping or railing,
That's our house-harmony. [*Aside.*
Lady Kix. What sayst, Jug?
Maid. The sweetest news!
Lady Kix. What is't, wench?
Maid. Throw down your doctor's drugs,
They're all but heretics; I bring certain remedy,
That has been taught and proved, and never failed.
Sir Ol. O that, that, that, or nothing!
Maid. There's a gentleman,
I haply have his name too, that has got
Nine children by one water that he useth:
It never misses; they come so fast upon him,
He was fain to give it over.
Lady Kix. His name, sweet Jug?
Maid. One Master Touchwood, a fine gentleman,
But run behind-hand much with getting children.
Sir Ol. Is't possible!
Maid. Why, sir, he'll undertake,
Using that water, within fifteen year,
For all your wealth, to make you a poor man,
You shall so swarm with children.
Sir Ol. I'll venture that, i'faith.
Lady Kix. That shall you, husband.

Maid. But I must tell you first, he's very dear.
Sir Ol. No matter, what serves wealth for?
Lady Kix. True, sweet husband;
There's land to come; put case[1] his water stands me
In some five hundred pound a pint,
'Twill fetch a thousand, and a kersten[2] soul,
And that's worth all, sweet husband: I'll about it.
[*Exeunt.*

SCENE II.

Before ALLWIT'S *House.*

Enter ALLWIT.

Allwit. I'll go bid gossips[3] presently myself,
That's all the work I'll do; nor need I stir,
But that it is my pleasure to walk forth,
And air myself a little: I am tied
To nothing in this business; what I do
Is merely recreation, not constraint.
Here's running to and fro! nurse upon nurse,
Three charwomen, besides maids and neighbours' children.
Fie, what a trouble have I rid my hands on!
It makes me sweat to think on't.

Enter Sir WALTER WHOREHOUND.

Sir Wal. How now, Jack?
Allwit. I'm going to bid gossips for your worship's child, sir;
A goodly girl, i'faith! give you joy on her;
She looks as if she had two thousand pound
To her portion, and run away with a tailor;

1 *i.e.* Suppose. 2 A corruption of Christian.
3 Godparents.

A fine plump black-eyed slut: under correction, sir,
I take delight to see her.—Nurse!

Enter Dry Nurse.

Dry N. Do you call, sir?
Allwit. I call not you, I call the wet nurse hither.
[*Exit* Dry Nurse.
Give me the wet nurse!—

Enter Wet Nurse *carrying child.*

Ay, 'tis thou; come hither,
Come hither:
Let's see her once again; I cannot choose
But buss her thrice an hour.
Wet N. You may be proud on't, sir;
'Tis the best piece of work that e'er you did.
Allwit. Think'st thou so, nurse? what sayst to Wat and Nick?
Wet N. They're pretty children both, but here's a wench
Will be a knocker.
Allwit. Pup,—sayst thou me so?—pup, little countess!—
Faith, sir, I thank your worship for this girl
Ten thousand times and upward.
Sir Wal. I am glad
I have her for you, sir.
Allwit. Here, take her in, nurse;
Wipe her, and give her spoon-meat.
Wet N. Wipe your mouth,[1] sir. [*Exit with the child.*
Allwit. And now about these gossips.
Sir Wal. Get but two;
I'll stand for one myself.
Allwit. To your own child, sir?
Sir Wal. The better policy, it prevents suspicion;
'Tis good to play with rumour at all weapons.

[1] Make a fool of yourself.—*Bullen.*

Allwit. Troth, I commend your care, sir; 'tis a thing
That I should ne'er have thought on.

Sir Wal. The more slave:
When man turns base, out goes his soul's pure flame,
The fat of ease o'erthrows[1] the eyes of shame.

Allwit. I'm studying who to get for godmother,
Suitable to your worship. Now I ha' thought on't.

Sir Wal. I'll ease you of that care, and please myself in't—
My love the goldsmith's daughter, if I send,
Her father will command her. [*Aside.*]—Davy Dahanna!

Enter DAVY.

Allwit. I'll fit your worship then with a male partner.

Sir Wal. What is he?

Allwit. A kind, proper gentleman,
Brother to Master Touchwood.

Sir Wal. I know Touchwood:
Has he a brother living?

Allwit. A neat bachelor.

Sir Wal. Now we know him, we will make shift with him:
Despatch, the time draws near.—Come hither, Davy.
[*Exit with* DAVY.

Allwit. In troth, I pity him; he ne'er stands still:
Poor knight, what pains he takes! sends this way one,
That way another; has not an hour's leisure:
I would not have thy toil for all thy pleasure.

Enter two Promoters.

Ha, how now? what are these that stand so close
At the street-corner, pricking up their ears
And snuffing up their noses, like rich men's dogs
When the first course goes in? By the mass, promoters;
'Tis so, I hold my life; and planted there

[1] Qy. "o'ergrows."—*Dyce.*

T' arrest the dead corps[1] of poor calves and sheep,
Like ravenous creditors, that will not suffer
The bodies of their poor departed debtors
To go to th' grave, but e'en in death to vex
And stay the corps with bills of Middlesex.
This Lent will fat the whoresons up with sweetbreads,
And lard their whores with lamb-stones: what their golls[2]
Can clutch goes presently to their Molls and Dolls:
The bawds will be so fat with what they earn,
Their chins[3] will hang like udders by Easter-eve,
And, being stroked, will give the milk of witches.
How did the mongrels hear my wife lies in?
Well, I may baffle 'em gallantly. [*Aside.*]—By your favour, gentlemen,
I am a stranger both unto the city
And to her carnal strictness.

1st Pro. Good; your will, sir?

Allwit. Pray, tell me where one dwells that kills this Lent?

1st Pro. How? kills?—Come hither, Dick; a bird, a bird!

2nd Pro. What is't that you would have?

Allwit. Faith, any flesh;
But I long especially for veal and green-sauce.

1st Pro. Green goose, you shall be sauced. [*Aside.*

Allwit. I've half a scornful stomach,
No fish will be admitted.

1st Pro. Not this Lent, sir?

Allwit. Lent? what cares colon[4] here for Lent?

1st Pro. You say well, sir;
Good reason that the colon of a gentleman,
As you were lately pleased to term your worship's, sir,
Should be fulfilled with answerable food,

[1] Corpses.
[2] A cant term for hands.
[3] A double chin was regarded as the distinguishing mark of a bawd.—*Bullen.*
[4] A part of the intestines.

To sharpen blood, delight health, and tickle nature.
Were you directed hither to this street, sir?

Allwit. That I was, ay, marry.

2nd Pro. And the butcher, belike,
Should kill and sell close in some upper room?

Allwit. Some apple-loft, as I take it, or a coal-house;
I know not which i'faith.

2nd Pro. Either will serve:
This butcher shall kiss Newgate, 'less he turn up
The bottom of the pocket of his apron.— [*Aside.*
You go to seek him?

Allwit. Where you shall not find him:
I'll buy, walk by your noses with my flesh,
Sheep-biting mongrels, hand-basket freebooters!
My wife lies in—a foutra[1] for promoters! [*Exit.*

1st Pro. That shall not serve your turn.—What a rogue's this!
How cunningly he came over us!

Enter Man *with a basket under his cloak.*

2nd Pro. Hush't, stand close!

Man. I have 'scaped well thus far; they say the knaves
Are wondrous hot and busy.

1st Pro. By your leave, sir,
We must see what you have under your cloak there.

Man. Have? I have nothing.

1st Pro. No? do you tell us that? what makes this lump
Stick out then? we must see, sir.

Man. What will you see, sir?
A pair of sheets and two of my wife's foul smocks
Going to the washers.

2nd Pro. O, we love that sight well!
You cannot please us better. What, do you gull us?
Call you these shirts and smocks?

[*Seizes basket and takes out of it a piece of meat.*

[1] A term of contempt.

Man. Now, a pox choke you!
You've cozened me and five of my wife's kindred
Of a good dinner; we must make it up now
With herrings and milk-pottage [*Exit.*

1st Pro. 'Tis all veal.

2nd Pro. All veal?
Pox, the worse luck! I promised faithfully
To send this morning a fat quarter of lamb
To a kind gentlewoman in Turnbull Street[1]
That longs, and how I'm crost!

1st Pro. Let us share this, and see what hap comes next then.

2nd Pro. Agreed. Stand close again, another booty:

Enter Man *with a basket.*

What's he?

1st Pro. Sir, by your favour.

Man. Meaning me, sir?

1st Pro. Good Master Oliver? cry thee mercy i'faith!
What hast thou there?

Man. A rack of mutton, sir,
And half a lamb; you know my mistress' diet.

1st Pro. Go, go, we see thee not; away, keep close!—
Heart, let him pass! thou'lt never have the wit
To know our benefactors.

2nd Pro. I have forgot him.

1st Pro. 'Tis Master Beggarland's man, the wealthy merchant,
That is in fee with us.

2nd Pro. Now I've a feeling of him. [*Exit* Man.

1st Pro. You know he purchased the whole Lent together,
Gave us ten groats a-piece on Ash Wednesday.

2nd Pro. True, true.

[1] A street in Clerkenwell noted as the residence of thieves and prostitutes.

1st Pro. A wench!

2nd Pro. Why, then, stand close indeed.

Enter Country Girl *with a basket.*

C. Girl. Women had need of wit, if they'll shift here,
And she that hath wit may shift anywhere. [*Aside.*

1st Pro. Look, look! poor fool, sh'as left the rump uncovered too,
More to betray her! this is like a murderer
That will outface the deed with a bloody band.

2nd Pro. What time of the year is't, sister?

C. Girl. O sweet gentlemen!
I'm a poor servant, let me go.

1st Pro. You shall, wench,
But this must stay with us.

C. Girl. O you undo me, sir!
'Tis for a wealthy gentlewoman that takes physic, sir;
The doctor does allow my mistress mutton.
O, as you tender the dear life of a gentlewoman!
I'll bring my master to you; he shall show you
A true authority from the higher powers,
And I'll run every foot.

2nd Pro. Well, leave your basket then,
And run and spare not.

C. Girl. Will you swear then to me
To keep it till I come?

1st Pro. Now by this light I will.

C. Girl. What say you, gentlemen?

2nd Pro. What a strange wench 'tis!—
Would we might perish else.

C. Girl. Nay, then I run, sir.
[*Leaves the basket, and exit.*

1st Pro. And ne'er return, I hope.

2nd Pro. A politic baggage! she makes us swear to keep it;
I prithee look what market she hath made.

1st Pro. Imprimis, sir, a good fat loin of mutton.
[*Taking out a loin of mutton.*
What comes next under this cloth? now for a quarter
Of lamb.

2nd Pro. No, for a shoulder of mutton.

1st Pro. Done!

2nd Pro. Why, done, sir!

1st Pro. By the mass, I feel I've lost
'Tis of more weight, i'faith.

2nd Pro. Some loin of veal?

1st Pro. No, faith, here's a lamb's head, I feel that plainly;
Why, I'll yet win my wager.

2nd Pro. Ha!

1st Pro. 'Swounds, what's here! [*Taking out a child.*

2nd Pro. A child!

1st Pro. A pox of all dissembling cunning whores!

2nd Pro. Here's an unlucky breakfast!

1st Pro. What shall's do?

2nd Pro. The quean made us swear to keep it too.

1st Pro. We might leave it else.

2nd Pro. Villainous strange!
Life, had she none to gull but poor promoters,
That watch hard for a living?

1st Pro. Half our gettings
Must run in sugar-sops and nurses' wages now,
Besides many a pound of soap and tallow;
We've need to get loins of mutton still, to save
Suet to change for candles.

2nd Pro. Nothing mads me
But this was a lamb's head with you; you felt it:
She has made calves' heads of us.

1st Pro. Prithee, no more on't;
There's time to get it up; it is not come
To Mid-Lent Sunday yet.

2nd Pro. I am so angry,
I'll watch no more to-day.

1st Pro. Faith, nor I neither.

2nd Pro. Why, then, I'll make a motion.

1st Pro. Well, what is't?

2nd Pro. Let's e'en go to the Checker at Queenhive,[1]
And roast the loin of mutton till young flood;
Then send the child to Branford.[2] [*Exeunt.*

SCENE III.

A Hall in ALLWIT'S *House.*

Enter ALLWIT *in one of* Sir WALTER'S *suits, and* DAVY *trussing*[3] *him.*

Allwit. 'Tis a busy day at our house, Davy.

Davy. Always the kursning[4] day, sir.

Allwit. Truss, truss me, Davy.

Davy. No matter an you were hanged, sir. [*Aside.*

Allwit. How does this suit fit me, Davy?

Davy. Excellent neatly;
My master's things were ever fit for you, sir,
E'en to a hair, you know.

Allwit. Thou'st hit it right, Davy:
We ever jumped in one this ten years, Davy;
So, well said.—

Enter Man *with a box.*

What art thou?

Man. Your comfit-maker's man, sir.

Allwit. O sweet youth!
In to the nurse, quick, quick, 'tis time, i'faith.
Your mistress will be here?

1 Queenhithe.
2 Brentford.
3 Tying the points of his trunk hose.
4 Christening.

Man. She was setting forth, sir. [*Exit.*

Allwit. Here comes our gossips now: O, I shall have
Such kissing work to-day.—

Enter two Puritans.

Sweet Mistress Underman
Welcome, i'faith.

1st Pur. Give you joy of your fine girl, sir:
Grant that her education may be pure,
And become one of the faithful!

Allwit. Thanks to your sisterly wishes, Mistress Underman.

2nd Pur. Are any of the brethren's wives yet come?

Allwit. There are some wives within, and some at home.

1st Pur. Verily, thanks, sir. [*Exeunt* Puritans.

Allwit. Verily you're an ass, forsooth:
I must fit all these times, or there's no music.
Here comes a friendly and familiar pair:

Enter two Gossips.

Now I like these wenches well.

1st Gos. How dost, sirrah?

Allwit. Faith, well, I thank you, neighbour;—and how dost thou?

2nd Gos. Want nothing but such getting, sir, as thine.

Allwit. My gettings, wench? they're poor.

1st Gos. Fie, that thou'lt say so;
Thou'st as fine children as a man can get.

Davy. Ay, as a man can get, and that's my master. [*Aside.*

Allwit. They're pretty foolish things, put to making in minutes,
I ne'er stand long about 'em. Will you walk in, wenches?
[*Exeunt* Gossips.

Enter TOUCHWOOD *junior and* MOLL.

Touch. jun. The happiest meeting that our souls could wish for!
Here is the ring ready; I'm beholden
Unto your father's haste, has kept his hour.

Moll. He never kept it better.

Enter Sir WALTER WHOREHOUND.

Touch. jun. Back, be silent.

Sir Wal. Mistress and partner, I will put you both
Into one cup.

Davy. Into one cup? most proper;
A fitting compliment for a goldsmith's daughter. [*Aside.*

Allwit. Yes, sir, that's he must be your worship's partner
In this day's business, Master Touchwood's brother.

Sir Wal. I embrace your acquaintance, sir.

Touch. jun. It vows your service, sir.

Sir Wal. It's near high time; come, Master Allwit.

Allwit. Ready, sir.

Sir Wal. Wilt please you walk?

Touch. jun. Sir, I obey your time. [*Exeunt.*

SCENE IV.

Before ALLWIT'S *House.*

Enter from the house Midwife *with the child,* LADY KIX *and other* Gossips, *who exeunt; then* MAUDLIN, Puritans, *and other* Gossips.

1st Gos. Good Mistress Yellowhammer——

Maud. In faith, I will not.

1st Gos. Indeed it [1] shall be yours.

[1] The two are entreating each other to take precedence.

Maud. I have sworn, i'faith.

1st Gos. I'll stand still then.

Maud. So, will you let the child
Go without company, and make me forsworn?

1st Gos. You are such another creature!

[*Exeunt* 1st Gossip *and* MAUDLIN.

2nd Gos. Before me?
I pray come down a little.

3rd Gos. Not a whit;
I hope I know my place.

2nd Gos. Your place? great wonder, sure!
Are you any better than a comfit-maker's wife?

3rd Gos. And that's as good at all times as a pothecary's.

2nd Gos. Ye lie! yet I forbear you too.

[*Exeunt* 2nd *and* 3rd Gossips.

1st. Pur. Come, sweet sister; we go
In unity, and show the fruits of peace,
Like children of the spirit.

2nd Pur. I love lowliness. [*Exeunt* Puritans.

4th Gos. True, so say I, though they strive more;
There comes as proud behind as goes before.

5th Gos. Every inch, i'faith. [*Exeunt.*

ACT THE THIRD.

SCENE I.

A Room in TOUCHWOOD *junior's lodgings.*

Enter TOUCHWOOD *junior and* Parson.

TOUCH. JUN. O sir, if e'er you felt the force of love,
Pity it in me!

Par. Yes, though I ne'er was married, sir,
I've felt the force of love from good men's daughters,
And some that will be maids yet three years hence.
Have you got a license?

Touch. jun. Here, 'tis ready, sir.

Par. That's well.

Touch. jun. The ring, and all things perfect; she'll steal hither.

Par. She shall be welcome, sir; I'll not be long
A clapping you together.

Touch. jun. O, here she's come, sir!

Enter MOLL *and* TOUCHWOOD *senior.*

Par. What's he?

Touch. jun. My honest brother.

Touch. sen. Quick, make haste, sirs!

Moll. You must despatch with all the speed you can,

For I shall be missed straight; I made hard shift
For this small time I have.

Par. Then I'll not linger,
Place that ring upon her finger:

[TOUCHWOOD *junior puts ring on* MOLL'S *finger.*

This the finger plays the part,
Whose master-vein shoots from the heart:
Now join hands—

Enter YELLOWHAMMER *and* Sir W. WHOREHOUND.

Yel. Which I will sever,
And so ne'er again meet, never!

Moll. O, we're betrayed!

Touch. jun. Hard fate!

Sir Wal. I'm struck with wonder!

Yel. Was this the politic fetch, thou mystical baggage,
Thou disobedient strumpet!—And were you
So wise to send for her to such an end?

Sir Wal. Now I disclaim the end; you'll make me mad.

Yel. And what are you, sir?

Touch. jun. An you cannot see
With those two glasses, put on a pair more.

Yel. I dreamed of anger still.—Here, take your ring, sir,— [*Taking ring off* MOLL'S *finger.*
Ha! this? life, 'tis the same! abominable!
Did not I sell this ring?

Touch. jun. I think you did;
You received money for't.

Yel. Heart, hark you, knight;
Here's no unconscionable villainy!
Set me a-work to make the wedding-ring,
And come with an intent to steal my daughter!
Did ever runaway match it!

Sir Wal. This your brother, sir?

Touch. sen. He can tell that as well as I.

Yel. The very posy mocks me to my face,—

"Love that's wise
Blinds parents' eyes."
I thank your wisdom, sir, for blinding of us;
We've good hope to recover our sight shortly:
In the meantime I will lock up this baggage
As carefully as my gold; she shall see
As little sun, if a close room or so
Can keep her from the light on't.

Moll. O sweet father,
For love's sake, pity me!

Yel. Away!

Moll. Farewell, sir;
All content bless thee! and take this for comfort,
Though violence keep me, thou canst lose me never,
I'm ever thine, although we part for ever.

Yel. Ay, we shall part you, minx. [*Exit with* MOLL.

Sir Wal. Your acquaintance, sir,
Came very lately, yet came too soon;
I must hereafter know you for no friend,
But one that I must shun like pestilence,
Or the disease of lust.

Touch. jun. Like enough, sir;
You ha' ta'en me at the worst time for words
That e'er ye picked out: faith, do not wrong me, sir.
[*Exit with* Parson.

Touch. sen. Look after him, and spare not: there he walks
That ne'er yet received baffling:[1] you are blest
More than ever I knew; go, take your rest. [*Exit.*

Sir Wal. I pardon you, you are both losers. [*Exit.*

[1] Endured insult.

SCENE II.

A Bedchamber; Mistress ALLWIT *discovered in bed.*

Enter Midwife *with the child,* LADY KIX, MAUDLIN, Puritans, *and other* Gossips.

1st Gos. How is it, woman? we have brought you home
A kursen[1] soul.

Mis. All. Ay, I thank your pains.

1st Pur. And, verily, well kursened, i' the right way,
Without idolatry or superstition,
After the pure manner of Amsterdam.[2]

Mis. All. Sit down, good neighbours.—Nurse.

Nurse. At hand, forsooth.

Mis. All. Look they have all low stools.

Nurse. They have, forsooth.

[*All the* Gossips *seat themselves.*

2nd Gos. Bring the child hither, nurse.—How say you now, gossip,
Is't not a chopping girl? so like the father.

3rd Gos. As if it had been spit out of his mouth!
Eyed, nosed, and browed, as like as a girl can be,
Only, indeed, it has the mother's mouth.

2nd Gos. The mother's mouth up and down, up and down.

3rd Gos. 'Tis a large child, she's but a little woman.

1st Pur. No, believe me,
A very spiny[3] creature, but all heart;
Well mettled, like the faithful, to endure
Her tribulation here, and raise up seed.

2nd Gos. She had a sore labour on't, I warrant you;
You can tell, neighbour?

3rd Gos. O, she had great speed;
We were afraid once, but she made us all

[1] Christened.
[3] Slender.
[2] Many Puritans took refuge at Amsterdam.

Have joyful hearts again; 'tis a good soul, i'faith;
The midwife found her a most cheerful daughter.

1st Pur. 'Tis the spirit; the sisters are all like her.

Enter Sir WALTER WHOREHOUND, *carrying a silver standing-cup and two spoons, and* ALLWIT.

2nd Gos. O, here comes the chief gossip, neighbours!
[*Exit* Nurse.

Sir Wal. The fatness of your wishes to you all, ladies!

3rd Gos. O dear, sweet gentleman, what fine words he has!
The fatness of our wishes!

2nd Gos. Calls us all ladies!

4th Gos. I promise you, a fine gentleman and a courteous.

2nd Gos. Methinks her husband shows like a clown to him.

3rd Gos. I would not care what clown my husband were too,
So I had such fine children.

2nd Gos. Sh'as all fine children, gossip.

3rd Gos. Ay, and see how fast they come!

1st Pur. Children are blessings,
If they be got with zeal by the brethren,
As I have five at home.

Sir Wal. The worst is past,
I hope, now, gossip.

Mis. All. So I hope too, good sir.

Allwit. What, then, so hope I too, for company;
I've nothing to do else.

Sir Wal. A poor remembrance, lady,
To the love of the babe; I pray, accept of it.
[*Giving cup and spoon.*

Mis. All. O, you are at too much charge, sir!

2nd Gos. Look, look, what has he given her? what is't, gossip?

3rd Gos. Now, by my faith, a fair high standing-cup
And two great 'postle-spoons,[1] one of them gilt.
1st Pur. Sure that was Judas then with the red beard.[2]
2nd Pur. I would not feed
My daughter with that spoon for all the world,
For fear of colouring her hair; red hair
The brethren like not, it consumes them much;
'Tis not the sisters' colour.

Re-enter Nurse *with comfits and wine.*

Allwit. Well said, nurse;
About, about with them among the gossips!
[Nurse *hands about the comfits.*
Now out comes all the tasselled handkerchers,
They're spread abroad between their knees already;
Now in goes the long fingers that are washed
Some thrice a day in urine; my wife uses it.
Now we shall have such pocketing; see how
They lurch[3] at the lower end! [*Aside.*
1st Pur. Come hither, nurse.
Allwit. Again? she has taken twice already. [*Aside.*
1st Pur. I had forgot a sister's child that's sick.
[*Taking comfits.*
Allwit. A pox! it seems your purity
Loves sweet things well that puts in thrice together.
Had this been all my cost now, I'd been beggared;
These women have no consciences at sweetmeats,[4]
Where'er they come; see an they've not culled out

[1] Spoons with a little figure of an apostle at the end of the handle; a common present of sponsors at christenings.

[2] Red, "the dissembling colour," is the traditional colour of Judas's hair. There is a prejudice against red hair among most Eastern nations.

[3] Filch.—*Bullen.*

[4] Bullen refers to Dekker's *Bachelor's Banquet*, cap. iii.:—"Consider then what cost and trouble it will be to him to have all things fine against the christening day: what store of sugar, biscuits, comfits and caraways, marmalade and marchpane, with all kind of sweet suckets and superfluous banqueting stuff, with a hundred other odd and needless trifles, which at that time must fill the pockets of dainty dames."

All the long plums too, they've left nothing here
But short wriggle-tail comfits, not worth mouthing:
No mar'l I heard a citizen complain once
That his wife's belly only broke his back;
Mine had been all in fitters[1] seven years since,
But for this worthy knight,
That with a prop upholds my wife and me,
And all my estate buried in Bucklersbury.[2] [*Aside.*

Mis. All. Here, Mistress Yellowhammer, and neighbours,
To you all that have taken pains with me,
All the good wives at once!

[*Drinks; after which* Nurse *hands round the wine.*

1st Pur. I'll answer for them;
They wish all health and strength, and that you may
Courageously go forward, to perform
The like and many such, like a true sister,
With motherly bearing. [*Drinks.*

Allwit. Now the cups troll about
To wet the gossips' whistles; it pours down, i'faith;
They never think of payment. [*Aside.*

1st Pur. Fill again, nurse. [*Drinks.*

Allwit. Now bless thee, two at once! I'll stay no longer;
It would kill me, an I paid for it.— [*Aside.*
Will't please you to walk down, and leave the women?

Sir Wal. With all my heart, Jack.

Allwit. Troth, I cannot blame you.

Sir Wal. Sit you all merry, ladies.

Gossips. Thank your worship, sir.

1st Pur. Thank your worship, sir.

Allwit. A pox twice tipple ye, you're last and lowest! [*Aside.*

[*Exeunt* Sir W. WHOREHOUND *and* ALLWIT.

1st Pur. Bring hither that same cup, nurse; I would fain
Drive away this—hup—antichristian grief. [*Drinks.*

[1] Pieces.

[2] Inhabited at the time chiefly by druggists, who were the principal sellers of sweetmeats.

3rd Gos. See, gossip, an she lies not in like a countess;
Would I had such a husband for my daughter!

4th Gos. Is not she toward marriage?

3rd Gos. O no, sweet gossip!

4th Gos. Why, she's nineteen.

3rd Gos. Ay, that she was last Lammas;
But she has a fault, gossip, a secret fault.

4th Gos. A fault? what is't?

3rd Gos. I'll tell you when I've drunk. [*Drinks.*

4th Gos. Wine can do that, I see, that friendship cannot. [*Aside.*

3rd Gos. And now, I'll tell you, gossip; she's too free. [*Exit* Nurse.

4th Gos. Too free?

3rd Gos. O ay, she cannot lie dry in her bed.

4th Gos. What, and nineteen?

3rd Gos. 'Tis as I tell you, gossip.

Re-enter Nurse, *and whispers* MAUDLIN.

Maud. Speak with me, nurse? who is't?

Nurse. A gentleman,
From Cambridge; I think it be your son, forsooth.

Maud. 'Tis my son Tim, i'faith; prithee, call him up
Among the women, 'twill embolden him well,— [*Exit* Nurse.
For he wants nothing but audacity.
Would the Welsh gentlewoman at home were here now! [*Aside.*

Lady Kix. Is your son come, forsooth?

Maud. Yes, from the university, forsooth.

Lady Kix. 'Tis great joy on ye.

Maud. There's a great marriage
Towards[1] for him.

Lady Kix. A marriage?

Maud. Yes, sure,
A huge heir in Wales at least to nineteen mountains.
Besides her goods and cattle.

[1] In preparation.

Re-enter Nurse *with* TIM.

Tim. O, I'm betrayed! [*Exit.*

Maud. What, gone again?—Run after him, good nurse;
He is so bashful, that's the spoil of youth: [*Exit* Nurse.
In the university they're kept still to men,
And ne'er trained up to women's company.

Lady Kix. 'Tis a great spoil of youth indeed.

Re-enter Nurse *and* TIM.

Nurse. Your mother will have it so.

Maud. Why, son! why Tim!
What, must I rise and fetch you? for shame, son!

Tim. Mother, you do intreat like a fresh-woman;
'Tis against the laws of the university
For any that has answered under bachelor
To thrust 'mongst married wives.

Maud. Come, we'll excuse you here.

Tim. Call up my tutor, mother, and I care not.

Maud. What, is your tutor come? have you brought him up?

Tim. I ha' not brought him up, he stands at door;
Negatur, there's logic to begin with you, mother.

Maud. Run, call the gentleman, nurse; he's my son's tutor.— [*Exit* Nurse.
Here, eat some plums. [*Offers comfits.*

Tim. Come I from Cambridge,
And offer me six plums?

Maud. Why, how now, Tim?
Will not your old tricks yet be left?

Tim. Served like a child,
When I have answered under bachelor!

Maud. You'll ne'er lin[1] till I make your tutor whip[2] you;

[1] Cease

[2] Undergraduates were frequently whipped in those days. Bullen mentions that, according to Aubrey, Milton, when a student at Cambridge, was whipped by his tutor, William Chappell; also that Chamberlain, in a letter to Carleton (1612), states that "a son of the Bishop of Bristol, of nineteen or twenty, killed himself

You know how I served you once at the free-school
In Paul's Churchyard?

Tim. O monstrous absurdity!
Ne'er was the like in Cambridge since my time;
'Life, whip a bachelor! you'd be laughed at soundly;
Let not my tutor hear you, 'twould be a jest
Through the whole university. No more words, mother.

Re-enter Nurse *with* Tutor.

Maud. Is this your tutor, Tim?

Tutor. Yes, surely, lady,
I am the man that brought him in league with logic,
And read the Dunces[1] to him.

Tim. That did he, mother;
But now I have 'em all in my own pate,
And can as well read 'em to others.

Tutor. That can he,
Mistress, for they flow naturally from him.

Maud. I am the more beholding to your pains, sir.

Tutor. *Non ideo sane.*

Maud. True, he was an idiot indeed
When he went out of London, but now he's well mended.
Did you receive the two goose-pies I sent you?

Tutor. And eat them heartily, thanks to your worship.

Maud. 'Tis my son Tim; I pray bid him welcome, gentlewomen.

Tim. Tim? hark you, Timotheus, mother, Timotheus.

Maud. How, shall I deny your name? Timotheus, quoth he!
Faith there's a name!—'Tis my son Tim, forsooth.

Lady Kix. You're welcome, master Tim. [*Kisses* TIM.

with a knife to avoid the disgrace of breeching, which his mother or mother-in-law (I know not whether) would need have put him to, for losing his money at tennis."

[1] The schoolmen, so named after Duns Scotus.

Tim. O this is horrible,
She wets as she kisses! [*Aside.*]—Your handkercher, sweet tutor,
To wipe them off as fast as they come on.

2nd Gos. Welcome from Cambridge. [*Kisses* TIM.

Tim. This is intolerable!
This woman has a villanous sweet breath,
Did she not stink of comfits. [*Aside.*]—Help me, sweet tutor,
Or I shall rub my lips off!

Tutor. I'll go kiss
The lower end the whilst.

Tim. Perhaps that's the sweeter,
And we shall despatch the sooner.

1st Pur. Let me come next:
Welcome from the wellspring of discipline,
That waters all the brethren.
[*Attempts to kiss* TIM, *but reels and falls.*

Tim. Hoist, I beseech thee!

3rd Gos. O bless the woman!—Mistress Underman—
[*They raise her up.*

1st Pur. 'Tis but the common affliction of the faithful;
We must embrace our falls.

Tim. I'm glad I escaped it;
It was some rotten kiss sure, it dropt down
Before it came at me.

Re-enter ALLWIT *with* DAVY.

Allwit. Here is a noise! not parted yet? heyday,
A looking-glass!—They've drunk so hard in plate,
That some of them had need of other vessels.—[*Aside.*
Yonder's the bravest show!

Gossips. Where, where, sir?

Allwit. Come along presently by the Pissing-conduit,[1]
With two brave drums and a standard-bearer.

[1] So called from its running in a small stream. It was also known as the "conduit in Cornhill." Shortyard (in Middleton's

Gossips. O brave!

Tim. Come, tutor. [*Exit with* Tutor.

Gossips. Farewell, sweet gossip!

Mis. All. I thank you all for your pains.

1st Pur. Feed and grow strong.

[*Exeunt* Lady KIX, MAUDLIN, *and all the* Gossips.

Allwit. You had more need to sleep than eat;
Go take a nap with some of the brethren, go,
And rise up a well-edified, boldified sister.
O, here's a day of toil well passed over,
Able to make a citizen hare-mad!
How hot they've made the room with their thick bums!
Dost not feel it, Davy?

Davy. Monstrous strong, sir.

Allwit. What's here under the stools?

Davy. Nothing but wet, sir;
Some wine spilt here belike.

Allwit. Is't no worse, think'st thou?
Fair needlework stools cost nothing with them, Davy.

Davy. Nor you neither, i'faith. [*Aside.*

Allwit. Look how they have laid them,
E'en as they lie themselves, with their heels up!
How they have shuffled up the rushes [1] too, Davy,
With their short figging little shittle-cock [2] heels!
These women can let nothing stand as they find it.
But what's the secret thou'st about to tell me,
My honest Davy?

Davy. If you should disclose it, sir——

Allwit. 'Life, rip my belly up to the throat then, Davy!

Davy. My master's upon marriage.

Michaelmas Term), who apes the fashionable observances of a gentleman, says, in reference to this conduit, "I tell you what I ha' done. Sometimes I carry my water all London over only to deliver it proudly at the Standard; and do I pass altogether unnoticed, think you?"

[1] With which the floors were always strewed.

[2] The original form of shuttlecock.

Allwit. Marriage, Davy?
Send me to hanging rather.
Davy. I have stung him! [*Aside.*
Allwit. When? where? what is she, Davy?
Davy. Even the same was gossip, and gave the spoon.
Allwit. I have no time to stay, nor scarce can speak:
I'll stop those wheels, or all the work will break. [*Exit.*
Davy. I knew 'twould prick. Thus do I fashion still
All mine own ends by him and his rank toil:
'Tis my desire to keep him still from marriage;
Being his poor nearest kinsman, I may fare
The better at his death; there my hopes build,
Since my Lady Kix is dry, and hath no child. [*Exit.*

SCENE III.

A Room in Sir OLIVER KIX'S *House.*

Enter TOUCHWOOD *senior and* TOUCHWOOD *junior.*

Touch. jun. You're in the happiest way t' enrich yourself
And pleasure me, brother, as man's feet can tread in;
For though she be locked up, her vow is fixed
Only to me; then time shall never grieve me,
For by that vow e'en absent I enjoy her,
Assuredly confirmed that none else shall,
Which will make tedious years seem gameful to me:
In the mean space, lose you no time, sweet brother;
You have the means to strike at this knight's fortunes,
And lay him level with his bankrout[1] merit;
Get but his wife with child, perch at tree-top,
And shake the golden fruit into her lap;
About it before she weep herself to a dry ground,
And whine out all her goodness.

[1] Bankrupt.

Touch. sen. Prithee, cease;
find a too much aptness in my blood
'or such a business, without provocation;
You might well spared this banquet of eringoes,
Artichokes, potatoes, and your buttered crab;[1]
They were fitter kept for your wedding-dinner.

Touch. jun. Nay, an you'll follow my suit, and save my purse too,
Fortune doats on me: he's in happy case
Finds such an honest friend i' the common-place.

Touch. sen. Life, what makes thee so merry? thou'st no cause
That I could hear of lately since thy crosses,
Unless there be news come with new additions.

Touch. jun. Why, there thou hast it right; I look for her
This evening, brother.

Touch. sen. How's that? look for her?

Touch. jun. I will deliver you of the wonder straight, brother:
By the firm secrecy and kind assistance
Of a good wench i' the house, who, made of pity,
Weighing the case her own, she's led through gutters,
Strange hidden ways, which none but love could find,
Or ha' the heart to venture: I expect her
Where you would little think.

Touch. sen. I care not where,
So she be safe, and yours.

Touch. jun. Hope tells me so;
But from your love and time my peace must grow.

Touch. sen. You know the worst then, brother.
[*Exit* TOUCHWOOD *jun.*]—Now to my Kix,
The barren he and she; they're i' the next room;
But to say which of their two humours hold them
Now at this instant, I cannot say truly.

1 All these were regarded as aphrodisiacs.

Sir Ol. [*within.*] Thou liest, barrenness!

Touch. sen. O, is't that time of day? give you joy o
your tongue,
There's nothing else good in you: this their life
The whole day, from eyes open to eyes shut,
Kissing or scolding, and then must be made friends;
Then rail the second part of the first fit out,
And then be pleased again, no man knows whicl
way:
Fall out like giants, and fall in like children;
Their fruit can witness as much.

Enter Sir OLIVER KIX *and* Lady KIX.

Sir Ol. 'Tis thy fault.

Lady Kix. Mine, drouth and coldness?

Sir Ol. Thine; 'tis thou art barren.

Lady Kix. I barren? O life, that I durst but speal
now
In mine own justice, in mine own right! I barren?
'Twas otherwise with me when I was at court;
I was ne'er called so till I was married.

Sir Ol. I'll be divorced.

Lady Kix. Be hanged! I need not wish it,
That will come too soon to thee: I may say
Marriage and hanging goes by destiny,
For all the goodness I can find in't yet.

Sir Ol. I'll give up house, and keep some fruitfu
whore,
Like an old bachelor, in a tradesman's chamber;
She and her children shall have all.

Lady Kix. Where be they?

Touch. sen. Pray, cease;
When there are friendlier courses took for you,
To get and multiply within your house
At your own proper costs, in spite of censure,
Methinks an honest peace might be established.

Sir Ol. What, with her? never.

Touch. sen. Sweet sir——

Sir Ol. You work all in vain.

Lady Kix. Then he doth all like thee.

Touch. sen. Let me entreat, sir——

Sir Ol. Singleness confound her!
took her with one smock.

Lady Kix. But, indeed, you
came not so single when you came from shipboard.

Sir Ol. Heart, she bit sore there! [*Aside.*]—Prithee, make us friends.

Touch. sen. Is't come to that? the peal begins to cease. [*Aside.*

Sir Ol. I'll sell all at an out-cry.[1]

Lady Kix. Do thy worst, slave!—
Good, sweet sir, bring us into love again.

Touch. sen. Some would think this impossible to compass.— [*Aside.*
Pray, let this storm fly over.

Sir Ol. Good sir, pardon me;
m master of this house, which I'll sell presently;
ll clap up bills this evening.

Touch. sen. Lady, friends, come!

Lady Kix. If ever ye loved woman, talk not on't, sir:
What, friends with him? good faith, do you think I'm mad?
With one that's scarce th' hinder quarter of a man?

Sir Ol. Thou art nothing of a woman.

Lady Kix. Would I were less than nothing! [*Weeps.*

Sir Ol. Nay, prithee, what dost mean?

Lady Kix. I cannot please you.

Sir Ol. I'faith, thou'rt a good soul; he lies that says it;
uss, buss, pretty rogue. [*Kisses her.*

Lady Kix. You care not for me.

Touch. sen. Can any man tell now which way they came in?
y this light, I'll be hanged then! [*Aside.*

[1] An auction announced by the common crier.—*Dyce.*

Sir Ol. Is the drink come?

Touch. sen. Here is a little vial of almond-milk—
That stood me in some threepence. [*Aside.*

Sir Ol. I hope to see thee, wench, within these few years,
Circled with children, pranking up a girl,
And putting jewels in her little ears;
Fine sport, i'faith!

Lady Kix. Ay, had you been aught, husband,
It had been done ere this time.

Sir Ol. Had I been aught?
Hang thee, hadst thou been aught! but a cross thing
I ever found thee.

Lady Kix. Thou'rt a grub, to say so.

Sir Ol. A pox on thee!

Touch. sen. By this light, they're out again
At the same door, and no man can tell which way!
[*Aside.*
Come, here's your drink, sir.

Sir Ol. I'll not take it now, sir,
An I were sure to get three boys ere midnight.

Lady Kix. Why, there thou show'st now of what breed thou com'st
To hinder generation: O thou villain,
That knows how crookedly the world goes with us
For want of heirs, yet put by all good fortune!

Sir Ol. Hang, strumpet! I will take it now in spite.

Touch. sen. Then you must ride upon't five hours.
[*Gives vial to* Sir OLIVER.

Sir Ol. I mean so.—
Within there!

Enter Servant.

Ser. Sir?

Sir Ol. Saddle the white mare: [*Exit* Servant.
I'll take a whore along, and ride to Ware.

Lady Kix. Ride to the devil!

Sir Ol. I'll plague you every way:
Look ye, do you see? 'tis gone. [*Drinks.*

Lady Kix. A pox go with it!

Sir Ol. Ay, curse, and spare not now.

Touch. sen. Stir up and down, sir;
You must not stand.

Sir Ol. Nay, I'm not given to standing.

Touch. sen. So much the better, sir, for the——

Sir Ol. I never could stand long in one place yet;
I learnt it of my father, ever figient.[1]
How if I crossed this, sir? [*Capers.*

Touch. sen. O, passing good, sir,
And would show well 'a horseback: when you come to your inn,
If you leapt over a joint-stool or two,
'Twere not amiss—although you brake your neck, sir. [*Aside.*

Sir Ol. What say you to a table thus high, sir?

Touch. sen. Nothing better, sir, if't be furnished with good victuals.
You remember how the bargain runs 'bout this business?

Sir Ol. Or else I had a bad head: you must receive, sir,
Four hundred pounds of me at four several payments;
One hundred pound now in hand.

Touch. sen. Right, that I have, sir.

Sir Ol. Another hundred when my wife is quick;
The third when she's brought a-bed; and the last hundred
When the child cries, for if't should be still-born,
It doth no good, sir.

Touch. sen. All this is even still:
A little faster, sir.

Sir Ol. Not a whit, sir;
I'm in an excellent pace for any physic.

[1] Fidgety.

Re-enter Servant.

Ser. Your white mare's ready.

Sir Ol. I shall up presently.— [*Exit* Servant.
One kiss and farewell. [*Kisses her.*

Lady Kix. Thou shalt have two, love.

Sir Ol. Expect me about three.

Lady Kix. With all my heart, sweet.

[*Exit* Sir OLIVER KIX.

Touch. sen. By this light, they've forgot their anger since,
And are as far in again as e'er they were!
Which way the devil came they? heart, I saw 'em not!
Their ways are beyond finding out. [*Aside.*]—Come, sweet lady.

Lady Kix. How must I take mine, sir?

Touch. sen. Clean contrary;
Yours must be taken lying.

Lady Kix. A-bed, sir?

Touch. sen. A-bed, or where you will, for your own ease;
Your coach will serve.

Lady Kix. The physic must needs please. [*Exeunt.*

ACT THE FOURTH.

SCENE I.

A Room in YELLOWHAMMER'S *House.*

Enter TIM *and* Tutor.

TIM. *Negatur argumentum*, tutor.

Tutor. Pro tibi, pupil, *stultus non est animal rationale.*

Tim. Falleris sane.

Tutor. Quæso ut taceas,—probo tibi——

Tim. Quomodo probas, domine?

Tutor. Stultus non habet rationem, ergo non est animal rationale.

Tim. Sic argumentaris, domine; stultus non habet rationem, ergo non est animal rationale; negatur argumentum again, tutor.

Tutor. Argumentum iterum probo tibi, domine; qui non participat de ratione, nullo modo potest vocari rationalis; but *stultus non participat de ratione, ergo stultus nullo modo potest dici rationalis.*

Tim. Participat.

Tutor. Sic disputas: qui participat, quomodo participat?

Tim. Ut homo, probabo tibi in syllogismo.

Tutor. Hunc proba.

Tim. Sic probo, domine; stultus est homo, sicut tu et ego sumus; homo est animal rationale, sicut stultus est animal rationale.

Enter MAUDLIN.

Maud. Here's nothing but disputing all the day long with 'em!

Tutor. Sic disputas; stultus est homo, sicut tu et ego sumus; homo est animal rationale, sicut stultus est animal rationale.

Maud. Your reasons are both good, whate'er they be.
Pray, give them over; faith, you'll tire yourselves;
What's the matter between you?

Tim. Nothing but reasoning
About a fool, mother.

Maud. About a fool, son?
Alas, what need you trouble your heads 'bout that!
None of us all but knows what a fool is.

Tim. Why, what's a fool, mother? I come to you now.

Maud. Why, one that's married before he has wit.

Tim. 'Tis pretty, i'faith, and well guessed of a woman never brought up at the university; but bring forth what fool you will, mother, I'll prove him to be as reasonable a creature as myself or my tutor here.

Maud. Fie, 'tis impossible!

Tutor. Nay, he shall do't, forsooth.

Tim. 'Tis the easiest thing to prove a fool by logic;
By logic I'll prove anything.

Maud. What, thou wilt not?

Tim. I'll prove a whore to be an honest woman.

Maud. Nay, by my faith, she must prove that herself,
Or logic will ne'er do't.

Tim. 'Twill do't, I tell you.

Maud. Some in this street would give a thousand pounds
That you could prove their wives so.

Tim. Faith, I can,
And all their daughters too, though they had three bastards.
When comes your tailor hither?

Maud. Why, what of him?

Tim. By logic I'll prove him to be a man,
Let him come when he will.

Maud. How hard at first

Was learning to him! truly, sir, I thought
He would never 'a took the Latin tongue:
How many accidences do you think he wore out
Ere he came to his grammar?

Tutor. Some three or four.

Maud. Believe me, sir, some four and thirty.

Tim. Pish, I made haberdines[1] of 'em in church-porches.

Maud. He was eight years in his grammar, and stuck horribly
At a foolish place there, call'd *as in præsenti.*

Tim. Pox, I have it here now.

Maud. He so shamed me once,
Before an honest gentleman that knew me
When I was a maid.

Tim. These women must have all out!

Maud. *Quid est grammatica?* says the gentleman to him,—
I shall remember by a sweet, sweet token,—
But nothing could he answer.

Tutor. How now, pupil, ha?
Quid est grammatica?

Tim. *Grammatica?* ha, ha, ha!

Maud. Nay, do not laugh, son, but let me hear you say't now:
There was one word went so prettily off
The gentleman's tongue, I shall remember it
The longest day of my life.

Tutor. Come, *quid est grammatica?*

Tim. Are you not ashamed, tutor, *grammatica?*
Why, *recte scribendi atque loquendi ars,*
Sir-reverence[2] of my mother.

Maud. That was it, i'faith: why now, son,
I see you're a deep scholar:—and, master tutor,

[1] "Perhaps Tim alludes to some childish sport: a kind of cod generally salted, was called *haberdine.*"—*Dyce.*

[2] A common form of apology.

A word, I pray; let us withdraw a little
Into my husband's chamber; I'll send in
The North Wales gentlewoman to him, she looks for wooing:
I'll put together both, and lock the door.

Tutor. I give great approbation to your conclusion.
[*Exeunt* MAUDLIN *and* Tutor.

Tim. I mar'l[1] what this gentlewoman should be
That I should have in marriage; she's a stranger to me;
I wonder what my parents mean, i' faith,
To match me with a stranger so,
A maid that's neither kiff[2] nor kin to me:
'Life, do they think I've no more care of my body
Than to lie with one that I ne'er knew, a mere stranger,
One that ne'er went to school with me neither,
Nor ever play-fellows together?
They're mightily o'erseen in it, methinks.
They say she has mountains to her marriage,
She's full of cattle, some two thousand runts:
Now, what the meaning of these runts[3] should be,
My tutor cannot tell me; I have look'd
In Rider's Dictionary[4] for the letter R,
And there I can hear no tidings of these runts neither;
Unless they should be Romford hogs, I know them not.

Enter Welshwoman.

And here she comes. If I know what to say to her now
In the way of marriage, I'm no graduate:
Methinks, i'faith, 'tis boldly done of her
To come into my chamber, being but a stranger;
She shall not say I am so proud yet but
I'll speak to her; marry, as I will order it,
She shall take no hold of my words, I'll warrant her.
[Welshwoman *curtsies.*

[1] Marvel. [2] Kith. [3] Oxen of small size.
[4] The familiar Latin dictionary of the seventeenth century; it was first published in 1589.

She looks and makes a curtsy.—
Salve tu quoque, puella pulcherrima; quid vis nescio nec sane curo,—
Tully's own phrase to a heart.

Welsh. I know not what he means: a suitor, quoth'a?
I hold my life he understands no English. [*Aside.*

Tim. Fertur, mehercule, tu virgo, Walliâ ut opibus abundas maximis.

Welsh. What's this *fertur* and *abundundis?*
He mocks me sure, and calls me a bundle of farts.

Tim. I have no Latin word now for their runts;
I'll make some shift or other: [*Aside.*
Iterum dico, opibus abundas maximis, montibus, et fontibus et ut ita dicam rontibus; attamen vero homunculus ego sum natura, simul[1] *et arte baccalaureus, lecto profecto non parato.*

Welsh. This is most strange: may be he can speak Welsh.
Avedera whee comrage, der due cog foginis.

Tim. Cog foggin? I scorn to cog[2] with her; I'll tell her so too in a word near her own language,—*Ego non cogo.*

Welsh. Rhegosin a whiggin harle ron corid ambro.

Tim. By my faith, she's a good scholar, I see that already;
She has the tongues plain; I hold my life sh'as travelled:
What will folks say? there goes the learned couple!
Faith, if the truth were known, she hath proceeded.[3]

Re-enter MAUDLIN.

Maud. How now? how speeds your business?

Tim. I'm glad
My mother's come to part us. [*Aside.*

Maud. How do you agree, forsooth?

[1] "Old ed. 'simule . . . parata.' I am by no means satisfied with my alterations; indeed, I do not quite understand the drift of Tim's oration."—*Dyce.*

[2] Dissemble.

[3] Taken a degree.

Welsh. As well as e'er we did before we met.

Maud. How's that?

Welsh. You put me to a man I understand not:
Your son's no Englishman, methinks.

Maud. No Englishman?
Bless my boy, and born i' the heart of London!

Welsh. I ha' been long enough in the chamber with him,
And I find neither Welsh nor English in him.

Maud. Why, Tim, how have you used the gentlewoman?

Tim. As well as a man might do, mother, in modest Latin.

Maud. Latin, fool?

Tim. And she recoiled in Hebrew.

Maud. In Hebrew, fool? 'tis Welsh.

Tim. All comes to one, mother.

Maud. She can speak English too.

Tim. Who told me so much?
Heart, an she can speak English, I'll clap to her;
I thought you'd marry me to a stranger.

Maud. You must forgive him; he's so inured to Latin,
He and his tutor, that he hath quite forgot
To use the Protestant tongue.

Welsh. 'Tis quickly pardoned, forsooth.

Maud. Tim, make amends and kiss her.—
He makes towards you, forsooth. [*They kiss.*

Tim. O delicious!
One may discover her country by her kissing:
'Tis a true saying, there's nothing tastes so sweet
As your Welsh mutton.—'Twas reported you could sing.

Maud. O, rarely, Tim, the sweetest British songs!

Tim. And 'tis my mind, I swear, before I marry,
I would see all my wife's good parts at once,
To view how rich I were

Maud. Thou shalt hear sweet music, Tim.—
Pray, forsooth.

Welsh. [*sings.*] [1]

Cupid is Venus' only joy,
But he is a wanton boy,
A very, very wanton boy;
He shoots at ladies' naked breasts,
He is the cause of most men's crests,
I mean upon the forehead,
Invisible but horrid;
'Twas he first thought upon the way
To keep a lady's lips in play.

Why should not Venus chide her son
For the pranks that he hath done,
The wanton pranks that he hath done?
He shoots his fiery darts so thick,
They hurt poor ladies to the quick,
Ah me, with cruel wounding!
His darts are so confounding,
That life and sense would soon decay,
But that he keeps their lips in play.

Can there be any part of bliss
In a quickly fleeting kiss,
A quickly fleeting kiss?
To one's pleasure leisures are but waste,
The slowest kiss makes too much haste,
And lose it ere we find it:
The pleasing sport they only know
That close above and close below.

Tim. I would not change my wife for a kingdom: I can do somewhat too in my own lodging.

Enter YELLOWHAMMER *and* ALLWIT.

Yel. Why, well said, Tim! the bells go merrily; I love such peals a' life.[2]—Wife, lead them in awhile;

[1] "Old ed. 'Musicke and Welche Song,' the words probably being adapted to some Welsh air."—*Dyce.*

[2] As my life; *i.e.*, extremely.

Here's a strange gentleman desires private conference.—
[*Exeunt* MAUDLIN, Welshwoman, *and* TIM.
You're welcome, sir, the more for your name's sake,
Good Master Yellowhammer: I love my name well:
And which o' the Yellowhammers take you descent from,
If I may be so bold with you? which, I pray?

Allwit. The Yellowhammers in Oxfordshire, near Abingdon.

Yel. And those are the best Yellowhammers, and truest bred;
I came from thence myself, though now a citizen:
I will be bold with you; you are most welcome.

Allwit. I hope the zeal I bring with me shall deserve it.

Yel. I hope no less: what is your will, sir?

Allwit. I understand, by rumours, you've a daughter,
Which my bold love shall henceforth title cousin.

Yel. I thank you for her, sir.

Allwit. I heard of her virtues
And other confirmed graces.

Yel. A plaguy girl, sir!

Allwit. Fame sets her out with richer ornaments
Than you are pleased to boast of; 'tis done modestly:
I hear she's towards marriage.

Yel. You hear truth, sir.

Allwit. And with a knight in town, Sir Walter Whorehound.

Yel. The very same, sir.

Allwit. I'm the sorrier for't.

Yel. The sorrier? why, cousin?

Allwit. 'Tis not too far past, is't?
It may be yet recalled?

Yel. Recalled! why, good sir?

Allwit. Resolve[1] me in that point, ye shall hear from me.

[1] Satisfy.

Yel. There's no contract past.

Allwit. I'm very joyful, sir.

Yel. But he's the man must bed her.

Allwit. By no means, coz;
She's quite undone then, and you'll curse the time
That e'er you made the match; he's an arrant whoremaster,
Consumes his time and state——[1]
Whom in my knowledge he hath kept this seven years;
Nay, coz, another man's wife too.

Yel. O, abominable!

Allwit. Maintains the whole house, apparels the husband,
Pays servants' wages, not so much but——[2]

Yel. Worse and worse; and doth the husband know this?

Allwit. Knows? ay, and glad he may too, 'tis his living:
As other trades thrive, butchers by selling flesh,
Poulters by vending conies, or the like, coz.

Yel. What an incomparable wittol's[3] this!

Allwit. Tush, what cares he for that? believe me, coz,
No more than I do.

Yel. What a base slave's that!

Allwit. All's one to him; he feeds and takes his ease,
Was ne'er the man that ever broke his sleep
To get a child yet, by his own confession,
And yet his wife has seven.

Yel. What, by Sir Walter?

Allwit. Sir Walter's like to keep 'em and maintain 'em
In excellent fashion; he dares do no less, sir.

Yel. 'Life, has he children too?

Allwit. Children! boys thus high,
In their Cato and Corderius.[4]

[1] There is a similar blank in the old edition.
[2] *Ibid.*
[3] A complaisant cuckold.
[4] Two old schoolbooks.

Yel. What? you jest, sir?

Allwit. Why, one can make a verse, and now's at Eton College.

Yel. O, this news has cut into my heart, coz!

Allwit. 'Thad eaten nearer, if it had not been prevented:
One Allwit's wife.

Yel. Allwit! 'foot, I have heard of him;
He had a girl kursened lately?

Allwit. Ay, that work
Did cost the knight above a hundred mark.

Yel. I'll mark him for a knave and villain for't;
A thousand thanks and blessings! I have done with him.

Allwit. Ha, ha, ha! this knight will stick by my ribs still;
I shall not lose him yet; no wife will come;
Where'er he woos, I find him still at home:
Ha, ha! [*Aside, and exit.*

Yel. Well, grant all this, say now his deeds are black,
Pray, what serves marriage but to call him back;
I've kept a whore myself, and had a bastard
By Mistress Anne, in *anno*——
I care not who knows it; he's now a jolly fellow,
Has been twice warden; so may his fruit be,
They were but base begot, and so was he.
The knight is rich, he shall be my son-in-law;
No matter, so the whore he keeps be wholesome,
My daughter takes no hurt then; so let them wed:
I'll have him sweat well ere they go to bed.

Re-enter MAUDLIN.

Maud. O husband, husband!

Yel. How now, Maudlin?

Maud. We are all undone; she's gone, she's gone!

Yel. Again? death, which way?

[1] There is a similar blank in the old edition.

Maud. Over the houses: lay[1] the water-side,
She's gone for ever else.

Yel. O venturous baggage! [*Exeunt.*

SCENE II.

Another Room in YELLOWHAMMER'S *House.*

Enter TIM *and* Tutor *Severally.*

Tim. Thieves, thieves! my sisters stolen: some thief hath got her:
O how miraculously did my father's plate 'scape!
'Twas all left out, tutor.

Tutor. Is't possible?

Tim. Besides three chains of pearl and a box of coral.
My sister's gone; let's look at Trig-stairs for her;
My mother's gone to lay the common stairs
At Puddle-wharf; and at the dock below
Stands my poor silly father; run, sweet tutor, run!
[*Exeunt.*

SCENE III.

A Street by the Thames.

Enter TOUCHWOOD *senior and* TOUCHWOOD *junior.*

Touch. sen. I had been taken, brother, by eight sergeants,
But for the honest watermen; I'm bound to them;
They are the most requitefull'st people living,
For as they get their means by gentlemen,
They're still the forwardest to help gentlemen:

[1] Scour.

You heard how one 'scaped out of the Blackfriars,
But a while since, from two or three varlets came
Into the house with all their rapiers drawn,
As if they'd dance the sword-dance on the stage,
With candles in their hands, like chandlers' ghosts;
Whilst the poor gentleman so pursued and banded,
Was by an honest pair of oars safely landed.

Touch. jun. I love them with my heart for't!

Enter several Watermen.

1st W. Your first man, sir.

2nd W. Shall I carry you, gentlemen, with a pair of oars?

Touch. sen. These be the honest fellows: take one pair,
And leave the rest for her.

Touch. jun. Barn Elms.

Touch. sen. No more, brother. [*Exit.*

1st W. Your first man.

2nd W. Shall I carry your worship?

Touch. jun. Go; and you honest watermen that stay,
Here's a French crown for you [*gives money*]: there comes a maid
With all speed to take water, row her lustily
To Barn Elms after me.

2nd W. To Barn Elms, good sir.—
Make ready the boat, Sam; we'll wait below.
[*Exeunt* Watermen.

Enter MOLL.

Touch. jun. What made you stay so long?

Moll. I found the way more dangerous than I looked for.

Touch. jun. Away, quick; there's a boat waits for you; and I'll
Take water at Paul's wharf, and overtake you.

Moll. Good sir, do; we cannot be too safe. [*Exeunt.*

Enter Sir WALTER WHOREHOUND, YELLOWHAMMER, TIM, *and* Tutor.

Sir Wal. Life, call you this close keeping?
Yel. She was kept
Under a double lock.
Sir Wal. A double devil!
Tim. That's a buff sergeant, tutor; he'll ne'er wear out.
Yel. How would you have women locked?
Tim. With padlocks, father;
The Venetian uses it; my tutor reads it.
Sir Wal. Heart, if she were so locked up, how got she out?
Yel. There was a little hole looked into the gutter;
But who would have dreamt of that?
Sir Wal. A wiser man would.
Tim. He says true, father; a wise man for love
Will seek every hole; my tutor knows it.
Tutor. Verum poeta dicit.
Tim. Dicit Virgilius, father
Yel. Prithee, talk of thy gills [1] somewhere else; sh'as played
The gill with me: where's your wise mother now?
Tim. Run mad, I think; I thought she would have drowned herself;
She would not stay for oars, but took a smelt-boat;
Sure I think she be gone a-fishing for her.
Yel. She'll catch a goodly dish of gudgeons now,
Will serve us all to supper.

Enter MAUDLIN, *drawing in* MOLL *by the hair, and* Watermen.

Maud. I'll tug thee home by the hair.
1st W. Good mistress, spare her!
Maud. Tend your own business.
1st W. You're a cruel mother.

[*Exeunt* Watermen.

[1] Lewd women.

Moll. O, my heart dies!
Maud. I'll make thee an example
For all the neighbours' daughters.
Moll. Farewell, life!
Maud. You that have tricks can counterfeit.
Yel. Hold, hold, Maudlin!
Maud. I've brought your jewel by the hair.
Yel. She's here, knight.
Sir Wal. Forbear, or I'll grow worse.
Tim. Look on her, tutor;
She hath brought her from the water like a mermaid;
She's but half my sister now, as far as the flesh goes,
The rest may be sold to fishwives.
Maud. Dissembling, cunning baggage!
Yel. Impudent strumpet!
Sir Wal. Either give over, both, or I'll give over.—
Why have you used me thus unkindly, mistress?
Wherein have I deserved?
Yel. You talk too fondly, sir:
We'll take another course and prevent all:
We might have done't long since; we'll lose no time now,
Nor trust to't any longer: to-morrow morn,
As early as sunrise, we'll have you joined.
Moll. O, bring me death to-night, love-pitying fates;
Let me not see to-morrow up on the world!
Yel. Are you content, sir? till then she shall be watched.
Maud. Baggage, you shall.
Tim. Why, father, my tutor and I
Will both watch in armour.
[*Exeunt* MAUDLIN, MOLL, *and* YELLOWHAMMER.
Tutor. How shall we do for weapons?
Tim. Take you
No care for that; if need be, I can send
For conquering metal, tutor, ne'er lost day yet.
'Tis but at Westminster; I am acquainted
With him that keeps the monuments; I can borrow

Harry the Fifth's sword; it will serve us both
To watch with. [*Exeunt* TIM *and* Tutor.

Sir Wal. I never was so near my wish
As this chance makes me: ere to-morrow noon
I shall receive two thousand pound in gold,
And a sweet maidenhead worth forty.

Re-enter TOUCHWOOD *junior and* Waterman.

Touch. jun. O, thy news splits me!

Water. Half-drowned, she cruelly tugged her by the hair,
Forced her disgracefully, not like a mother.

Touch. jun. Enough; leave me, like my joys.— [*Exit* Waterman.
Sir, saw you not a wretched maid pass this way?
Heart, villain, is it thou?

Sir Wal. Yes, slave, 'tis I.

Touch. jun. I must break through thee then: there is no stop
That checks my tongue[1] and all my hopeful fortunes,
That breast excepted, and I must have way.

Sir Wal. Sir, I believe 'twill hold your life in play.

Touch. jun. Sir, you will gain the heart in my breast first.

Sir Wal. There is no dealing then; think on the dowry
For two thousand pounds. [*They fight.*

Touch. jun. O, now 'tis quit, sir.

Sir Wal. And being of even hand, I'll play no longer.

Touch. jun. No longer, slave?

Sir Wal. I've certain things to think on,
Before I dare go further.

Touch. jun. But one bout!
I'll follow thee to death, but ha' it out. [*Exeunt.*

[1] "*i.e.* Perhaps, suit—if it be not a misprint."—*Dyce.*

ACT THE FIFTH.

SCENE I.

A Room in ALLWIT'S *House.*

Enter ALLWIT, Mistress ALLWIT, *and* DAVY.

MIS. ALL. A misery of a house!

Allwit. What shall become of us!

Davy. I think his wound be mortal.

Allwit. Think'st thou so, Davy?
Then am I mortal too, but a dead man, Davy;
This is no world for me, whene'er he goes;
I must e'en truss up all, and after him, Davy;
A sheet with two knots, and away.

Davy. O see, sir!

Enter Sir WALTER WHOREHOUND *led in by two* Servants, *who place him in a chair.*

How faint he goes! two of my fellows lead him.

Mis. All. O me! [*Swoons.*

Allwit. Heyday, my wife's laid down too; here's like to be
A good house kept, when we're all together down:
Take pains with her, good Davy, cheer her up there;
Let me come to his worship, let me come.

Sir Wal. Touch me not, villain; my wound aches at thee,
Thou poison to my heart!

Allwit. He raves already;
His senses are quite gone, he knows me not.—

Look up, an't like your worship; heave those eyes,
Call me to mind; is your remembrance left?
Look in my face; who am I, an't like your worship?
Sir Wal. If anything be worse than slave or villain,
Thou art the man!
Allwit. Alas, his poor worship's weakness!
He will begin to know me by little and little.
Sir Wal. No devil can be like thee!
Allwit. Ah, poor gentleman.
Methinks the pain that thou endurest mads thee.
Sir Wal. Thou know'st me to be wicked; for thy baseness
Kept the eyes open still on all my sins;
None knew the dear account my soul stood charged with
So well as thou, yet, like hell's flattering angel,
Wouldst never tell me on't, lett'st me go on,
And join with death in sleep; that if I had not
Waked now by chance, even by a stranger's pity,
I had everlastingly slept out all hope
Of grace and mercy.
Allwit. Now he's worse and worse.
Wife, to him, wife; thou wast wont to do good on him.
Mis. All. How is it with you, sir?
Sir Wal. Not as with you,
Thou loathsome strumpet! Some good, pitying man
Remove my sins out of my sight a little;
I tremble to behold her, she keeps back
All comfort while she stays. Is this a time,
Unconscionable woman, to see thee?
Art thou so cruel to the peace of man,
Not to give liberty now? the devil himself
Shows a far fairer reverence and respect
To goodness than thyself; he dares not do this,
But parts in time of penitence, hides his face;
When man withdraws from him, he leaves the place:
Hast thou less manners and more impudence

Than thy instructor? prithee, show thy modesty,
If the least grain be left, and get thee from me:
Thou shouldst be rather locked many rooms hence
From the poor miserable sight of me,
If either love or grace had part in thee.

Mis. All. He's lost for ever! [*Aside.*

Allwit. Run, sweet Davy, quickly,
And fetch the children hither; sight of them
Will make him cheerful straight. [*Exit* DAVY.

Sir Wal. O death! is this
A place for you to weep? what tears are those!
Get you away with them, I shall fare the worse
As long as they're a-weeping, they work against me;
There's nothing but thy appetite in that sorrow,
Thou weep'st for lust; I feel it in the slackness
Of comforts coming towards me; I was well
Till thou began'st t' undo me: this shows like
The fruitless sorrow of a careless mother,
That brings her son with dalliance to the gallows,
And then stands by and weeps to see him suffer.

Re-enter DAVY *with* NICK, WAT, *and other children.*

Davy. There are the children, sir, an't like your worship,
Your last fine girl; in troth, she smiles;
Look, look, in faith, sir.

Sir Wal. O my vengeance!
Let me for ever hide my cursèd face
From sight of those that darken all my hopes,
And stand between me and the sight of Heaven!
Who sees me now—O, and those so near me,
May rightly say I am o'ergrown with sin.
O, how my offences wrestle with my repentance!
It hath scarce breath;
Still my adulterous guilt hovers aloft,
And with her black wings beats down all my prayers
Ere they be half-way up. What's he knows now

How long I have to live? O, what comes then?
My taste grows bitter; the round world all gall now;
Her pleasing pleasures now hath poisoned me,
Which I exchanged my soul for!
Make way a hundred sighs at once for me!

Allwit. Speak to him, Nick.

Nick. I dare not, I'm afraid.

Allwit. Tell him he hurts his wounds, Wat, with making moan.

Sir Wal. Wretched, death of seven! [1]

Allwit. Come let's be talking
Somewhat to keep him alive. Ah, sirrah Wat,
And did my lord bestow that jewel on thee
For an epistle thou mad'st in Latin? thou
Art a good forward boy, there's great joy on thee.

Sir Wal. O sorrow!

Allwit. Heart, will nothing comfort him?
If he be so far gone, 'tis time to moan. [*Aside.*
Here's pen and ink, and paper, and all things ready;
Will't please your worship for to make your will?

Sir Wal. My will! yes, yes, what else? who writes apace now?

Allwit. That can your man Davy, an't like your worship;
A fair, fast, legible hand.

Sir Wal. Set it down then. [DAVY *writes.*
Imprimis, I bequeath to yonder wittol
Three times his weight in curses.

Allwit. How!

Sir Wal. All plagues
Of body and of mind.

Allwit. Write them not down, Davy.

Davy. It is his will; I must.

Sir Wal. Together also
With such a sickness ten days ere his death.

[1] His seven children by Allwit's wife.

Allwit. There's a sweet legacy! I'm almost choked with't. [*Aside.*

Sir Wal. Next, I bequeath to that foul whore his wife
All barrenness of joy, a drouth of virtue,
And dearth of all repentance: for her end,
The common misery of an English strumpet,
In French and Dutch; beholding, ere she dies,
Confusion of her brats before her eyes,
And never shed a tear for't.

Enter 3rd Servant.

3rd Ser. Where's the knight?—
O sir, the gentleman you wounded is
Newly departed!

Sir Wal. Dead? lift, lift, who helps me?

Allwit. Let the law lift you now, that must have all;
I have done lifting on you, and my wife too.

3rd Ser. You were best lock yourself close.

Allwit. Not in my house, sir;
I'll harbour no such persons as men-slayers;
Lock yourself where you will.

Sir Wal. What's this?

Mis. All. Why, husband!

Allwit. I know what I do, wife.

Mis. All. You cannot tell yet;
For having killed the man in his defence,
Neither his life nor estate will be touched, husband.

Allwit. Away, wife! hear a fool! his lands will hang him.

Sir Wal. Am I denied a chamber?—What say you, forsooth?

Mis. All. Alas, sir, I am one that would have all well,
But must obey my husband.—Prithee, love,
Let the poor gentleman stay, being so sore wounded:
There's a close chamber at one end of the garret
We never use; let him have that, I prithee.

Allwit. We never use? you forgot sickness then,
And physic-times; is't not a place for easement?
Sir Wal. O, death! do I hear this with part
Of former life in me?—

Enter 4*th* Servant.

What's the news now?
4th Ser. Troth, worse and worse; you're like to lose your land,
If the law save your life, sir, or the surgeon.
Allwit. Hark you there, wife.
Sir Wal. Why, how, sir?
4th Ser. Sir Oliver Kix's wife is new quickened;
That child undoes you, sir.
Sir Wal. All ill at once!
Allwit. I wonder what he makes here with his consorts?
Cannot our house be private to ourselves,
But we must have such guests? I pray, depart, sirs,
And take your murderer along with you;
Good he were apprehended ere he go,
Has killed some honest gentleman; send for officers.
Sir Wal. I'll soon save you that labour.
Allwit. I must tell you, sir,
You have been somewhat bolder in my house
Than I could well like of; I suffered you
Till it stuck here at my heart; I tell you truly
I thought y'had been familiar with my wife once.
Mis. All. With me! I'll see him hanged first; I defy him,
And all such gentlemen in the like extremity.
Sir Wal. If ever eyes were open, these are they:
Gamesters, farewell, I've nothing left to play.
Allwit. And therefore get you gone, sir.
[*Exit* Sir WALTER, *led off by* Servants.
Davy. Of all wittols
Be thou the head—thou the grand whore of spittles!
[*Exit.*

Allwit. So, since he's like now to be rid of all,
I am right glad I'm so well rid of him.

Mis. All. I knew he durst not stay when you named officers.

Allwit. That stopped his spirits straight. What shall we do now, wife?

Mis. All. As we were wont to do.

Allwit. We're richly furnished, wife,
With household stuff.

Mis. All. Let's let out lodgings then,
And take a house in the Strand.

Allwit. In troth, a match, wench!
We're simply stocked with cloth-of-tissue cushions
To furnish out bay-windows; pish, what not
That's quaint and costly, from the top to the bottom;
Life, for furniture we may lodge a countess:
There's a close-stool of tawny velvet too,
Now I think on it, wife.

Mis. All. There's that should be, sir;
Your nose must be in everything.

Allwit. I've done, wench.
And let this stand in every gallant's chamber,—
There is no gamester like a politic sinner,
For whoe'er games, the box is sure a winner. [*Exeunt.*

SCENE II.

A Room in YELLOWHAMMER'S *House.*

Enter YELLOWHAMMER *and* MAUDLIN.

Maud. O husband, husband, she will die, she will die!
There is no sign but death.

Yel. 'Twill be our shame then.

Maud. O, how she's changed in compass of an hour!

Yel. Ah, my poor girl! good faith, thou wert too cruel
To drag her by the hair.
Maud. You'd have done as much, sir.
To curb her of her humour.
Yel. 'Tis curbed sweetly;
She catched her bane o' th' water.

Enter TIM.

Maud. How now, Tim?
Tim. Faith, busy, mother, about an epitaph
Upon my sister's death.
Maud. Death? she's not dead, I hope?
Tim. No, but she means to be, and that's as good,
And when a thing's done, 'tis done; you taught me that, mother.
Yel. What is your tutor doing?
Tim. Making one too, in principal pure Latin,
Culled out of Ovid *de Tristibus.*
Yel. How does your sister look? is she not changed?
Tim. Changed? gold into white money was ne'er so changed
As is my sister's colour into paleness.

Enter MOLL, *led in by* Servants, *who place her in a chair.*

Yel. O, here she's brought; see how she looks like death!
Tim. Looks she like death, and ne'er a word made yet?
I must go beat my brains against a bed-post,
And get before my tutor. [*Exit.*
Yel. Speak, how dost thou?
Moll. I hope I shall be well, for I'm as sick
At heart as I can be.
Yel. 'Las, my poor girl!
The doctor's making a most sovereign drink for thee,
The worst ingredience dissolved pearl and amber;
We spare no cost, girl.

Moll. Your love comes too late,
Yet timely thanks reward it. What is comfort,
When the poor patient's heart is past relief?
It is no doctor's art can cure my grief.

Yel. All is cast away, then;
Prithee, look upon me cheerfully.

Maud. Sing but a strain or two; thou wilt not think
How 'twill revive thy spirits; strive with thy fit,
Prithee, sweet Moll.

Moll. You shall have my good will, mother.

Maud. Why, well said, wench.

Moll. [*sings.*]

Weep eyes, break heart!
My love and I must part.
Cruel fates true love do soonest sever:
O, I shall see thee never, never, never!
O, happy is the maid whose life takes end
Ere it knows parent's frown or loss of friend!
Weep eyes, break heart!
My love and I must part.

Maud. O, I could die with music!—Well sung, girl.

Moll. If you call't so, it was.

Yel. She plays the swan,
And sings herself to death.

Enter TOUCHWOOD *senior.*

Touch. sen. By your leave, sir.

Yel. What are you, sir? or what's your business, pray?

Touch. sen. I may be now admitted, though the brother
Of him your hate pursued: it spreads no further.
Your malice sets in death, does it not, sir?

Yel. In death?

Touch. sen. He's dead: 'twas a dear love to him,
It cost him but his life, that was all, sir;
He paid enough, poor gentleman, for his love.

Yel. There's all our ill removed, if she were well now.— [*Aside.*
Impute not, sir, his end to any hate
That sprung from us; he had a fair wound brought that.

Touch. sen. That helped him forward, I must needs confess;
But the restraint of love, and your unkindness,
Those were the wounds that from his heart drew blood;
But being past help, let words forget it too:
Scarcely three minutes ere his eyelids closed,
And took eternal leave of this world's light,
He wrote this letter, which by oath he boun me
To give to her own hands; that's all my business.

Yel. You may perform it then; there she sits.

Touch. sen. O, with a following look!

Yel. Ay, trust me, sir,
I think she'll follow him quickly.

Touch. sen. Here's some gold
He willed me to distribute faithfully
Amongst your servants. [*Gives gold to* Servants.

Yel. 'Las, what doth he mean, sir?

Touch. sen. How cheer you, mistress?

Moll. I must learn of you, sir.

Touch. sen. Here is a letter from a friend of yours,
[*Giving letter to* MOLL.
And where that fails in satisfaction,
I have a sad tongue ready to supply.

Moll. How does he, ere I look on't?

Touch. sen. Seldom better;
Has a contented health now,

Moll. I'm most glad on't.

Maud. Dead, sir?

Yel. He is: now, wife, let's but get the girl
Upon her legs again, and to church roundly with her.

Moll. O, sick to death, he tells me: how does he after this?

Touch. sen. Faith, feels no pain at all; he's dead, sweet mistress.

Moll. Peace close mine eyes! [*Swoons.*

Yel. The girl! look to the girl, wife!

Maud. Moll, daughter, sweet girl, speak! look but once up,
Thou shalt have all the wishes of thy heart
That wealth can purchase!

Yel. O, she's gone for ever!
That letter broke her heart.

Touch. sen. As good now then
As let her lie in torment, and then break it.

Enter SUSAN.

Maud. O Susan, she thou lovedst so dear is gone!

Susan. O sweet maid!

Touch. sen. This is she that helped her still.—
I've a reward here for thee.

Yel. Take her in,
Remove her from my sight, our shame and sorrow.

Touch. sen. Stay, let me help thee, 'tis the last cold kindness
I can perform for my sweet brother's sake.

[*Exeunt* TOUCHWOOD *senior*, SUSAN, *and* Servants, *carrying out* MOLL.

Yel. All the whole street will hate us, and the world
Point me out cruel: it's our best course, wife,
After we've given order for the funeral,
T' absent ourselves till she be laid in ground.

Maud. Where shall we spend that time!

Yel. I'll tell thee where, wench:
Go to some private church, and marry Tim
To the rich Brecknock gentlewoman.

Maud. Mass, a match;
We'll not lose all at once, somewhat we'll catch.

[*Exeunt.*

SCENE III.

A Room in Sir OLIVER KIX'S *House.*

Enter Sir OLIVER KIX *and* Servants.

Sir Ol. Ho, my wife's quickened; I'm a man for ever!
I think I have bestirred my stumps, i'faith.
Run, get your fellows all together instantly,
Then to the parish church and ring the bells.

1st Ser. It shall be done, sir. [*Exit.*

Sir Ol. Upon my love
I charge you, villain, that you make a bonfire
Before the door at night.

2nd Ser. A bonfire, sir?

Sir Ol. A thwacking one, I charge you.

2nd Ser. This is monstrous. [*Aside, and exit.*

Sir Ol. Run, tell a hundred pound out for the gentleman
That gave my wife the drink, the first thing you do.

3rd Ser. A hundred pounds, sir?

Sir Ol. A bargain : as our joy grows,
We must remember still from whence it flows,
Or else we prove ungrateful multipliers :
[*Exit* 3rd Servant.
The child is coming, and the land comes after;
The news of this will make a poor Sir Walter :
I've strook it home, i'faith.

4th Ser. That you have, marry, sir;
But will not your worship go to the funeral
Of both these lovers?

Sir Ol. Both? go both together?

4th Ser. Ay, sir, the gentleman's brother will have it so :
'Twill be the pitifull'st sight! there is such running,
Such rumours, and such throngs, a pair of lovers

Had never more spectators, more men's pities,
Or women's wet eyes.

Sir Ol. My wife helps the number then.

4th Ser. There is such drawing out of handkerchers;
And those that have no handkerchers lift up aprons.

Sir Ol. Her parents may have joyful hearts at this:
I would not have my cruelty so talked on
To any child of mine for a monopoly.

4th Ser. I believe you, sir.
Tis cast[1] so, too, that both their coffins meet,
Which will be lamentable.

Sir Ol. Come, we'll see't. [*Exeunt.*

SCENE IV.

Near a Church.

Recorders[2] *dolefully playing, enter at one door the coffin of* TOUCHWOOD *junior, solemnly decked, his sword upon it, attended by many gentlemen in black, among whom are* Sir OLIVER KIX, ALLWIT, *and* Parson, TOUCHWOOD *senior being the chief mourner: at the other door the coffin of* MOLL, *adorned with a garland of flowers, and epitaphs pinned on it, attended by many matrons and maids, among whom are* Lady KIX, Mistress ALLWIT, *and* SUSAN; *the coffins are set down, one right over against the other; and while all the company seem to weep and mourn, there is a sad song in the music-room.*[3]

Touch. sen. Never could death boast of a richer prize
From the first parent; let the world bring forth
A pair of truer hearts. To speak but truth

[1] Contrived. [2] Flageolets.
[3] Collier suggests that one of the boxes of the theatre was appropriated to the musicians.

Of this departed gentleman, in a brother
Might, by hard censure, be called flattery,
Which makes me rather silent in his right
Than so to be delivered to the thoughts
Of any envious hearer, starved in virtue,
And therefore pining to hear others thrive;
But for this maid, whom envy cannot hurt
With all her poisons, having left to ages
The true, chaste monument of her living name,
Which no time can deface, I say of her
The full truth freely, without fear of censure:
What nature could there shrine, that might redeem
Perfection home to woman, but in her
Was fully glorious? beauty set in goodness
Speaks what she was; that jewel so infixed,
There was no want of anything of life
To make these virtuous precedents man and wife,

Allwit. Great pity of their deaths!

1st Mour. Never more pity!

Lady Kix. It makes a hundred weeping eyes, sweet gossip.

Touch sen. I cannot think there's any one amongst you
In this full fair assembly, maid, man, or wife,
Whose heart would not have sprung with joy and gladness
To have seen their marriage-day.

2nd Mour. It would have made
A thousand joyful hearts.

Touch. sen. Up then apace,
And take your fortunes, make these joyful hearts;
Here's none but friends.

[MOLL *and* TOUCHWOOD *junior rise out of their coffins.*

All. Alive, sir? O sweet, dear couple!

Touch. sen. Nay, do not hinder 'em now, stand from about 'em;
If she be caught again, and have this time,

I'll ne'er plot further for 'em, nor this honest chamber-maid,
That helped all at a push.

Touch. jun. Good sir, apace.

Parson. Hands join now, but hearts for ever,
[MOLL *and* TOUCHWOOD *junior join hands.*
Which no parent's mood shall sever.
You shall forsake all widows, wives, and maids—
You lords, knights, gentlemen, and men of trades;—
And if in haste any article misses,
Go interline it with a brace of kisses.

Touch. sen. Here's a thing trolled nimbly.—Give you joy, brother;
Were't not better thou shouldst have her than the maid should die?

Mis. All. To you, sweet mistress bride.

All. Joy, joy to you both.

Touch. sen. Here be your wedding-sheets you brought along with you;
You may both go to bed when you please too.

Touch jun. My joy wants utterance.

Touch. sen. Utter all at night
Then, brother.

Moll. I am silent with delight.

Touch. sen. Sister, delight will silence any woman;
But you'll find your tongue again 'mong maid servants,
Now you keep house, sister.

2nd Mour. Never was hour so filled with joy and wonder.

Touch. sen. To tell you the full story of this chamber-maid,
And of her kindness in this business to us,
'Twould ask an hour's discourse; in brief, 'twas she
That wrought it to this purpose cunningly.

3rd Mour. We shall all love her for't.

4th Mour. See, who comes here now

Enter YELLOWHAMMER *and* MAUDLIN.

Touch. sen. A storm, a storm! but we are sheltered for it.

Yel. I will prevent[1] you all, and mock you thus,
You and your expectations; I stand happy,
Both in your lives, and your hearts' combination.

Touch. sen. Here's a strange day again!

Yel. The knight's proved villain;
All's come out now, his niece an arrant baggage;
My poor boy Tim is cast away this morning,
Even before breakfast, married a whore
Next to his heart.

Mourners. A whore!

Yel. His niece, forsooth.

Allwit. I think we rid our hands in good time of him.

Mis. All. I knew he was past the best when I gave him over,—
What is become of him, pray, sir?

Yel. Who, the knight?
He lies i' th' Knights' ward;[2]—now your belly, lady,
[*To* Lady KIX.
Begins to blossom, there's no peace for him,
His creditors are so greedy.

Sir Ol. Master Touchwood,
Hear'st thou this news? I'm so endeared to thee
For my wife's fruitfulness, that I charge you both,
Your wife and thee, to live no more asunder
For the world's frowns; I've purse, and bed, and board for you:
Be not afraid to go to your business roundly;
Get children, and I'll keep them.

Touch. sen. Say you so, sir?

Sir Ol. Prove me with three at a birth, an thou dar'st now.

[1] Anticipate.
[2] A ward in the prison.

Touch. sen. Take heed how you dare a man, while you live, sir,
That has good skill at his weapon.
Sir Ol. 'Foot, I dare you, sir!

Enter TIM, Welshwoman, *and* Tutor.

Yel. Look, gentlemen, if e'er you saw the picture
Of the unfortunate marriage, yonder 'tis.
Welsh. Nay, good sweet Tim——
Tim. Come from the university
To marry a whore in London, with my tutor too!
O tempora! O mores!
Tutor. Prithee, Tim, be patient.
Tim. I bought a jade at Cambridge;
I'll let her out to execution, tutor,
For eighteenpence a-day, or Brainford[1] horse-races;
She'll serve to carry seven miles out of town well.
Where be these mountains? I was promised mountains
But there's such a mist, I can see none of 'em.
What are become of those two thousand runts?
Let's have a bout with them in the meantime;
A vengeance runt thee!
Maud. Good sweet Tim, have patience.
Tim. Flectere[2] si nequeo superos, Acheronta movebo, mother.
Maud. I think you have married her in logic, Tim.
You told me once by logic you would prove
A whore an honest woman; prove her so, Tim,
And take her for thy labour.
Tim. Troth, I thank you:
I grant you, I may prove another man's wife so,
But not mine own.
Maud. There's no remedy now, Tim;
You must prove her so as well as you may.
Tim. Why then

[1] Brentford. [2] Virg. *Æn.* vii. 312.

My tutor and I will about her as well as we can:
Uxor non est meretrix ergo falleris.

Welsh. Sir, if your logic cannot prove me honest,
There's a thing called marriage, and that makes me honest.

Maud. O, there's a trick beyond your logic, Tim!

Tim. I perceive then a woman may be honest
According to the English print, when she's
A whore in the Latin; so much for marriage and logic:
I'll love her for her wit, I'll pick out my runts there;
And for my mountains, I'll mount upon——[1]

Yel. So fortune seldom deals two marriages
With one hand, and both lucky; the best is,
One feast will serve them both: marry, for room,
I'll have the dinner kept in Goldsmiths' Hall,
To which, kind gallants, I invite you all.

[*Exeunt.*

[1] There is a similar blank in the old edition.

WOMEN BEWARE WOMEN.

THE tragedy of *Women beware Women* was not published till 1657, thirty years after Middleton's death. It appeared with *More Dissemblers besides Women*, in a volume entitled *Two New Playes*.

The following address, by Humphrey Moseley, the publisher, is prefixed to the volume:

"TO THE READER.

"When these amongst others of Mr. Thomas Middleton's excellent poems came to my hands, I was not a little confident but that his name would prove as great an inducement for thee to read as me to print them; since those issues of his brain that have already seen the sun have by their worth gained themselves a free entertainment amongst all that are ingenious: and I am most certain that these will no way lessen his reputation nor hinder his admission to any noble and recreative spirits. All that I require at thy hands is to continue the author in his deserved esteem, and to accept of my endeavours, which have ever been to please thee. Farewell."

Middleton was indebted to a novel called *Hyppolito and Isabella*, translated in 1628.

UPON THE TRAGEDY OF MY FAMILIAR ACQUAINTANCE, THO. MIDDLETON.

Women beware Women; 'tis a true text
Never to be forgot; drabs of state vext
Have plots, poisons, mischiefs that seldom miss,
To murder virtue with a venom-kiss.
Witness this worthy tragedy, exprest
By him that well deserved among the best
Of poets in his time: he knew the rage,
Madness of women crossed, and for the stage
Fitted their humours; hell-bred malice, strife
Acted in state, presented to the life.
I that have seen't can say, having just cause,
Never came tragedy off with more applause.

NATH. RICHARDS.[1]

[1] Richards, who belonged to Caius College, Cambridge, wrote the tragedy of *Messalina, the Roman Empress*, 1640, and *Poems, Sacred and Satyricall*, 1641.

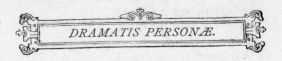

DRAMATIS PERSONÆ.

DUKE OF FLORENCE.
LORD CARDINAL, brother of the Duke.
FABRICIO, father of Isabella.
HIPPOLITO, brother of Fabricio.
GUARDIANO, uncle of the Ward.
The Ward, a rich young heir.
LEANTIO, a factor,[1] husband of Bianca.
SORDIDO, servant of the Ward.
Cardinals, Knights, States[2] of Florence, Citizens, &c.

LIVIA, sister of Fabricio and Hippolito.
ISABELLA, daughter of Fabricio
BIANCA, wife of Leantio.
Mother of Leantio.
Ladies.

SCENE—FLORENCE.

[1] A merchant's agent or clerk. [2] Nobles.

WOMEN BEWARE WOMEN.

ACT THE FIRST.

SCENE I.

An outer Room in the House of LEANTIO's Mother.

Enter LEANTIO, BIANCA, *and* Mother.

MOTH. Thy sight was never yet more precious to me;
Welcome with all th' affection of a mother,
That comfort can express from natural love!
Since thy birth-joy—a mother's chiefest gladness,
After sh'as undergone her curse of sorrows—
Thou wast not more dear to me than this hour
Presents thee to my heart: welcome again!

Lean. 'Las, poor affectionate soul, how her joys speak to me!
I have observ'd it often, and I know it is
The fortune commonly of knavish children
To have the lovings't mothers. [*Aside.*

Moth. What's this gentlewoman?

Lean. O, you have named the most unvaluedst[1] purchase
That youth of man had ever knowledge of!
As often as I look upon that treasure,
And know it to be mine—there lies the blessing—
It joys me that I ever was ordained
To have a being, and to live 'mongst men;
Which is a fearful living, and a poor one,
Let a man truly think on't:
To have the toil and griefs of fourscore years
Put up in a white sheet, tied with two knots;
Methinks it should strike earthquakes in adulterers,
When even the very sheets they commit sin in
May prove, for aught they know, all their last garments.
O what a mark were there for women then!
But beauty, able to content a conqueror
Whom earth could scarce content, keeps me in compass:
I find no wish in me bent sinfully
To this man's sister, or to that man's wife;
In love's name let 'em keep their honesties,
And cleave to their own husbands,—'tis their duties:
Now when I go to church I can pray handsomely,
Nor come like gallants only to see faces,
As if lust went to market still on Sundays.
I must confess I'm guilty of one sin, mother,
More than I brought into the world with me,
But that I glory in; 'tis theft, but noble
As ever greatness yet shot up withal.

Moth. How's that?

Lean. Never to be repented, mother,
Though sin be death; I had died, if I had not sinned;
And here's my masterpiece; do you now behold her!
Look on her well, she's mine; look on her better;
Now say if't be not the best piece of theft
That ever was committed? and I've my pardon for't,—
'Tis sealed from Heaven by marriage.

[1] Most invaluable.

Moth. Married to her!

Lean. You must keep counsel, mother, I'm undone else;
If it be known, I've lost her; do but think now
What that loss is,—life's but a trifle to't.
From Venice, her consent and I have brought her
From parents great in wealth, more now in rage;
But let storms spend their furies; now we've got
A shelter o'er our quiet innocent loves,
We are contented: little money sh'as brought me;
View but her face, you may see all her dowry,
Save that which lies locked up in hidden virtues,
Like jewels kept in cabinets.

Moth. You're to blame,
If your obedience will give way to a check,
To wrong such a perfection.

Lean. How?

Moth. Such a creature,
To draw her from her fortune, which, no doubt,
At the full time might have proved rich and noble;
You know not what you've done; my life can give you
But little helps, and my death lesser hopes;
And hitherto your own means has but made shift
To keep you single, and that hardly too:
What ableness have you to do her right then
In maintenance fitting her birth and virtues?
Which every woman of necessity looks for,
And most to go above it, not confined
By their conditions, virtues, bloods, or births,
But flowing to affections, wills, and humours.

Lean. Speak low, sweet mother; you're able to spoil as many
As come within the hearing; if it be not
Your fortune to mar all, I have much marvel.
I pray do not you teach her to rebel,
When she is in a good way to obedience;
To rise with other women in commotion

Against their husbands for six gowns a-year,
And so maintain their cause, when they're once up,
In all things else that require cost enough.
They're all of 'em a kind of spirits soon raised,
But not so soon laid, mother ; as, for example,
A woman's belly is got up in a trice,—
A simple charge ere't be laid down again :
So ever in all their quarrels and their courses ;
And I'm a proud man I hear nothing of 'em,
They're very still, I thank my happiness,
And sound asleep, pray let not your tongue wake 'em
If you can but rest quiet, she's contented
With all conditions that my fortunes bring her to ;
To keep close, as a wife that loves her husband ;
To go after the rate of my ability,
Not the licentious swing of her own will,
Like some of her old school-fellows ; she intends
To take out other works in a new sampler,
And frame the fashion of an honest love,
Which knows no wants, but, mocking poverty,
Brings forth more children, to make rich men wonder
At divine providence, that feeds mouths of infants,
And sends them none to feed, but stuffs their rooms
With fruitful bags, their beds with barren wombs.
Good mother, make not you things worse than they are
Out of your too much openness ; pray take heed on't,
Nor imitate the envy of old people,
That strive to mar good sport because they're perfect :
I would have you more pitiful to youth,
Especially to your own flesh and blood.
I'll prove an excellent husband, here's my hand,
Lay in provision, follow my business roundly,
And make you a grandmother in forty weeks.
Go, pray salute her, bid her welcome cheerfully.

Moth. [*kissing* BIANCA]. Gentlewoman, thus much is a debt of courtesy,
Which fashionable strangers pay each other

At a kind meeting: then there's more than one
Due to the knowledge I have of your nearness;
I'm bold to come again, and now salute you
By the name of daughter, which may challenge more
Than ordinary respect.

Lean. Why, this is well now,
And I think few mothers of threescore will mend it.
[*Aside.*

Moth. What I can bid you welcome to, is mean,
But make it all your own; we're full of wants,
And cannot welcome worth.

Lean. Now this is scurvy,
And spoke as if a woman lacked her teeth;
These old folks talk of nothing but defects,
Because they grow so full of 'em themselves. [*Aside.*

Bian. Kind mother, there is nothing can be wanting
To her that does enjoy all her desires:
Heaven send a quiet peace with this man's love,
And I'm as rich as virtue can be poor,
Which were enough after the rate of mind
To erect temples for content placed here.
I have forsook friends, fortunes, and my country,
And hourly I rejoice in't. Here's my friends,
And few is the good number.—Thy successes,
Howe'er they look, I will still name my fortunes;
Hopeful or spiteful, they shall all be welcome:
Who invites many guests has of all sorts,
As he that traffics much drinks of all fortunes,
Yet they must all be welcome, and used well.
I'll call this place the place of my birth now,
And rightly too, for here my love was born,
And that's the birthday of a woman's joys.
You have not bid me welcome since I came.

Lean. That I did questionless.

Bian. No, sure—how was't?
I've quite forgot it.

Lean. Thus. [*Kisses her.*

Bian. O, sir, 'tis true,
Now I remember well; I've done thee wrong,
Pray take 't again, sir. [*Kisses him.*
Lean. How many of these wrongs
Could I put up in an hour, and turn up the glass
For twice as many more!
Moth. Will't please you to walk in, daughter?
Bian. Thanks, sweet mother;
The voice of her that bare me is not more pleasing.
[*Exit with* Mother.
Lean. Though my own care and my rich master's trust
Lay their commands both on my factorship,
This day and night I'll know no other business
But her and her dear welcome. 'Tis bitterness
To think upon to-morrow! that I must leave
Her still to the sweet hopes of the week's end;
That pleasure should be so restrained and curbed
After the course of a rich work-master,
That never pays till Saturday night! marry,
It comes together in a round sum then,
And does more good, you'll say. O fair-eyed Florence,
Didst thou but know what a most matchless jewel
Thou now art mistress of, a pride would take thee,
Able to shoot destruction through the bloods
Of all thy youthful sons! but 'tis great policy
To keep choice treasures in obscurest places;
Should we show thieves our wealth, 'twould make 'em bolder;
Temptation is a devil will not stick
To fasten upon a saint; take heed of that:
The jewel is cased up from all men's eyes;
Who could imagine now a gem were kept
Of that great value under this plain roof?
But how in times of absence? what assurance
Of this restraint then? Yes, yes, there's one with her:
Old mothers know the world; and such as these,
When sons lock chests, are good to look to keys. [*Exit.*

SCENE II.

A Garden attached to FABRICIO'S *House.*

Enter GUARDIANO, FABRICIO, *and* LIVIA.

Guar. What, has your daughter seen him yet? know you that?

Fab. No matter, she shall love him.

Guar. Nay, let's have fair play;
He has been now my ward some fifteen year,
And 'tis my purpose, as time calls upon me,
By custom seconded and such moral virtues,
To tender him a wife. Now, sir, this wife
I'd fain elect out of a daughter of yours;
You see my meaning's fair: if now this daughter
So tendered,—let me come to your own phrase, sir,—
Should offer to refuse him, I were hanselled.—
Thus am I fain to calculate all my words
For the meridian of a foolish old man,
To take his understanding. [*Aside.*]—What do you answer, sir?

Fab. I say still, she shall love him.

Guar. Yet again?
And shall she have no reason for this love?

Fab. Why, do you think that women love with reason?

Guar. I perceive fools are not at all hours foolish,
No more than wise men wise. [*Aside.*

Fab. I had a wife,
She ran mad for me! she had no reason for't,
For aught I could perceive.—What think you, lady sister?

Guar. 'Twas a fit match that, being both out of their wits;
A loving wife, it seemed
She strove to come as near you as she could. [*Aside.*

Fab. And if her daughter prove not mad for love too,

She takes not after her ; nor after me,
If she prefer reason before my pleasure.—
You're an experienced widow, lady sister,
I pray, let your opinion come amongst us.
Liv. I must offend you then, if truth will do't,
And take my niece's part, and call't injustice
To force her love to one she never saw :
Maids should both see and like, all little enough ;
If they love truly after that, 'tis well.
Counting the time, she takes one man till death ;
That's a hard task, I tell you ; but one may
Inquire at three years' end amongst young wives,
And mark how the game goes.
Fab. Why, is not man
Tied to the same observance, lady sister,
And in one woman ?
Liv. 'Tis enough for him ;
Besides, he tastes of many sundry dishes
That we poor wretches never lay our lips to,
As obedience forsooth, subjection, duty, and such kick-
shaws,
All of our making, but served in to them ;
And if we lick a finger then sometimes,
We're not to blame, your best cooks often use it.
Fab. Thou'rt a sweet lady sister and a witty.
Liv. A witty ! O the bud of commendation,
Fit for a girl of sixteen ! I am blown, man ;
I should be wise by this time ; and, for instance,
I've buried my two husbands in good fashion,
And never mean more to marry.
Guar. No ! why so, lady ?
Liv. Because the third shall never bury me :
I think I'm more than witty. How think you, sir ?
Fab. I have paid often fees to a counsellor
Has had a weaker brain.
Liv. Then I must tell you
Your money was soon parted.

Guar. Like enow.[1]
Liv. Where is my niece? let her be sent for straight,
If you have any hope 'twill prove a wedding;
'Tis fit, i'faith, she should have one sight of him
And stop upon't, and not be joined in haste,
As if they went to stock a new-found land.
Fab. Look out her uncle, and you're sure of her,
Those two are ne'er asunder; they've been heard
In argument at midnight; moonshine nights
Are noondays with them; they walk out their sleeps,
Or rather at those hours appear like those
That walk in 'em, for so they did to me.
Look you, I told you truth; they're like a chain,
Draw but one link, all follows.

Enter HIPPOLITO *and* ISABELLA.

Guar. O affinity,
What piece of excellent workmanship art thou!
'Tis work clean wrought, for there's no lust but love in't,
And that abundantly; when in stranger things
There is no love at all but what lust brings.
Fab. On with your mask! for 'tis your part to see now,
And not be seen: go to, make use of your time;
See what you mean to like; nay, and I charge you,
Like what you see: do you hear me? there's no dallying;
The gentleman's almost twenty, and 'tis time
He were getting lawful heirs, and you a-breeding on 'em.
Isa. Good father——
Fab. Tell not me of tongues and rumours:
You'll say the gentleman is somewhat simple;
The better for a husband, were you wise,
For those that marry fools live ladies' lives.

[1] In the old edition: "Light her now, brother," which is evidently corrupt. "Like enow" was suggested by Bullen; it is difficult to account for "brother," it cannot well be fitted into the following line.

On with the mask! I'll hear no more: he's rich;
The fool's hid under bushels.
Liv. Not so hid neither
But here's a foul great piece of him, methinks;
What will he be when he comes altogether?

Enter the Ward *with a trap-stick, and* Sordido.

Ward. Beat him?
I beat him out o' the field with his own cat-stick,
Yet gave him the first hand.
Sor. O strange!
Ward. I did it;
Then he set jacks[1] on me.
Sor. What, my lady's tailor?
Ward. Ay, and I beat him too.
Sor. Nay, that's no wonder,
He's used to beating.
Ward. Nay, I tickled him
When I came once to my tippings.
Sor. Now you talk on 'em,
There was a poulterer's wife made a great complaint
Of you last night to your guardianer, that you struck
A bump in her child's head as big as an egg.
Ward. An egg may prove a chicken, then in time
The poulterer's wife will get by't: when I am
In game, I'm furious; came my mother's eyes
In my way, I would not lose a fair end; no,
Were she alive, but with one tooth in her head,
I should venture the striking out of that:
I think of nobody when I'm in play,
I am so earnest. Coads me, my guardianer!
Prithee, lay up my cat and cat-stick[2] safe.
Sor. Where, sir? i' the chimney-corner?
Ward. Chimney-corner!
Sor. Yes, sir; your cats are always safe i' the chimney-corner,
Unless they burn their coats.

[1] Fellows.

[2] Referring to the game of tip-cat.

Ward. Marry, that I am afraid on!

Sor. Why, then, I will bestow your cat i' the gutter,
And there she's safe, I'm sure.

Ward. If I but live
To keep a house, I'll make thee a great man,
If meat and drink can do't. I can stoop gallantly,
And pitch out when I list; I'm dog at a hole:
I mar'l[1] my guardianer does not seek a wife for me;
I protest I'll have a bout with the maids else,
Or contract myself at midnight to the larder-woman,
In presence of a fool[2] or a sack-posset.

Guar. Ward!

Ward. I feel myself after any exercise
Horribly prone: let me but ride, I'm lusty;
A cock-horse, straight, i'faith!

Guar. Why, ward, I say!

Ward. I'll forswear eating eggs in moonshine nights;
There's ne'er a one I eat but turns into a cock
In four-and-twenty hours: if my hot blood
Be not took down in time, sure 'twill crow shortly.

Guar. Do you hear, sir? follow me, I must new-school you.

Ward. School me? I scorn that now, I am past schooling:
I'm not so base to learn to write and read;
I was born to better fortunes in my cradle.

[*Exeunt* GUARDIANO, *the* Ward, *and* SORDIDO.

Fab. How do you like him, girl? this is your husband:
Like him, or like him not, wench, you shall have him,
And you shall love him.

Liv. O, soft there, brother! though you be a justice
Your warrant cannot be served out of your liberty;
You may compel, out of the power of father,
Things merely harsh to a maid's flesh and blood;

[1] Marvel.

[2] "A play on the words *fool* and *fowl* is intended. Cf. 3 *Henry VI.*, v. 6, ll. 18–20."—*Bullen.*

But when you come to love, there the soil alters,
You're in another country, where your laws
Are no more set by than the cacklings of geese
In Rome's great Capitol.

Fab. Marry him she shall then,
Let her agree upon love afterwards. [*Exit.*

Liv. You speak now, brother, like an honest mortal
That walks upon th' earth with a staff; you were up
I' the clouds before; you would command love,
And so do most old folks that go without it.—
My best and dearest brother, I could dwell here;
There is not such another seat on earth,
Where all good parts better express themselves.

Hip. You'll make me blush anon.

Liv. 'Tis but like saying grace before a feast then,
And that's most comely; thou art all a feast,
And she that has thee a most happy guest.
Prithee, cheer up thy niece with special counsel. [*Exit.*

Hip. I would 'twere fit to speak to her what I would; but
'Twas not a thing ordained, Heaven has forbid it;
And 'tis most meet that I should rather perish
Than the decree divine receive least blemish.
Feed inward, you my sorrows, make no noise,
Consume me silent, let me be stark dead
Ere the world know I'm sick. You see my honesty;
If you befriend me, so. [*Aside.*

Isa. Marry a fool!
Can there be greater misery to a woman
That means to keep her days true to her husband,
And know no other man? so virtue wills it.
Why, how can I obey and honour him,
But I must needs commit idolatry?
A fool is but the image of a man,
And that but ill made neither. O the heartbreakings
Of miserable maids, where love's enforced!
The best condition is but bad enough;

When women have their choices, commonly
They do but buy their thraldoms, and bring great portions
To men to keep 'em in subjection ;
As if a fearful prisoner should bribe
The keeper to be good to him, yet lies in still,
And glad of a good usage, a good look sometimes.
By'r lady, no misery surmounts a woman's ;
Men buy their slaves, but women buy their masters
Yet honesty and love makes all this happy,
And, next to angels', the most blessed estate.
That providence, that has made every poison
Good for some use, and sets four warring elements
At peace in man, can make a harmony
In things that are most strange to human reason.
O, but this marriage ! [*Aside.*]—What are you sad too, uncle ?
Faith, then there's a whole household down together :
Where shall I go to seek my comfort now,
When my best friend's distressed ? what is't afflicts you, sir ?

Hip. Faith, nothing but one grief, that will not leave me,
And now 'tis welcome ; every man has something
To bring him to his end, and this will serve,
Joined with your father's cruelty to you,—
That helps it forward.

Isa. O, be cheered, sweet uncle !
How long has 't been upon you ? I ne'er spied it ;
What a dull sight have I ! how long, I pray, sir ?

Hip. Since I first saw you, niece, and left Bologna.

Isa. And could you deal so unkindly with my heart,
To keep it up so long hid from my pity ?
Alas ! how shall I trust your love hereafter ?
Have we passed through so many arguments,
And missed of that still, the most needful one ?
Walked out whole nights together in discourses,

And the main point forgot? we're to blame both;
This is an obstinate, wilful forgetfulness,
And faulty on both parts: let's lose no time now;
Begin, good uncle, you that feel 't; what is it?

Hip. You of all creatures, niece, must never hear on't,
'Tis not a thing ordained for you to know.

Isa. Not I, sir? all my joys that word cuts off;
You made profession once you loved me best;
'Twas but profession.

Hip. Yes, I do't too truly,
And fear I shall be chid for't. Know the worst then;
I love thee dearlier than an uncle can.

Isa. Why, so you ever said, and I believed it.

Hip. So simple is the goodness of her thoughts,
They understand not yet th' unhallowed language
Of a near sinner; I must yet be forced,
Though blushes be my venture, to come nearer.— [*Aside.*
As a man loves his wife, so love I thee.

Isa. What's that?
Methought I heard ill news come toward me,
Which commonly we understand too soon,
Then over-quick at hearing; I'll prevent it,
Though my joys fare the harder, welcome it:
It shall ne'er come so near mine ear again.
Farewell all friendly solaces and discourses;
I'll learn to live without ye, for your dangers
Are greater than your comforts. What's become
Of truth in love, if such we cannot trust,
When blood, that should be love, is mixed with lust? [*Exit.*

Hip. The worst can be but death, and let it come;
He that lives joyless, every day's his doom. [*Exit.*

SCENE III.

Street before the House of LEANTIO's Mother.

Enter LEANTIO.

Lean. Methinks I'm even as dull now at departure,
As men observe great gallants the next day
After a revel; you shall see 'em look
Much of my fashion, if you mark 'em well.
'Tis even a second hell to part from pleasure
When man has got a smack on't: as many holydays
Coming together makes your poor heads idle
A great while after, and are said to stick
Fast in their fingers' ends,—even so does game
In a new-married couple; for the time
It spoils all thrift, and indeed lies a-bed
'T invent all the new ways for great expenses.
[BIANCA *and* MOTHER *appear above.*
See an she be not got on purpose now
Into the window to look after me!
I've no power to go now, an I should be hanged;
Farewell all business; I desire no more
Than I see yonder: let the goods at key[1]
Look to themselves; why should I toil my youth out?
It is but begging two or three year sooner,
And stay with her continually: is't a match?
O, fie, what a religion have I leaped into!
Get out again, for shame! the man loves best
When his care's most, that shows his zeal to love:
Fondness is but the idiot to affection,
That plays at hot-cockles with rich merchants' wives,
Good to make sport withal when the chest's full,
And the long warehouse cracks. 'Tis time of day
For us to be more wise; 'tis early with us;
And if they lose the morning of their affairs,
They commonly lose the best part of the day:

[1] Quay.

Those that are wealthy, and have got enough,
'Tis after sunset with 'em; they may rest,
Grow fat with ease, banquet, and toy, and play,
When such as I enter the heat o' the day,
And I'll do't cheerfully.

Bian. I perceive, sir,
You're not gone yet; I've good hope you'll stay now.

Lean. Farewell; I must not.

Bian. Come, come, pray return;
To-morrow, adding but a little care more,
Will despatch all as well; believe me 'twill, sir,

Lean. I could well wish myself where you would have me;
But love that's wanton must be ruled awhile
By that that's careful, or all goes to ruin:
As fitting is a government in love
As in a kingdom; where 'tis all mere lust,
'Tis like an insurrection in the people,
That raised in self-will, wars against all reason;
But love that is respective for increase
Is like a good king, that keeps all in peace.
Once more, farewell.

Bian. But this one night, I prithee!

Lean. Alas, I'm in for twenty, if I stay,
And then for forty more! I've such luck to flesh,
I never bought a horse but he bore double.
If I stay any longer, I shall turn
An everlasting spendthrift: as you love
To be maintained well, do not call me again,
For then I shall not care which end goes forward.
Again, farewell to thee.

Bian. Since it must, farewell too. [*Exit* LEANTIO.

Moth. Faith, daughter, you're to blame; you take the course
To make him an ill husband, troth you do;
And that disease is catching, I can tell you,
Ay, and soon taken by a young man 's blood,
And that with little urging. Nay, fie, see now,

What cause have you to weep? would I had no more,
That have lived threescore years! there were a cause,
An 'twere well thought on. Trust me, you're to blame;
His absence cannot last five days at utmost:
Why should those tears be fetched forth? cannot love
Be even as well expressed in a good look,
But it must see her face still in a fountain?
It shows like a country maid dressing her head
By a dish of water: come, 'tis an old custom
To weep for love.

Enter several Boys, *several* Citizens, *and an* Apprentice.

1st Boy. Now they come, now they come!
2nd Boy. The duke
3rd Boy. The states![1]
1st Cit. How near, boy?
1st Boy. I' the next street, sir, hard at hand.
1st Cit. You, sirrah, get a standing for your mistress,
The best in all the city.
Appren. I have't for her, sir;
'Twas a thing I provided for her over-night,
'Tis ready at her pleasure.
1st Cit. Fetch her to't then:
Away, sir; [*Exeunt* Boys, Citizens, *and* Apprentice.
Bian. What's the meaning of this hurry?
Can you tell, mother?
Moth. What a memory
Have I! I see by that years come upon me:
Why, 'tis a yearly custom and solemnity,
Religiously observed by the duke and states,
To St. Mark's temple, the fifteenth of April;
See, if my dull brains had not quite forgot it!
'Twas happily questioned of thee; I had gone down else,
Sat like a drone below, and never thought on't.
I would not, to be ten years younger again,
That you had lost the sight: now you shall see
Our duke, a goodly gentleman of his years.

[1] Nobles.

Bian. Is he old then?

Moth. About some fifty-five.

Bian. That's no great age in man; he's then at best
For wisdom and for judgment.

Moth. The lord cardinal,
His noble brother—there's a comely gentleman,
And greater in devotion than in blood.

Bian. He's worthy to be marked.

Moth. You shall behold
All our chief states of Florence: you came fortunately
Against this solemn day.

Bian. I hope so always. [*Music within.*

Moth. I hear 'em near us now: do you stand easily?

Bian. Exceeding well, good mother.

Moth. Take this stool.

Bian. I need it not, I thank you.

Moth. Use your will then.

Enter six Knights *bare-headed, then two* Cardinals, *then the* LORD CARDINAL, *then the* DUKE; *after him the states of* Florence *by two and two, with variety of music and song. They pass over the stage in great pomp and exeunt.*

Moth. How like you, daughter?

Bian. 'Tis a noble state;
Methinks my soul could dwell upon the reverence
Of such a solemn and most worthy custom.
Did not the duke look up? methought he saw us.

Moth. That's every one's conceit that sees a duke;
If he look steadfastly, he looks straight at them,
When he, perhaps, good, careful gentleman,
Never minds any, but the look he casts
Is at his own intentions, and his object
Only the public good.

Bian. Most likely so.

Moth. Come, come, we'll end this argument below.
[*Exeunt above.*

ACT THE SECOND.

SCENE I.

An Apartment in LIVIA'S *House.*

Enter HIPPOLITO *and* LIVIA.

LIV. A strange affection, brother! when I
think on't, I wonder how thou cam'st by't.
Hip. Even as easily [ofttimes
As man comes by destruction, which
He wears in his own bosom.
Liv. Is the world
So populous in women, and creation
So prodigal in beauty, and so various,
Yet does love turn thy point to thine own blood?
'Tis somewhat too unkindly: must thy eye
Dwell evilly on the fairness of thy kindred,
And seek not where it should? it is confined
Now in a narrower prison than was made for't;
It is allowed a stranger; and where bounty
Is made the great man's honour, 'tis ill husbandry
To spare, and servants shall have small thanks for't;
So he Heaven's bounty seems to scorn and mock
That spares free means, and spends of his own stock.
Hip. Ne'er was man's misery so soon summed up,
Counting how truly.
Liv. Nay, I love you so,
That I shall venture much to keep a change from you

So fearful as this grief will bring upon you;
Faith, it even kills me when I see you faint
Under a reprehension, and I'll leave it,
Though I know nothing can be better for you.
Prithee, sweet brother, let not passion waste
The goodness of thy time and of thy fortune:
Thou keep'st the treasure of that life I love
As dearly as mine own; and if you think
My former words too bitter, which were ministered
By truth and zeal, 'tis but a hazarding
Of grace and virtue, and I can bring forth
As pleasant fruits as sensuality wishes
In all her teeming longings; this I can do.

Hip. O, nothing that can make my wishes perfect!

Liv. I would that love of yours were pawned to't, brother,
And as soon lost that way as I could win!
Sir, I could give as shrewd a lift to chastity
As any she that wears a tongue in Florence;
Sh'ad need be a good horsewoman, and sit fast,
Whom my strong argument could not fling at last.
Prithee, take courage, man; though I should counsel
Another to despair, yet I am pitiful
To thy afflictions, and will venture hard—
I will not name for what, it is not handsome;
Find you the proof and praise me.

Hip. Then I fear me
I shall not praise you in haste.

Liv. This is the comfort,
You are not the first, brother, has attempted
Things more forbidden than this seems to be.
I'll minister all cordials now to you,
Because I'll cheer you up, sir.

Hip. I'm past hope.

Liv. Love, thou shalt see me do a strange cure then,
As e'er was wrought on a disease so mortal
And near akin to shame. When shall you see her?

Hip. Never in comfort more.
Liv. You're so impatient too!
Hip. Will you believe? death, sh'as forsworn my company,
And sealed it with a blush.
Liv. So, I perceive
All lies upon my hands then; well, the more glory
When the work's finished.

Enter Servant.

How now, sir? the news?
Ser. Madam, your niece, the virtuous Isabella,
Is lighted now to see you.
Liv. That's great fortune;
Sir, your stars bless you simply.—Lead her in.
[*Exit* Servant.
Hip. What's this to me?
Liv. Your absence, gentle brother;
I must bestir my wits for you.
Hip. Ay, to great purpose. [*Exit.*
Liv. Beshrew you, would I loved you not so well!
I'll go to bed, and leave this deed undone:
I am the fondest where I once affect;
The carefull'st of their healths and of their ease, forsooth,
That I look still but slenderly to mine own:
I take a course to pity him so much now,
That I've none left for modesty and myself.
This 'tis to grow so liberal: you've few sisters
That love their brothers' ease 'bove their own honesties;
But if you question my affections,
That will be found my fault.

Enter ISABELLA.

Niece, your love's welcome.
Alas! what draws that paleness to thy cheeks?
This enforced marriage towards?[1]
Isa. It helps, good aunt,

[1] At hand.

Amongst some other griefs; but those I'll keep
Locked up in modest silence, for they're sorrows
Would shame the tongue more than they grieve the
thought.

Liv. Indeed, the ward is simple.

Isa. Simple! that were well;
Why, one might make good shift with such a husband,
But he's a fool entailed, he halts downright in't.

Liv. And knowing this, I hope 'tis at your choice
To take or refuse, niece.

Isa. You see it is not.
I loathe him more than beauty can hate death,
Or age her spiteful neighbour.

Liv. Let 't appear then.

Isa. How can I, being born with that obedience
That must submit unto a father's will?
If he command, I must of force consent.

Liv. Alas, poor soul! be not offended, prithee,
If I set by the name of niece awhile,
And bring in pity in a stranger fashion;
It lies here in this breast would cross this match.

Isa. How! cross it, aunt?

Liv. Ay, and give thee more liberty
Than thou hast reason yet to apprehend.

Isa. Sweet aunt, in goodness keep not hid from me
What may befriend my life!

Liv. Yes, yes, I must!
When I return to reputation,
And think upon the solemn vow I made
To your dead mother, my most loving sister;
As long as I've her memory 'twixt mine eyelids,
Look for no pity now.

Isa. Kind, sweet, dear aunt——

Liv. No, 'twas a secret I've took special care of,
Delivered by your mother on her death-bed,
That's nine years now, and I'll not part from't yet,
Though ne'er was fitter time, nor greater cause for't.

Isa. As you desire the praises of a virgin——
Liv. Good sorrow, I would do thee any kindness
Not wronging secrecy or reputation.
Isa. Neither of which, as I have hope of fruitfulness,
Shall receive wrong from me.
Liv. Nay, 'twould be your own wrong
As much as any's, should it come to that once.
Isa. I need no better means to work persuasion then.
Liv. Let it suffice, you may refuse this fool,
Or you may take him as you see occasion,
For your advantage; the best wits will do't;
You've liberty enough in your own will,
You cannot be enforced; there grows the flower,
If you could pick it out, makes whole life sweet to you.
That which you call your father's command's nothing,
Then your obedience must needs be as little:
If you can make shift here to taste your happiness,
Or pick out aught that likes you, much good do you;
You see your cheer, I'll make you no set dinner.
Isa. And, trust me, I may starve for all the good
I can find yet in this: sweet aunt, deal plainlier.
Liv. Say I should trust you now upon an oath,
And give you, in a secret, that would start you,
How am I sure of you in faith and silence?
Isa. Equal assurance may I find in mercy
As you for that in me!
Liv. It shall suffice:
Then know, however custom has made good,
For reputation's sake, the names of niece
And aunt 'twixt you and I, we're nothing less.
Isa. How's that?
Liv. I told you I should start your blood;
You are no more allied to any of us,
Save what the courtesy of opinion casts
Upon your mother's memory and your name,
Than the merest stranger is, or one begot
At Naples when the husband lies at Rome;

There's so much odds betwixt us. Since your knowledge
Wished more instruction, and I have your oath
In pledge for silence, it makes me talk the freelier.
Did never the report of that famed Spaniard,
Marquis of Corïa, since your time was ripe
For understanding, fill your ear with wonder?

Isa. Yes; what of him? I've heard his deeds of honour
Often related when we lived in Naples.

Liv. You heard the praises of your father then.

Isa. My father!

Liv. That was he; but all the business
So carefully and so discreetly carried,
That fame received no spot by't, not a blemish;
Your mother was so wary to her end,
None knew it but her conscience and her friend,
Till penitent confession made it mine,
And now my pity yours, it had been long else;
And I hope care and love alike in you,
Made good by oath, will see it take no wrong now.
How weak his commands now whom you call father!
How vain all his enforcements, your obedience!
And what a largeness in your will and liberty,
To take, or to reject, or to do both!
For fools will serve to father wise men's children:
All this you've time to think on. O my wench,
Nothing o'erthrows our sex but indiscretion!
We might do well else of a brittle people
As any under the great canopy:
I pray, forget not but to call me aunt still;
Take heed of that, it may be marked in time else:
But keep your thoughts to yourself, from all the world,
Kindred, or dearest friend; nay, I entreat you,
From him that all this while you have called uncle;
And though you love him dearly, as I know
His deserts claim as much even from a stranger,
Yet let not him know this, I prithee, do not;

As ever thou hast hope of second pity,
If thou shouldst stand in need on't, do not do't.
Isa. Believe my oath, I will not.
Liv. Why, well said.—
Who shows more craft t' undo a maidenhead,
I'll resign my part to her. [*Aside.*

Enter HIPPOLITO.

She's thine own; go.
Hip. Alas, fair flattery cannot cure my sorrows!
[*Exit* LIVIA.
Isa. Have I passed so much time in ignorance,
And never had the means to know myself
Till this blessed hour? thanks to her virtuous pity
That brought it now to light; would I had known it
But one day sooner! he had then received
In favours, what, poor gentleman, he took
In bitter words; a slight and harsh reward
For one of his deserts. [*Aside.*
Hip. There seems to me now
More anger and distraction in her looks:
I'm gone; I'll not endure a second storm;
The memory of the first is not past yet. [*Aside.*
Isa. Are you returned, you comforts of my life,
In this man's presence? I will keep you fast now,
And sooner part eternally from the world
Than my good joys in you. [*Aside.*]—Prithee, forgive me,
I did but chide in jest; the best loves use it
Sometimes; it sets an edge upon affection:
When we invite our best friends to a feast,
'Tis not all sweetmeats that we set before them;
There's somewhat sharp and salt, both to whet appetite
And make 'em taste their wine well; so, methinks,
After a friendly, sharp, and savoury chiding,
A kiss tastes wondrous well, and full o' the grape;
How think'st thou? does't not? [*Kisses him.*

Hip. 'Tis so excellent,
I know not how to praise it, what to say to't!
Isa. This marriage shall go forward.
Hip. With the ward?
Are you in earnest?
Isa. 'Twould be ill for us else.
Hip. For us! how means she that? [*Aside.*
Isa. Troth, I begin
To be so well, methinks, within this hour,
For all this match able to kill one's heart,
Nothing can pull me down now; should my father
Provide a worse fool yet—which I should think
Were a hard thing to compass—I'd have him either;
The worse the better, none can come amiss now,
If he want wit enough; so discretion love me,
Desert and judgment, I've content sufficient.
She that comes once to be a housekeeper
Must not look every day to fare well, sir,
Like a young waiting-gentlewoman in service,
For she feeds commonly as her lady does,
No good bit passes her but she gets a taste on't;
But when she comes to keep house for herself,
She's glad of some choice cates then once a-week,
Or twice at most, and glad if she can get 'em;
So must affection learn to fare with thankfulness:
Pray, make your love no stranger, sir, that's all,—
Though you be one yourself, and know not on't,
And I have sworn you must not. [*Aside, and exit.*
Hip. This is beyond me!
Never came joys so unexpectedly
To meet desires in man: how came she thus?
What has she done to her, can any tell?
'Tis beyond sorcery this, drugs, or love-powders;
Some art that has no name, sure; strange to me
Of all the wonders I e'er met withal
Throughout my ten years' travels; but I'm thankful for't,
This marriage now must of necessity forward;

It is the only veil wit can devise
To keep our acts hid from sin-piercing eyes. [*Exit.*

SCENE II.

Another Apartment in LIVIA'S *House: a chess-board set out.*

Enter LIVIA *and* GUARDIANO.

Liv. How, sir? a gentlewoman so young, so fair,
As you set forth, spied from the widow's window?
Guar. She.
Liv. Our Sunday-dinner woman?
Guar. And Thursday-supper woman, the same still:
I know not how she came by her, but I'll swear
She's the prime gallant for a face in Florence,
And no doubt other parts follow their leader.
The duke himself first spied her at the window,
Then, in a rapture—as if admiration
Were poor when it were single—beckoned me,
And pointed to the wonder warily,
As one that feared she would draw in her splendour
Too soon, if too much gazed at: I ne'er knew him
So infinitely taken with a woman;
Nor can I blame his appetite, or tax
His raptures of slight folly; she's a creature
Able to draw a state from serious business,
And make it their best piece to do her service.
What course shall we devise? has spoke twice now.
Liv. Twice?
Guar. 'Tis beyond your apprehension
How strangely that one look has catched his heart:
'Twould prove but too much worth in wealth and favour
To those should work his peace.

Liv. And if I do't not,
Or at least come as near it—if your art
Will take a little pains and second me—
As any wench in Florence of my standing,
I'll quite give o'er, and shut up shop in cunning.
Guar. 'Tis for the duke; and if I fail your purpose,
All means to come by riches or advancement
Miss me, and skip me over!
Liv. Let the old woman then
Be sent for with all speed, then I'll begin.
Guar. A good conclusion follow, and a sweet one,
After this stale beginning with old ware!
Within there!

Enter Servant.

Ser. Sir, do you call?
Guar. Come near, list hither. [*Whispers.*
Liv. I long myself to see this absolute creature,
That wins the heart of love and praise so much.
Guar. Go, sir, make haste.
Liv. Say I entreat her company:
Do you hear, sir?
Ser. Yes, madam. [*Exit.*
Liv. That brings her quickly.
Guar. I would 'twere done! the duke waits the good hour,
And I wait the good fortune that may spring from't.
I've had a lucky hand these fifteen year
At such court-passage[1] with three dice in a dish.—

Enter FABRICIO.

Signor Fabricio!
Fab. O sir,
I bring an alteration in my mouth now.
Guar. An alteration?—No wise speech, I hope;
He means not to talk wisely, does he, trow?— [*Aside.*
Good; what's the change, I pray, sir?

[1] A game with dice.

Fab. A new change.

Guar. Another yet? faith, there's enough already.

Fab. My daughter loves him now.

Guar. What, does she, sir?

Fab. Affects him beyond thought: who but the ward, forsooth?
No talk but of the ward; she would have him
To choose 'bove all the men she ever saw:
My will goes not so fast as her consent now;
Her duty gets before my command still.

Guar. Why, then, sir, if you'll have me speak my thoughts,
I smell 'twill be a match.

Fab. Ay, and a sweet young couple,
If I have any judgment.

Guar. Faith, that's little.— [*Aside.*
Let her be sent to-morrow, before noon,
And handsomely tricked up, for 'bout that time
I mean to bring her in, and tender her to him.

Fab. I warrant you for handsome; I will see
Her things laid ready, every one in order,
And have some part of her tricked up to-night.

Guar. Why, well said.

Fab. 'Twas a use her mother had;
When she was invited to an early wedding,
She'd dress her head o'er night, sponge up herself,
And give her neck three lathers.

Guar. Ne'er a halter? [*Aside.*

Fab. On with her chain of pearl, her ruby bracelets,
Lay ready all her tricks and jiggembobs.

Guar. So must your daughter.

Fab. I'll about it straight, sir. [*Exit.*

Liv. How he sweats in the foolish zeal of fatherhood,
After six ounces an hour, and seems
To toil as much as if his cares were wise ones!

Guar. You've let his folly blood in the right vein, lady.

Liv. And here comes his sweet son-in-law that shall be;
They're both allied in wit before the marriage;
What will they be hereafter, when they're nearer!
Yet they can go no further than the fool;
There's the world's end in both of 'em.

Enter the Ward *and* SORDIDO, *one with a shittlecock, the other with a battledoor.*

Guar. Now, young heir.
Ward. What's the next business after shittlecock now?
Guar. To-morrow you shall see the gentlewoman
Must be your wife.
Ward. There's even another thing too,
Must be kept up with a pair of battledoors:
My wife! what can she do?
Guar. Nay, that's a question you should ask yourself, ward,
When you're alone together.
Ward. That's as I list;
A wife's to be asked anywhere, I hope;
I'll ask her in a congregation,
If I've a mind to't, and so save a license.
My guardianer has no more wit than an herb-woman,
That sells away all her sweet herbs and nosegays,
And keeps a stinking breath for her own pottage.
Sor. Let me be at the choosing of your beloved,
If you desire a woman of good parts.
Ward. Thou shalt, sweet Sordido.
Sor. I have a plaguy guess; let me alone to see what she is: if I but look upon her—'way! I know all the faults to a hair that you may refuse her for.
Ward. Dost thou? I prithee, let me hear 'em, Sordido.
Sor. Well, mark 'em, then; I have 'em all in rhyme:
The wife your guardianer ought to tender

Should be pretty, straight, and slender;
Her hair not short, her foot not long,
Her hand not huge, nor too, too loud her tongue;
No pearl in eye, nor ruby in her nose,
No burn or cut but what the catalogue shows;
She must have teeth, and that no black ones,
And kiss most sweet when she does smack once;
Her skin must be both white and plumped,
Her body straight, not hopper-rumped,
Or wriggle sideways like a crab;
She must be neither slut nor drab,
Nor go too splay-foot with her shoes,
To make her smock lick up the dews;
And two things more, which I forgot to tell ye,
She neither must have bump in back nor belly:
These are the faults that will not make her pass.

Ward. And if I spy not these I'm a rank ass.

Sor. Nay, more; by right, sir, you should see her naked,
For that's the ancient order.

Ward. See her naked?
That were good sport i'faith: I'll have the books turned o'er,
And if I find her naked on record,
She shall not have a rag on: but stay, stay;
How if she should desire to see me so too?
I were in a sweet case then; such a foul skin!

Sor. But you've a clean shirt, and that makes amends, sir.

Ward. I will not see her naked for that trick though. [*Exit.*

Sor. Then take her with all faults with her clothes on,
And they may hide a number with a bum-roll.[1]
Faith, choosing of a wench in a huge farthingale
Is like the buying of ware under a great pent-house;

[1] Bustle. The bum-roll was worn by ladies who could not afford farthingales.

What with the deceit of one,
And the false light[1] of th' other, mark my speeches,
He may have a diseased wench in's bed,
And rotten stuff in's breeches. [*Exit.*

Guar. It may take handsomely.

Liv. I see small hindrance.—

Re-enter Servant, *showing in* Mother.

How now? so soon returned?

Guar. She's come.

Liv. That's well.— [*Exit* Servant.
Widow, come, come, I've a great quarrel to you;
Faith, I must chide you, that you must be sent for;
You make yourself so strange, never come at us,
And yet so near a neighbour, and so unkind;
Troth, you're to blame; you cannot be more welcome
To any house in Florence, that I'll tell you.

Moth. My thanks must needs acknowledge so much, madam.

Liv. How can you be so strange then? I sit here
Sometimes whole days together without company,
When business draws this gentleman from home,
And should be happy in society
Which I so well affect as that of yours:
I know you're alone too; why should not we,
Like two kind neighbours, then, supply the wants
Of one another, having tongue-discourse,
Experience in the world, and such kind helps
To laugh down time, and meet age merrily?

Moth. Age, madam! you speak mirth; 'tis at my door,
But a long journey from your ladyship yet.

Liv. My faith, I'm nine-and-thirty, every stroke, wench;
And 'tis a general observation

[1] An allusion to the darkening of shops by dishonest tradesmen.

'Mongst knights—wives or widows we account ourselves
Then old, when young men's eyes leave looking at's;
'Tis a true rule amongst us, and ne'er failed yet
In any but in one, that I remember;
Indeed, she had a friend at nine-and-forty;
Marry, she paid well for him, and in th' end
He kept a quean or two with her own money,
That robbed her of her plate and cut her throat.

Moth. She had her punishment in this world, madam,
And a fair warning to all other women
That they live chaste at fifty.

Liv. Ay, or never, wench.
Come, now I have thy company, I'll not part with't
Till after supper.

Moth. Yes, I must crave pardon, madam.

Liv. I swear you shall stay supper; we've no strangers, woman,
None but my sojourners and I, this gentleman
And the young heir his ward; you know our company.

Moth. Some other time I'll make bold with you, madam.

Guar. Nay, pray stay, widow.

Liv. Faith, she shall not go:
Do you think I'll be forsworn?

Moth. 'Tis a great while
Till supper-time; I'll take my leave then now, madam,
And come again i' th' evening, since your ladyship
Will have it so.

Liv. I' th' evening? by my troth, wench,
I'll keep you while I have you: you've great business, sure,
To sit alone at home; I wonder strangely
What pleasure you take in't; were't to me now,
I should be ever at one neighbour's house
Or other all day long: having no charge,
Or none to chide you, if you go or stay,
Who may live merrier, ay, or more at heart's ease?

Come, we'll to chess or draughts; there are an hundred tricks
To drive out time till supper, never fear't, wench.

Moth. I'll but make one step home, and return straight, madam.

Liv. Come, I'll not trust you; you use more excuses
To your kind friends than ever I knew any.
What business can you have, if you be sure
You've locked the doors? and, that being all you have,
I know you're careful on't. One afternoon
So much to spend here! say I should entreat you now
To lie a night or two, or a week, with me,
Or leave your own house for a month together;
It were a kindness that long neighbourhood
And friendship might well hope to prevail in;
Would you deny such a request? i'faith,
Speak truth, and freely.

Moth. I were then uncivil, madam.

Liv. Go to then; set your men; we'll have whole nights
Of mirth together, ere we be much older, wench.

[LIVIA *and* Mother *sit down to the chess-board.*

Moth. As good now tell her then, for she will know't;
I've always found her a most friendly lady. [*Aside.*

Liv. Why, widow, where's your mind?

Moth. Troth, even at home, madam:
To tell you truth, I left a gentlewoman
Even sitting all alone, which is uncomfortable,
Especially to young bloods.

Liv. Another excuse!

Moth. No; as I hope for health, madam, that's a truth:
Please you to send and see.

Liv. What gentlewoman? pish!

Moth. Wife to my son, indeed; but not known, madam,
To any but yourself.

Liv. Now I beshrew you;
Could you be so unkind to her and me,
To come and not bring her? faith, 'tis not friendly.

Moth. I feared to be too bold.

Liv. Too bold! O, what's become
Of the true hearty love was wont to be
'Mongst neighbours in old time!

Moth. And she's a stranger, madam.

Liv. The more should be her welcome: when is courtesy
In better practice than when 'tis employed
In entertaining strangers? I could chide, i'faith:
Leave her behind, poor gentlewoman! alone too!
Make some amends, and send for her betimes, go.

Moth. Please you, command one of your servants, madam.

Liv. Within there!

Re-enter Servant.

Ser. Madam.

Liv. Attend the gentlewoman.[1]

Moth. It must be carried wondrous privately
From my son's knowledge, he'll break out in storms else.—
Hark you, sir. [*Whispers the* Servant, *who then goes out.*

Liv. [*to Guar.*] Now comes in the heat of your part.

Guar. True, I know't, lady; and if I be out,
May the duke banish me from all employments,
Wanton or serious!

Liv. So, have you sent, widow?

Moth. Yes, madam, he's almost at home by this.

Liv. And, faith, let me entreat you that henceforward
All such unkind faults may be swept from friendship,
Which does but dim the lustre; and think thus much,
It is a wrong to me, that have ability

1 "This is one of those scenes," remarks Lamb, "which has the air of being an immediate transcript from life. Livia, the 'good neighbour,' is as real a creature as one of Chaucer's characters. She is such another jolly housewife as the Wife of Bath."

To bid friends welcome, when you keep 'em from me;
You cannot set greater dishonour near me;
For bounty is the credit and the glory
Of those that have enough. I see you're sorry,
And the good 'mends is made by't.

Re-enter Servant, *showing in* BIANCA.

Moth. Here she is, madam. [*Exit* Servant.

Bian. I wonder how she comes to send for me now. [*Aside.*

Liv. Gentlewoman, you're most welcome; trust me, you are,
As courtesy can make one, or respect
Due to the presence of you.

Bian. I give you thanks, lady.

Liv. I heard you were alone, and 't had appeared
An ill condition in me, though I knew you not,
Nor ever saw you—yet humanity
Thinks every case her own—t' have kept your company
Here from you, and left you all solitary:
I rather ventured upon boldness then,
As the least fault, and wished your presence here;
A thing most happily motioned of that gentleman,
Whom I request you, for his care and pity,
To honour and reward with your acquaintance;
A gentleman that ladies' rights stands for,
That's his profession.

Bian. 'Tis a noble one,
And honours my acquaintance.

Guar. All my intentions
Are servants to such mistresses.

Bian. 'Tis your modesty,
It seems, that makes your deserts speak so low, sir.

Liv. Come, widow.—Look you, lady, here's our business; [*Pointing to the chess-board.*
Are we not well employed, think you? an old quarrel
Between us, that will ne'er be at an end.

Bian. No? and, methinks, there's men enough to part
you, lady.

Liv. Ho, but they set us on, let us come off
As well as we can, poor souls; men care no farther.
I pray, sit down, forsooth, if you've the patience
To look upon two weak and tedious gamesters.

Guar. Faith, madam, set these by till evening,
You'll have enough on't then; the gentlewoman,
Being a stranger, would take more delight
To see your rooms and pictures.

Liv. Marry, good sir,
And well remembered; I beseech you, show 'em her,
That will beguile time well; pray heartily, do, sir,
I'll do as much for you: here, take these keys;
[*Gives keys to* GUARDIANO.
Show her the monument too, and that's a thing
Every one sees not; you can witness that, widow.

Moth. And that's worth sight indeed, madam.

Bian. Kind lady,
I fear I came to be a trouble to you.

Liv. O, nothing less, forsooth!

Bian. And to this courteous gentleman,
That wears a kindness in his breast so noble
And bounteous to the welcome of a stranger.

Guar. If you but give acceptance to my service,
You do the greatest grace and honour to me
That courtesy can merit.

Bian. I were to blame else,
And out of fashion much. I pray you, lead, sir.

Liv. After a game or two, we're for you, gentlefolks.

Guar. We wish no better seconds in society
Than your discourses, madam, and your partner's there.

Moth. I thank your praise; I listened to you, sir,
Though, when you spoke, there came a paltry rook
Full in my way, and chokes up all my game.
[*Exeunt* GUARDIANO *and* BIANCA.

Liv. Alas, poor widow, I shall be too hard for thee!

Moth. You're cunning at the game, I'll be sworn, madam.

Liv. It will be found so, ere I give you over.— [*Aside.*
She that can place her man well——

Moth. As you do, madam.

Liv. As I shall, wench, can never lose her game:
Nay, nay, the black king's mine.

Moth. Cry you mercy, madam!

Liv. And this my queen.

Moth. I see't now.

Liv. Here's a duke[1]
Will strike a sure stroke for the game anon;
Your pawn cannot come back to relieve itself.

Moth. I know that, madam.

Liv. You play well the whilst:
How she belies her skill! I hold two ducats,
I give you check and mate to your white king,
Simplicity itself, your saintish king there.

Moth. Well, ere now, lady,
I've seen the fall of subtlety; jest on.

Liv. Ay, but simplicity receives two for one.

Moth. What remedy but patience!

Enter GUARDIANO *and* BIANCA *above.*

Bian. Trust me, sir,
Mine eye ne'er met with fairer ornaments.

Guar. Nay, livelier, I'm persuaded neither Florence
Nor Venice can produce.

Bian. Sir, my opinion
Takes your part highly.

Guar. There's a better piece
Yet than all these.

Bian. Not possible, sir!

Guar. Believe it,
You'll say so when you see't: turn but your eye now,

[1] Rook.

You're upon't presently.

[*Draws a curtain, and discovers the* DUKE; *then exit.*]

Bian. O sir!

Duke. He's gone, beauty:
Pish, look not after him; he's but a vapour,
That, when the sun appears, is seen no more.

Bian. O, treachery to honour!

Duke. Prithee, tremble not;
I feel thy breast shake like a turtle panting
Under a loving hand that makes much on't:
Why art so fearful? as I'm friend to brightness,
There's nothing but respect and honour near thee:
You know me, you have seen me; here's a heart
Can witness I have seen thee.

Bian. The more's my danger.

Duke. The more's thy happiness. Pish, strive not, [sweet;
This strength were excellent employed in love now,
But here 'tis spent amiss: strive not to seek
Thy liberty, and keep me still in prison;
I'faith, you shall not out till I'm released now;
We'll be both freed together, or stay still by't,
So is captivity pleasant.

Bian. O my lord!

Duke. I am not here in vain; have but the leisure
To think on that, and thou'lt be soon resolved:
The lifting of thy voice is but like one
That does exalt his enemy, who, proving high,
Lays all the plots to confound him that raised him.
Take warning, I beseech thee; thou seem'st to me
A creature so composed of gentleness,
And delicate meekness—such as bless the faces
Of figures that are drawn for goddesses,
And makes art proud to look upon her work—
I should be sorry the least force should lay
An unkind touch upon thee.

Bian. O my extremity!
My lord, what seek you?

Duke. Love.
Bian. 'Tis gone already;
I have a husband.
Duke. That's a single comfort;
Take a friend to him.
Bian. That's a double mischief,
Or else there's no religion.
Duke. Do not tremble
At fears of thine own making.
Bian. Nor, great lord,
Make me not bold with death and deeds of ruin,
Because they fear not you; me they must fright;
Then am I best in health: should thunder speak,
And none regard it, it had lost the name,
And were as good be still. I'm not like those
That take their soundest sleeps in greatest tempests;
Then wake I most, the weather fearfullest,
And call for strength to virtue.
Duke. Sure, I think
Thou know'st the way to please me: I affect
A passionate pleading 'bove an easy yielding;
But never pitied any—they deserve none—
That will not pity me. I can command,
Think upon that; yet if thou truly knewest
The infinite pleasure my affection takes
In gentle, fair entreatings, when love's businesses
Are carried courteously 'twixt heart and heart,
You'd make more haste to please me.
Bian. Why should you seek, sir,
To take away that you can never give?
Duke. But I give better in exchange,—wealth, honour;
She that is fortunate in a duke's favour
'Lights on a tree that bears all women's wishes:
If your own mother saw you pluck fruit there,
She would commend your wit, and praise the time
Of your nativity; take hold of glory.
Do not I know you've cast away your life

Upon necessities, means merely doubtful
To keep you in indifferent health and fashion—
A thing I heard too lately, and soon pitied—
And can you be so much your beauty's enemy,
To kiss away a month or two in wedlock,
And weep whole years in wants for ever after?]
Come, play the wise wench, and provide for ever;
Let storms come when they list, they find thee sheltered.
Should any doubt arise, let nothing trouble thee;
Put trust in our love for the managing
Of all to thy heart's peace: we'll walk together,
And show a thankful joy for both our fortunes.
[*Exeunt* DUKE *and* BIANCA *above.*

Liv. Did not I say my duke would fetch you o'er, widow?

Moth. I think you spoke in earnest when you said it, madam.

Liv. And my black king makes all the haste he can too.

Moth. Well, madam, we may meet with him in time yet.

Liv. I've given thee blind mate twice.

Moth. You may see, madam,
My eyes begin to fail.

Liv. I'll swear they do, wench.

Re-enter GUARDIANO.

Guar. I can but smile as often as I think on't:
How prettily the poor fool was beguiled!
How unexpectedly! it's a witty age;
Never were finer snares for women's honesties
Than are devised in these days; no spider's web
Made of a daintier thread than are now practised
To catch love's flesh-fly by the silver wing:
Yet, to prepare her stomach by degrees
To Cupid's feast, because I saw 'twas queasy,

I showed her naked pictures by the way,
A bit to stay the appetite. Well, advancement,
I venture hard to find thee; if thou com'st
With a greater title set upon thy crest,
I'll take that first cross patiently, and wait
Until some other comes greater than that;
I'll endure all. [*Aside.*

Liv. The game's even at the best now: you may see, widow,
How all things draw to an end.

Moth. Even so do I, madam.

Liv. I pray, take some of your neighbours along with you.

Moth. They must be those are almost twice your years then,
If they be chose fit matches for my time, madam.

Liv. Has not my duke bestirred himself?

Moth. Yes, faith, madam;
Has done me all the mischief in this game.

Liv. Has showed himself in's kind.

Moth. In's kind, call you it?
I may swear that.

Liv. Yes, faith, and keep your oath.

Guar. Hark, list! there's somebody coming down: 'tis she. [*Aside.*

Re-enter BIANCA.

Bian. Now bless me from a blasting! I saw that now,
Fearful for any woman's eye to look on;
Infectious mists and mildews hang at's eyes,
The weather of a doomsday dwells upon him:
Yet since mine honour's leprous, why should I
Preserve that fair that caused the leprosy?
Come, poison all at once. [*Aside.*]—Thou in whose baseness
The bane of virtue broods, I'm bound in soul
Eternally to curse thy smooth-browed treachery,

That wore the fair veil of a friendly welcome,
And I a stranger; think upon't, 'tis worth it;
Murders piled up upon a guilty spirit,
At his last breath will not lie heavier
Than this betraying act upon thy conscience:
Beware of offering the first-fruits to sin;
His weight is deadly who commits with strumpets,
After they've been abased, and made for use;
If they offend to the death, as wise men know,
How much more they, then, that first make 'em so!
I give thee that to feed on. I'm made bold now,
I thank thy treachery; sin and I'm acquainted,
No couple greater; and I'm like that great one,
Who, making politic use of a base villain,
He likes the treason well, but hates the traitor
So I hate thee, slave!

Guar. Well, so the duke love me,
I fare not much amiss then; two great feasts
Do seldom come together in one day,
We must not look for 'em.

Bian. What, at it still, mother?

Moth. You see we sit by't: are you so soon returned?

Liv. So lively and so cheerful! a good sign that. [*Aside.*

Moth. You have not seen all since, sure?

Bian. That have I, mother,
The monument and all: I'm so beholding
To this kind, honest, courteous gentleman,
You'd little think it, mother; showed me all,
Had me from place to place so fashionably;
The kindness of some people, how 't exceeds!
Faith, I've seen that I little thought to see
I' the morning when I rose.

Moth. Nay, so I told you
Before you saw't, it would prove worth your sight.—
I give you great thanks for my daughter, sir,
And all your kindness towards her.

Guar. O, good widow,
Much good may't do her !—forty weeks hence, i'faith.
[*Aside.*

Re-enter Servant.

Liv. Now, sir?
Ser. May't please you, madam, to walk in;
Supper's upon the table.
Liv. Yes, we come.— [*Exit* Servant.
Will't please you, gentlewoman?
Bian. Thanks, virtuous lady.—
You're a damned bawd. [*Aside to* LIVIA.]—I'll follow you, forsooth;
Pray, take my mother in ;—an old ass go with you !—
[*Aside.*
This gentleman and I vow not to part.
Liv. Then get you both before.
Bian. There lies his art.
[*Exeunt* BIANCA *and* GUARDIANO.
Liv. Widow, I'll follow you. [*Exit* Mother.] Is't so? "damned bawd!"
Are you so bitter? 'tis but want of use:
Her tender modesty is sea-sick a little,
Being not accustomed to the breaking billow
Of woman's wavering faith blown with temptations:
'Tis but a qualm of honour, 'twill away;
A little bitter for the time, but lasts not:
Sin tastes at the first draught like wormwood-water,
But drunk again, 'tis nectar ever after. [*Exit.*

ACT THE THIRD.

SCENE I.

A Room in the House of Leantio's Mother.

Enter Mother.

MOTH. I would my son would either keep at home,
Or I were in my grave!
She was but one day abroad, but ever since
She's grown so cutted,[1] there's no speaking to her:
Whether the sight of great cheer at my lady's,
And such mean fare at home, work discontent in her,
I know not; but I'm sure she's strangely altered.
I'll ne'er keep daughter-in-law i' th' house with me
Again, if I had an hundred: when read I of any
That agreed long together, but she and her mother
Fell out in the first quarter? nay, sometime
A grudging or a scolding the first week, by'r lady!
So takes the new disease, methinks, in my house:
I'm weary of my part; there's nothing likes her;
I know not how to please her here a' late:
And here she comes.

Enter Bianca.

Bian. This is the strangest house
For all defects as ever gentlewoman
Made shift withal to pass away her love in:

[1] Cross, querulous.

Why is there not a cushion-cloth of drawn-work,
Or some fair cut-work pinned up in my bed-chamber,
A silver and gilt casting-bottle[1] hung by't?—
Nay, since I am content to be so kind to you,
To spare you for a silver basin and ewer,
Which one of my fashion looks for of duty;
She's never offered under where she sleeps.

Moth. She talks of things here my whole state's not worth. [mother,

Bian. Never a green silk quilt is there i' th' house,
To cast upon my bed?

Moth. No, by troth, is there,
Nor orange-tawny neither.

Bian. Here's a house
For a young gentlewoman to be got with child in!

Moth. Yes, simple though you make it, there has been three
Got in a year in't, since you move me to't,
And all as sweet-faced children and as lovely
As you'll be mother of: I will not spare you:
What, cannot children be begot, think you,
Without gilt casting-bottles? yes, and as sweet ones:
The miller's daughter brings forth as white[2] boys
As she that bathes herself with milk and bean-flour![3]
'Tis an old saying, One may keep good cheer
In a mean house; so may true love affect
After the rate of princes in a cottage.

Bian. Troth, you speak wondrous well for your old house here;
'Twill shortly fall down at your feet to thank you,
Or stoop, when you go to bed, like a good child,
To ask you blessing. Must I live in want

[1] A bottle for sprinkling perfumes. [2] A term of endearment.

[3] Middleton refers again to these baths, as the right thing for "a beauty of nineteen," in *The Old Law*, act ii. sc. 2:—

"Alas! I should be tumbling in cold baths now,
Under each armpit a fine bean-flour bag
To screw out whiteness when I list."

Because my fortune matched me with your son?
Wives do not give away themselves to husbands
To the end to be quite cast away; they look
To be the better used and tendered rather,
Highlier respected, and maintained the richer;
They're well rewarded else for the free gift
Of their whole life to a husband! I ask less now
Than what I had at home when I was a maid,
And at my father's house; kept short of that
Which a wife knows she must have, nay, and will—
Will, mother, if she be not a fool born;
And report went of me, that I could wrangle
For what I wanted when I was two hours old:
And, by that copy, this land still I hold:
You hear me, mother. [*Exit.*

Moth. Ay, too plain, methinks;
And were I somewhat deafer when you spake,
'Twere ne'er a whit the worse for my quietness.
'Tis the most sudden'st, strangest alteration,
And the most subtlest, that e'er wit at threescore
Was puzzled to find out: I know no cause for't; but
She's no more like the gentlewoman at first,
Than I'm like her that never lay with man yet,—
And she's a very young thing, where'er she be.
When she first lighted here, I told her then [forsooth,
How mean she should find all things; she was pleased,
None better: I laid open all defects to her,
She was contented still; but the devil's in her,
Nothing contents her now. To-night my son
Promised to be at home; would he were come once,
For I am weary of my charge, and life too!
She'd be served all in silver, by her good will,
By night and day; she hates the name of pewterer
More than sick men the noise, or diseased bones
That quake at fall o' th' hammer, seeming to have
A fellow feeling with't at every blow.
What course shall I think on? she frets me so! [*Exit.*

Enter LEANTIO.

Lean. How near am I now to a happiness
That earth exceeds not! not another like it:
The treasures of the deep are not so precious
As are the concealed comforts of a man
Locked up in woman's love. I scent the air
Of blessings when I come but near the house:
What a delicious breath marriage sends forth!
The violet-bed's not sweeter. Honest wedlock
Is like a banqueting-house built in a garden,
On which the spring's chaste flowers take delight
To cast their modest odours; when base lust,
With all her powders, paintings, and best pride,
Is but a fair house built by a ditch-side.
When I behold a glorious dangerous strumpet,
Sparkling in beauty and destruction too,
Both at a twinkling, I do liken straight
Her beautified body to a goodly temple
That's built on vaults where carcasses lie rotting;
And so, by little and little, I shrink back again,
And quench desire with a cool meditation;
And I'm as well methinks. Now for a welcome
Able to draw men's envies upon man;
A kiss now, that will hang upon my lip
As sweet as morning-dew upon a rose,
And full as long; after a five days' fast
She'll be so greedy now, and cling about me,
I take care how I shall be rid of her:
And here't begins.

Re-enter BIANCA *and* Mother.

Bian. O sir, you're welcome home!
Moth. O, is he come? I'm glad on't.
Lean. Is that all?
Why, this is dreadful now as sudden death
To some rich man, that flatters all his sins
With promise of repentance when he's old,

And dies in the midway before he comes to't.— [*Aside.*
Sure you're not well, Bianca; how dost, prithee?
Bian. I have been better than I am at this time.
Lean. Alas, I thought so!
Bian. Nay, I've been worse too
Than now you see me, sir.
Lean. I'm glad thou mend'st yet,
I feel my heart mend too: how came it to thee?
Has anything disliked[1] thee in my absence?
Bian. No, certain; I have had the best content
That Florence can afford.
Lean. Thou mak'st the best on't.—
Speak, mother; what's the cause? you must needs know.
Moth. Troth, I know none, son; let her speak herself;
Unless it be the same gave Lucifer
A tumbling cast,—that's pride.
Bian. Methinks this house stands nothing to my mind;
I'd have some pleasant lodging i' th' high street, sir;
Or if 'twere near the court, sir, that were much better:
'Tis a sweet recreation for a gentlewoman
To stand in a bay-window and see gallants.
Lean. Now I've another temper, a mere stranger
To that of yours, it seems; I should delight
To see none but yourself.
Bian. I praise not that;
Too fond is as unseemly as too churlish:
I would not have a husband of that proneness
To kiss me before company for a world;
Beside, 'tis tedious to see one thing still, sir,
Be it the best that ever heart affected;
Nay, were't yourself, whose love had power, you know,
To bring me from my friends, I'd not stand thus
And gaze upon you always, troth, I could not, sir;
As good be blind and have no use of sight,
As look on one thing still: what's the eye's treasure
But change of objects? you are learnèd, sir,

[1] Displeased.

And know I speak not ill: 'tis full as virtuous
For woman's eye to look on several men,
As for her heart, sir, to be fixed on one.

Lean. Now thou com'st home to me; a kiss for that word.

Bian. No matter for a kiss, sir; let it pass;
'Tis but a toy, we'll not so much as mind it;
Let's talk of other business, and forget it.
What news now of the pirates? any stirring?
Prithee, discourse a little.

Moth. I'm glad he's here yet,
To see her tricks himself; I had lied monstrously
If I had told 'em first. [*Aside.*

Lean. Speak, what's the humour, sweet,
You make your lip so strange? this was not wont.

Bian. Is there no kindness betwixt man and wife,
Unless they make a pigeon-house of friendship,
And be still billing? 'tis the idlest fondness
That ever was invented, and 'tis pity
It's grown a fashion for poor gentlewomen;
There's many a disease kissed in a year by't,
And a French curtsy made to't: alas, sir!
Think of the world, how we shall live; grow serious;
We have been married a whole fortnight now.

Lean. How? a whole fortnight! why, is that so long?

Bian. 'Tis time to leave off dalliance; 'tis a doctrine
Of your own teaching, if you be remembered;
And I was bound to obey it.

Moth. Here's one fits him;
This was well catched, i'faith, son; like a fellow
That rids another country of a plague,
And brings it home with him to his own house.
[*Aside.—Knocking within.*
Who knocks?

Lean. Who's there now?—Withdraw you, Bianca;
Thou art a gem no stranger's eye must see,
Howe'er thou'rt pleased now to look dull on me.—
[*Exit* BIANCA.

Enter Messenger.

You're welcome, sir; to whom your business, pray?
Mess. To one I see not here now.
Lean. Who should that be, sir?
Mess. A young gentlewoman I was sent to.
Lean. A young gentlewoman?
Mess. Ay, sir, about sixteen: why look you wildly, sir?
Lean. At your strange error; you've mistook the house, sir?
There's none such here, I assure you.
Mess. I assure you too
The man that sent me cannot be mistook.
Lean. Why, who is't sent you, sir?
Mess. The duke.
Lean. The duke?
Mess. Yes; he entreats her company at a banquet
At Lady Livia's house.
Lean. Troth, shall I tell you, sir,
It is the most errоneous business
That e'er your honest pains was abused with;
I pray, forgive me if I smile a little,
I cannot choose, i'faith, sir, at an error
So comical as this,—I mean no harm though:
His grace has been most wondrous ill informed:
Pray, so return it, sir. What should her name be?
Mess. That I shall tell you straight too—Bianca Capello.
Lean. How, sir? Bianca? what do you call th' other.
Mess. Capello. Sir, it seems you know no such then?
Lean. Who should this be? I never heard o' the name.
Mess. Then 'tis a sure mistake.
Lean. What if you inquired
In the next street, sir? I saw gallants there
In the new houses that are built of late;
Ten to one there you find her.

Mess. Nay, no matter;
I will return the mistake, and seek no further.

Lean. Use your own will and pleasure, sir, you're welcome. [*Exit* Messenger.
What shall I think of first?—Come forth, Bianca!

Re-enter BIANCA.

Thou art betrayed, I fear me.

Bian. Betrayed! how, sir?

Lean. The duke knows thee.

Bian. Knows me! how know you that, sir?

Lean. Has got thy name.

Bian. Ay, and my good name too,
That's worse o' the twain. [*Aside.*

Lean. How comes this work about?

Bian. How should the duke know me? can you guess, mother?

Moth. Not I, with all my wits; sure we kept house close.

Lean. Kept close! not all the locks in Italy
Can keep you women so; you have been gadding,
And ventured out at twilight to the court-green yonder,
And met the gallant bowlers coming home;
Without your masks too, both of you, I'll be hanged else:
Thou hast been seen, Bianca, by some stranger;
Never excuse it.

Bian. I'll not seek the way, sir;
Do you think you've married me to mew me up,
Not to be seen? what would you make of me?

Lean. A good wife, nothing else.

Bian. Why, so are some
That are seen every day, else the devil take 'em.

Lean. No more, then; I believe all virtuous in thee,
Without an argument; 'twas but thy hard chance
To be seen somewhere, there lies all the mischief:
But I've devised a riddance.

Moth. Now I can tell you, son,
The time and place.

Lean. When? where?

Moth. What wits have I!
When you last took your leave, if you remember,
You left us both at window.

Lean. Right, I know that.

Moth. And not the third part of an hour after,
The duke passed by, in a great solemnity,
To St. Mark's temple, and, to my apprehension,
He looked up twice to the window.

Lean. O, there quickened
The mischief of this hour!

Bian. If you call't mischief,
It is a thing I fear I am conceived with. [*Aside.*

Lean. Looked he up twice, and could you take no warning?

Moth. Why, once may do as much harm, son, as a thousand;
Do not you know one spark has fired an house
As well as a whole furnace?

Lean. My heart flames for't:
Yet let's be wise, and keep all smothered closely;
I have bethought a means: is the door fast?

Moth. I locked it myself after him.

Lean. You know, mother,
At the end of the dark parlour there's a place
So artificially contrived for a conveyance,
No search could ever find it; when my father
Kept in for manslaughter, it was his sanctuary;
There will I lock my life's best treasure up,
Bianca.

Bian. Would you keep me closer yet? [sir:
Have you the conscience? you're best e'en choke me up,
You make me fearful of your health and wits,
You cleave to such wild courses; what's the matter?

Lean. Why, are you so insensible of your danger
To ask that now? the duke himself has sent for you
To Lady Livia's to a banquet, forsooth.

Bian. Now I beshrew you heartily, has he so!
And you the man would never yet vouchsafe
To tell me on't till now? you show your loyalty
And honesty at once; and so farewell, sir.
Lean. Bianca, whither now?
Bian. Why, to the duke, sir;
You say he sent for me.
Lean. But thou dost not mean
To go, I hope?
Bian. No? I shall prove unmannerly,
Rude, and uncivil, mad, and imitate you!—
Come, mother, come, follow his humour no longer;
We shall be all executed for treason shortly.
Moth. Not I, i'faith; I'll first obey the duke,
And taste of a good banquet; I'm of thy mind:
I'll step but up and fetch two handkerchiefs
To pocket up some sweetmeats, and o'ertake thee.
[*Exit.*
Bian. Why, here's an old wench would trot into a bawd now
For some dry sucket,[1] or a colt in march-pane.[2]
[*Aside, and exit.*
Lean. O thou, the ripe time of man's misery, wedlock,
When all his thoughts, like overladen trees,
Crack with the fruits they bear, in cares, in jealousies!
O, that's a fruit that ripens hastily,
After 'tis knit to marriage! it begins,
As soon as the sun shines upon the bride,
A little to show colour. Blessèd powers,
Whence comes this alteration? the distractions,
The fears and doubts it brings, are numberless;
And yet the cause I know not. What a peace
Has he that never marries! if he knew
The benefit he enjoyed, or had the fortune

1 Sweatmeat.
2 A composition of almonds, sugar, etc., moulded into various shapes.

To come and speak with me, he should know then
Th' infinite wealth he had, and discern rightly
The greatness of his treasure by my loss:
Nay, what a quietness has he 'bove mine
That wears his youth out in a strumpet's arms,
And never spends more care upon a woman
Than at the time of lust; but walks away;
And if he find her dead at his return,
His pity is soon done,—he breaks a sigh
In many parts, and gives her but a piece on't:
But all the fears, shames, jealousies, costs and troubles,
And still renewed cares of a marriage-bed,
Live in the issue, when the wife is dead.

Re-enter Messenger.

Mess. A good perfection to your thoughts!
Lean. The news, sir?
Mess. Though you were pleased of late to pin an error on me,
You must not shift another in your stead too:
The duke has sent me for you.
Lean. How! for me, sir?—
I see then 'tis my theft; we're both betrayed:
Well, I'm not the first has stol'n away a maid;
My countrymen have used it. [*Aside.*]—I'll along with you, sir. [*Exeunt.*

SCENE II.

An Apartment in LIVIA'S *House: a Banquet set out.*

Enter GUARDIANO *and the* Ward.

Guar. Take you especial note of such a gentlewoman,
She's here on purpose; I've invited her,
Her father, and her uncle, to this banquet;

Mark her behaviour well, it does concern you ;
And what her good parts are, as far as time
And place can modestly require a knowledge of,
Shall be laid open to your understanding.
You know I'm both your guardian and your uncle ;
My care of you is double, ward and nephew,
And I'll express it here.

Ward. Faith, I should know her
Now by her mark among a thousand women ;
A little pretty deft and tidy thing, you say?

Guar. Right.

Ward. With a lusty sprouting sprig in her hair?

Guar. Thou goest the right way still ; take one mark more,—
Thou shalt ne'er find her hand out of her uncle's,
Or else his out of hers, if she be near him ;
The love of kindred never yet stuck closer
Than theirs to one another ; he that weds her,
Marries her uncle's heart too.

Ward. Say you so, sir?
Then I'll be asked i' the church to both of them.

[*Cornets within.*

Guar. Fall back ; here comes the duke.

Ward. He brings a gentlewoman,
I should fall forward rather.

Enter the DUKE *leading in* BIANCA, FABRICIO, HIPPOLITO, LIVIA, Mother, ISABELLA, Gentlemen, *and* Attendants.

Duke. Come, Bianca,
Of purpose sent into the world to show
Perfection once in woman ; I'll believe
Henceforward they have every one a soul too,
'Gainst all the uncourteous opinions
That man's uncivil rudeness ever held of 'em :
Glory of Florence, light into mine arms!

Bian. Yon comes a grudging man will chide you, sir ;

Enter LEANTIO.

The storm is now in's heart, and would get nearer,
And fall here, if it durst ; it pours down yonder.

Duke. If that be he, the weather shall soon clear;
List, and I'll tell thee how. [*Whispers* BIANCA.

Lean. A kissing too !
I see 'tis plain lust now, adultery 'boldened ;
What will it prove anon, when 'tis stuffed full
Of wine and sweetmeats, being so impudent fasting?
[*Aside.*

Duke. We've heard of your good parts, sir, which we honour
With our embrace and love.—Is not the captainship
Of Rouans' citadel, since the late deceased
Supplied by any yet?

Gentleman. By none, my lord.

Duke. Take it, the place is yours then ; and as faithfulness
And desert grows, our favour shall grow with 't :
[LEANTIO *kneels.*
Rise now, the captain of our fort at Rouans.

Lean. [*rising.*] The service of whole life give your grace thanks !

Duke. Come, sit, Bianca.
[DUKE, BIANCA, *&c., seat themselves.*

Lean. This is some good yet,
And more than e'er I looked for ; a fine bit
To stay a cuckold's stomach : all preferment
That springs from sin and lust it shoots up quickly,
As gardeners' crops do in the rotten'st grounds ;
So is all means raised from base prostitution
Even like a salad growing upon a dunghill.
I'm like a thing that never was yet heard of,
Half merry and half mad ; much like a fellow
That eats his meat with a good appetite,
And wears a plague-sore that would fright a country ;
Or rather like the barren,[1] hardened ass,

[1] Stupid.

That feeds on thistles till he bleeds again;
And such is the condition of my misery. [*Aside.*
Liv. Is that your son, widow?
Moth. Yes; did your ladyship
Never know that till now?
Liv. No, trust me, did I,—
Nor ever truly felt the power of love
And pity to a man, till now I knew him.
I have enough to buy me my desires,
And yet to spare, that's one good comfort. [*Aside.*]—
Hark you,
Pray, let me speak with you, sir, before you go.
Lean. With me, lady? you shall, I'm at your service.—
What will she say now, trow? more goodness yet?
[*Aside.*
Ward. I see her now, I'm sure; the ape's so little,
I shall scarce feel her; I have seen almost
As tall as she sold in the fair for tenpence:
See how she simpers it, as if marmalade
Would not melt in her mouth! she might have the kindness, i'faith,
To send me a gilded bull from her own trencher,
A ram, a goat, or somewhat to be nibbling:
These women, when they come to sweet things once,
They forget all their friends, they grow so greedy,
Nay, oftentimes their husbands.
Duke. Here's a health now, gallants,
To the best beauty at this day in Florence.
Bian. Whoe'er she be, she shall not go unpledged, sir.
Duke. Nay, you're excused for this.
Bian. Who, I, my lord?
Duke. Yes, by the law of Bacchus; plead your benefit,
You are not bound to pledge your own health, lady.
Bian. That's a good way, my lord, to keep me dry.
Duke. Nay, then, I'll not offend Venus so much,
Let Bacchus seek his 'mends in another court;
Here's to thyself, Bianca. [DUKE *and others drink.*

Bian. Nothing comes
More welcome to that name than your grace.
Lean. So, so;
Here stands the poor thief now that stole the treasure,
And he's not thought on. Ours is near kin now
To a twin-misery born into the world;
First the hard-conscienced worldling, he hoards wealth [up,
Then comes the next, and he feasts all upon't;
One's damned for getting, th' other for spending on't.
O equal justice, thou hast met my sin
With a full weight! I'm rightly now opprest,
All her friends' heavy hearts lie in my breast. [*Aside.*
Duke. Methinks there is no spirit 'mongst us, gallants,
But what divinely sparkles from the eyes
Of bright Bianca; we sat all in darkness
But for that splendour. Who was't told us lately
Of a match-making right, a marriage-tender?
Guar. 'Twas I, my lord.
Duke. 'Twas you indeed. Where is she?
Guar. This is the gentlewoman.
Fab. My lord, my daughter.
Duke. Why, here's some stirring yet.
Fab. She's a dear child to me.
Duke. That must needs be, you say she is your daughter.
Fab. Nay, my good lord, dear to my purse, I mean,
Beside my person, I ne'er reckoned that.
Sh'as the full qualities of a gentlewoman;
I've brought her up to music, dancing, what not,
That may commend her sex, and stir her husband.
Duke. And which is he now?
Guar. This young heir, my lord.
Duke. What is he brought up to?
Hip. To cat and trap. [*Aside.*
Guar. My lord, he's a great ward, wealthy but simple.
His part consists in acres.
Duke. O, wise-acres.

Guar. You've spoke him in a word, sir.
Bian. 'Las, poor gentlewoman!
She's ill-bestead, unless she'as dealt the wiselier,
And laid in more provision for her youth;
Fools will not keep in summer.
Lean. No, nor such wives
From whores in winter. [*Aside.*
Duke. Yea, the voice too, sir?
Fab. Ay, and a sweet breast[1] too, my lord, I hope
Or I have cast away my money wisely;
She took her pricksong[2] earlier my lord,
Than any of her kindred ever did;
A rare child, though I say't: but I'd not have
The baggage hear so much, 'twould make her swell straight,
And maids of all things must not be puffed up.
Duke. Let's turn us to a better banquet, then;
For music bids the soul of man to a feast,
And that's indeed a noble entertainment,
Worthy Bianca's self: you shall perceive, beauty,
Our Florentine damsels are not brought up idly.
Bian. They're wiser of themselves it seems, my lord,
And can take gifts when goodness offers 'em.
Lean. True, and damnation has taught you that wisdom; [*Music.*
You can take gifts too. O, that music mocks me!
[*Aside.*
Liv. I am as dumb to any language now
But love's, as one that never learned to speak.
I am not yet so old but he may think of me;
My own fault, I've been idle a long time;
But I'll begin the week, and paint to-morrow,
So follow my true labour day by day;
I never thrived so well as when I used it. [*Aside.*

[1] Voice.
[2] "Harmony written or pricked down, in opposition to plain-song, where the descant rested with the will of the singer."—Chappell's *Popular Music*, quoted by Bullen.

Isa. [*sings.*] What harder chance can fall to woman,
Who was born to cleave to some man,
Than to bestow her time, youth, beauty,
Life's observance, honour, duty,
On a thing for no use good
But to make physic work, or blood
Force fresh in an old lady's cheek?
She that would be
Mother of fools, let her compound with me.

Ward. Here's a tune indeed! pish,
I had rather hear one ballad sung i' the nose now
Of the lamentable drowning of fat sheep and oxen,
Than all these simpering tunes played upon cat's-guts,
And sung by little kitlings [*Aside.*

Fab. How like you her breast now, my lord?

Bian. Her breast?
He talks as if his daughter had given suck
Before she were married, as her betters have;
The next he praises sure will be her nipples. [*Aside.*

Duke. Methinks now such a voice to such a husband
Is like a jewel of unvalued worth
Hung at a fool's ear. [*Aside to* BIANCA.

Fab. May it please your grace
To give her leave to show another quality?

Duke. Marry, as many good ones as you will, sir;
The more the better welcome.

Lean. But the less
The better practised: that soul's black indeed
That cannot commend virtue; but who keeps it?
Th' extortioner will say to a sick beggar,
Heaven comfort thee! though he give none himself;
This good is common. [*Aside.*

Fab. Will it please you now, sir,
To entreat your ward to take her by the hand,
And lead her in a dance before the duke?

Guar. That will I, sir; 'tis needful.—Hark you, nephew.
[*Whispers* Ward.

Fab. Nay, you shall see, young heir, what you've for your money,
Without fraud or imposture.

Ward. Dance with her?
Not I, sweet guardianer, do not urge my heart to't,
'Tis clean against my blood; dance with a stranger?
Let who will do't, I'll not begin first with her.

Hip. No, fear't not, fool; sh'as took a better order. [*Aside.*

Guar. Why, who shall take her then?

Ward. Some other gentleman:
Look, there's her uncle, a fine-timbered reveller,
Perhaps he knows the manner of her dancing too;
I'll have him do't before me—I've sworn, guardianer—
Then may I learn the better.

Guar. Thou'lt be an ass still!

Ward. Ay, all that, uncle, shall not fool me out:
Pish, I stick closer to myself than so.

Guar. I must entreat you, sir, to take your niece
And dance with her; my ward's a little wilful,
He'd have you show him the way.

Hip. Me, sir? he shall
Command it at all hours; pray, tell him so.

Guar. I thank you for him; he has not wit, himself, sir.

Hip. Come, my life's peace—I've a strange office on't here:
'Tis some man's luck to keep the joys he likes
Concealed for his own bosom, but my fortune
To set 'em out now for another's liking;
Like the mad misery of necessitous man,
That parts from his good horse with many praises,
And goes on foot himself: need must be obeyed
In every action; it mars man and maid. [*Aside.*

[*Music.* HIPPOLITO *and* ISABELLA *dance, making obeisance to the* DUKE, *and to each other, both before and after the dance.*

Duke. Signor Fabricio, you're a happy father;

Your cares and pains are fortunate you see,
Your cost bears noble fruits.—Hippolito, thanks.

Fab. Here's some amends for all my charges yet;
She wins both prick and praise[1] where'er she comes.

Duke. How lik'st, Bianca?

Bian. All things well, my lord,
But this poor gentlewoman's fortune, that's the worst.

Duke. There is no doubt, Bianca, she'll find leisure
To make that good enough; he's rich and simple.

Bian. She has the better hope o' th' upper hand, indeed,
Which women strive for most.

Guar. Do't when I bid you, sir.

Ward. I'll venture but a hornpipe with her, guardianer,
Or some such married man's dance.

Guar. Well, venture something, sir.

Ward. I have rhyme for what I do.

Guar. But little reason, I think.

Ward. Plain men dance the measures,[2] the cinquapace[3] the gay;
Cuckolds dance the hornpipe, and farmers dance the hay;[4]
Your soldiers dance the round, and maidens that grow big;
Your drunkards, the canaries;[5] your whore and bawd, the jig.
Here's your eight kind of dancers; he that finds
The ninth let him pay the minstrels.

Duke. O, here he appears once in his own person;
I thought he would have married her by attorney,
And lain with her so to.

Bian. Nay, my kind lord,
There's very seldom any found so foolish
To give away his part there.

1 "Prick and praise," a proverbial expression; the prick was the point in the centre of the target at archery.
2 A slow stately dance.
3 *Cinque-pace*, a lively French dance of five steps.
4 A rustic dance.
5 A quick dance.

Lean. Bitter scoff!
Yet I must do't! with what a cruel pride
The glory of her sin strikes by my afflictions! [*Aside.*

[*The* Ward *and* ISABELLA *dance; he ridiculously imitating* HIPPOLITO.

Duke. This thing will make shift, sirs, to make a husband
For aught I see in him.—How think'st, Bianca?
Bian. Faith, an ill-favoured shift, my lord, methinks;
If he would take some voyage when he's married,
Dangerous, or long enough, and scarce be seen
Once in nine year together, a wife then
Might make indifferent shift to be content with him.
Duke. A kiss [*kisses her*]; that wit deserves to be made much on.—
Come, our caroch![1]
Guar. Stands ready for your grace.
Duke. My thanks to all your loves.—Come, fair Bianca,
We have took special care of you and provided
Your lodging near us now.
Bian. Your love is great, my lord.
Duke. Once more, our thanks to all.
Omnes. All blest honours guard you!

[*Cornets flourishing, exeunt all but* LEANTIO *and* LIVIA.

Lean. O hast thou left me then, Bianca, utterly?
Bianca, now I miss thee! O, return,
And save the faith of woman! I ne'er felt
The loss of thee till now; 'tis an affliction
Of greater weight than youth was made to bear;
As if a punishment of after-life
Were faln upon man here, so new it is
To flesh and blood, so strange, so insupportable;
A torment even mistook, as if a body
Whose death were drowning, must needs therefore suffer it
In scalding oil. [*Aside.*
Liv. Sweet sir——

[1] Coach. Fr. *carrosse.*

Lean. As long as mine eye saw thee,
I half enjoyed thee. [*Aside.*

Liv. Sir——

Lean. Canst thou forget
The dear pains my love took? how it has watched
Whole nights together, in all weathers, for thee,
Yet stood in heart more merry than the tempest
That sung about mine ears—like dangerous flatterers,
That can set all their mischief to sweet tunes—
And then received thee, from thy father's window,
Into these arms at midnight: when we embraced
As if we had been statues only made for't,
To show art's life, so silent were our comforts,
And kissed as if our lips had grown together? [*Aside.*

Liv. This makes me madder to enjoy him now. [*Aside.*

Lean. Canst thou forget all this, and better joys
That we met after this, which then new kisses
Took pride to praise? [*Aside.*

Liv. I shall grow madder yet. [*Aside.*]—Sir——

Lean. This cannot be but of some close bawd's working.— [*Aside.*
Cry mercy, lady! what would you say to me?
My sorrow makes me so unmannerly,
So comfort bless me, I had quite forgot you.

Liv. Nothing, but even, in pity to that passion,[1]
Would give your grief good counsel.

Lean. Marry, and welcome, lady;
It never could come better.

Liv. Then first, sir,
To make away all your good thoughts at once of her,
Know most assuredly she is a strumpet.

Lean. Ha! "most assuredly?" speak not a thing
So vile so certainly, leave it more doubtful.

Liv. Then I must leave all truth, and spare my knowledge
A sin which I too lately found and wept for.

[1] Sorrow.

Lean. Found you it?
Liv. Ay, with wet eyes.
Lean. O perjurious friendship! [sir.
Liv. You missed your fortunes when you met with her,
Young gentlemen that only love for beauty,
They love not wisely; such a marriage rather
Proves the destruction of affection;
It brings on want, and want's the key of whoredom.
I think y'had small means with her?
Lean. O, not any, lady.
Liv. Alas, poor gentleman! what meant'st thou, sir,
Quite to undo thyself with thine own kind heart?
Thou art too good and pitiful to woman:
Marry, sir, thank thy stars for this blest fortune,
That rids the summer of thy youth so well
From many beggars, that had lain a-sunning
In thy beams only else, till thou hadst wasted
The whole days of thy life in heat and labour.
What would you say now to a creature found
As pitiful to you, and, as it were,
Even sent on purpose from the whole sex general,
To requite all that kindness you have shown to't?
Lean. What's that, madam?
Liv. Nay, a gentlewoman, and one able
To reward good things, ay, and bears a conscience to't:
Couldst thou love such a one, that, blow all fortunes,
Would never see thee want?
Nay, more, maintain thee to thine enemy's envy,
And shall not spend a care for't, stir a thought,
Nor break a sleep? unless love's music waked thee,
No storm of fortune should: look upon me,
And know that woman.
Lean. O my life's wealth, Bianca!
Liv. Still with her name? will nothing wear it out?
[*Aside.*
That deep sigh went but for a strumpet, sir.
Lean. It can go for no other that loves me.

Liv. He's vexed in mind: I came too soon to him;
Where's my discretion now, my skill, my judgment?
I'm cunning in all arts but my own love.
'Tis as unseasonable to tempt him now
So soon, as for a widow to be courted
Following her husband's corse, or to make bargain
By the grave-side, and take a young man there:
Her strange departure stands like a hearse[1] yet
Before his eyes, which time will take down shortly.
[*Aside, and exit.*

Lean. Is she my wife till death, yet no more mine?
That's a hard measure: then what's marriage good for?
Methinks, by right I should not now be living,
And then 'twere all well. What a happiness
Had I been made of, had I never seen her!
For nothing makes man's loss grievous to him
But knowledge of the worth of what he loses;
For what he never had, he never misses.
She's gone for ever, utterly; there is
As much redemption of a soul from hell,
As a fair woman's body from his palace.
Why should my love last longer than her truth?
What is there good in woman to be loved,
When only that which makes her so has left her?
I cannot love her now, but I must like
Her sin and my own shame too, and be guilty
Of law's breach with her, and mine own abusing;
All which were monstrous: then my safest course,
For health of mind and body, is to turn
My heart and hate her, most extremely hate her;
I have no other way: those virtuous powers,
Which were chaste witnesses of both our troths,
Can witness she breaks first. And I'm rewarded
With captainship o' the fort; a place of credit,

[1] "In imitation of which [cenotaph] our *hearses* here in England are set up in churches, during the continuance of a yeare or the space of certaine monthes.' Weever—cited in Todd's Johnson's *Dict.* v. *Hearse.*"—*Dyce.*

I must confess, but poor; my factorship
Shall not exchange means with't: he that died last in't,
He was no drunkard, yet he died a beggar
For all his thrift: besides, the place not fits me;
It suits my resolution, not my breeding.

Re-enter LIVIA.

Liv. I've tried all ways I can, and have not power
To keep from sight of him. [*Aside.*]—How are you now, [sir?

Lean. I feel a better ease, madam.

Liv. Thanks to blessedness!
You will do well, I warrant you, fear't not, sir,
Join but your own good will to't: he's not wise
That loves his pain or sickness, or grows fond
Of a disease whose property is to vex him,
And spitefully drink his blood up: out upon't sir!
Youth knows no greater loss. I pray, let's walk, sir;
You never saw the beauty of my house yet,
Nor how abundantly fortune has blest me
In worldly treasure; trust me, I've enough, sir,
To make my friend a rich man in my life,
A great man at my death; yourself will say so.
If you want anything, and spare to speak,
Troth, I'll condemn you for a wilful man, sir.

Lean. Why, sure,
This can be but the flattery of some dream.

Liv. Now, by this kiss, my love, my soul, and riches,
'Tis all true substance! [*Kisses him.*
Come, you shall see my wealth; take what you list;
The gallanter you go, the more you please me:
I will allow you too your page and footman,
Your race-horses, or any various pleasure
Exercised youth delights in; but to me
Only, sir, wear your heart of constant stuff;
Do but you love enough, I'll give enough.

Lean. Troth, then, I'll love enough, and take enough.

Liv. Then we are both pleased enough. [*Exeunt.*

SCENE III.

A Room in FABRICIO'S *House.*

Enter on one side GUARDIANO *and* ISABELLA, *on the other the* Ward *and* SORDIDO.

Guar. Now, nephew, here's the gentlewoman again.

Ward. Mass, here she's come again! mark her now, Sordido.

Guar. This is the maid my love and care has chose
Out for your wife, and so I tender her to you;
Yourself has been eye-witness of some qualities
That speak a courtly breeding, and are costly:
I bring you both to talk together now;
'Tis time you grew familiar in your tongues,
To-morrow you join hand, and one ring ties you,
And one bed holds you; if you like the choice,
Her father and her friends are i' the next room,
And stay to see the contract ere they part:
Therefore, despatch, good ward, be sweet and short;
Like her, or like her not, there's but two ways,
And one your body, th' other your purse pays.

Ward. I warrant you, guardianer, I'll not stand all day thrumming,
But quickly shoot my bolt at your next coming.

Guar. Well said: good fortune to your birding then! [*Exit.*

Ward. I never missed mark yet.

Sor. Troth, I think, master, if the truth were known,
You never shot at any but the kitchen wench,
And that was a she-woodcock,[1] a mere innocent,[2]
That was oft lost and cried[3] at eight-and-twenty.

Ward. No more of that meat, Sordido, here's eggs o' the spit now;
We must turn gingerly: draw out the catalogue
Of all the faults of women.

[1] Simpleton. [2] Idiot. [3] Meaning, by the public crier.

Sor. How? all the faults? have you so little reason, to think so much paper will lie in my breeches? why, ten carts will not carry it, if you set down but the bawds. All the faults? pray, let's be content with a few of 'em; and if they were less, you would find 'em enough, I warrant you: look you, sir.

Isa. But that I have th' advantage of the fool,
As much as woman's heart can wish and joy at,
What an infernal torment 'twere to be
Thus bought and sold, and turned and pryed into,
When, alas,
The worst bit's too good for him! and the comfort is,
Has but a cater's[1] place on't, and provides
All for another's table: yet how curious
The ass is! like some nice professor on't,
That buys up all the daintiest food i' the markets,
And seldom licks his lips after a taste on't. [*Aside.*

Sor. Now to her, now you've scanned all her parts over.

Ward. But at which end shall I begin now, Sordido?

Sor. O, ever at a woman's lip, while you live, sir; do you ask that question?

Ward. Methinks, Sordido, sh'as but a crabbed face to begin with.

Sor. A crabbed face? that will save money.

Ward. How? save money, Sordido?

Sor. Ay, sir; for, having a crabbed face of her own she'll eat the less verjuice[2] with her mutton; 'twill save verjuice at year's end, sir.

Ward. Nay, an your jests begin to be saucy once, I'll make you eat your meat without mustard.

Sor. And that in some kind is a punishment.

Ward. Gentlewoman, they say 'tis your pleasure to be my wife, and you shall know shortly whether it be mine or no to be your husband; and thereupon thus I first

[1] Caterer's.

[2] Verjuice, a favourite sauce of the day, was made from crab-apples.

enter upon you. [*Kisses her.*]—O most delicious scent! methinks it tasted as if a man had stept into a comfit-maker's shop to let a cart go by, all the while I kissed her.—It is reported, gentlewoman, you'll run mad for me, if you have me not.

Isa. I should be in great danger of my wits, sir,
For being so forward.—Should this ass kick backward now! [*Aside.*

Ward. Alas, poor soul! and is that hair your own?

Isa. My own? yes, sure, sir; I owe nothing for't.

Ward. 'Tis a good hearing; I shall have the less to pay when I have married you.—Look, do her eyes stand well?

Sor. They cannot stand better than in her head, I think: where would you have them? and for her nose, 'tis of a very good last.

Ward. I have known as good as that has not lasted a year through.

Sor. That's in the using of a thing; will not any strong bridge fall down in time, if we do nothing but beat at the bottom? a nose of buff would not last always, sir, especially if it came into the camp once.

Ward. But, Sordido, how shall we do to make her laugh, that I may see what teeth she has? for I'll not bate her a tooth, nor take a black one into the bargain.

Sor. Why, do but you fall in talk with her, you cannot choose but, one time or other, make her laugh, sir.

Ward. It shall go hard but I will.—Pray, what qualities have you beside singing and dancing? can you play at shittlecock, forsooth?

Isa. Ay, and at stool-ball[1] too, sir; I've great luck at it.

Ward. Why, can you catch a ball well?

Isa. I have catched two in my lap at one game.

Ward. What! have you, woman? I must have you learn
To play at trap too, then you're full and whole.

[1] An old game at which the ball was driven from stool to stool.

Isa. Anything that you please to bring me up to,
I shall take pains to practise.

Ward. 'Twill not do, Sordido;
We shall ne'er get her mouth opened wide enough.

Sor. No, sir? that's strange; then here's a trick for your learning.

[SORDIDO *yawns,* ISABELLA *yawns also, but covers her mouth with a handkerchief.*

Look now, look now! quick, quick there!

Ward. Pox of that scurvy mannerly trick with handkerchief!
It hindered me a little, but I'm satisfied:
When a fair woman gapes, and stops her mouth so,
It shows like a cloth-stopple in a cream-pot:
I have fair hope of her teeth now, Sordido.

Sor. Why, then, you've all well, sir! for aught I see,
She's right and straight enough now as she stands:
They'll commonly lie crooked, that's no matter;
Wise gamesters
Never find fault with that, let 'em lie still so.

Ward. I'd fain mark how she goes, and then I have all; for of all creatures I cannot abide a splay-footed woman; she's an unlucky thing to meet in a morning; her heels keep together so, as if she were beginning an Irish dance still, and the wriggling of her bum playing the tune to't: but I have bethought a cleanly shift to find it; dab down as you see me, and peep of one side when her back's towards you—I'll show you the way.

Sor. And you shall find me apt enough to peeping;
I have been one of them has seen mad sights
Under your scaffolds.

Ward. Will't please you walk, forsooth,
A turn or two by yourself? you're so pleasing to me,
I take delight to view you on both sides.

Isa. I shall be glad to fetch a walk to your love, sir;

'Twill get affection a good stomach, sir,—
Which I had need have to fall to such coarse victuals.
[*Aside.*

[ISABELLA *walks while the* Ward *and* SORDIDO *stoop down to look at her.*

Ward. Now go thy ways for a clean-treading wench,
As ever man in modesty peeped under!

Sor. I see the sweetest sight to please my master!
Never went Frenchman righter upon ropes,
Than she on Florentine rushes.[1]

Ward. 'Tis enough, forsooth.

Isa. And how do you like me now, sir?

Ward. Faith, so well,
I never mean to part with thee, sweetheart,
Under some sixteen children, and all boys.

Isa. You'll be at simple pains, if you prove kind,
And breed 'em all in your teeth.[2]

Ward. Nay by my faith,
What serves your belly for? 'twould make my cheeks
Look like blown bagpipes.

Re-enter GUARDIANO.

Guar. How now, ward and nephew,
Gentlewoman and niece! speak, is it so or not?

Ward. 'Tis so; we're both agreed, sir.

Guar. In to your kindred then;
There's friends, and wine, and music waits to welcome you.

Ward. Then I'll be drunk for joy.

Sor. And I for company;
I cannot break my nose in a better action. [*Exeunt.*

[1] With which the floors used to be strewn.

[2] "In allusion to a superstitious idea, that an affectionate husband had the toothache while his wife was breeding."—Editor of 1816.

ACT THE FOURTH.

SCENE I.

BIANCA'S *Lodging at Court.*

Enter BIANCA, *attended by two* Ladies.

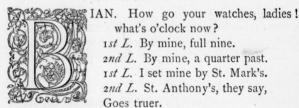

BIAN. How go your watches, ladies! what's o'clock now?

1st L. By mine, full nine.

2nd L. By mine, a quarter past.

1st L. I set mine by St. Mark's.

2nd L. St. Anthony's, they say,
Goes truer.

1st L. That's but your opinion, madam,
Because you love a gentleman o' the name.

2nd L. He's a true gentleman then.

1st L. So may he be
That comes to me to-night, for aught you know.

Bian. I'll end this strife straight: I set mine by the sun;
I love to set by the best, one shall not then
Be troubled to set often.

2nd L. You do wisely in't.

Bian. If I should set my watch, as some girls do,
By every clock i' the town, 'twould ne'er go true;
And too much turning of the dial's point,
Or tampering with the spring, might in small time
Spoil the whole work too; here it wants of nine now.

1st L. It does indeed, forsooth; mine's nearest truth yet.

2nd L. Yet I've found her lying with an advocate, which showed
Like two false clocks together in one parish.
Bian. So now I thank you, ladies; I desire
Awhile to be alone.
1st L. And I am nobody,
Methinks, unless I've one or other with me.—
Faith, my desire and hers will ne'er be sisters.
[*Aside.—Exeunt* Ladies.
Bian. How strangely woman's fortune comes about!
This was the farthest way to come to me,
All would have judged that knew me born in Venice,
And there with many jealous eyes brought up,
That never thought they had me sure enough
But when they were upon me; yet my hap
To meet it here, so far off from my birth-place,
My friends, or kindred! 'tis not good, in sadness,[1]
To keep a maid so strict in her young days;
Restraint
Breeds wandering thoughts, as many fasting days
A great desire to see flesh stirring again:
I'll ne'er use any girl of mine so strictly;
Howe'er they're kept, their fortunes find 'em out;
I see't in me: if they be got in court,
I'll ne'er forbid 'em the country; nor the court,
Though they be born i' the country: they will come to't,
And fetch their falls a thousand mile about,
Where one would little think on't.

Enter LEANTIO, *richly dressed.*

Lean. I long to see how my despiser looks
Now she's come here to court: these are her lodgings;
She's simply now advanced: I took her out
Of no such window, I remember, first;
That was a great deal lower, and less carved. [*Aside.*

[1] Seriously.

Bian. How now! what silkworm's this, i' the name of pride?
What, is it he?
Lean. A bow i' th' ham to your greatness;
You must have now three legs[1] I take it, must you not?
Bian. Then I must take another, I shall want else
The service I should have; you have but two there.
Lean. You're richly placed.
Bian. Methinks you're wondrous brave,[2] sir.
Lean. A sumptuous lodging.
Bian. You've an excellent suit there.
Lean. A chair of velvet.
Bian. Is your cloak lined through, sir?
Lean. You're very stately here.
Bian. Faith, something proud, sir.
Lean. Stay, stay, let's see your cloth-of-silver slippers.
Bian. Who's your shoemaker? has made you a neat boot.
Lean. Will you have a pair? the duke will lend you spurs.
Bian. Yes, when I ride.
Lean. 'Tis a brave life you lead.
Bian. I could ne'er see you in such good clothes
In my time.
Lean. In your time?
Bian. Sure I think, sir,
We both thrive best asunder.
Lean. You're a whore!
Bian. Fear nothing, sir.
Lean. An impudent, spiteful strumpet!
Bian. O, sir, you give me thanks for your captainship!
I thought you had forgot all your good manners.
Lean. And, to spite thee as much, look there; there read, [*Giving letter.*
Vex, gnaw; thou shalt find there I'm not love-starved.
The world was never yet so cold or pitiless,

[1] Bows, obeisances. [2] Finely attired.

But there was ever still more charity found out
Than at one proud fool's door; and 'twere hard, faith,
If I could not pass that. Read to thy shame there;
A cheerful and a beauteous benefactor too,
As e'er erected the good works of love.

Bian. Lady Livia!
Is't possible? her worship was my pandress;
She dote, and send, and give, and all to him!
Why, here's a bawd plagued home! [*Aside.*]—You're simply happy, sir;
Yet I'll not envy you.

Lean. No, court-saint, not thou!
You keep some friend of a new fashion:
There's no harm in your devil, he's a suckling,
But he will breed teeth shortly, will he not?

Bian. Take heed you play not then too long with him.

Lean. Yes, and the great one too: I shall find time
To play a hot religious bout with some of you,
And, perhaps, drive you and your course of sins
To their eternal kennels. I speak softly now,
'Tis manners in a noble woman's lodgings,
And I well know all my degrees of duty;
But come I to your everlasting parting once,
Thunder shall seem soft music to that tempest.

Bian. 'Twas said last week there would be change of weather,
When the moon hung so, and belike you heard it.

Lean. Why, here's sin made, and ne'er a conscience put to't,—
A monster with all forehead and no eyes!
Why do I talk to thee of sense or virtue,
That art as dark as death? and as much madness
To set light before thee, as to lead blind folks
To see the monuments, which they may smell as soon
As they behold,—marry, ofttimes their heads,
For want of light, may feel the hardness of 'em:

So shall thy blind pride my revenge and anger,
That canst not see it now; and it may fall
At such an hour when thou least seest of all:
So, to an ignorance darker than thy womb
I leave thy perjured soul; a plague will come! [*Exit.*

Bian. Get you gone first, and then I fear no greater;
Nor thee will I fear long; I'll have this sauciness
Soon banished from these lodgings, and the rooms
Perfumed well after the corrupt air it leaves:
His breath has made me almost sick, in troth:
A poor, base start-up! life, because has got
Fair clothes by foul means, comes to rail and show 'em!

Enter the DUKE.

Duke. Who's that?

Bian. Cry you mercy, sir!

Duke. Prithee, who's that?

Bian. The former thing, my lord, to whom you gave
The captainship; he eats his meat with grudging still.

Duke. Still?

Bian. He comes vaunting here of his new love,
And the new clothes she gave him, Lady Livia;
Who but she now his mistress!

Duke. Lady Livia?
Be sure of what you say.

Bian. He showed me her name, sir,
In perfumed paper, her vows, her letter,
With an intent to spite me; so his heart said,
And his threats made it good; they were as spiteful
As ever malice uttered, and as dangerous,
Should his hand follow the copy.

Duke. But that must not:
Do not you vex your mind; prithee, to bed, go;
All shall be well and quiet.

Bian. I love peace, sir.

Duke. And so do all that love; take you no care for't,

It shall be still provided to your hand.—
[*Exit* BIANCA.
Who's near us there?

Enter Servant.

Ser. My lord?
Duke. Seek out Hippolito,
Brother to Lady Livia, with all speed.
Ser. He was the last man I saw, my lord.
Duke. Make haste.— [*Exit* Servant.
He is a blood soon stirred; and as he's quick
To apprehend a wrong, he's bold and sudden
In bringing forth a ruin: I know, likewise,
The reputation of his sister's honour's
As dear to him as life-blood to his heart;
Besides, I'll flatter him with a goodness to her,—
Which I now thought on, but ne'er meant to practice,
Because I know her base,—and that wind drives him:
The ulcerous reputation feels the poise
Of lightest wrongs, as sores are vexed with flies.
He comes.—

Enter HIPPOLITO.

Hippolito, welcome.
Hip. My loved lord!
Duke. How does that lusty widow, thy kind sister?
Is she not sped yet of a second husband?
A bed-fellow she has, I ask not that,
I know she's sped of him.
Hip. Of him, my lord?
Duke. Yes, of a bed-fellow: is the news so strange to you?
Hip. I hope 'tis so to all.
Duke. I wish it were, sir,
But 'tis confessed too fast: her ignorant pleasures,
Only by lust instructed, have received
Into their services an impudent boaster,
One that does raise his glory from her shame,

And tells the mid-day sun what's done in darkness ;
Yet, blinded with her appetite, wastes her wealth,
Buys her disgraces at a dearer rate
Than bounteous housekeepers purchase their honour.
Nothing sads me so much, as that, in love
To thee and to thy blood, I had picked out
A worthy match for her, the great Vincentio,
High in our favour and in all men's thoughts.

Hip. O thou destruction of all happy fortunes,
Unsated blood ! Know you the name, my lord,
Of her abuser?

Duke. One Leantio.

Hip. He's a factor.

Duke. He ne'er made so brave a voyage,
By his own talk.

Hip. The poor old widow's son.
I humbly take my leave.

Duke. I see 'tis done.— [*Aside.*
Give her good counsel, make her see her error ;
I know she'll hearken to you.

Hip. Yes, my lord,
I make no doubt, as I shall take the course
Which she shall never know till it be acted,
And when she wakes to honour, then she'll thank me for't :
I'll imitate the pities of old surgeons
To this lost limb, who, ere they show their art,
Cast one asleep, then cut the diseased part ;
So, out of love to her I pity most,
She shall not feel him going till he's lost ;
Then she'll commend the cure. [*Exit.*

Duke. The great cure's [1] past ;
I count this done already ; his wrath's sure,
And speaks an injury deep : farewell, Leantio,
This place will never hear thee murmur more.—

[1] "Cure" was sometimes used in the sense of "care."

Enter the Cardinal *and* Servants.

Our noble brother, welcome !
Car. Set those lights down :
Depart till you be called. [*Exeunt* Servants.
Duke. There's serious business
Fixed in his look ; nay, it inclines a little
To the dark colour of a discontentment.— [*Aside.*
Brother, what is't commands your eye so powerfully ?
Speak, you seem lost.
Car. The thing I look on seems so,
To my eyes lost for ever.
Duke. You look on me.
Car. What a grief 'tis to a religious feeling.
To think a man should have a friend so goodly,
So wise, so noble, nay, a duke, a brother,
And all this certainly damned !
Duke. How !
Car. 'Tis no wonder,
If your great sin can do't : dare you look up
For thinking of a vengeance ? dare you sleep
For fear of never waking but to death ?
And dedicate unto a strumpet's love
The strength of your affections, zeal, and health ?
Here you stand now, can you assure your pleasures
You shall once more enjoy her, but once more ?
Alas, you cannot ! what a misery 'tis then,
To be more certain of eternal death
Than of a next embrace ! nay, shall I show you
How more unfortunate you stand in sin
Than the low, private man : all his offences,
Like enclosed grounds, keep but about himself,
And seldom stretch beyond his own soul's bounds ;
And when a man grows miserable, 'tis some comfort
When he's no further charged than with himself,
'Tis a sweet ease to wretchedness : but, great man,
Every sin thou committ'st shows like a flame

Upon a mountain, 'tis seen far about,
And, with a big wind made of popular breath,
The sparkles fly through cities, here one takes,
Another catches there, and in short time
Waste all to cinders; but remember still,
What burnt the valleys first came from the hill:
Every offence draws his particular pain,
But 'tis example proves the great man's bane.
The sins of mean men lie like scattered parcels
Of an unperfect bill; but when such fall,
Then comes example, and that sums up all:
And this your reason grants; if men of good lives,
Who by their virtuous actions stir up others
To noble and religious imitation,
Receive the greater glory after death,
As sin must needs confess, what may they feel
In height of torments and in weight of vengeance,
Not only they themselves not doing well,
But sets a light up to show men to hell?

Duke. If you have done, I have; no more, sweet brother!

Car. I know time spent in goodness is too tedious;
This had not been a moment's space in lust now:
How dare you venture on eternal pain,
That cannot bear a minute's reprehension?
Methinks you should endure to hear that talked of
Which you so strive to suffer. O, my brother,
What were you, if that you were taken now!
My heart weeps blood to think on't; 'tis a work
Of infinite mercy, you can never merit,
That yet you are not death-struck, no, not yet;
I dare not stay you long, for fear you should not
Have time enough allowed you to repent in:
There's but this wall [*pointing to his body*] betwixt you and destruction,
When you're at strongest, and but poor thin clay:
Think upon't, brother; can you come so near it

For a fair strumpet's love, and fall into
A torment that knows neither end nor bottom
For beauty but the deepness of a skin,
And that not of their own neither? Is she a thing
Whom sickness dare not visit, or age look on,
Or death resist? does the worm shun her grave?
If not, as your soul knows it, why should lust
Bring man to lasting pain for rotten dust?

Duke. Brother of spotless honour, let me weep
The first of my repentance in thy bosom,
And show the blest fruits of a thankful spirit:
And if I e'er keep woman more, unlawfully,
May I want penitence at my greatest need!
And wise men know there is no barren place
Threatens more famine than a dearth in grace.

Car. Why, here's a conversion is at this time, brother,
Sung for a hymn in Heaven, and at this instant
The powers of darkness groan, makes all hell sorry:
First I praise Heaven, then in my work I glory.
Who's there attends without?

Re-enter Servants.

1st Ser. My lord?

Car. Take up those lights; there was a thicker darkness
When they came first.—The peace of a fair soul
Keep with my noble brother!

Duke. Joys be with you, sir!

[*Exeunt* Cardinal *and* Servants.

She lies alone to-night for't, and must still,
Though it be hard to conquer; but I've vowed
Never to know her as a strumpet more,
And I must save my oath: if fury fail not,
Her husband dies to-night, or, at the most,
Lives not to see the morning spent to-morrow;
Then will I make her lawfully mine own,

Without this sin and horror. Now I'm chidden,
For what I shall enjoy then unforbidden;
And I'll not freeze in stoves: 'tis but a while;
Live like a hopeful bridegroom, chaste from flesh,
And pleasure then will seem new, fair, and fresh.

[*Exit.*

SCENE II.

A Hall in LIVIA'S *House.*

Enter HIPPOLITO.

Hip. The morning so far wasted, yet his baseness
So impudent! see if the very sun
Do not blush at him!
Dare he do thus much, and know me alive?
Put case one must be vicious, as I know myself
Monstrously guilty, there's a blind time made for't,
He might use only that,—'twere conscionable;
Art, silence, closeness, subtlety, and darkness,
Are fit for such a business; but there's no pity
To be bestowed on an apparent sinner,
An impudent daylight lecher. The great zeal
I bear to her advancement in this match
With Lord Vincentio, as the duke has wrought it,
To the perpetual honour of our house,
Puts fire into my blood to purge the air
Of this corruption, fear it spread too far,
And poison the whole hopes of this fair fortune.
I love her good so dearly, that no brother
Shall venture farther for a sister's glory
Than I for her preferment.

Enter LEANTIO *and a* Page.

Lean. Once again

I'll see that glistering whore, shines like a serpent
Now the court sun's upon her. [*Aside.*]—Page.

Page. Anon, sir.

Lean. I'll go in state too. [*Aside.*]—See the coach be ready. [*Exit* Page.
I'll hurry away presently.

Hip. Yes, you shall hurry,
And the devil after you: take that at setting forth; [*Strikes him.*
Now, an you'll draw, we're upon equal terms, sir.
Thou took'st advantage of my name in honour
Upon my sister; I ne'er saw the stroke
Come, till I found my reputation bleeding;
And therefore count it I no sin to valour
To serve thy lust so: now we're of even hand,
Take your best course against me. You must die.

Lean. How close sticks envy to man's happiness!
When I was poor, and little cared for life,
I had no such means offered me to die,
No man's wrath minded me.—Slave, I turn this to thee, [*Draws.*
To call thee to account for a wound lately
Of a base stamp upon me.

Hip. 'Twas most fit
For a base metal: come and fetch one now
More noble then, for I will use thee fairer
Than thou hast done thine own soul, or our honour; [*They fight.*
And there I think 'tis for thee. [LEANTIO *falls.*

[*Voices within.*] Help, help! O, part 'em!

Lean. False wife, I feel now thou'st prayed heartily for me:
Rise, strumpet, by my fall! thy lust may reign now:
My heart-string and the marriage-knot that tied thee,
Break both together. [*Dies.*

Hip. There I heard the sound on't,
And never liked string better.

Enter GUARDIANO, LIVIA, ISABELLA, *the* Ward, *and* SORDIDO.

Liv. 'Tis my brother!
Are you hurt, sir?
Hip. Not anything.
Liv. Blest fortune!
Shift for thyself: what is he thou hast killed?
Hip. Our honour's enemy.
Guar. Know you this man, lady?
Liv. Leantio! my love's joy!—Wounds stick upon thee
As deadly as thy sins! art thou not hurt—
The devil take that fortune!—and he dead?
Drop plagues into thy bowels without voice,
Secret and fearful!—Run for officers;
Let him be apprehended with all speed,
For fear he 'scape away; lay hands on him,
We cannot be too sure, 'tis wilful murder:
You do Heaven's vengeance and the law just service:
You know him not as I do; he's a villain
As monstrous as a prodigy and as dreadful.
Hip. Will you but entertain a noble patience
Till you but hear the reason, worthy sister?
Liv. The reason! that's a jest hell falls a-laughing at:
Is there a reason found for the destruction
Of our more lawful loves, and was there none
To kill the black lust 'twixt thy niece and thee,
That has kept close so long?
Guar. How's that, good madam?
Liv. Too true, sir; there she stands, let her deny't:
The deed cries shortly in the midwife's arms,
Unless the parent's sins strike it still-born;
And if you be not deaf and ignorant,
You'll hear strange notes ere long.—Look upon me, wench;
'Twas I betrayed thy honour subtlely to him,

Under a false tale; it light upon me now.—
His arm has paid me home upon thy breast,
My sweet, beloved Leantio!

Guar. Was my judgment
And care in choice so devilishly abused,
So beyond shamefully? all the world will grin at me.

Ward. O Sordido, Sordido, I'm damned, I'm damned.

Sor. Damned? why, sir?

Ward. One of the wicked; dost not see't? a cuckold, a plain reprobate cuckold!

Sor. Nay, an you be damned for that, be of good cheer, sir, you've gallant company of all professions; I'll have a wife next Sunday too, because I'll along with you myself.

Ward. That will be some comfort yet.

Liv. You, sir, that bear your load of injuries,
As I of sorrows, lend me your grieved strength
To this sad burden [*pointing to the body of* LEANTIO], who in life wore actions,
Flames were not nimbler: we will talk of things
May have the luck to break our hearts together.

Guar. I'll list to nothing but revenge and anger,
Whose counsels I will follow.

[*Exeunt* LIVIA *and* GUARDIANO, *with the body of* LEANTIO.

Sor. A wife, quoth 'a?
Here's a sweet plum-tree of your guardianer's graffing!

Ward. Nay, there's a worse name belongs to this fruit yet, an you could hit on't, a more open one; for he that marries a whore looks like a fellow bound all his lifetime to a medlar-tree, and that's good stuff; 'tis no sooner ripe but it looks rotten, and so do some queans at nineteen. A pox on't! I thought there was some knavery a-broach, for something stirred in her belly the first night I lay with her.

Sor. What, what, sir?

Ward. This is she brought up so courtly, can sing,

and dance!—and tumble too, methinks; I'll never marry wife again that has so many qualities.

Sor. Indeed, they are seldom good, master; for likely when they are taught so many, they will have one trick more of their own finding out. Well, give me a wench but with one good quality, to lie with none but her husband, and that's bringing up enough for any woman breathing.

Ward. This was the fault when she was tendered to me; you never looked to this.

Sor. Alas, how would you have me see through a great farthingale, sir? I cannot peep through a millstone, or in the going, to see what's done i' the bottom.

Ward. Her father praised her breast;[1] sh'ad the voice, forsooth! I marvelled she sung so small indeed, being no maid: now I perceive there's a young quirister in her belly, this breeds a singing in my head, I'm sure.

Sor. 'Tis but the tune of your wife's cinquapace[2] danced in a feather-bed: faith, go lie down, master; but take heed your horns do not make holes in the pillowbeers.[3]—I would not batter brows with him for a hogshead of angels;[4] he would prick my skull as full of holes as a scrivener's sand-box.

[*Aside.—Exeunt* Ward *and* SORDIDO.

Isa. Was ever maid so cruelly beguiled,
To the confusion of life, soul, and honour,
All of one woman's murdering! I'd fain bring
Her name no nearer to my blood than woman,
And 'tis too much of that. O, shame and horror!
In that small distance from yon man to me
Lies sin enough to make a whole world perish.—
[*Aside.*
'Tis time we parted, sir, and left the sight
Of one another; nothing can be worse
To hurt repentance, for our very eyes

[1] Voice. [2] See note *ante*, p. 325.
[3] Pillow-cases. [4] Gold coins.

Are far more poisonous to religion
Than basilisks to them: if any goodness
Rest in you, hope of comforts, fear of judgments,
My request is, I ne'er may see you more;
And so I turn me from you everlastingly,
So is my hope to miss you: but for her
That durst so dally with a sin so dangerous,
And lay a snare so spitefully for my youth,
If the least means but favour my revenge,
That I may practice the like cruel cunning
Upon her life as she has on mine honour,
I'll act it without pity.

Hip. Here's a care
Of reputation and a sister's fortune
Sweetly rewarded by her! would a silence,
As great as that which keeps among the graves,
Had everlastingly chained up her tongue!
My love to her has made mine miserable.

Re-enter GUARDIANO *and* LIVIA.

Guar. If you can but dissemble your heart's griefs now,—
Be but a woman so far.

Liv. Peace; I'll strive, sir.

Guar. As I can wear my injuries in a smile:
Here's an occasion offered, that gives anger
Both liberty and safety to perform
Things worth the fire it holds, without the fear
Of danger or of law; for mischiefs acted
Under the privilege of a marriage-triumph,
At the duke's hasty nuptials, will be thought
Things merely accidental, all's [3] by chance,
Not got of their own natures.

Liv. I conceive you, sir,
Even to a longing for performance o'n't;

[1] All as.

And here behold some fruits.—[*Kneels to* HIPPOLITO *and* ISABELLA.]—Forgive me both:
What I am now, returned to sense and judgment,
Is not the same rage and distraction
Presented lately to you,—that rude form
Is gone for ever; I am now myself,
That speaks all peace and friendship, and these tears
Are the true springs of hearty, penitent sorrow
For those foul wrongs which my forgetful fury
Slandered your virtues with: this gentleman
Is well resolved[1] now.

Guar. I was never otherways;
I knew, alas, 'twas but your anger spake it,
And I ne'er thought on't more.

Hip. [*raising* LIVIA.] Pray, rise, good sister.

Isa. Here's even as sweet amends made for a wrong now,
As one that gives a wound, and pays the surgeon;
All the smart's nothing, the great loss of blood,
Or the time of hindrance: well, I had a mother,
I can dissemble too. [*Aside.*]—What wrongs have slipt
Through anger's ignorance, aunt, my heart forgives.

Guar. Why, that's tuneful now!

Hip. And what I did, sister,
Was all for honour's cause, which time to come
Will approve to you.

Liv. Being awaked to goodness,
I understand so much, sir, and praise now
The fortune of your arm and of your safety;
For by his death you've rid me of a sin
As costly as e'er woman doated on:
'T has pleased the duke so well too, that behold, sir,
[*Giving paper.*
Has sent you here your pardon, which I kissed
With most affectionate comfort: when 'twas brought,

[1] Satisfied.

Then was my fit just past; it came so well, methought,
To glad my heart.

Hip. I see his grace thinks on me.

Liv. There's no talk now but of the preparation
For the great marriage.

Hip. Does he marry her, then?

Liv. With all speed, suddenly, as fast as cost
Can be laid on with many thousand hands.
This gentleman and I had once a purpose
To have honoured the first marriage of the duke
With an invention of his own; 'twas ready,
The pains well past, most of the charge bestowed on't,
Then came the death of your good mother, niece,
And turned the glory of it all to black:
'Tis a device would fit these times so well too,
Art's treasury not better: if you'll join,
It shall be done; the cost shall be mine.

Hip. You've my voice first; 'twill well approve my thankfulness
For the duke's love and favour.

Liv. What say you, niece?

Isa. I am content to make one.

Guar. The plot's full then;
Your pages, madam, will make shift for Cupids.

Liv. That will they, sir.

Guar. You'll play your old part still.

Liv. What is it? good troth, I have even forgot it.

Guar. Why, Juno Pronuba, the marriage goddess.

Liv. 'Tis right indeed.

Guar. And you shall play the Nymph,
That offers sacrifice to appease her wrath.

Isa. Sacrifice, good sir?

Liv. Must I be appeased then?

Guar. That's as you list yourself, as you see cause.

Liv. Methinks 'twould show the more state in her deity
To be incensed.

Isa. 'Twould; but my sacrifice
Shall take a course to appease you;—or I'll fail in't,
And teach a sinful bawd to play a goddess.
[*Aside, and exit.*

Guar. For our parts, we'll not be ambitious, sir:
Please you, walk in and see the project drawn,
Then take your choice.

Hip. I weigh not, so I have one.
[*Exeunt* GUARDIANO *and* HIPPOLITO.

Liv. How much ado have I to restrain fury
From breaking into curses! O, how painful 'tis
To keep great sorrow smothered! sure, I think
'Tis harder to dissemble grief than love.
Leantio, here the weight of thy loss lies,
Which nothing but destruction can suffice. [*Exit.*

SCENE III.

Before the DUKE'S Palace.

Hautboys. Enter the DUKE *and* BIANCA *richly attired, attended by* Lords, Cardinals, Ladies *and others: as they are passing in great state over the stage, enter the* Cardinal, *meeting them.*

Car. Cease, cease! religious honours done to sin
Disparage virtue's reverence, and will pull
Heaven's thunder upon Florence: holy ceremonies
Were made for sacred uses, not for sinful.
Are these the fruits of your repentance, brother?
Better it had been you had never sorrowed,
Than to abuse the benefit, and return
To worse than where sin left you.
Vowed you then never to keep strumpet more,
And are you now so swift in your desires

To knit your honours and your life fast to her?
Is not sin sure enough to wretched man,
But he must bind himself in chains to't! worse;
Must marriage, the immaculate robe of honour,
That renders virtue glorious, fair, and fruitful
To her great master, be now made the garment
Of leprosy and foulness? Is this penitence
To sanctify hot lust? what is it otherwise
Than worship done to devils? Is this the best
Amends that sin can make after her riots?
As if a drunkard, to appease Heaven's wrath,
Should offer up his surfeit for a sacrifice:
If that be comely, then lust's offerings are
On wedlock's sacred altar.

Duke. Here you're bitter
Without cause, brother; what I vowed I keep,
As safe as you your conscience; and this needs not;
I taste more wrath in't than I do religion,
And envy more than goodness: the path now
I tread is honest, leads to lawful love,
Which virtue in her strictness would not check:
I vowed no more to keep a sensual woman;
'Tis done, I mean to make a lawful wife of her.

Car. He that taught you that craft,
Call him not master long, he will undo you;
Grow not too cunning for your soul, good brother:
Is it enough to use adulterous thefts,
And then take sanctuary in marriage?
I grant, so long as an offender keeps
Close in a privileged temple, his life's safe;
But if he ever venture to come out,
And so be taken, then he surely dies for't:
So now you're safe; but when you leave this body,
Man's only privileged temple upon earth,
In which the guilty soul takes sanctuary,
Then you'll perceive what wrongs chaste vows endure
When lust usurps the bed that should be pure.

Bian. Sir, I have read you over all this while
In silence, and I find great knowledge in you
And severe learning; yet, 'mongst all your virtues
I see not charity written, which some call
The first-born of religion, and I wonder
I cannot see't in yours: believe it, sir,
There is no virtue can be sooner missed,
Or later welcomed; it begins the rest,
And sets 'em all in order: Heaven and angels
Take great delight in a converted sinner;
Why should you then, a servant and professor,
Differ so much from them? If every woman
That commits evil should be therefore kept
Back in desires of goodness, how should virtue
Be known and honoured? From a man that's blind,
To take a burning taper 'tis no wrong,
He never misses it; but to take light
From one that sees, that's injury and spite.
Pray, whether is religion better served,
When lives that are licentious are made honest,
Than when they still run through a sinful blood?
'Tis nothing virtue's temples to deface;
But build the ruins, there's a work of grace!

Duke. I kiss thee for that spirit; thou'st praised thy wit
A modest way.—On, on, there!

[*Hautboys. Exeunt all except the* Cardinal.

Car. Lust is bold,
And will have vengeance speak ere't be controlled.

[*Exit.*

ACT THE FIFTH.

SCENE I.

A great Hall in the DUKE'S *Palace.*

Enter GUARDIANO *and the* Ward.

GUAR. Speak, hast thou any sense of thy abuse?
Dost thou know what wrong's done thee?

Ward. I were an ass else;
I cannot wash my face but I am feeling on't.

Guar. Here, take this caltrop[1] then [*giving caltrop*], convey it secretly
Into the place I showed you: look you, sir,
This is the trap-door to't.

Ward. I know't of old, uncle, since the last triumph;[2] here rose up a devil with one eye, I remember, with a company of fireworks at's tail.

Guar. Prithee, leave squibbing now; mark me, and fail not;
But when thou hear'st me give a stamp, down with't,
The villain's caught then.

Ward. If I miss you, hang me: I love to catch a villain, and your stamp[3] shall go current I warrant you. But how shall I rise up and let him down too all at one hole? that will be a horrible puzzle. You know I have a part in't, I play Slander.

[1] An instrument having four iron spikes used to impede cavalry.
[2] Show.
[3] Halfpenny.

Guar. True, but never make you ready for't.

Ward. No? my clothes are bought and all, and a foul fiend's head, with a long, contumelious tongue i' the chaps on't, a very fit shape for Slander i' th' out-parishes.

Guar. It shall not come so far; thou understand'st
it not.

Ward. O, O!

Guar. He shall lie deep enough ere that time,
And stick first upon those.

Ward. Now I conceive you, guardianer.

Guar. Away!
List to the privy stamp, that's all thy part.

Ward. Stamp my horns in a mortar, if I miss you, and give the powder in white wine to sick cuckolds, a very present remedy for the headache. [*Exit.*

Guar. If this should any way miscarry now—
As, if the fool be nimble enough, 'tis certain—
The pages, that present the swift-winged Cupids,
Are taught to hit him with their shafts of love,
Fitting his part, which I have cunningly poisoned:
He cannot 'scàpe my fury; and those ills
Will be laid all on fortune, not our wills;
That's all the sport on't: for who will imagine
That, at the celebration of this night,
Any mischance that haps can flow from spite? [*Exit.*

Flourish. Enter above DUKE, BIANCA, Lord Cardinal, FABRICIO, *other* Cardinals, *and* Lords *and* Ladies *in state.*

Duke. Now, our fair duchess, your delight shall witness
How you're beloved and honoured; all the glories
Bestowed upon the gladness of this night
Are done for your bright sake.

Bian. I am the more
In debt, my lord, to love and courtesies
That offer up themselves so bounteously
To do me honoured grace, without my merit.

Duke. A goodness set in greatness; how it sparkles
Afar off, like pure diamonds set in gold!
How perfect my desires were, might I witness
But a fair noble peace 'twixt your two spirits!
The reconcilement would be more sweet to me
Than longer life to him that fears to die.—
Good sir—

Car. I profess peace, and am content.

Duke. I'll see the seal upon't, and then 'tis firm.

Car. You shall have all you wish. [*Kisses* BIANCA.

Duke. I've all indeed now. [me;

Bian. But I've made surer work; this shall not blind
He that begins so early to reprove,
Quickly rid him, or look for little love:
Beware a brother's envy; he's next heir too.
Cardinal, you die this night; the plot's laid surely;
In time of sports death may steal in securely,
Then 'tis least thought on;
For he that's most religious, holy friend,
Does not at all hours think upon his end;
He has his times of frailty, and his thoughts
Their transportations too through flesh and blood,
For all his zeal, his learning, and his light,
As well as we, poor soul, that sin by night. [*Aside.*

Duke [*looking at a paper.*] What's this, Fabricio?

Fab. Marry, my lord, the model
Of what's presented.

Duke. O, we thank their loves.—
Sweet duchess, take your seat; list to the argument.
[*Reads.*

There is a Nymph that haunts the woods and springs,
  In love with two at once, and they with her;
Equal it runs; but, to decide these things,
  The cause to mighty Juno they refer,
She being the marriage-goddess: the two lovers
  They offer sighs, the Nymph a sacrifice,
All to please Juno, who by signs discovers
  How the event shall be; so that strife dies:

Then springs a second; for the man refused
Grows discontent, and, out of love abused,
He raises Slander up, like a black fiend,
To disgrace th' other, which pays him i' the end.

Bian. In troth, my lord, a pretty, pleasing argument,
And fits th' occasion well: envy and slander
Are things soon raised against two faithful lovers;
But comfort is, they're not long unrewarded. [*Music.*
Duke. This music shows they're upon entrance now.
Bian. Then enter all my wishes. [*Aside.*

Enter HYMEN *in a yellow robe,* GANYMEDE *in a blue robe powdered with stars, and* HEBE *in a white robe with golden stars, each bearing a covered cup: they dance a short dance, and then make obeisance to the* DUKE, *&c.*

Hym. To thee, fair bride, Hymen offers up
Of nuptial joys this the celestial cup;
Taste it, and thou shalt ever find
Love in thy bed, peace in thy mind.

Bian. We'll taste you, sure; 'twere pity to disgrace
So pretty a beginning.
[*Takes cup from* HYMEN, *and drinks.*
Duke. 'Twas spoke nobly.
Gan. Two cups of nectar have we begged from Jove;
Hebe, give that to innocence, I this to love:
Take heed of stumbling more, look to your way;
Remember still the *Via Lactea.*
[GANYMEDE *and* HEBE *respectively offer their cups to the* DUKE *and* Cardinal, *who drink.*
Hebe. Well, Ganymede, you've more faults, though not so known;
I spilled one cup, but you've filched many a one.
Hym. No more; forbear for Hymen's sake;
In love we met, and so let's part.
[*Exeunt* HYMEN, GANYMEDE, *and* HEBE.

Duke. But, soft; here's no such persons in the argument

As these three, Hymen, Hebe, Ganymede;
The actors that this model here discovers
Are only four,—Juno, a Nymph, two lovers.

Bian. This is some antemasque[1] belike, my lord,
To entertain time.—Now my peace is perfect,
Let sports come on apace. [*Aside.*]—Now is their time,
my lord: [*Music.*
Hark you! you hear from 'em.

Duke. The Nymph indeed!

Enter two Nymphs *bearing tapers lighted; then* ISABELLA *as a* Nymph, *dressed with flowers and garlands, carrying a censer with fire in it: they set the censer and tapers on* JUNO'S *altar with much reverence, singing this ditty in parts:*

Juno, nuptial goddess,
Thou that rul'st o'er coupled bodies,
Tiest man to woman, never to forsake her,
Thou only powerful marriage-maker,
Pity this amazed affection!
I love both, and both love me;
Nor know I where to give rejection,
My heart likes so equally,
Till thou sett'st right my peace of life,
And with thy power conclude this strife.

Isa. Now, with my thanks, depart you to the springs,
I to these wells of love. [*Exeunt the two* Nymphs.]—
Thou sacred goddess
And queen of nuptials, daughter to great Saturn,
Sister and wife to Jove, imperial Juno,
Pity this passionate conflict in my breast,
This tedious war 'twixt two affections;
Crown me with victory, and my heart's at peace!

Enter HIPPOLITO *and* GUARDIANO *as* Shepherds.

Hip. Make me that happy man, thou mighty goddess!

Guar. But I live most in hope, if truest love
Merit the greatest comfort.

[1] A burlesque interlude in the masque.

Isa. I love both
With such an even and fair affection,
I know not which to speak for, which to wish for,
Till thou, great arbitress 'twixt lovers' hearts,
By thy auspicious grace design the man ;
Which pity I implore !

Hip. and Guar. We all implore it !

Isa. And after sighs—contrition's truest odours—
I offer to thy powerful deity
This precious incense [*waving the censer*] ; may it ascend peacefully !—
(And if it keep true touch, my good aunt Juno,
'Twill try your immortality ere't be long :
I fear you'll ne'er get so nigh Heaven again,
When you're once down.) [*Aside.*

[LIVIA *descends as* JUNO, *attended by* Pages *as* Cupids.

Liv. Though you and your affections
Seem all as dark to our illustrious brightness
As night's inheritance, hell, we pity you,
And your requests are granted. You ask signs,
They shall be given you ; we'll be gracious to you :
He of those twain which we determine for you,
Love's arrows shall wound twice ; the latter wound
Betokens love in age ; for so are all
Whose love continues firmly all their lifetime
Twice wounded at their marriage, else affection
Dies when youth ends.—
(This savour overcomes me !) [*Aside.*
Now, for a sign of wealth and golden days,
Bright-eyed prosperity—which all couples love,
Ay, and makes love—take that ; our brother Jove
Never denies us of his burning treasure
To express bounty. [ISABELLA *falls down and dies.*

Duke. She falls down upon't ;
What's the conceit of that ?

Fab. As o'erjoyed belike :
Too much prosperity o'erjoys us all,
And she has her lapful, it seems, my lord.

Duke. This swerves a little from the argument though:
Look you, my lords. [*Showing paper.*

Guar. All's fast: now comes my part to tole[1] him hither;
Then, with a stamp given, he's despatched as cunningly. [*Aside.*

Hip. [*raising the body of* ISA.] Stark dead! O treachery! cruelly made away!

[GUARDIANO *stamps, and falls through a trap-door.*

How's that?

Fab. Look, there's one of the lovers dropped away too!

Duke. Why, sure, this plot's drawn false; here's no such thing.

Liv. O, I am sick to the death! let me down quickly,
This fume is deadly; O, 't has poison'd me!
My subtlety is sped, her art has quitted me;
My own ambition pulls me down to ruin. [*Falls down and dies.*

Hip. Nay, then, I kiss thy cold lips, and applaud
This thy revenge in death. [*Kisses the body of* ISABELLA.

Fab. Look, Juno's down too!

[Cupids *shoot at* HIPPOLITO.

What makes she there? her pride should keep aloft:
She was wont to scorn the earth in other shows;
Methinks her peacock's feathers are much pulled.

Hip. O, death runs through my blood in a wild flame too!
Plague of those Cupids! some lay hold on 'em,
Let 'em not escape; they've spoiled me, the shaft's deadly.

Duke. I've lost myself in this quite.

Hip. My great lords,
We're all confounded.

Duke. How?

Hip. Dead; and I worse.

Fab. Dead! my girl dead? I hope
My sister Juno has not served me so.

[1] Allure.

Hip. Lust and forgetfulness has been amongst us,
And we are brought to nothing: some blest charity
Lend me the speeding pity of his sword,
To quench this fire in blood! Leantio's death
Has brought all this upon us—now I taste it—
And made us lay plots to confound each other;
Th' event so proves it; and man's understanding
Is riper at his fall than all his lifetime.
She, in a madness for her lover's death,
Revealed a fearful lust in our near bloods,
For which I'm punished dreadfully and unlooked for;
Proved her own ruin too; vengeance met vengeance,
Like a set match, as if the plagues of sin
Had been agreed to meet here altogether:
But how her fawning partner fell I reach not,
Unless caught by some springe of his own setting,—
For, on my pain, he never dreamed of dying;
The plot was all his own, and he had cunning
Enough to save himself: but 'tis the property
Of guilty deeds to draw your wise men downward:
Therefore the wonder ceases. O, this torment!
Duke. Our guard below there!

Enter a Lord *with a* Guard.

Lord. My lord?
Hip. Run and meet death then,
And cut off time and pain! [*Runs on a sword and dies.*
Lord. Behold, my lord,
Has run his breast upon a weapon's point!
Duke. Upon the first night of our nuptial honours
Destruction play her triumph, and great mischiefs
Mask in expected pleasures! 'tis prodigious!
They're things most fearfully ominous; I like 'em not.—
Remove these ruined bodies from our eyes.
[*The* Guard *removes the bodies of* ISABELLA, LIVIA, *and* HIPPOLITO.

Bian. Not yet, no change? when falls he to the earth? [*Aside.*

Lord. Please but your excellence to peruse that paper, [*Gives paper to the* DUKE.
Which is a brief confession from the heart
Of him that fell first, ere his soul departed;
And there the darkness of these deeds speaks plainly,
'Tis the full scope, the manner, and intent:
His ward, that ignorantly let him down,
Fear put to present flight at the voice of him.

Bian. Not yet? [*Aside.*

Duke. Read, read, for I am lost in sight and strength! [*Falls.*

Car. My noble brother!

Bian. O, the curse of wretchedness!
My deadly hand is fall'n upon my lord:
Destruction, take me to thee! give me way;
The pains and plagues of a lost soul upon him
That hinders me a moment!

Duke. My heart swells bigger yet; help here, break't ope!
My breast flies open next. [*Dies.*

Bian. O, with the poison
That was prepared for thee! thee, cardinal,
'Twas meant for thee.

Car. Poor prince!

Bian. Accursèd error!
Give me thy last breath, thou infected bosom,
And wrap two spirits in one poisoned vapour!
Thus, thus, reward thy murderer, and turn death [*Kisses the body of the* DUKE.
Into a parting kiss! my soul stands ready at my lips,
Even vexed to stay one minute after thee.

Car. The greatest sorrow and astonishment
That ever struck the general peace of Florence
Dwells in this hour.

Bian. So, my desires are satisfied,

I feel death's power within me.
Thou hast prevailed in something, cursèd poison;
Though thy chief force was spent in my lord's bosom;
But my deformity in spirit's more foul,
A blemished face best fits a leprous soul.
What make I here? these are all strangers to me,
Not known but by their malice now thou'rt gone,
Nor do I seek their pities.

[*Drinks from the poisoned cup.*[1]

Car. O restrain
Her ignorant, wilful hand!

Bian. Now do; 'tis done.
Leantio, now I feel the breach of marriage
At my heart-breaking. O, the deadly snares
That women set for women, without pity
Either to soul or honour! learn by me
To know your foes: in this belief I die,—
Like our own sex we have no enemy.

Lord. See, my lord,
What shift sh'as made to be her own destruction!

Bian. Pride, greatness, honour, beauty, youth, ambition,
You must all down together, there's no help for't:
Yet this my gladness is, that I remove
Tasting the same death in a cup of love. [*Dies.*

Car. Sin, what thou art, these ruins show too piteously;
Two kings on one throne cannot sit together,
But one must needs down, for his title's wrong;
So where lust reigns, that prince cannot reign long.

[*Exeunt omens.*

[1] "Which she had prepared for the Cardinal and which Ganymede had by mistake presented to the duke."—*Dyce.*

THE SPANISH GIPSY.

THE *Spanish Gipsy*, written by Middleton and William Rowley, was acted at court in 1623 and 1624. It was published for the first time in 1653 and again in 1661. The story of Roderigo and Clara is taken directly from a novel by Cervantes, *La Fuerze de la Sangre*; the gipsy portions of the play were suggested by another novel by Cervantes, *La Gitanilla*, which has furnished hints for so many later plays and novels.

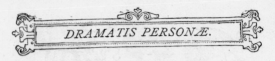

DRAMATIS PERSONÆ.

FERNANDO DE AZEVIDA, corregidor of Madrid.

PEDRO DE CORTES, } two old Dons.
FRANCISCO DE CARCOMO, }

RODERIGO, son of Fernando.

LOUIS DE CASTRO.

DIEGO, his friend.

JOHN, son of Francisco.

SANCHO, a foolish gentleman and ward to Pedro.

SOTO, a merry fellow, his man.

ALVAREZ DE CASTILLA, an old lord disguised as the father of the gipsies.

CARLO, }
ANTONIO, } disguised as gipsies.
and others, }

Servants.

MARIA, wife of Pedro.

CLARA, their daughter.

GUIAMARA, wife of Alvarez and sister to Fernando, disguised as the mother of the gipsies, and called by the name of Eugenia.

CONSTANZA, daughter of Fernando, disguised as a young Spanish gipsy, and called by the name of Pretiosa.

CHRISTIANA, a gentlewoman disguised as a gipsy.

CARDOCHIA, a young hostess to the gipsies.

SCENE—MADRID and its neighbourhood.

371 *THE SPANISH GIPSY.*

ACT THE FIRST.

SCENE I.

The Neighbourhood of Madrid.

Enter Roderigo, Louis, *and* Diego.

LOUIS. Roderigo!

Diego. Art mad?

Rod. Yes, not so much with wine: it's as rare to see a Spaniard a drunkard as a German sober, an Italian no whoremonger, an Englishman to pay his debts. I am no borachio;[1] sack, malaga, nor canary breeds the calenture[2] in my brains; mine eye mads me, not my cups.

Louis. What wouldst have us do?

Rod. Do?

Diego. So far as 'tis fit for gentlemen we'll venture.

Rod. I ask no more. I ha' seen a thing has bewitched me; a delicate body, but this in the waist [*showing the size by a sign*]; foot and leg tempting; the face I had only a glimpse of, but the fruit must needs be delicious, the tree being so beautiful.

[1] Drunkard. Literally a Spanish term for a vessel made of skins in which wine is kept.

[2] Sun-stroke, delirium.

Louis. Prithee, to the point.

Rod. Here 'tis: an old gentleman—no matter who he is—an old gentlewoman—I ha' nothing to do with her—but a young creature that follows them, daughter or servant, or whatsoever she be, her I must have: they are coming this way: shall I have her? I must have her.

Diego. How, how?

Louis. Thou speakest impossibilities.

Rod. Easy, easy, easy! I'll seize the young girl; stop you the old man; stay you the old woman.

Louis. How then?

Rod. I'll fly off with the young bird, that's all; many of our Spanish gallants act these merry parts every night. They are weak and old, we young and sprightly: will you assist me?

Louis. Troth, Roderigo, anything in the way of honour.

Rod. For a wench, man, any course is honourable.

Louis. Nay, not any; her father, if he be her father, may be noble.

Rod. I am as noble.

Louis. Would the adventure were so!

Rod. Stand close, they come.

Enter PEDRO, MARIA, *and* CLARA.

Ped. 'Tis late; would we were in Madrill! [1]

Mar. Go faster, my lord.

Ped. Clara, keep close.

[LOUIS *and* DIEGO *hold* PEDRO *and* MARIA, *while* RODERIGO *seizes* CLARA.

Cla. Help, help, help!

Rod. Are you crying out? I'll be your midwife.

[*Exit, bearing off* CLARA.

Ped. What mean you, gentlemen?

Mar. Villains! thieves! murderers!

[1] Madrid.

Ped. Do you not know me? I am De Cortes,
Pedro de Cortes.

Louis. De Cortes?—Diego, come away.

[*Exit with* DIEGO.

Ped. Clara!—where is my daughter?

Mar. Clara!—these villains
Have robbed us of our comfort, and will, I fear,
Her of her honour.

Ped. This had not wont to be
Our Spanish fashion; but now our gallants,
Our gentry, our young dons, heated with wine,—
A fire our countrymen do seldom sit at,—
Commit these outrages.—Clara!—Maria,
Let's homeward; I will raise Madrill to find
These traitors to all goodness.—Clara!

Mar. Clara! [*Exeunt.*

SCENE II.

Another Place in the Neighbourhood of Madrid.

Enter LOUIS *and* DIEGO.

Louis. O Diego, I am lost, I am mad!

Diego. So we are all.

Louis. 'Tis not with wine; I'm drunk with too much horror,
Inflamed with rage, to see us two made bawds
To Roderigo's lust: did not the old man
Name De Cortes, Pedro de Cortes?

Diego. Sure he did.

Louis. O Diego, as thou lov'st me, nay, on the forfeit
Of thine own life or mine, seal up thy lips,
Let 'em not name De Cortes! stay, stay, stay!
Roderigo has into his father's house
A passage through a garden——

Diego. Yes, my lord.
Louis. Thither I must, find Roderigo out,
And check him, check him home: if he but dare—
No more!—Diego, along! my soul does fight
A thousand battles blacker than this night. [*Exeunt.*

SCENE III.

A Bed-chamber in FERNANDO'S *House.*

RODERIGO *and* CLARA *discovered.*

Cla. Though the black veil of night hath overclouded
The world in darkness, yet ere many hours
The sun will rise again, and then this act
Of my dishonour will appear before you
More black than is the canopy that shrouds it:
What are you, pray? what are you?
Rod. Husht—a friend, a friend.
Cla. A friend? be then a gentle ravisher,
An honourable villain: as you have
Disrobed my youth of nature's goodliest portion,
My virgin purity, so with your sword
Let out that blood which is infected now
By your soul-staining lust.
Rod. Pish!
Cla. Are you noble?
I know you then will marry me; say!
Rod. Umh.
Cla. Not speak to me? are wanton devils dumb?
How are so many harmless virgins wrought
By falsehood of prevailing words to yield
Too easy forfeits of their shames and liberty,
If every orator of folly plead
In silence, like this untongued piece of violence?
You shall not from me. [*Holding him.*

Rod. Phew!—no more.
Cla. You shall not:
Who'er you are, disease of nature's sloth,
Birth of some monstrous sin, or scourge of virtue,
Heaven's wrath and mankind's burden, I will hold you;
I will: be rough, and therein merciful,
I will not loose my hold else.
Rod. There; 'tis gold. [*Offers money.*
Cla. Gold? why, alas! for what? the hire of pleasure
Perhaps is payment, mine is misery;
I need no wages for a ruined name,
More than a bleeding heart.
Rod. Nay, then, you're troublesome;
I'll lock you safe enough. [*Shakes her off, and exit.*
Cla. They cannot fear
Whom grief hath armed with hate and scorn of life.
Revenge, I kneel to thee! alas! 'gainst whom?
By what name shall I pull confusion down
From justice on his head that hath betrayed me?
I know not where I am: up, I beseech thee,
Thou lady regent of the air, the moon,
And lead me by thy light to some brave vengeance!
It is a chamber sure; the guilty bed,
Sad evidence against my loss of honour,
Assures so much. What's here, a window-curtain?
O Heaven, the stars appear too: ha, a chamber,
A goodly one? dwells rape in such a paradise?
Help me, my quickened senses! 'tis a garden
To which this window guides the covetous prospect,
A large one and a fair one; in the midst
A curious alabaster fountain stands,
Framed like—like what? no matter—swift, remembrance!
Rich furniture within too? and what's this?
A precious crucifix! I have enough.
[*Takes the crucifix, and conceals it in her bosom.*
Assist me, O you powers that guard the innocent!

Re-enter RODERIGO.

Rod. Now.
Cla. Welcome, if you come armèd in destruction:
I am prepared to die.
Rod. Tell me your name,
And what you are.
Cla. You urge me to a sin
As cruel as your lust; I dare not grant it.
Think on the violence of my defame;
And if you mean to write upon my grave
An epitaph of peace, forbear to question
Or whence or who I am. I know the heat
Of your desires is, after the performance
Of such a hellish act, by this time drowned
In cooler streams of penance;[1] and for my part,
I have washed off the leprosy that cleaves
To my just shame in true and honest tears;
I must not leave a mention of my wrongs,
The stain of my unspotted birth, to memory;
Let it lie buried with me in the dust;
That never time hereafter may report
How such a one as you have made me live.
Be resolute, and do not stagger; do not,
For I am nothing.
Rod. Sweet, let me enjoy thee
Now with a free allowance.
Cla. Ha, enjoy me?
Insufferable villain!
Rod. Peace, speak low;
I mean no second force; and since I find
Such goodness in an unknown frame of virtue,
Forgive my foul attempt, which I shall grieve for
So heartily, that could you be yourself
Eye-witness to my constant vowed repentance,
Trust me, you'd pity me.

[1] Penitence.

Cla. Sir, you can speak now.
Rod. So much I am the executioner
Of mine own trespass, that I have no heart
Nor reason to disclose my name or quality;
You must excuse me that; but, trust me, fair one,
Were this ill deed undone, this deed of wickedness,
I would be proud to court your love like him
Whom my first birth presented to the world.
This for your satisfaction: what remains,
That you can challenge as a service from me,
I both expect and beg it.
Cla. First, that you swear,
Neither in riot of your mirth, in passion
Of friendship, or in folly of discourse,
To speak of wrongs done to a ravished maid.
Rod. As I love truth, I swear!
Cla. Next, that you lead me
Near to the place you met me, and there leave me
To my last fortunes, ere the morning rise.
Rod. Say more.
Cla. Live a new man: if e'er you marry—
O me, my heart's a-breaking—but if e'er
You marry, in a constant love to her
That shall be then your wife, redeem the fault
Of my undoing. I am lost for ever:
Pray, use no more words.
Rod. You must give me leave
To veil you close.
Cla. Do what you will; no time
Can ransom me from sorrows or dishonours.
[RODERIGO *throws a veil over her.*
Shall we now go?
Rod. My shame may live without me,
But in my soul I bear my guilt about me.
Lend me your hand; now follow. [*Exeunt.*

SCENE IV.

Before FERNANDO'S *House.*

Enter LOUIS, DIEGO, *and* Servant.

Louis. Not yet come in, not yet?
Ser. No, I'll assure your lordship; I've seldom known him
Keep out so long; my lord usually observes
More seasonable hours.
Louis. What time of night is't?
Ser. On the stroke of three.
Louis. The stroke of three? 'tis wondrous strange! Dost hear?——
Ser. My lord?
Louis. Ere six I will be here again;
Tell thy lord so; ere six; 'a must not sleep;
Or if 'a do, I shall be bold to wake him;
Be sure thou tell'st him, do.
Ser. My lord, I shall. [*Enters the house.*
Louis. Diego,
Walk thou the street that leads about the Prado;
I'll round the west part of the city: meet me
At the Inquisition-chapel; if we miss him,
We'll both back to his lodgings.
Diego. At the chapel?
Louis. Ay, there we'll meet.
Diego. Agreed, I this way.
[*Exit* LOUIS: *as* DIEGO *is going out,*

Enter JOHN *reading.*

John. She is not noble, true; wise nature meant
Affection should ennoble her descent,
For love and beauty keeps as rich a seat
Of sweetness in the mean-born as the great.
I am resolved. [*Exit.*

Diego. 'Tis Roderigo certainly,
Yet his voice makes me doubt; but I'll o'erhear him.
[*Exit.*

SCENE V.

A Street.

Enter LOUIS.

Louis. That I, I, only I should be the man
Made accessary and a party both
To mine own torment, at a time so near
The birth of all those comforts I have travailed with
So many, many hours of hopes and fears;
Now at the instant—

Enter RODERIGO.

Ha! stand! thy name,
Truly and speedily.
Rod. Don Louis?
Louis. The same;
But who art thou? speak!
Rod. Roderigo.
Louis. Tell me,
As you're a noble gentleman, as ever
You hope to be enrolled amongst the virtuous,
As you love goodness, as you wish t' inherit
The blessedness and fellowship of angels,
As you're my friend, as you are Roderigo,
As you are anything that would deserve
A worthy name, where have you been to-night?
O, how have you disposed of that fair creature
Whom you led captive from me? speak, O speak!
Where, how, when, in what usage have you left her?
Truth, I require all truth.
Rod. Though I might question

The strangeness of your importunity,
Yet, 'cause I note distraction in the height
Of curiosity, I will be plain
And brief.

Louis. I thank you, sir.

Rod. Instead of feeding
Too wantonly upon so rich a banquet,
I found, even in that beauty that invited me,
Such a commanding majesty of chaste
And humbly glorious virtue, that it did not
More check my rash attempt than draw to ebb
The float[1] of those desires, which in an instant
Were cooled in their own streams of shame and folly.

Louis. Now all increase of honours
Fall in full showers on thee, Roderigo,
The best man living!

Rod. You are much transported
With this discourse, methinks.

Louis. Yes, I am.
She told ye her name too?

Rod. I could not urge it
By any importunity.

Louis. Better still!
Where did you leave her?

Rod. Where I found her; farther
She would by no means grant me to wait on her:
O, Louis, I am lost!

Louis This self-same lady
Was she to whom I have been long a suitor,
And shortly hope to marry.

Rod. She your mistress, then? Louis, since friendship
And noble honesty conjure our loves
To a continued league, here I unclasp
The secrets of my heart. O, I have had
A glimpse of such a creature, that deserves

[1] Flood.

A temple! if thou lov'st her—and I blame thee not,
For who can look on her, and not give up
His life unto her service?—if thou lov'st her,
For pity's sake conceal her; let me not
As much as know her name, there's a temptation in't
Let me not know her dwelling, birth, or quality,
Or anything that she calls hers, but thee;
In thee, my friend, I'll see her: and t' avoid
The surfeits and those rareties that tempt me,
So much I prize the happiness of friendship,
That I will leave the city——

Louis. Leave it?

Rod. Speed me
For Salamanca; court my studies now
For physic 'gainst infection of the mind.

Louis. You do amaze me.

Rod. Here to live, and live
Without her, is impossible and wretched.
For Heaven's sake, never tell her what I was,
Or that you knew me! and when I find that absence
Hath lost her to my memory, I'll dare
To see ye again. Meantime, the cause that draws me
From hence shall be to all the world untold;
No friend but thou alone, for whose sake only
I undertake this voluntary exile,
Shall be partaker of my griefs: thy hand,
Farewell; and all the pleasures, joys, contents,
That bless a constant lover, henceforth crown thee
A happy bridegroom!

Louis. You have conquered friendship
Beyond example.

Enter DIEGO.

Diego. Ha, ha, ha! some one
That hath slept well to-night, should a' but see me
Thus merry by myself, might justly think
I were not well in my wits.

Louis. Diego?

Diego. Yes,
'Tis I, and I have had a fine fegary,[1]
The rarest wild-goose chase!

Louis. 'T had made thee melancholy.

Diego. Don Roderigo here? 'tis well you met him;
For though I missed him, yet I met an accident
Has almost made me burst with laughter.

Louis. How so?

Diego. I'll tell you: as we parted, I perceived
A walking thing before me, strangely tickled
With rare conceited raptures; him I dogged
Supposing 't had been Roderigo landed
From his new pinnace, deep in contemplation
Of the sweet voyage he stole to-night.

Rod. You're pleasant.

Louis. Prithee, who was't?

Rod. Not I.

Diego. You're i' the right, not you indeed;
For 'twas that noble gentleman Don John,
Son to the Count Francisco de Carcomo.

Louis. In love, it seems?

Diego. Yes, peppered, on my life;
Much good may't do him; I'd not be so lined
For my cap full of double pistolets.

Louis. What should his mistress be?

Diego. That's yet a riddle
Beyond my resolution; but of late
I have observed him oft to frequent the sports
The gipsies newly come to th' city present.

Louis. It is said there is a creature with 'em,
Though young of years, yet of such absolute beauty,
Dexterity of wit, and general qualities,
That Spain reports her not without admiration.

Diego. Have you seen her?

Louis. Never.

[1] Vagary.

Diego. Nor you, my lord?
Rod. I not remember.
Diego. Why, then, you never saw the prettiest toy
That ever sang or danced.
Louis. Is she a gipsy?
Diego. In her condition, not in her complexion:
I tell you once more, 'tis a spark of beauty
Able to set a world at gaze; the sweetest,
The wittiest rogue! shall's see 'em? they've fine gambols
Are mightily frequented; court and city
Flock to 'em, but the country does 'em worship:
This little ape gets money by the sack-full,
It trolls upon her.
Louis. Will ye with us, friend?
Rod. You know my other projects; sights to me
Are but vexations.
Louis. O, you must be merry!—
Diego, we'll to th' gipsies.
Diego. Best take heed
You be not snapped.
Louis. How snapped?
Diego. By that little fairy;
'T has a shrewd tempting face and a notable tongue.
Louis. I fear not either.
Diego. Go, then.
Louis. Will you with us?
Rod. I'll come after.— [*Exeunt* LOUIS *and* DIEGO
Pleasure and youth like smiling evils woo us
To taste new follies; tasted, they undo us. [*Exit.*

ACT THE SECOND.

SCENE I.

A Room in an Inn.

Enter ALVAREZ, CARLO, *and* ANTONIO, *disguised as gipsies.*

ALV. Come, my brave boys! the tailor's shears has cut us into shapes fitting our trades.

Car. A trade free as a mason's.

Ant. A trade brave as a courtier's; for some of them do but shark, and so do we.

Alv. Gipsies, but no tanned ones; no red-ochre rascals umbered with soot and bacon as the English gipsies are, that sally out upon pullen,[1] lie in ambuscado for a rope of onions, as if they were Welsh freebooters; no, our stile has higher steps to climb over, Spanish gipsies, noble gipsies.

Car. I never knew nobility in baseness.

Alv. Baseness? the arts of Cocoquismo and Germania,[2] used by our Spanish pickaroes[3]—I mean filching, foist-

[1] Poultry.

[2] "Alvarez proceeds to explain his meaning; but I may just observe that *Cocoquismo* should perhaps be *Cacoquismo*, formed from the Spanish *caco*, a pickpocket (unless indeed it has some affinity with the phrase *hacer cocos*, to wheedle), and that *Germania* signifies, in that language, the jargon of the gipsies. See Neuman's *Span. and Engl. Dict.* in vv."—*Dyce.*

[3] Rogues.

ing,[1] nimming, jilting—we defy[2]; none in our college shall study 'em! such graduates we degrade.

Ant. I am glad Spain has an honest company.

Alv. We'll entertain no mountebanking stroll,
No piper, fiddler, tumbler through small hoops,
No ape-carrier, baboon-bearer;
We must have nothing stale, trivial, or base:
Am I your major-domo, your teniente,[3]
Your captain, your commander?

Ant. Who but you?

Alv. So then: now being entered Madrill, the enchanted circle of Spain, have a care to your new lessons.

Car.
Ant. } We listen.

Alv. Plough deep furrows, to catch deep root in th' opinion of the best grandoes, dukes, marquesses, condes, and other titulados; show your sports to none but them: what can you do with three or four fools in a dish, and a blockhead cut into sippets?

Ant. Scurvy meat!

Alv. The Lacedemonians threw their beards over their shoulders, to observe what men did behind them as well as before; you must do't.

Car. We shall never do't.

Ant. Our muzzles are too short.

Alv. Be not English gipsies, in whose company a man's not sure of the ears of his head, they so pilfer! no such angling; what you pull to land catch fair: there is no iron so foul but may be gilded; and our gipsy profession, how base soever in show, may acquire commendations.

Car. Gipsies, and yet pick no pockets?

Alv. Infamous and roguy! so handle your webs, that they never come to be woven in the loom of justice: take anything that's given you, purses, knives, handkerchers, rosaries, tweezers, any toy, any money! refuse

[1] Pocket-picking. [2] Renounce. [3] Lieutenant. (*Span.*)

not a maravedi,[1] a blank:[2] feather by feather birds build nests, grain pecked up after grain makes pullen fat.

Ant. The best is, we Spaniards are no great feeders.

Alv. If one city cannot maintain us, away to another! our horses must have wings. Does Madrill yield no money? Seville shall; is Seville closefisted? Valladoly is open; so Cordova, so Toledo. Do not our Spanish wines please us? Italian can then, French can. Preferment's bow is hard to draw, set all your strengths to it; what you get, keep; all the world is a second Rochelle;[3] make all sure, for you must not look to have your dinner served in with trumpets.

Car. No, no, sack-buts shall serve us.

Alv. When you have money, hide it; sell all our horses but one.

Ant. Why one?

Alv. 'Tis enough to carry our apparel and trinkets, and the less our ambler eats, our cheer is the better. None be sluttish, none thievish, none lazy; all bees, no drones, and our hives shall yield us honey.

Enter GUIAMARA, CONSTANZA, CHRISTIANA, *disguised as gipsies, and* CARDOCHIA.

Const. See, father, how I'm fitted; how do you like
This our new stock of clothes?

Alv. My sweet girl, excellent.—
See their old robes be safe.

Card. That, sir, I'll look to:
Whilst in my house you lie, what thief soever
Lays hands upon your goods, call but to me,
I'll make thee satisfaction.

Alv. Thanks, good hostess!

[1] A small Spanish copper coin.

[2] A small silver coin with an alloy of baser metal.

[3] "Rochelle was a general asylum for those persecuted Protestants who knew not where to go; and Alvarez intimates that the whole world was equally open to people who had no settled home."—Editor of 1816.

Card. People already throng into the inn,
And call for you into their private rooms.

Alv. No chamber-comedies: hostess, ply you your tide; flow let 'em to a full sea, but we'll show no pastime till after dinner, and that in a full ring of good people, the best, the noblest; no closet-sweetmeats, pray tell 'em so.

Card. I shall. [*Exit.*

Alv. How old is Pretiosa?

Gui. Twelve and upwards.

Const. I am in my teens, assure you, mother; as little as I am, I have been taken for an elephant, castles and lordships offered to be set upon me, if I would bear 'em: why, your smallest clocks are the prettiest things to carry about gentlemen.

Gui. Nay, child, thou wilt be tempted.

Const. Tempted? though I am no mark in respect of a huge butt, yet I can tell you great bubbers [1] have shot at me, and shot golden arrows, but I myself gave aim, thus,—wide, four bows; short, three and a half: they that crack me shall find me as hard as a nut of Galicia; a parrot I am, but my teeth too tender to crack a wanton's almond.

Alv. Thou art my noble girl: a many dons
Will not believe but that thou art a boy
In woman's clothes; and to try that conclusion,
To see if thou be'st alcumy [2] or no,
They'll throw down gold in musses; [3] but, Pretiosa,
Let these proud sakers [4] and gerfalcons fly,
Do not thou move a wing; be to thyself
Thyself, and not a changeling.

Const. How? not a changeling?
Yes, father, I will play the changeling;

[1] "A vulgarised form of *bibbers*, Constanza having used the word *butt* in the double sense of *mark* and *liquor-vessel.*"—*Dyce.*

[2] Alloyed metal.

[3] To be scrambled for. There was a children's game called muss.

[4] The peregrine hawk.

I'll change myself into a thousand shapes,
To court our brave spectators; I'll change my postures
Into a thousand different variations,
To draw even ladies' eyes to follow mine;
I'll change my voice into a thousand tones,
To chain attention: not a changeling, father?
None but myself shall play the changeling.

Alv. Do what thou wilt, Pretiosa. [*A knocking within.*
What noise is this?

Re-enter CARDOCHIA.

Card. Here's gentlemen swear all the oaths in Spain they have seen you, must see you, and will see you.

Alv. To drown this noise let 'em enter. [*Exit* CARD.

Enter SANCHO *and* SOTO.

San. Is your playhouse an inn, a gentleman cannot see you without crumpling his taffeta cloak?

Soto. Nay, more than a gentleman, his man being a diminutive don too.

San. Is this the little ape does the fine tricks?

Const. Come aloft, Jack little ape!

San. Would my jack might come aloft! please you to set the watermill with the ivory cogs in't a-grinding my handful of purging comfits. [*Offers comfits.*

Soto. My master desires to have you loose from your company.

Const. Am I pigeon, think you, to be caught with cummin-seeds? a fly to glue my wings to sweetmeats, and so be ta'en?

San. When do your gambols begin?

Alv. Not till we ha' dined.

San. 'Foot, then your bellies will be so full, you'll be able to do nothing.—Soto, prithee, set a good face on't, for I cannot, and give the little monkey that letter.

Soto. Walk off and hum to yourself. [SANCHO *retires.*]

—I dedicate, sweet Destiny, into whose hand every Spaniard desires to put a distaff, these lines of love.

[*Offering a paper to* CONSTANZA.

Gui. What love? what's the matter?

Soto. Grave Mother Bumby,[1] the mark's out a' your mouth.

Alv. What's the paper? from whom comes it?

Soto. The commodity wrapped up in the paper are verses; the warming-pan that puts heat into 'em, yon fire-brained bastard of Helicon.

San. Hum, hum.

Alv. What's your master's name?

Soto. His name is Don Tomazo Portacareco, nuncle to young Don Hortado de Mendonza, cousin-german to the Conde de Tindilla, and natural brother to Francisco de Bavadilla, one of the commendadors of Alcantara, a gentleman of long standing.

Alv. And of as long a style.

Const. Verses? I love good ones; let me see 'em.

[*Taking paper.*

San. [*advancing.*] Good ones? if they were not good ones, they should not come from me; at the name of verses I can stand on no ground.

Const. Here's gold too! whose is this?

San. Whose but yours? If there be any fault in the verses, I can mend it extempore; for a stitch in a man's stocking not taken up in time, ravels out all the rest.

Soto. Botcherly poetry, botcherly! [*Aside.*

Const. Verses and gold! these then are golden verses.

San. Had every verse a pearl in the eye, it should be thine.

Const. A pearl in mine eye![2] I thank you for that; do you wish me blind?

[1] A fortune-teller frequently alluded to; Lyly wrote a play called *Mother Bombie*.

[2] Referring to a disease of the eye.

San. Ay, by this light do I, that you may look upon nobody's rhymes but mine.

Const. I should be blind indeed then.

Alv. Pray, sir, read your verses.

San. Shall I sing 'em or say 'em?

Alv. Which you can best.

Soto. Both scurvily. [*Aside.*

San. I'll set out a throat then.

Soto. Do, master, and I'll run division behind your back.

San. [*sings.*] O that I were a bee to sing
Hum, buz, buz, hum! I first would bring
Home honey to your hive, and there leave my sting.

Soto. [*sings.*] He maunders.

San. [*sings.*] O that I were a goose, to feed
At your barn door! such corn I need,
Nor would I bite, but goslings breed.

Soto. [*sings.*] And ganders.

San. [*sings.*] O that I were your needle's eye!
How through your linen would I fly,
And never leave one stitch awry!

Soto. [*sings.*] He'll touse ye.

San. [*sings.*] O would I were one of your hairs,
That you might comb out all my cares,
And kill the nits of my despairs!

Soto. [*sings.*] O lousy!

San. How? lousy? can rhymes be lousy?

Const. No, no, they're excellent.

Alv. But are these all your own?

San. Mine own? would I might never see ink drop out of the nose of any goose-quill more, if velvet cloaks have not clapped me for 'em! Do you like 'em?

Const. Past all compare?
They shall be writ out: when you've as good or better,
For these and those, pray, book me down your debtor:
Your paper is long-lived, having two souls,
Verses and gold.

San. Would both those were in thy pretty little body, sweet gipsy!

Const. A pistolet and this paper? 'twould choke me.

Soto. No more than a bribe does a constable: the verses will easily into your head, then buy what you like with the gold, and put it into your belly. I hope I ha' chawed a good reason for you.

San. Will you chaw my jennet ready, sir?

Soto. And eat him down, if you say the word. [*Exit.*

San. Now the coxcomb my man is gone, because you're but a country company of strolls, I think your stock is threadbare; here, mend it with this cloak.

[*Giving his cloak.*

Alv. What do you mean, sir?

San. This scarf, this feather, and this hat.

[*Giving his scarf, &c.*

Alv. Dear signor!——

San. If they be never so dear:—pox o' this hot ruff! little gipsy, wear thou that. [*Giving his ruff.*

Alv. Your meaning, sir?

San. My meaning is, not to be an ass, to carry a burden when I need not. If you show your gambols forty leagues hence, I'll gallop to 'em.—Farewell, old greybeard;—adieu, mother mumble-crust;—to-morrow, my little wart of beauty. [*Exit.*

Enter behind JOHN, *muffled.*

Alv. So, harvest will come in; such sunshine days
Will bring in golden sheaves, our markets raise:
Away to your task.

[*Exeunt* ALVAREZ, CHRISTIANA, CARLO, *and* ANTONIO; *and as* GUIAMARA *and* CONSTANZA *are going out,* JOHN *pulls the latter back.*

Const. Mother! grandmother!

John. Two rows of kindred in one mouth?

Gui. Be not uncivil, sir; thus have you used her thrice.

John. Thrice? three thousand more: may I not use mine own?

Const. Your own! by what tenure?

John. Cupid entails this land upon me; I have wooed thee, thou art coy: by this air, I am a bull of Tarifa, wild, mad for thee! you trowed I was some copper coin; I am a knight of Spain; Don Francisco de Carcomo my father, I Don John his son; this paper tells you more. [*Gives paper.*]—Grumble not, old granam; here's gold [*gives money*]; for I must, by this white hand, marry this cherry-lipped, sweet-mouthed villain.

Const. There's a thing called *quando.*

John. Instantly.

Gui. Art thou so willing?

John. Peace, threescore and five!

Const. Marry me? eat a chicken ere it be out o' th' shell? I'll wear no shackles; liberty is sweet; that I have, that I'll hold. Marry me? can gold and lead mix together? a diamond and a button of crystal fit one ring? You are too high for me, I am too low; you too great, I too little.

Gui. I pray, leave her, sir, and take your gold again.

Const. Or if you doat, as you say, let me try you do this.

John. Anything; kill the great Turk, pluck out the Mogul's eye-teeth; in earnest, Pretiosa, anything!

Const. Your task is soon set down; turn gipsy for two years, be one of us; if in that time you mislike not me nor I you, here's my hand: farewell. [*Exit.*

Gui. There's enough for your gold.—Witty child!

[*Aside, and exit.*

John. Turn gipsy for two years? a capering trade;
And I in th' end may keep a dancing-school,
Having served for it; gipsy I must turn.
O beauty, the sun's fires cannot so burn! [*Exit.*

SCENE II.

A Room in the House of PEDRO.

Enter CLARA.

Cla. I have offended; yet, O Heaven, thou know'st
How much I have abhorred, even from my birth,
A thought that tended to immodest folly!
Yet I have fallen; thoughts with disgraces strive,
And thus I live, and thus I die alive.

Enter PEDRO *and* MARIA.

Ped. Fie, Clara, thou dost court calamity too much.
Mar. Yes, girl, thou dost.
Ped. Why should we fret our eyes out with our tears,
Weary Heaven with complaints? 'tis fruitless, childish
Impatience; for when mischief hath wound up
The full weight of the ravisher's foul life
To an equal height of ripe iniquity,
The poise will, by degrees, sink down his soul
To a much lower, much more lasting ruin
Than our joint wrongs can challenge.
Mar. Darkness itself
Will change night's sable brow into a sunbeam
For a discovery; and be thou sure,
Whenever we can learn what monster 'twas
Hath robbed thee of the jewel held so precious,
Our vengeance shall be noble.
Ped. Royal, anything:
Till then let's live securely; to proclaim
Our sadness were mere vanity.
Cla. 'A needs not;
I'll study to be merry.
Ped. We are punished,
Maria, justly; covetousness to match
Our daughter to that matchless piece of ignorance,
Our foolish ward, hath drawn this curse upon us.

Mar. I fear it has.
Ped. Off with this face of grief:
Here comes Don Louis.

Enter LOUIS *and* DIEGO.

Noble Sir.
Louis. My lord,
I trust I have your and your lady's leave
T' exchange a word with your fair daughter.
Ped. Leave
And welcome.—Hark, Maria.—Your ear too.
Diego. Mine, my lord?
Louis. Dear Clara, I have often sued for love,
And now desire you would at last be pleased
To style me yours.
Cla. Mine eyes ne'er saw that gentleman
Whom I more nobly in my heart respected
Than I have you, yet you must, sir, excuse me,
If I resolve to use awhile that freedom
My younger days allow.
Louis. But shall I hope?
Cla. You will do injury to better fortunes.
To your own merit, greatness, and advancement,
Which I beseech you not to slack.
Louis. Then hear me:
If ever I embrace another choice,
Until I know you elsewhere matched, may all
The chief of my desires find scorn and ruin!
Cla. O me!
Louis. Why sigh you, lady?
Cla. 'Deed, my lord,
I am not well.
Louis. Then all discourse is tedious;
I'll choose some fitter time; till when, fair Clara——
Cla. You shall not be unwelcome hither, sir;
That's all that I dare promise.
Louis. Diego.

Diego. My lord?
Louis. What says Don Pedro?
Diego. He'll go with you.
Louis. Leave us.— [*Exit* DIEGO.
Shall I, my lord, entreat your privacy?
Ped. Withdraw, Maria; we'll follow presently.
[*Exeunt* MARIA *and* CLARA.
Louis. The great corregidor, whose politic stream
Of popularity glides on the shore
Of every vulgar praise, hath often urged me
To be a suitor to his Catholic Majesty
For a repeal from banishment for him
Who slew my father; compliments in vows
And strange well-studied promises of friendship;
But what is new to me, still as he courts
Assistance for Alvarez, my grand enemy,
Still he protests how ignorant he is
Whether Alvarez be alive or dead.
To-morrow is the day we have appointed
For meeting, at the Lord Francisco's house,
The Earl of Carcomo; now, my good lord,
The sum of my request is, you will please
To lend your presence there, and witness wherein
Our joint accord consists.
Ped. You shall command it.
Louis. But first, as you are noble, I beseech you
Help me with your advice what you conceive
Of great Fernando's importunity,
Or whether you imagine that Alvarez
Survive or not?
Ped. It is a question, sir,
Beyond my resolution: I remember
The difference betwixt your noble father
And Conde de Alvarez; how it sprung
From a mere trifle first, a cast [1] of hawks,
Whose made the swifter flight, whose could mount highest,

[1] A couple.

Lie longest on the wing: from change of words
Their controversy grew to blows, from blows
To parties, thence to faction; and, in short,
I well remember how our streets were frighted
With brawls, whose end was blood; till, when no friends
Could mediate their discords, by the king
A reconciliation was enforced,
Death threatened to the first occasioner
Of breach, besides the confiscation
Of lands and honours: yet at last they met
Again; again they drew to sides, renewed
Their ancient quarrel; in which dismal uproar
Your father hand to hand fell by Alvarez:
Alvarez fled; and after him the doom
Of exile was sent out: he, as report
Was bold to voice, retired himself to Rhodes
His lands and honours by the king bestowed
On you, but then an infant.

Louis. Ha, an infant?

Ped. His wife, the sister to the corregidor,
With a young daughter, and some few that followed
her,
By stealth were shipped for Rhodes, and by a storm
Shipwrecked at sea: but for the banished Conde,
'Twas never yet known what became of him:
Here's all I can inform you.

Louis. A repeal?
Yes, I will sue for't, beg for't, buy it, anything
That may by possibility of friends
Or money, I'll attempt.

Ped. 'Tis a brave charity.

Louis. Alas! poor lady, I could mourn for her!
Her loss was usury more than I covet;
But for the man, I'd sell my patrimony
For his repeal, and run about the world
To find him out; there is no peace can dwell
About my father's tomb, till I have sacrified

Some portion of revenge to his wronged ashes.
You will along with me?

Ped. You need not question it. [furies

Louis. I have strange thoughts about me: two such
Revel amidst my joys as well may move
Distraction in a saint, vengeance and love.
I'll follow, sir.

Ped. Pray, lead the way, you know it.— [*Exit* LOUIS.

Enter SANCHO *without his cloak, hat, &c., and* SOTO.

How now? from whence come you, sir?

San. From flaying myself, sir.

Soto. From playing with fencers, sir; and they have beat him out of his clothes, sir.

Ped. Cloak, band, rapier, all lost at dice?

San. Nor cards neither.

Soto. This was one of my master's dog-days, and he would not sweat too much.

San. It was mine own goose, and I laid the giblets upon another coxcomb's trencher: you are my guardian, best beg me for a fool[1] now.

Soto. He that begs one begs t'other. [*Aside.*

Ped. Does any gentleman give away his things thus?

San. Yes, and gentlewomen give away their things too.

Soto. To gulls sometimes, and are cony-catched for their labour.

Ped. Wilt thou ever play the coxcomb?

San. If no other parts be given me, what would you have me do?

Ped. Thy father was as brave a Spaniard
As ever spake the haut[2] Castilian tongue.

San. Put me in clothes, I'll be as brave[3] as he.

Ped. This is the ninth time thou hast played the ass,
Flinging away thy trappings and thy cloth
To cover others, and go naked thyself.

[1] *i.e.* A lunatic. See note *ante*, p. 150. [2] Haughty. (Fr. *haut.*)
[3] A play upon the word which means finely attired as well as valiant.

San. I'll make 'em up ten, because I'll be even with you.

Ped. Once more your broken walls shall have new hangings.

Soto. To be well hung is all our desire.

Ped. And what course take you next?

San. What course? why, my man Soto and I will go make some maps.

Ped. What maps?

Soto. Not such maps[1] as you wash houses with, but maps of countries.

San. I have an uncle in Seville, I'll go see him; an aunt in Siena in Italy, I'll go see her.

Soto. A cousin of mine in Rome, I'll go to him with a mortar.

San. There's a courtesan in Venice, I'll go tickle her.

Soto. Another in England, I'll go tackle her.

Ped. So, so! and where's the money to do all this?

San. If my woods, being cut down, cannot fill this pocket, cut 'em into trapsticks.

Soto. And if his acres, being sold for a maravedi a turf for larks in cages, cannot fill this pocket, give 'em to gold-finders.[3]

Ped. You'll gallop both to the gallows; so fare you well. [*Exit.*

San. And be hanged you! new clothes, you'd best.

Soto. Four cloaks, that you may give away three, and keep one.

San. We'll live as merrily as beggars; let's both turn [gipsies.

Soto. By any means; if they cog,[4] we'll lie; if they toss, we'll tumble.

San. Both in a belly, rather than fail.

Soto. Come, then, we'll be gipsified.

San. And tipsified too.

Soto. And we will show such tricks and such rare [gambols,
As shall put down the elephant and camels. [*Exeunt.*

[1] Mops. [2] A cap resembling a mortar in shape.
[3] A jocular term for a cleanser of cesspools. [4] Cheat.

ACT THE THIRD.

SCENE I.

A Street.

Enter RODERIGO *disguised as an Italian.*

ROD. A thousand stings are in me: O, what vile prisons
Make we our bodies to our immortal souls!
Brave tenants to bad houses; 'tis a dear rent
They pay for naughty lodging: the soul, the mistress;
The body, the caroch[1] that carries her;
Sins the swift wheels that hurry her away;
Our will, the coachman rashly driving on,
Till coach and carriage both are quite o'erthrown.
My body yet 'scapes bruises; that known thief
Is not yet called to th' bar: there's no true sense
Of pain but what the law of conscience
Condemns us to; I feel that. Who would lose
A kingdom for a cottage? an estate
Of perpetuity for a man's life
For annuity of that life, pleasure? a spark
To those celestial fires that burn about us;
A painted star to that bright firmament
Of constellations which each night are set
Lighting our way; yet thither how few get

[1] Coach.

How many thousand in Madrill drink off
The cup of lust, and laughing, in one month,
Not whining as I do! Should this sad lady
Now meet me, do I know her? should this temple,
By me profaned, lie in the ruins here,
The pieces would scarce show her me: would they did!
She's mistress to Don Louis; by his steps,
And this disguise, I'll find her. To Salamanca
Thy father thinks thou'rt gone; no, close here stay;
Where'er thou travell'st, scorpions stop thy way.
Who are these?

Enter SANCHO *and* SOTO *disguised as Gipsies.*

San. Soto, how do I show?

Soto. Like a rusty armour new scoured; but, master, how show I?

San. Like an ass with a new piebald saddle on his back.

Soto. If the devil were a tailor, he would scarce know us in these gaberdines.[1]

San. If a tailor were the devil, I'd not give a louse for him, if he should bring up this fashion amongst gentlemen, and make it common.

Rod. The freshness of the morning be upon you both!

San. The saltness of the evening be upon you single!

Rod. Be not displeased, that I abruptly thus
Break in upon your favours; your strange habits
Invite me with desire to understand
Both what you are and whence, because no country—
And I have measured some—shows me your like.

Soto. Our like? no, we should be sorry we or our clothes should be like fish, new, stale, and stinking in three days.

San. If you ask whence we are, we are Egyptian Spaniards; if what we are, *ut*, *re*, *mi*, *fa*, *sol*, jugglers, tumblers, anything, anywhere, everywhere.

[1] Coarse upper garments.

Rod. A good fate hither leads me by the hand.— [*Aside.*
Your quality I love; the scenical school
Has been my tutor long in Italy,
For that's my country; there have I put on
Sometimes the shape of a comedian,
And now and then some other.

San. A player! a brother of the tiring house![1]

Soto. A bird of the same feather!

San. Welcome! wu't turn gipsy?

Rod. I can nor dance nor sing; but if my pen
From my invention can strike music-tunes,
My head and brains are yours.

Soto. A calf's head and brains were better for my stomach.

San. A rib of poetry!

Soto. A modicum of the Muses! a horse-shoe of Helicon!

San. A magpie of Parnassus! welcome again! I am a firebrand of Phœbus myself; we'll invoke together, so you will not steal my plot.

Rod. 'Tis not my fashion.

San. But now-a-days 'tis all the fashion.

Soto. What was the last thing you writ? a comedy?

Rod. No! 'twas a sad, too sad a tragedy.
Under these eaves I'll shelter me.

San. See, here comes our company; do our tops spin as you would have 'em?

Soto. If not, whip us round.

Enter ALVAREZ, GUIAMARA, CONSTANZA, CHRISTIANA, CARLO, ANTONIO, *and others, disguised as before.*

San. I sent you a letter to tell you we were upon a march.

Alv. And you are welcome.—Yet these fools will trouble us! [*Aside.*

[1] Theatrical dressing-room.

Gui. Rich fools shall buy our trouble.

San. Hang lands! it's nothing but trees, stones, and dirt. Old father, I have gold to keep up our stock. Precious Pretiosa, for whose sake I have thus transformed myself out of a gentleman into a gipsy, thou shalt not want sweet rhymes, my little musk-cat; for besides myself, here's an Italian poet, on whom I pray throw your welcomes.

Alv., Gui., &c. He's welcome!

Const. Sir, you're most welcome; I love a poet,
So he writes chastely; if your pen can sell me
Any smooth quaint romances, which I may sing,
You shall have bays and silver.

Rod. Pretty heart, no selling;
What comes from me is free.

San. And me too.

Alv. We shall be glad to use you, sir: our sports
Must be an orchard, bearing several trees,
And fruits of several taste; one pleasure dulls.
A time may come when we, besides these pastimes,
May from the grandoes and the dons of Spain
Have leave to try our skill even on the stage,
And then your wits may help us.

San. And mine too.

Rod. They are your servants.

Const. Trip softly through the streets till we arrive,
You know at whose house, father.

San. [*sings.*]

Trip it, gipsies, trip it fine,
Show tricks and lofty capers;
At threading needles we repine,
And leaping over rapiers:
Pindy-pandy rascal toys!
We scorn cutting purses;
Though we live by making noise,
For cheating none can curse us.

Over high ways, over low,
And over stones and gravel,
Though we trip it on the toe,
And thus for silver travel;
Though our dances waste our backs,
At night fat capons mend them,
Eggs well brewed in buttered sack,
Our wenches say befriend them.

O that all the world were mad!
Then should we have fine dancing;
Hobby-horses would be had,
And brave girls keep a-prancing;
Beggars would on cock-horse ride,
And boobies fall a-roaring,
And cuckolds, though no horns be spied,
Be one another goring.

Welcome, poet, to our ging![1]
Make rhymes, we'll give thee reason;
Canary bees thy brains shall sting,
Mull-sack did ne'er speak treason;
Peter-see-me[2] shall wash thy noul[3]
And malaga glasses fox[4] thee;
If, poet, thou toss not bowl for bowl,
Thou shalt not kiss a doxy. [*Exeunt.*

SCENE II.

A Garden belonging to FRANCISCO'S *House.*

Enter FERNANDO, FRANCISCO, JOHN, PEDRO, MARIA, LOUIS, *and* DIEGO.

Fer. Louis de Castro, since you circled are
In such a golden ring of worthy friends,

[1] Gang. [2] *i.e. Pedro Ximenes,* a sweet Spanish wine.
[3] Noddle. [4] Intoxicate.

Pray, let me question you about that business
You and I last conferred on.

Louis. My lord, I wish it.

Fer. Then, gentlemen, though you all know this man,
Yet now look on him well, and you shall find
Such mines of Spanish honour in his bosom
As but in few are treasured.

Louis. O, my good lord——

Fer. He's son to that De Castro o'er whose tomb
Fame stands writing a book, which will take up
The age of time to fill it with the stories
Of his great acts, and that his honoured father
Fell in the quarrel of those families,
His own and Don Alvarez de Castillas.

Fran. The volumes of those quarrels is too large
And too wide printed in our memory.

Louis. Would it had ne'er come forth!

Fran., Ped., &c. So wish we all.

Fer. But here's a son as matchless as the father,
For his mind's bravery; he lets blood his spleen,
Tears out the leaf in which the picture stands
Of slain De Castro, casts a hill of sand
On all revenge, and stifles it.

Fran., Ped., &c. 'Tis done nobly!

Fer. For I by him am courted to solicit
The king for the repeal of poor Alvarez,
Who lives a banished man, some say, in Naples.

Ped. Some say in Aragon.

Louis. No matter where;
That paper folds in it my hand and heart,
Petitioning the royalty of Spain
To free the good old man, and call him home:
But what hope hath your lordship that these beams
Of grace shall shine upon me?

Fer. The word royal.

Fran., Ped., &c. And that's enough.

Louis. Then since this sluice is drawn up to increase

The stream, with pardon of these honoured friends
Let me set ope another, and that's this;
That you, my lord Don Pedro, and this lady
Your noble wife, would in this fair assembly,
If still you hold me tenant to your favour,
Repeat the promise you so oft have made me,
Touching the beauteous Clara for my wife.

Ped. What I possess in her, before these lords
I freely once more give you.

Mar. And what's mine,
To you, as right heir to it, I resign.

Fer., Fran., &c. What would you more? [head.

Louis. What would I more? the tree bows down his
Gently to have me touch it, but when I offer
To pluck the fruit, the top branch grows so high
To mock my reaching hand, up it does fly;
I have the mother's smile, the daughter's frown.

Fran., Ped., &c. O, you must woo hard!

Fer. Woo her well; she's thine own.

John. That law holds not 'mongst gipsies; I shoot hard,
And am wide off from the mark. [*Aside.*

[*Flourish within.*

Fer. Is this, my lord, your music?

Fran. None of mine.

Enter SOTO *disguised as before, with a cornet in his hand.*

Soto. A crew of gipsies with desire
To show their sports are at your gates a-fire.

Fran. How, how, my gates a-fire, knave?

John. Art panting? I am a-fire I'm sure! [*Aside.*

Fer. What are the things they do?

Soto. They frisk, they caper, dance and sing,
Tell fortunes too, which is a very fine thing;
They tumble—how? not up and down,
As tumblers do, but from town to town:
Antics they have and gipsy-masquing,
And toys which you may have for asking:

They come to devour nor wine nor good cheer,
But to earn money, if any be here;
But being asked, as I suppose,
Your answer will be, in your t'other hose;
For there's not a gipsy amongst 'em that begs,
But gets his living by his tongue and legs.
If therefore you please, dons, they shall come in:
Now I have ended, let them begin.

Fer., *Ped.*, *&c.* Ay, ay, by any means.

Fran. But, fellow, bring you music along with you too?

Soto. Yes, my lord, both loud music and still music; the loud is that which you have heard, and the still is that which no man can hear. [*Exit.*

Fer. A fine knave!

Fran. There's report of a fair gipsy,
A pretty little toy, whom all our gallants
In Madrill flock to look on: this she, trow?

John. Yes, sure 'tis she—I should be sorry else.
[*Aside.*

Enter ALVAREZ, GUIAMARA, CONSTANZA, CHRISTIANA, CARLO, ANTONIO, RODERIGO, SANCHO, SOTO, *and others, disguised, as before, with the following Song.*

Come, follow your leader, follow;
Our convoy be Mars and Apollo!
The van comes brave up here;
(*Answer.*)—As hotly comes the rear:
Chorus. Our knackers are the fifes and drums,
Sa, sa, the gipsies' army comes!

Horsemen we need not fear,
There's none but footmen here;
The horse sure charge without;
Or if they wheel about,
Our knackers are the shot that fly,
Pit-a-pat rattling in the sky.

If once the great ordnance play,
That's laughing, yet run not away,
But stand the push of pike,
Scorn can but basely strike;
Then let our armies join and sing,
And pit-a-pat make our knackers ring.

Arm, arm! what bands are those?
They cannot be sure our foes;
We'll not draw up our force,
Nor muster any horse;
For since they pleased to view our sight,
Let's this way, this way give delight.

A council of war let's call,
Look either to stand or fall;
If our weak army stands,
Thank all these noble hands;
Whose gates of love being open thrown,
We enter, and then the town's our own.

Fer. A very dainty thing!

Fran. A handsome creature!

Ped. Look what a pretty pit there's in her chin!

John. Pit? 'tis a grave to bury lovers in.

Rod. My father? disguise guard me! [*Aside.*

San. Soto, there's De Cortes my guardian, but he smells not us.

Soto. Peace, brother gipsy.—Would any one here know his fortune?

Fer., Fran., &c. Good fortunes all of us!

Ped. 'Tis I, sir, needs a good one: come, sir, what's mine?

Mar. Mine and my husband's fortunes keep together; Who is't tells mine?

San. I, I; hold up, madam; fear not your pocket, for I ha' but two hands. [*Examining her hands.*

You are sad, or mad, or glad,
For a couple of cocks that cannot be had;
Yet when abroad they have picked store of grain.
Doodle-doo they will cry on your dunghills again.

Mar. Indeed I miss an idle gentleman,
And a thing of his a fool, but neither sad
Nor mad for them: would that were all the lead
Lying at my heart!

Ped. [*while* SOTO *examines his hand.*] What look'st thou on so long?

Soto. So long! do you think good fortunes are fresh herrings, to come in shoals? bad fortunes are like mackerel at midsummer: you have had a sore loss of late.

Ped. I have indeed; what is't?

Soto. I wonder it makes you not mad, for—
Through a gap in your ground thence late have been stole
A very fine ass and a very fine foal;
Take heed, for I speak not by habs and by nabs,[1]
Ere long you'll be horribly troubled with scabs.

Ped. I am now so; go, silly fool.

Soto. I ha' gi'n't him. [*Aside.*

San. O Soto, that ass and foal fattens me!

Fer. The mother of the gipsies, what can she do?
I'll have a bout with her.

John. I with the gipsy daughter.

Fran. To her, boy.

Gui. [*examining* FERNANDO's *hand.*]
From you went a dove away,
Which ere this had been more white
Than the silver robe of day;
Her eyes, the moon has none so bright.
Sate she now upon your hand,
Not the crown of Spain could buy it;
But 'tis flown to such a land,
Never more shall you come nigh it:

[1] At random.

Ha! yes, if palmistry tell true,
This dove again may fly to you.

Fer. Thou art a lying witch; I'll hear no more.

San. If you be so hot, sir, we can cool you with a song.

Soto. And when that song's done, we'll heat you again with a dance.

Louis. Stay, dear sir; send for Clara, let her know her fortune.

Mar. 'Tis too well known.

Louis. 'Twill make her
Merry to be in this brave company.

Ped. Good Diego, fetch her. [*Exit* DIEGO.

Fran. What's that old man? has he cunning too?

Gui., Car., &c. More than all we!

Louis. Has he? I'll try his spectacles.

Fer. Ha! Roderigo there? the scholar
That went to Salamanca takes his degrees
I' th' school of gipsies? let the fish alone,
Give him line: this is the dove—the dove?—the raven
That beldam mocked me with. [*Aside.*

Louis. [*while* ALVAREZ *examines his hand.*] What worms pick you out there now?

Alv. This:

When this line the other crosses,
Art tells me 'tis a book of losses:—
Bend your hand thus:—O, here I find
You have lost a ship in a great wind.

Louis. Lying rogue, I ne'er had any.

Alv. Hark, as I gather,
That great ship was De Castro called, your father.

Louis. And I must hew that rock that split him.

Alv. Nay, an you threaten—— [*Retires.*

Fran. And what's, Don John, thy fortune?
Thou'rt long fumbling at it.

John. She tells me tales of the moon, sir.

Const. And now 'tis come to the sun, sir.

[*To* FRAN.] Your son would ride, the youth would run,
The youth would sail, the youth would fly;
He's tying a knot will ne'er be done,
He shoots, and yet has ne'er an eye:
You have two, 'twere good you lent him one,
And a heart too, for he has none.

Fran. Hoyday! lend one of mine eyes?

San. They give us nothing; we'd best put on a bold face and ask it.

[*Sings.*] Now that from the hive
You gathered have the honey,
Our bees but poorly thrive
Unless the banks be sunny;
Then let your sun and moon,
Your gold and silver shine,
My thanks shall humming fly to you,
Chorus. And mine, and mine, and mine.
[FRAN., FER., *&c.*, *give money.*

ALV. [*sings.*] See, see, you gipsy toys,
You mad girls, you merry boys,
A boon voyage we have made,
Loud peals must then be had;
If I a gipsy be,
A crack-rope I'm for thee:
O, here's a golden ring!
Such clappers please a king,
Chorus. Such clappers please a king.

ALV. [*sings.*] You pleased may pass away;
Then let your bell-ropes stay;
Now chime, 'tis holyday,
Chorus. Now chime, 'tis holyday.

Const. No more of this, pray, father; fall to your dancing. [CONST., CAR., *&c.*, *dance.*

Louis. Clara will come too late now.

Fer. 'Tis great pity,
Besides your songs, dances, and other pastimes,

You do not, as our Spanish actors do,
Make trial of a stage.

Alv. We are, sir, about it;
So please your high authority to sign us
Some warrant to confirm us.

Fer. My hand shall do't,
And bring the best in Spain to see your sports.

Alv. Which is set off, this gentleman, a scholar——

Rod. Pox on you! [*Aside.*

Alv. Will write for us.

Fer. A Spaniard, sir?

Rod. No, my lord, an Italian.

Fer. Denies
His country too? my son sings gipsy-ballads! [*Aside.*
Keep as you are, we'll see your poet's vein,
And yours for playing: time is not ill spent
That's thus laid out in harmless merriment.

[*Exeunt* ALVAREZ, GUIAMARA, CONSTANZA, CHRISTIANA, CARLO, ANTONIO, RODERIGO, SANCHO, SOTO, *and others dancing.*

Ped. My lord of Carcomo, for this entertainment
You shall command our loves.

Fran. You're nobly welcome.

Ped. The evening grows upon us: lords, to all
A happy time of day.

Fer. The like to you, Don Pedro.

Louis. To my heart's sole lady
Pray let my service humbly be remembered;
We only missed her presence.

Mar. I shall truly
Report your worthy love. [*Exeunt* PEDRO *and* MARIA.

Fer. You shall no further;
Indeed, my lords, you shall not.

Fran. With your favour,
We will attend you home.[1]

[1] Dyce suggests that the scene here changes to the neighbourhood of Fernando's house.

Re-enter DIEGO.

Diego. Where's Don Pedro?—
O sir!
Louis. Why, what's the matter?
Diego. The Lady Clara,
Passing near to my lord corregidor's house,
Met with a strange mischance.
Fer. How? what mischance?
Diego. The jester that so late arrived at court,
And there was welcome for his country's sake,
By importunity of some friends, it seems,
Had borrowed from the gentleman of your horse
The backing of your mettled Barbary;
On which being mounted, whilst a number gazed
To hear what jests he could perform on horseback,
The headstrong beast, unused to such a rider,
Bears the press of people on before him;
With which throng the Lady Clara meeting,
Fainted, and there fell down, not bruised, I hope,
But frighted and entranced.
Louis. Ill-destined mischief!
Fer. Where have you left her?
Diego. At your house, my lord;
A servant coming forth, and knowing who
The lady was, conveyed her to a chamber;
A surgeon, too, is sent for.
Fer. Had she been my daughter,
My care could not be greater than it shall be
For her recure.
Louis. But if she miscarry,
I am the most unhappy man that lives. [*Exit.*
Fer. Diego, coast about the fields,
And overtake Don Pedro and his wife;
They newly parted from us.
Diego. I'll run speedily. [*Exit.*
Fer. A strange mischance: but what I have, my Lord

Francisco, this day noted, I may tell you;
An accident of merriment and wonder.
Fran. Indeed, my lord!
Fer. I have not thoughts enough
About me to imagine what th' event
Can come to; 'tis indeed about my son;
Hereafter you may counsel me.
Fran. Most gladly.—

Re-enter LOUIS.

How fares the lady?
Louis. Callèd back to life,
But full of sadness.
Fer. Talks she nothing?
Louis. Nothing;
For when the women that attend on her
Demanded how she did, she turned about,
And answered with a sigh: when I came near,
And by the love I bore her begged a word
Of hope to comfort me in her well-doing,
Before she would reply, from her fair eyes
She greets me with a bracelet of her tears,
Then wished me not to doubt; she was too well;
Entreats that she may sleep without disturbance
Or company until her father came:
And thus I left her.
Fran. Sir, she's past the worst;
Young maids are oft so troubled.
Fer. Here come they
You talk of.—

Re-enter PEDRO *and* MARIA.

Sir, your daughter, for your comfort,
Is now upon amendment.
Mar. O, my lord,
You speak an angel's voice!
Fer. Pray, in and visit her;

I'll follow instantly. [*Exeunt* PEDRO *and* MARIA.]—
You shall not part
Without a cup of wine, my lord.

Fra. 'Tis now
Too troublesome a time.—Which way take you,
Don Louis?

Louis. No matter which; for till I hear
My Clara be recovered, I am nothing.—
My lord corregidor, I am your servant
For this free entertainment.

Fer. You have conquered me
In noble courtesy.

Louis. O, that no art
But love itself can cure a love-sick heart! [*Exeunt.*

SCENE III.

A Room in FERNANDO'S *House.*

CLARA *discovered seated in a chair,* PEDRO *and* MARIA *standing by.*

Mar. Clara, hope of mine age!

Ped. Soul of my comfort!
Kill us not both at once: why dost thou speed
Thine eye in such a progress 'bout these walls?

Cla. Yon large window
Yields some fair prospect; good my lord, look out
And tell me what you see there.

Ped. Easy suit:
Clara, it overviews a spacious garden,
Amidst which stands an alabaster fountain,
A goodly one.

Cla. Indeed, my lord!

Mar. Thy griefs grow wild,

And will mislead thy judgment through thy weakness,
If thou obey thy weakness.

Cla. Who owns these glorious buildings?

Ped. Don Fernando
De Azevida, the corregidor
Of Madrill, a true noble gentleman.

Cla. May I not see him?

Mar. See him, Clara? why?

Cla. A truly noble gentleman, you said, sir?

Ped. I did: lo, here he comes in person.—

Enter FERNANDO.

We are,
My lord, your servants.

Fer. Good, no compliment.—
Young lady, there attends below a surgeon
Of worthy fame and practice; is't your pleasure
To be his patient?

Cla. With your favour, sir,
May I impart some few but needful words
Of secrecy to you, to you yourself,
None but yourself?

Fer. You may.

Ped. Must I not hear 'em?

Mar. Nor I?

Cla. O yes.—Pray, sit, my lord.

Fer. Say on.

Cla. You have been married?

Fer. To a wife, young lady,
Who, while the Heavens did lend her me, was fruitful
In all those virtues which styles woman good.

Cla. And you had children by her?

Fer. Had, 'tis true;
Now have but one, a son, and he yet lives;
The daughter, as if in her birth the mother
Had perfected the errand she was sent for
Into the world, from that hour took her life

In which the other that gave it her lost hers;
Yet shortly she unhappily, but fatally,
Perished at sea.

Cla. Sad story!

Fer. Roderigo,
My son——

Cla. How is he called, sir?

Fer. Roderigo:
He lives at Salamanca; and I fear
That neither time, persuasions, nor his fortunes,
Can draw him thence.

Cla. My lord, d'ye know this crucifix?[1]

[*Showing the crucifix.*

Fer. You drive me to amazement! 'twas my son's,
A legacy bequeathed him from his mother
Upon her deathbed, dear to him as life;
On earth there cannot be another treasure
He values at like rate as he does this.

Cla. O, then I am a cast-away!

Mar. How's that?

Ped. Alas! she will grow frantic!

Cla. In my bosom,
Next to my heart, my lord, I have laid up,
In bloody characters, a tale of horror.
Pray, read the paper; and if there you find

[*Giving a paper.*

Ought that concerns a maid undone and miserable,
Made so by one[2] of yours, call back the piety
Of nature to the goodness of a judge,
An upright judge, not of a partial father;
For do not wonder that I live to suffer
Such a full weight of wrongs, but wonder rather
That I have lived to speak them: thou, great man,
Yet read, read on, and as thou readst consider

[1] It will be remembered that Clara had concealed on her person the crucifix she found in the room to which Roderigo had conveyed her. See *ante*, p. 375.

[2] "Qy. 'son'?"—*Dyce*.

What I have suffered, what thou ought'st to do,
Thine own name, fatherhood, and my dishonour:
Be just as Heaven and fate are, that by miracle
Have in my weakness wrought a strange discovery:
Truth copied from my heart is texted there:
Let now my shame be th'roughly understood;
Sins are heard farthest when they cry in blood.

Fer. True, true, they do not cry but holla here;
This is the trumpet of a soul drowned deep
In the unfathomed seas of matchless sorrows.
I must lock fast the door. [*Exit.*

Mar. I have no words
To call for vengeance.

Ped. I am lost in marvel.

Re-enter FERNANDO.

Fer. Sit,[1] pray sit as you sat before. White paper,
This should be innocence; these letters gules
Should be the honest oracles of revenge:
What's beauty but a perfect white and red?
Both here well mixed limn truth so beautiful,
That to distrust it, as I am a father,
Speaks me as foul as rape hath spoken my son;
'Tis true?

Cla. 'Tis true.

Fer. Then mark me how I kneel
Before the high tribunal of your injuries. [*Kneels*
Thou too, too-much-wronged maid, scorn not my tears
For these are tears of rage, not tears of love,—
Thou father of this too, too-much-wronged maid,—
Thou mother of her counsels and her cares,
I do not plead for pity to a villain;
O, let him die as he hath lived, dishonourably,
Basely and cursedly! I plead for pity
To my till now untainted blood and honour:

[1] Dyce, following the old eds., prints "Sir."

Teach me how I may now be just and cruel,
For henceforth I am childless.

Cla. Pray, sir, rise;
You wrong your place and age.

Fer. [*rising.*] Point me my grave
In some obscure by-path, where never memory
Nor mention of my name may be found out.

Cla. My lord, I can weep with you, nay, weep for ye,
As you for me; your passions are instructions,
And prompt my faltering tongue to beg at least
A noble satisfaction, though not revenge.

Fer. Speak that again.

Cla. Can you procure no balm
To heal a wounded name?

Fer, O, thou'rt as fair
In mercy as in beauty! wilt thou live,
And I'll be thy physician?

Cla. I'll be yours.

Fer. Don Pedro, we'll to counsel;
This daughter shall be ours.—Sleep, sleep, young angel,
My care shall wake about thee.

Cla. Heaven is gracious,
And I am eased!

Fer. We will be yet more private;
Night curtains o'er the world; soft dreams rest with thee!
The best revenge is to reform our crimes,
Then time crowns sorrows, sorrows sweeten times.

[*Exeunt all except* CLARA, *on whom the scene shuts.*

ACT THE FOURTH.

SCENE I.

A Court before an Inn.

ALVAREZ, GUIAMARO, CONSTANZA, CHRISTIANA, SANCHO, SOTO, ANTONIO, CARLO, RODERIGO, *and others discovered disguised, as before. A shout within. Enter* JOHN.

ALV., *Gui.*, *&c.* Welcome, welcome, welcome!

Soto. More sacks to the mill.

San. More thieves to the sacks.

Alv. Peace!

Const. I give you now my welcome without noise.

John. 'Tis music to me. [*Offering to kiss* CONSTANZA.

Alv., *Gui.*, *&c.* O sir!

San. You must not be in your mutton before we are out of our veal.

Soto. Stay for vinegar to your oysters; no opening till [then.

Gui. No kissing till you're sworn.

John. Swear me then quickly,
I have brought gold for my admission.

Alv. What you bring leave, and what you leave count [lost.

San. I brought all my teeth, two are struck out; them I count lost, so must you.

Soto. I brought all my wits; half I count lost, so must you.

John. To be as you are, I lose father, friends,

Birth, fortunes, all the world: what will you do
With the beast I rode on hither?

San. A beast? is't a mule? send him to Muly Crag-a-whee in Barbary.

Soto. Is't an ass? give it to a lawyer, for in Spain they ride upon none else.

John. Kill him by any means, lest, being pursued,
The beast betray me.

Soto. He's a beast betrays any man.

San. Except a bailiff to be pumped.

John. Pray, bury the carcass and the furniture.

San. Do, do; bury the ass's household stuff, and in his skin sew any man that's mad for a woman.

Alv. Do so then, bury it: now to your oath.

Gui. All things are ready.

Alv. [*sings.*] Thy best hand lay on this turf of grass,
There thy heart lies, vow not to pass
From us two years for sun nor snow,
For[1] hill nor dale, howe'er winds blow;
Vow the hard earth to be thy bed,
With her green cushions under thy head;
Flower-banks or moss to be thy board,
Water thy wine——

San. [*sings.*] And drink like a lord.

Chorus. Kings can have but coronations;
We are as proud of gipsy-fashions:
Dance, sing, and in a well-mixed border
Close this new brother of our order.

Alv. [*sings.*] What we get with us come share,
You to get must vow to care;
Nor strike gipsy, nor stand by
When strangers strike, but fight, or die;
Our gipsy-wenches are not common,
You must not kiss a fellow's leman[2];

[1] Bullen suggested, "O'er hill, o'er dale, howe'er winds blow."
[2] Mistress.

Nor to your own, for one you must,
In songs send errands of base lust.

Chorus. Dance, sing, and in a well-mixed border
Close this new brother of our order.

John. [*sings.*] On this turf of grass I vow
Your laws to keep, your laws allow.

All. A gipsy! a gipsy! a gipsy!

Gui. [*sings.*] Now choose what maid has yet no mate,
She's yours.

John. [*sings.*] Here then fix I my fate.

[*Takes* CONSTANZA *by the hand and offers to kiss her.*

San. Again fall to before you ha' washed?

Soto. Your nose in the manger before the oats are measured, jade so hungry?

Alv. [*sings.*] Set foot to foot; those garlands hold;
Now mark well what more is told.
By cross arms, the lover's sign,
Vow, as these flowers themselves entwine,
Of April's wealth building a throne
Round, so your love to one or none;
By those touches of your feet,
You must each night embracing meet,
Chaste, howe'er disjoined by day;
You the sun with her must play,
She to you the marigold,
To none but you her leaves unfold;
Wake she or sleep, your eyes so charm,
Want, woe, nor weather do her harm.

Car. [*sings.*] This is your market now of kisses,
Buy and sell free each other blisses.

John. Most willingly.

Chorus. Holydays, high-days, gipsy-fairs,
When kisses are fairings, and hearts meet in pairs.

Alv. All ceremonies end here: welcome, brother gipsy!

San. And the better to instruct thee, mark what a brave life 'tis all the year long.

[*Sings.*] Brave Don, cast your eyes
On our gipsy fashions:
In our antic hey-de-guize [1]
We go beyond all nations;
Plump Dutch
At us grutch,
So do English, so do French,
He that lopes [2]
On the ropes,
Show me such another wench.

We no camels have to show,
Nor elephant with growt [3] head;
We can dance, he cannot go,
Because the beast is corn-fed;
No blind bears
Shedding tears,
For a collier's whipping;
Apes nor dogs,
Quick as frogs,
Over cudgels skipping.

Jack-in-boxes,[4] nor decoys,
Puppets, nor such poor things,
Nor are we those roaring boys
That cozen fools with gilt rings;
For an ocean,
Not such a motion [5]
As the city Nineveh;
Dancing, singing,
And fine ringing,
You these sports shall hear and see.

Come now, what shall his name be?

[1] A rustic dance. [2] Leaps. [3] Great.
[4] Sharpers who substituted empty boxes for boxes containing money. See Dekker's *Lanthorn and Candlelight.*
[5] Puppet-show.

Const. His name shall now be Andrew.—Friend
Andrew, mark me :
Two years I am to try you : prove fine gold,
The uncracked diamond of my faith shall hold.
John. My vows are rocks of adamant.
Const. Two years you are to try me : black when I turn
May I meet youth and want, old age and scorn!
John. King's diadems shall not buy thee.
Car. Do you think
You can endure the life, and love it?
John. As usurers doat upon their treasure.
Soto. But when your face shall be tanned
Like a sailor's worky-day hand——
San. When your feet shall be galled,
And your noddle be malled——
Soto. When the woods you must forage,
And not meet with poor pease-porridge——
San. Be all to-be-dabbled, yet lie in no sheet——
Soto. With winter's frost, hail, snow, and sleet;
What life will you say it is then?
John. As now, the sweetest.
Diego [*within.*] Away! away! the corregidor has sent for [you.
San. [*sings.*] Hence merrily fine to get money!
Dry are the fields, the banks are sunny,
Silver is sweeter far than honey;
Fly like swallows,
We for our conies must get mallows;
Who loves not his dill,[1] let him die at the gallows.
Hence, bonny girls, foot it trimly,
Smug up your beetle-brows, none look grimly;
To show a pretty foot, O 'tis seemly!
[*Exeunt all except* SOTO: *as he is going out,*

Enter CARDOCHIA, *who stays him.*

Card. Do you hear, you gipsy? gipsy!

[1] Another form of "dell," meaning a girl who is still a virgin.

Soto. Me?

Card. There's a young gipsy newly entertained;
Sweet gipsy, call him back for one two words,
And here's a jewel for thee.

Soto. I'll send him.

Card. What's his name?

Soto. Andrew. [*Exit.*

Card. A very handsome fellow; I ha' seen courtiers
Jet[1] up and down in their full bravery,[2]
Yet here's a gipsy worth a drove of 'em.

Re-enter JOHN.

John. With me, sweetheart?

Card. Your name is Andrew?

John. Yes.

Card. You can tell fortunes, Andrew?

John. I could once.
But now I ha' lost that knowledge; I'm in haste,
And cannot stay to tell you yours.

Card. I cannot tell yours then;
And 'cause you're in haste, I'm quick; I am a maid——

John. So, so, a maid quick?

Card. Juanna Cardochia,
That's mine own name; I am my mother's heir
Here to this house, and two more.

John. I buy no lands.

Card. They shall be given you, with some plate and money,
And free possession during life of me,
So the match like you; for so well I love you,
That I, in pity of this trade of gipsying,
Being base, idle, and slavish, offer you
A state to settle you, my youth and beauty,
Desired by some brave Spaniards, so I may call you
My husband: shall I, Andrew?

John. 'Las! pretty soul,

[1] Strut. [2] Finery.

Better stars guide you! may that hand of Cupid
Ache, ever shot this arrow at your heart!
Sticks there one such indeed?

Card. I would there did not,
Since you'll not pluck it out.

John. Good sweet, I cannot;
For marriage, 'tis a law amongst us gipsies
We match in our own tribes; for me to wear you,
I should but wear you out.

Card. I do not care;
Wear what you can out, all my life, my wealth,
Ruin me, so you lend me but your love,
A little of your love!

John. Would I could give it,
For you are worth a world of better men,
For your free noble mind! all my best wishes
Stay with you; I must hence.

Card. Wear for my sake
This jewel.

John. I'll not rob you, I'll take nothing.

Card. Wear it about your neck but one poor moon;
If in that time your eye be as 'tis now,
Send my jewel home again, and I protest
I'll never more think on you; deny not this,
Put it about your neck.

John. Well then, 'tis done. [*Putting on jewel.*

Card. And vow to keep it there.

John. By all the goodness
I wish attend your fortunes, I do vow it! [*Exit.*

Card. Scorned! thou hast tempered poison to kill me
Thyself shall drink; since I cannot enjoy thee,
My revenge shall.

Enter DIEGO.

Diego. Where are the gipsies?

Card. Gone.
Diego, do you love me?

Diego. Love thee, Juanna?
Is my life mine? it is but mine so long
As it shall do thee service.
Card. There's a young gipsy newly entertained.
Diego. A handsome rascal; what of him?
Card. That slave in obscene language courted me,
Drew reals[1] out, and would have bought my body,
Diego, from thee.
Diego. Is he so itchy? I'll cure him.
Card. Thou shalt not touch the villain, I'll spin his fate;
Woman strikes sure, fall the blow ne'er so late.
Diego. Strike on, since thou wilt be a striker.[2]
[*Exeunt.*

SCENE II.

A Room in FERNANDO'S *House.*

Enter FERNANDO, FRANCISCO, PEDRO, *and* LOUIS.

Fer. See, Don Louis; an arm,
The strongest arm in Spain, to the full length
Is stretched to pluck old Count Alvarez home
From his sad banishment.
Louis. With longing eyes,
My lord, I expect the man: your lordship's pardon,
Some business calls me from you.
Fer. Prithee, Don Louis,
Unless th' occasion be too violent,
Stay and be merry with us; all the gipsies
Will be here presently.
Louis. I'll attend your lordship
Before their sports be done.

[1] Spanish coins worth about 2½d.
[2] Cant term for a libertine.

Fer. Be your own carver. [*Exit* LOUIS.
[*To* FRAN.] Not yet shake off these fetters? I see a son
Is heavy when a father carries him
On his old heart.

Fran. Could I set up my rest [1]
That he were lost, or taken prisoner,
I could hold truce with sorrow; but to have him
Vanish I know not how, gone none knows whither,
'Tis that mads me.

Ped. You said he sent a letter.

Fran. A letter? a mere riddle; he's gone to seek
His fortune in the wars; what wars have we?
Suppose we had, goes any man to th' field
Naked, unfurnished both of arms and money?

Fer. Come, come, he's gone a-wenching; we in our youth
Ran the self-same bias.

Enter DIEGO.

Diego. The gipsies, my lord, are come.

Fer. Are they? let them enter. [*Exit* DIEGO.
My lord De Cortes, send for your wife and daughter;
Good company is good physic: take the pains
To seat yourselves in my great chamber. See,
They are here.— [*Exeunt* FRANCISCO *and* PEDRO.

Enter ALVAREZ, GUIAMARA, CONSTANZA, CHRISTIANA, JOHN, RODERIGO, ANTONIO, CARLO, SANCHO, *and* SOTO, *disguised as before.*

What's your number?

San. The figure of nine casts us all up, my lord.

Fer. Nine? let me see—you are ten, sure.

Soto. That's our poet, he stands for a cipher.

Fer. Ciphers make numbers:—what plays have you?

[1] Be sure.

Alv. Five or six, my lord.

Fer. It's well so many already.

Soto. We are promised a very merry tragedy, if all hit right, of Cobby Nobby.

Fer. So, so; a merry tragedy! there is a way
Which the Italians and the Frenchmen use,
That is, on a word given, or some slight plot,
The actors will extempore fashion out
Scenes neat and witty.

Alv. We can do that, my lord;
Please you bestow the subject.

Fer. Can you?—Come hither,
You master poet: to save you a labour,
Look you, against your coming I projected
This comic passage [*producing a paper*]; your drama, that's the scene——

Rod. Ay, ay, my lord.

Fer. I lay in our own country, Spain.

Rod. 'Tis best so.

Fer. Here's a brave part for this old gipsy; look you,
The father: read the plot; this young she gipsy,
This lady: now the son, play him yourself.

Rod. My lord, I am no player.

Fer. Pray, at this time,
The plot being full, to please my noble friends,
Because your brains must into theirs put language,
Act thou the son's part; I'll reward your pains.

Rod. Protest, my lord——

Fer. Nay, nay, shake off protesting;
When I was young, sir, I have played myself.

San. Yourself, my lord? you were but a poor company then.

Fer. Yes, full enough, honest fellow.—Will you do it?

Rod. I'll venture.

Fer. I thank you: let this father be a Don
Of a brave spirit.—Old gipsy, observe me——

Alv. Yes, my lord.

Fer. Play him up high; not like a pantaloon,
But hotly, nobly, checking this his son,
Whom make a very rake-hell, a deboshed [1] fellow.
This point, I think, will show well.

Rod. This of the picture?
It will indeed, my lord.

San. My lord, what part play I?

Fer. What parts dost use to play?

San. If your lordship has ever a coxcomb, I think I could fit you.

Fer. I thank your coxcombship.

Soto. Put a coxcomb upon a lord!

Fer. There are parts to serve you all; go, go, make ready,
And call for what you want. [*Exit.*

Alv. Give me the plot; our wits are put to trial.
What's the son's name? Lorenzo: that's your part.
[*To* RODERIGO.
Look only you to that; these I'll dispose:
Old Don Avero, mine; Hialdo, Lollio,
Two servants,—you for them. [*To* SANCHO *and* SOTO.

San. One of the foolish knaves give me; I'll be Hialdo.

Soto. And I, Lollio.

San. Is there a banquet in the play? we may call for what we will.

Rod. Yes, here is a banquet.

San. I'll go, then, and bespeak an ocean of sweetmeats, marmalade, and custards.

Alv. Make haste to know what you must do.

San. Do? call for enough; and when my belly is full, fill my pockets.

Soto. To a banquet there must be wine; fortune's a scurvy whore, if she makes not my head sound like a rattle, and my heels dance the canaries.[2]

[1] Debauched.
[2] A brisk lively dance, at times accompanied by castanets.

Alv. So, so; despatch whilst we employ our brains
To set things off to th' life.
Rod. I'll be straight with you.—
[*Exeunt all except* RODERIGO.
Why does my father put this trick on me;
Spies he me through my vizard? if he does,
He's not the King of Spain, and 'tis no treason;
If his invention jet upon a stage,
Why should not I use action? A deboshed fellow!
A very rake-hell! this reflects on me,
And I'll retort it: grown a poet, father?
No matter in what strain your play must run,
But I shall fit you for a roaring son. [*Exit.*

SCENE III.

A large Apartment in FERNANDO'S *House.*

Enter FERNANDO, FRANCISCO, PEDRO, DIEGO, MARIA, CLARA, *and* Servants.

Fer. Come, ladies, take your places. [*Flourish within.*]
This their music?
'Tis very handsome: O, I wish this room
Were freighted but with pleasures, noble friends,
As are to you my welcomes!—Begin there, masters.

San. [*within.*] Presently, my lord; we want but a cold capon for a property.

Fer. Call, call for one.

Enter SANCHO *as* Prologue.

Now they begin.

San. Both short and sweet some say is best;
We will not only be sweet, but short:
Take you pepper in the nose,[1] you mar our sport.

Fer. By no means pepper.

[1] *i.e.* If you are angry.

San. Of your love measure us forth but one span;
We do though not the best, the best we can. [*Exit.*

Fer. A good honest gipsy!

Enter ALVAREZ (*as* AVERO), *and* SOTO (*as* LOLLIO).

Alv. Slave, where's my son, Lorenzo?

Soto. I have sought him, my lord, in all four elements: in earth, my shoes are full of gravel; in water, I drop at nose with sweating; in air, wheresoever I heard noise of fiddlers, or the wide mouths of gallon pots roaring; and in fire, what chimney soever I saw smoking with good cheer, for my master's dinner, as I was in hope.

Alv. Not yet come home? before on this old tree
Shall grow a branch so blasted, I'll hew it off,
And bury it at my foot! Didst thou inquire
At my brother's?

Soto. At your sister's.

Alv. At my wife's father's?

Soto. At your uncle's mother's: no such sheep has broke through their hedge; no such calf as your son sucks or bleats in their ground.

Alv. I am unblessed to have but one son only,
One staff to bear my age up, one taper left
To light me to my grave, and that burns dimly;
That leaves me darkling hid in clouds of woe:
He that should prop me is mine overthrow.

Fer. Well done, old fellow! is't not?

Fran., *Ped.*, *&c.* Yes, yes, my lord.

Soto. Here comes his man Hialdo.

Enter SANCHO (*as* HIALDO).

Alv. Where's the prodigal your master, sirrah?

San. Eating acorns amongst swine, draff amongst hogs, and gnawing bones amongst dogs: has lost all his money at dice, his wits with his money, and his honesty with both; for he bum-fiddles me, makes the drawers curvet, pitches the plate over the bar, scores up the vintner's name in the Ramhead, flirts his wife under the nose, and bids you with a pox send him more money.

Alv. Art thou one of his curs to bite me too?
To nail thee to the earth were to do justice.

San. Here comes Bucephalus my prancing master; nail me now who dares.

Enter RODERIGO (*as* LORENZO).

Rod. I sit like an owl in the ivy-bush of a tavern; Hialdo, I have drawn red wine from the vintner's own hogshead.

San. Here's two more, pierce them too.

Rod. Old Don, whom I call father, am I thy son? if I be, flesh me with gold, fat me with silver; had I Spain in this hand, and Portugal in this, puff it should fly: where's the money I sent for?
I'll tickle you for a rake-hell! [*Aside.*

San. Not a marvedi.[1]

Alv. Thou shalt have none of me.

Soto. Hold his nose to the grin'stone, my lord.

Rod. I shall have none?

Alv. Charge me a case[2] of pistols;
What I have built I'll ruin: shall I suffer
A slave to set his foot upon my heart?
A son? a barbarous villain? or if heaven save t
Now from my justice, yet my curse pursues thee.

Rod. Hialdo, carbonado[3] thou the old rogue my father.

San. Whilst you slice into collops the rusty gammon his man there.

Rod. No money? Can taverns stand without anon, anon? fiddlers live without scraping? taffeta[4] girls look plump without pampering? If you will not lard me with money, give me a ship, furnish me to sea.

Alv. To have thee hanged for piracy?

San. Trim, tram, hang master, hang man!

Rod. Then send me to the West Indies, buy me some office there.

Alv. To have thy throat cut for thy quarrelling?

Rod. Else send me and my ningle[5] Hialdo to the wars.

San. A match; we'll fight dog, fight bear.

Enter ANTONIO (*as* HERNANDO).

Alv. O dear Hernando, welcome!—Clap wings to your heels, [*To* SOTO.

[1] A small copper coin. [2] Pair.
[3] *i.e.* Cut into rashers for broiling.
[4] Dainty, nice. [5] *i.e.* Mine ingle—favourite.

And pray my worthy friends bestow upon me
Their present visitation.— [*Exit* SOTO.
Lorenzo, see the anger of a father;
Although it be as loud and quick as thunder,
Yet 'tis done instantly: cast off thy wildness,
Be mine, be mine, for I to call thee home
Have, with my honoured friend here, Don Hernando,
Provided thee a wife.

Rod. A wife! is she handsome? is she rich? is she fair? is she witty? is she honest? hang honesty! has she a sweet face, cherry-cheek, strawberry-lip, white skin, dainty eye, pretty foot, delicate legs, as there's a girl now?

Ant. It is a creature both for birth and fortunes,
And for most excellent graces of the mind,
Few like her are in Spain.

Rod. When shall I see her?—
Now, father, pray take your curse off.

Alv. I do: the lady
Lives from Madrill very near fourteen leagues,
But thou shalt see her picture.

Rod. That! that! most ladies in these days are but very fine pictures.

Enter CARLO, JOHN, GUIAMARA, CONSTANZA, *and* CHRISTIANA (*as friends of* AVERO).

Alv. Ladies, to you first welcome; my lords, Alonzo,
And you worthy marquis, thanks for these honours.—
Away you! [*Exit* SANCHO.
To th' cause now of this meeting. My son Lorenzo,
Whose wildness you all know, comes now to th' lure,
Sits gently; has called home his wandering thoughts,
And now will marry.

Const. A good wife fate send him!

Gui. One staid may settle him.

Rod. Fly to the mark, sir; show me the wench, or her face, or anything I may know 'tis a woman fit for me.

Alv. She is not here herself, but here's her picture.
[*Shows a picture.*

Fer. My Lord De Carcomo, pray, observe this.

Fran. I do, attentively.—Don Pedro, mark it.

Re-enter SOTO.

Soto [*to* JOHN.] If you ha' done your part, yonder's a wench would ha' a bout with you. [*Exit.*

John. Me? [*Exit.*

Diego. A wench! [*Exit.*

Alv. Why stand you staring at it? how do you like her?

Rod. Are you in earnest?

Alv. Yes, sir, in earnest.

Rod. I am not so hungry after flesh to make the devil a cuckold.

Ant. Look not upon the face, but on the goodness
That dwells within her.

Rod. Set fire on the tenement!

Alv. She's rich; nobly descended.

Rod. Did ever nobility look so scurvily?

Alv. I'm sunk in fortunes, she may raise us both.

Rod. Sink, let her to her granam! marry a witch? have you fetched a wife for me out of Lapland? an old midwife in a velvet hat were a goddess to this: that a red lip?

Const. There's a red nose.

Rod. That a yellow hair?

Gui. Why, her teeth may be yellow.

Rod. Where's the full eye?

Chris. She has full blabber-cheeks.

Alv. Set up thy rest,[1] her marriest thou or none.

Rod. None then: were all the water in the world one sea, all kingdoms one mountain, I would climb on all fours up to the top of that hill, and headlong hurl myself into that abyss of waves, ere I would touch the skin of such rough haberdine,[2] for the breath of her picture stinks hither.

A noise within. Re-enter, in a hurry, JOHN, DIEGO, SANCHO, *and* SOTO, *with* CARDOCHIA.

Fer. What tumult's this?

San. Murder, murder, murder!

Soto. One of our gipsies is in danger of hanging, hanging!

Ped. Who is hurt?

[1] Make up your mind. [2] Salted cod-fish.

Diego. 'Tis I, my lord, stabbed by this gipsy.

John. He struck me first, and I'll not take a blow
From any Spaniard breathing.

Ped. Are you so brave?

Fer. Break up your play; lock all the doors.

Diego. I faint, my lord.

Fran. Have him to a surgeon.—

[Servants *remove* DIEGO.

How fell they out?

Card. O, my good lord, these gipsies when they lodged
At my house, I had a jewel from my pocket
Stolen by this villain.

John. 'Tis most false, my lords;
Her own hands gave it me.

Const. She that calls him villain,
Or says he stole——

Fer. Hoyday! we hear your scolding.

Card. And the hurt gentleman finding it in his bosom,
For that he stabbed him.

Fer. Hence with all the gipsies!

Ped. Ruffians and thieves; to prison with 'em all!

Alv. My lord, we'll leave engagements in plate and money
For all our safe forthcomings; punish not all
For one's offence; we'll prove ourselves no thieves.

San. O Soto, I make buttons![1]

Soto. Would I could make some, and leave this trade!

Fer. Iron him then, let the rest go free; but stir not
One foot out of Madrill. Bring you in your witness.

[*Exeunt* JOHN *in custody of* Servants, ALVAREZ, GUIAMARA, CONSTANZA, CHRISTIANA, ANTONIO, CARLO, *and* CARDOCHIA.

Soto. Prick him with a pin, or pinch him by the elbow; anything.

San. My lord Don Pedro, I am your ward; we have spent a little money to get a horrible deal of wit, and now I am weary of it.

[1] *i.e.* I'm in great fear.

Ped. My runaways turned jugglers, fortune-tellers?

Soto. No great fortunes.

Fer. To prison with 'em both: a gentleman play the ass!

San. If all gentlemen that play the ass should to prison, you must widen your jails.—Come, Soto, I scorn to beg; set thy foot to mine, and kick at shackles.

Fer. So so; away with 'em!

Soto. Send all our company after, and we'll play there, and be as merry as you here.

[*Exeunt* SANCHO *and* SOTO *with* Servants.

Fer. Our comedy turned tragical! Please you, lords, walk:
This actor here and I must change a word,
And I come to you.

Fran., *Ped.*, *&c.* Well, my lord, your pleasure.

[*Exeunt all except* FERNANDO *and* RODERIGO.

Fer. Why, couldst thou think in any base disguise
To blind my sight? fathers have eagles' eyes.
But pray, sir, why was this done? why, when I thought you
Fast locked in Salamanca at your study,
Leaped you into a gipsy?

Rod. Sir, with your pardon,
I shall at fit time to you show cause for all.

Fer. Meantime, sir, you have got a trade to live by:
Best to turn player; an excellent ruffian, ha!
But know, sir, when I had found you out, I gave you
This project of set purpose; 'tis all myself;
What the old gipsy spake must be my language;
Nothing are left me but my offices
And thin-faced honours; and this very creature,
By you so scorned, must raise me by your marrying her.

Rod. You would not build your glory on my ruins?

Fer. The rascal has belied the lady,
She is not half so bad; all's one, she's rich.

Rod. O, will you sell the joys of my full youth
To dunghill muck? seek out some wretch's daughter,

Whose soul is lost for gold then: you're more noble
Than t' have your son, the top-branch of your house,
Grow in a heap of rubbish: I must marry a thing
I shall be ashamed to own, ashamed to bring her
Before a sunbeam.

Fer. I cannot help it, sir;
Resolve upon't, and do't.

Rod. And do't, and die!
Is there no face in Spain for you to pick out
But one to fright me? when you sat the play here,
There was a beauty, to be lord of which
I would against an army throw defiance.

Fer. She? alas!

Rod. How? she! at every hair of hers
There hangs a very angel; this! I'm ready
To drop down looking at it: sir, I beseech you
Bury me in this earth [*kneels*], on which I'm humbled
To beg your blessing on me, for a gipsy,
Rather than—O, I know not what to term it!
Pray, what is that young pensive piece of beauty?
Your voice for her; I eyed her all the scene.

Fer. I saw you did.

Rod. Methought 'twas a sweet creature.

Fer. Well, though my present state stands now on ice,
I'll let it crack and fall rather than bar thee
Of thy content; this lady shall go by then.

Rod. Hang let her there, or anywhere!

Fer. That young lannard,[1]
Whom you have such a mind to, if you can whistle her
To come to fist, make trial; play the young falconer;
I will nor mar your marriage nor yet make;
Beauty, no wealth,—wealth, ugliness,—which you will take.

Rod. I thank you, sir. [*Exit* FERNANDO.]—Put on your mask, good madam. [*To the picture.*
The sun will spoil your face else. [*Exit.*

[1] A species of hawk.

ACT THE FIFTH.

SCENE I.

A Room in FERNANDO'S *House.*

FERNANDO, FRANCISCO, PEDRO, RODERIGO, CLARA, *and* MARIA, *pass over the stage from church; as the others exeunt,* FERNANDO *stays* RODERIGO.

FER. Thou hast now the wife of thy desires.

Rod. Sir, I have, [life
And in her every blessing that makes
Loth to be parted with.

Fer. Noble she is, [beauty,
And fair; has to enrich her blood and
Plenty of wit, discourse, behaviour, carriage.

Rod. I owe you duty for a double birth,
Being in this happiness begot again,
Without which I had been a man of wretchedness.

Fer. Then henceforth, boy, learn to obey thy fate;
Tis fallen upon thee; know it, and embrace it;
'Thy wife's a wanton.

Rod. A wanton?

Fer. Examine through the progress of thy youth
What capital sin, what great one 'tis, for 'tis
A great one thou'st committed.

Rod. I, a great one?

Fer. Else Heaven is not so wrathful to pour on thee
A misery so full of bitterness:
I am thy father; think on't, and be just;
Come, do not dally.

Rod. Pray, my lord

Fer. Fool, 'twere
Impossible that justice should rain down
In such a frightful horror without cause.
Sir, I will know it; rather blush thou didst
An act thou dar'st not name, than that it has
A name to be known by.
Rod. Turn from me then,
And as my guilt sighs out this monster,—rape,
O, do not lend an ear?
Fer. Rape? fearful!
Rod. Hence,
Hence springs my due reward.
Fer. Thou'rt none of mine,
Or if thou be'st, thou dost belie the stamp
Of thy nativity.
Rod. Forgive me!
Fer. Had she,
Poor wrongèd soul, whoe'er she was, no friend,
Nor father, to revenge? had she no tongue
To roar her injuries?
Rod. Alas! I know her not!
Fer. Peace! thou wilt blaze a sin beyond all precedent:
Young man, thou shouldst have married her; the devil
Of lust that riots in thy eye should there
Have let fall love and pity, not on this stranger
Whom thou hast doted on.
Rod. O, had I married her,
I had been then the happiest man alive!

Re-enter CLARA, MARIA, *and* PEDRO, *from behind the arras.*

Cla. As I the happiest woman, being married:
Look on me, sir.
Ped. You shall not find a change
So full of fears as your most noble father,
In his wise trial, urged.
Mar. Indeed you shall not,
The forfeit of her shame shall be her pawn,

Rod. Why, pray, d'ye mock my sorrows? now, O, now,
My horrors flow about me!
Fer. No, thy comforts,
Thy blessings, Roderigo.
Cla. By this crucifix [*Showing crucifix.*
You may remember me.
Rod. Ha! art thou
That lady wrongèd?
Cla. I was, but now am
Righted in noble satisfaction.
Rod. How can I turn mine eyes, and not behold
On every side my shame?
Fer. No more: hereafter
We shall have time to talk at large of all:
Love her that's now thine own; do, Roderigo;
She's far from what I charactered.
Cla. My care
Shall live about me to deserve your love.
Rod. Excellent Clara!—Fathers both, and mother,
I will redeem my fault.
Fer., Ped., Mar. Our blessings dwell on ye!

Re-enter FRANCISCO *with* LOUIS.

Louis. Married to Roderigo?
Fran. Judge yourself:
See where they are. [*Exit.*
Louis. Is this your husband, lady?
Cla. He is, sir: Heaven's great hand, that on record
Fore-points the equal union of all hearts,
Long since decreed what this day hath been perfected
Louis. 'Tis well then; I am free, it seems.
Cla. Make smooth,
My lord, those clouds, which on your brow deliver
Emblems of storm; I will, as far as honour
May privilege, deserve a noble friendship
As you from me deserve a worthy memory.

Louis. Your husband has proved himself a friend to me
Trusty and tried; he's welcome, I may say,
From the university.
Rod. To a new school
Of happy knowledge, Louis.
Louis. Sir, I am
Not so poor as to put this injury up:
The best blood flows within you is the price.
Rod. Louis, for this time calm your anger; and if
I do not give you noble satisfaction,
Call me to what account you please.
Louis. So, so.—I come for justice t'ye,
And you shall grant it.
Fer. Shall and will.
Louis. With speed too;
My poor friend bleeds the whiles.
Fer. You shall yourself,
Before we part, receive the satisfaction
You come for.—Who attends?
Servant [*within.*] My lord?
Fer. The prisoner!
Servant [*within.*] He attends your lordship's pleasure.

Enter CONSTANZA, GUIAMARA, *and* ALVAREZ.

Louis. What would this girl?
Foh, no tricks; get you to your cabin, huswife;
We have no ear for ballads.
Fer. Take her away.
Cla. A wondrous lovely creature!
Const. Noble gentlemen,
If a poor maid's, a gipsy-virgin's tears
May soften the hard edge of angry justice,
Then grant me gracious hearing; as you're merciful,
I beg my husband's life!
Fer. Thy husband's, little one?
Const. Gentle sir, our plighted troths are chronicled

In that white book above which notes the secrets
Of every thought and heart; he is my husband
I am his wife.

Louis. Rather his whore.

Const. Now, trust me,
You're no good man to say so; I am honest,
'Deed, la, I am; a poor soul, that deserves not
Such a bad word: were you a better man
Than you are, you do me wrong.

Louis. The toy grows angry!

Cla. And it becomes her sweetly; troth, my lord,
I pity her.

Rod. I thank you, sweet.

Louis. Your husband,
You'll say, is no thief.

Const. Upon my conscience,
He is not.

Louis. Dares not strike a man.

Const. Unworthily
He dares not; but if trod upon, a worm
Will turn again.

Louis. That turning turns your worm
Off from the ladder, minion.

Const. Sir, I hope
You're not his judge; you are too young, too choleric,
Too passionate; the price of life or death
Requires a much more grave consideration
Than your years warrant: here sit they, like gods,
Upon whose heads the reverend badge of time
Hath sealed the proof of wisdom; to these oracles
Of riper judgment, lower in my heart [*Kneels.*
Than on my knees, I offer up my suit,
My lawful suit, which begs they would be gentle
To their own fames, their own immortal stories.
O, do not think, my lords, compassion thrown
On a base low estate, on humble people,
Less meritorious than if you had favoured

The faults of great men! and indeed great men
Have oftentimes great faults: he whom I plead for
Is free; the soul of innocence itself
Is not more white: will you pity him?
I see it in your eyes, 'tis a sweet sunbeam,
Let it shine out; and to adorn your praise,
The prayers of the poor shall crown your days,
And theirs are sometimes heard.
Fer. Beshrew the girl,
She has almost melted me to tears!
Louis. Hence, trifler!—Call in my friends!

Enter JOHN, DIEGO, CARDOCHIA, *and* Servants.

What hope of ease?
Diego. Good hope, but still I smart;
The worst is in my pain.
Louis. The price is high
Shall buy thy vengeance: to receive a wound
By a base villain's hand, it maddens me.
John. Men subject to th' extremity of law
Should carry peace about 'em to their graves;
Else, were you nobler than the blood you boast of,
Could any way, my lord, derive you, know
I would return sharp answer to your slanders;
But it suffices, I am none of ought
Your rage misterms me.
Louis. None of 'em? no rascal?
John. No rascal?
Louis. Nor no thief?
John. Ask her that's my accuser: could your eyes
Pierce through the secrets of her foul desires,
You might without a partial judgment look into
A woman's lust and malice.
Card. My good lords,
What I have articled against this fellow,
I justify for truth.
John. On then, no more:

This being true she says, I have deserved
To die.
Fer. We sit not here to bandy words,
But minister the law, and that condemns thee
For theft unto the gallows.
Const. O my misery!
Are you all marble-breasted? are your bosoms
Hooped-round with steel? to cast away a man,
More worthy life and honours than a thousand
Of such as only pray unto the shadow
Of abused greatness!
John. 'Tis in vain to storm;
My fate is here determinèd.
Const. Lost creature,
Art thou grown dull too? is my love so cheap
That thou court'st thy destruction 'cause I love thee?—
My lords, my lords!—Speak, Andrew, prithee, now,
Be not so cruel to thyself and me;
One word of thine will do't.
Fer. Away with him!
To-morrow is his day of execution.
John. Even when you will.
Const. Stay, man; thou shalt not go,
Here are more women yet.—Sweet madam, speak!
You, lady, you methinks should have some feeling
Of tenderness; you may be touched as I am:
Troth, were't your cause, I'd weep with you, and join
In earnest suit for one you held so dear.
Cla. My lord, pray speak in his behalf.
Rod. I would,
But dare not; 'tis a fault so clear and manifest.
Louis. Back with him to his dungeon!
John. Heaven can tell
I sorrow not to die, but to leave her
Who whiles I live is my life's comforter.
[*Exit with* Servants.

Card. Now shall I be revenged!
[*Aside, and exit with* DIEGO.

Const. O me unhappy! [*Swoons.*

Fer. See, the girl falls!
Some one look to her.

Cla. 'Las, poor maid!

Gui. Pretiosa!
She does recover: mine honourable lord——

Fer. In vain: what is't?

Gui. Be pleased to give me private audience;
I will discover something shall advantage
The noblest of this land.

Fer. Well, I will hear thee;
Bring in the girl.

[*Exeunt* FERNANDO, MARIA, PEDRO, CLARA, RODERIGO, GUIAMARA, *and* CONSTANZA: ALVAREZ *stays* LOUIS.

Louis. Ought with me; what is't?
I care not for thy company, old ruffian;
Rascal, art impudent?

Alv. To beg your service.

Louis. Hang yourself!

Alv. By your father's soul, sir, hear me!

Louis. Despatch!

Alv. First promise me you'll get reprieve
For the condemnèd man, and by my art
I'll make you master of what your heart on earth
Can wish for or desire.

Louis. Thou liest; thou canst not!

Alv. Try me.

Louis. Do that, and then, as I am noble,
I will not only give thy friend his life,
But royally reward thee, love thee ever.

Alv. I take your word; what would you?

Louis. If thou mock'st me,
'Twere better thou wert damned!

Alv. Sir, I am resolute.

Louis. Resolve me, then, whether the Count Alvarez
Who slew my father, be alive or dead?

Alv. Is this the mighty matter? the count lives.

Louis. How?

Alv. The count lives.

Louis. O fate! Now tell me where,
And be my better genius.

Alv. I can do't:
In Spain 'a lives; more, not far from Madrill,
But in disguise, much altered.

Louis. Wonderful scholar!
Miracle of artists! Alvarez living?
And near Madrill too? now, for Heaven's sake, where?
That's all, and I am thine.

Alv. Walk off, my lord,
To the next field, you shall know all.

Louis. Apace, then!
I listen to thee with a greedy ear:
The miserable and the fortunate
Are alike in this, they cannot change their fate. [*Exeunt.*

SCENE II.

A Field.

Enter ALVAREZ *and* LOUIS.

Alv. Good, good: you would fain kill him, and revenge
Your father's death?

Louis. I would.

Alv. Bravely, or scurvily?

Louis. Not basely, for the world!

Alv. We are secure. [*Produces two swords.*
Young Louis, two more trusty blades than these
Spain has not in her armoury: with this

Alvarez slew thy father; and this other
Was that the King of France wore when great Charles
In a set battle took him prisoner;
Both I resign to thee.

Louis. This is a new mystery.

Alv. Now see this naked bosom; turn the points
Of either on this bulwark, if thou covet'st,
Out of a sprightly youth and manly thirst
Of vengeance, blood; if blood be thy ambition,
Then call to mind the fatal blow that struck
De Castro, thy brave father, to his grave;
Remember who it was that gave that blow,
His enemy Alvarez: hear, and be sudden,
Behold Alvarez!

Louis. Death, I am deluded!

Alv. Thou art incredulous; as fate is certain,
I am the man.

Louis. Thou that butcher?

Alv. Tremble not, young man, trust me, I have wept
Religiously to wash off from my conscience
The stain of my offence: twelve years and more,
Like to a restless pilgrim I have run
From foreign lands to lands to find out death.
I'm weary of my life; give me a sword:
That thou mayst know with what a perfect zeal
I honour old De Castro's memory,
I'll fight with thee; I would not have thy hand
Dipped in a wilful murder; I could wish
For one hour's space I could pluck back from time
But thirty of my years, that in my fall
Thou might'st deserve report: now if thou conquer'st,
Thou canst not triumph; I'm half dead already,
Yet I'll not start a foot.

Louis. Breathes there a spirit
In such a heap of age?

Alv. O, that I had
A son of equal growth with thee, to tug

For reputation! by thy father's ashes,
I would not kill thee for another Spain,
Yet now I'll do my best. Thou art amazed;
Come on.

Louis. Twelve tedious winters' banishment?
'Twas a long time.

Alv. Could they redeem thy father,
Would every age had been twelve ages, Louis,
And I for penance every age a-dying!
But 'tis too late to wish.

Louis. I am o'ercome;
Your nobleness hath conquered me: here ends
All strife between our families, and henceforth
Acknowledge me for yours.

Alv. O, thou reviv'st
Fresh horrors to my fact![1] for in thy gentleness
I see my sin anew.

Louis. Our peace is made;
Your life shall be my care: 'twill be glad news
To all our noble friends.

Alv. Since Heaven will have it so,
I thank thee, glorious majesty! My son,
For I will call thee so, ere the next morrow
Salute the world, thou shalt know stranger mysteries.

Louis. I have enough to feed on: sir, I'll follow ye.
[*Exeunt.*

SCENE III.

A Room in FERNANDO'S *House.*

Enter FERNANDO, GUIAMARA, *and* CONSTANZA.

Fer. Don John, son to the Count of Carcomo?
Woman, take heed thou trifle not.

[1] Guilt.

Gui. Is this,
My lord, so strange?
Fer. Beauty in youth, and wit
To set it forth, I see, transforms the best
Into what shape love fancies.
Const. Will you yet
Give me my husband's life?
Fer. Why, little one,
He is not married to thee.
Const. In his faith
He is; and faith and troth I hope bind faster
Than any other ceremonies can;
Do they not, pray, my lord?
Fer. Yes, where the parties
Pledged are not too unequal in degree,
As he and thou art.
Const. This is new divinity.
Gui. My lord, behold this child well: in her face
You may observe, by curious insight, something
More than belongs to every common birth.
Fer. True, 'tis a pretty child.
Gui. The glass of misery
Is, after many a change of desperate fortune,
At length run out: you had a daughter called
Constanza?
Fer. Ha!
Gui. A sister, Guiamara,
Wife to the Count Alvarez?
Fer. Peace, O, peace!
Gui. And to that sister's charge you did commit
Your infant daughter, in whose birth your wife,
Her mother, died?
Fer. Woman thou art too cruel!
Const. What d'ye mean, granam? 'las, the nobleman
Grows angry!
Fer. Not I, indeed I do not:—
But why d'ye use me thus?

Gui. Your child and sister,
As you supposed, were drowned?
Fer. Drowned? talking creature!
Supposed?
Gui. They live; Fernando, from my hand,
Thy sister's hand, receive thine own Constanza,
The sweetest, best child living.
Const. Do you mock me?
Fer. Torment me on; yet more, more yet, and spare not,
My heart is now a-breaking; now!
Gui. O brother!
Am I so far removed off from your memory,
As that you will not know me? I expected
Another welcome home: look on this casket,
[*Showing casket.*
The legacy your lady left her daughter,
When to her son she gave her crucifix.
Fer. Right, right; I know ye now.
Gui. In all my sorrows,
My comfort has been here, she should be yours,
Be yours at last.—Constanza, kneel, sweet child,
To thy old father.
Const. How? my father? [*Kneels.*
Fer. Let not
Extremity of joys ravish life from me
Too soon, Heaven, I beseech thee! Thou art my sister,
My sister Guiamara! How have mine eyes
Been darkened all this while! 'tis she!
Gui. 'Tis, brother;
And this Constanza, now no more a stranger,
No Pretiosa henceforth.
Fer. My soul's treasure,
Live to an age of goodness; and so thrive
In all thy ways, that thou mayst die to live
Const. But must I call you father?

Fer. Thou wilt rob me else
Of that felicity, for whose sake only
I am ambitious of being young again:
Rise, rise, mine own Constanza!

Const. [*rising.*] 'Tis a new name,
But 'tis a pretty one; I may be bold
To make a suit t'ye?

Fer. Anything.

Const. O father,
And if you be my father, think upon
Don John my husband! without him, alas,
I can be nothing!

Fer. As I without thee;
Let me alone, Constanza.—Tell me, tell me,
Lives yet Alvarez?

Gui. In your house.

Fer. Enough:
Cloy me not; let me by degrees digest
My joys.—Within, my Lords Francisco, Pedro!
Come all at once! I have a world within me;
I am not mortal sure, I am not mortal:

Enter FRANCISCO, PEDRO, MARIA, RODERIGO, *and* CLARA.

My honourable lords, partake my blessings;
The Count Alvarez lives here in my house;
Your son, my Lord Francisco, Don John, is
The condemned man falsely accused of theft;
This, my Lord Pedro, is my sister Guiamara;
Madam, this is Constanza, mine own child,
And I am a wondrous merry man.—Without!
The prisoner!

Enter ALVAREZ, LOUIS, JOHN, DIEGO, SANCHO, SOTO, *and* CARDOCHIA.

Louis. Here, free and acquitted,
By her whose folly drew her to this error;

And she for satisfaction is assured[1]
To my wronged friend.

Card. I crave your pardons;
He whose I am speaks for me.

Diego. We both beg it!

Fer. Excellent! admirable! my dear brother!

Alv. Never a happy man till now; young Louis
And I are reconciled.

Louis. For ever, faithfully,
Religiously.

Fran., Ped., &c. My noble lord, most welcome!

Alv. To all my heart pays what it owes, due thanks;
Most, most, brave youth, to thee!

John. I all this while
Stand but a looker-on; and though my father
May justly tax the violence of my passions,
Yet if this lady, lady of my life,
Must be denied, let me be as I was,
And die betimes.

Const. You promised me——

Fer. I did.—
My lord of Carcomo, you see their hearts
Are joined already, so let our consents
To this wished marriage.

Fran. I forgive thine errors;
Give me thy hand.

Fer. [*to Constanza*]. Me thine.—But wilt thou love
My daughter, my Constanza?

John. As my bliss.

Const. I thee as life, youth, beauty, anything
That makes life comfortable.

Fer. Live together
One, ever one!

Fran., Rod., &c. And Heaven crown your happiness!

Ped. Now, sir, how like you a prison?

[1] Affianced.

San. As gallants do a tavern, being stopped for a reckoning, scurvily.

Soto. Though you caged us up never so close, we sung like cuckoos.

Fer. Well, well, you be yourself now.

San. Myself?—am I out of my wits, Soto?

Fer. Here now are none but honourable friends:
Will you, to give a farewell to the life
You ha' led as gipsies, these being now found none,
But noble in their births, altered in fortunes,
Give it a merry shaking by the hand,
And cry adieu to folly?

San. We'll shake our hands, and our heels, if you'll give us leave. [*A dance.*

Fer. On, brides and bridegrooms! to your Spanish feasts
Invite with bent knees all these noble guests.
[*Exeunt omnes.*

FINIS

PRINTED BY J. S. VIRTUE AND CO., LIMITED, CITY ROAD, LONDON.